www.wadsworth.com

wadsworth.com is the World Wide Web site for Wadsworth and is your direct source to dozens of online resources.

At *wadsworth.com* you can find out about supplements, demonstration software, and student resources. You can also send email to many of our authors and preview new publications and exciting new technologies.

wadsworth.com
Changing the way the world learns®

Dedication

To my mother, a retired small business owner, who taught me to work with passion and commitment; in memory of my father, a professor of business administration, who taught me to see the positives and opportunities for learning in any situation; and to both of them for showing me how to always treat people with kindness and respect.
T. P.

Management of Human Service Programs

THIRD EDITION

Judith A. Lewis
Governors State University

Michael D. Lewis
Governors State University

Thomas Packard
San Diego State University

Federico Souflée, Jr.

BROOKS/COLE

THOMSON LEARNING   Australia • Canada • Mexico • Singapore • Spain United Kingdom • United States

BROOKS/COLE

THOMSON LEARNING™

Counseling Editor: Julie Martinez
Editorial Assistant: Cat Broz
Marketing Manager: Caroline Concilla
Project Editor: Teri Hyde
Print Buyer: Tandra Jorgensen
Permissions Editor: Joohee Lee
Production Service: Heidi Marschner
Copy Editor: Laura E. Larson

Cover Designer: Laurie Anderson
Cover Images: (top to bottom) PhotoDisk,
Inc., Mitch Hrdlicka, Mel Curtis,
Jack Hollingsworth, Ryan McVay
Cover Printer: Phoenix Color Corp. (MD)
Compositor: Color Type, San Diego
Printer: Maple Vail (NY)

**Library of Congress
Cataloging-in-Publication Data**
Management of human service programs / Judith A.
    Lewis . . . [et al.].—3rd ed.
        p. cm.
    Rev. ed. of: Management of human service
        programs / Judith A. Lewis, 2nd ed. c1991.
    Includes bibliographical references and index.
    ISBN 0-534-36886-7
    1. Human services—management. 2. Human
        services—United States—Management—
        Case studies.
    I. Lewis, Judith A., [date] II. Lewis, Judith A.
        [date] Management of human service
        programs.
HV41 .M2765 2000
361'.0068—dc21   00-034980

Wadsworth/Thomson Learning
10 Davis Drive
Belmont, CA 94002-3098
USA

For information about our products, contact us:
Thomson Learning Academic Resource Center
1-800-423-0563
http://www.wadsworth.com

International Headquarters
Thomson Learning
International Division
290 Harbor Drive, 2nd Floor
Stamford, CT 06902-7477
USA

UK/Europe/Middle East/South Africa
Thomson Learning
Berkshire House
168-173 High Holborn
London WC1V 7AA
United Kingdom

Asia
Thomson Learning
60 Albert Street #15-01
Albert Complex
Singapore 189969

Canada
Nelson/Thomson Learning
1120 Birchmount Road
Scarborough, Ontario M1K 5G4
Canada

Preface

The effectiveness and survival of human service programs increasingly depends on how well they are managed. In spite of recent ongoing and notable improvements of human services management methods, deficiencies in particular settings have been apparent for years, ranging from the William Aramony scandal at United Way of America to the regular defunding and closure of small community-based organizations. This third edition of *Management of Human Service Programs* recognizes that human service managers will need well-developed management and leadership knowledge and skills, a solid foundation of professional values, and critical thinking abilities to execute management responsibilities purposefully, effectively, and efficiently.

The book provides an overview of the managerial and leadership functions that make human services work. It has been designed primarily as a resource for current or emerging managers and for people who see themselves as direct service professionals who believe management knowledge will increase their effectiveness. Many human service programs are managed by professional helpers rather than by experts in the field of management. Management experts sometimes have professional degrees such as the MSW and have also had formal management training, but some come from other sectors such as business and lack the values and knowledge base of human services technologies. Even those human service providers who avoid moving into full-time supervisory positions find that they must perform a variety of administrative functions and that they must understand how human service systems are planned, organized, and evaluated.

Thus, this book is appropriate for experienced managers who were trained some years ago and want updates on current practice, professionals who were promoted to supervisory or management positions without training, students expecting to soon enter management, and students and nonmanagers who don't plan to become managers soon but may in the future. It should also be useful for those with no managerial aspirations but who want to better understand how their supervisors and managers think and what their concerns, priorities, worldviews, and work days are like. Understanding a managerial perspective should make a worker more effective in managing the complexities of agency life and influencing upward in the hierarchy to make agencies and programs more responsive.

Because of an increased recognition that services must be effectively run, most human services degree programs now offer courses that introduce students to the field of management. This text is appropriate for such a course, whether students are expected to work in community agencies, educational institutions, health care organizations, mental health centers, or any of a number of other settings that fall under the definition of human services. It is targeted for programmatic-, not necessarily executive-, level managers. We believe it is best suited for a first-year graduate course or perhaps in some cases a senior-level course. When supplemented by other readings, it could be used in an advanced management course for students with no prior management knowledge.

Beyond the material covered here, executives in public sector organizations will need additional training in public administration, such as governmental funding, legal issues, and working with elected officials. Executives in large not-for-profit (and, increasingly, for-profit) organizations will likewise need to go beyond the content of this book to learn more about subjects such as boards of directors, risk management, and accounting.

In this book, readers are introduced to theory and practice in relation to the functions that form the basis of human service management and leadership. Each chapter includes discussion questions and cases providing a number of realistic situations that allow readers to examine the challenges that human service workers face every day. The questions following the cases do not have "right" answers but serve to guide explorations of the issues involved. Many chapters also have suggested exercises that will allow readers to apply management concepts to hypothetical situations.

These cases, as well as the examples included within the body of the text, have all been based on ideas and suggestions provided by more than fifty practicing human service managers. The settings and people described, however, are fictitious.

We emphasize the importance of alignment among the various organizational systems and the role of leadership in pulling things together. We have tried to balance theory and practice throughout the book and to include illustrations that apply to a number of human service settings. We hope readers will gain an awareness of management and its applications and will be able to add to the effectiveness of their own organizations.

New to This Edition

A lot has happened in the human services since the second edition was published, from the evolution of increasingly complex environments to new practice models and research findings. We have tried to address these new developments by adding material on emerging trends and models from the human services, general management, and business and by updating references where possible. A separate chapter on environmental trends and relations has been added, which includes new developments such as asset mapping and community collaboratives. Strategic planning, organizational visioning, and program design have increased prominence. The chapter on structure has been split into one on organization theory and one on organization design, with more attention to the process of organization design and new models such as learning organizations and reinventing government. A new chapter on the design of information systems has been added.

New content has been added in areas including diversity, outcomes measurement, and new approaches to evaluation. To keep the book at a length making it appropriate for a one-semester course, detail on some topics, including needs assessments and experimental evaluation designs, which are typically covered in other graduate courses, has been eliminated. The sections on leadership and organizational change have been significantly reworked and put into a new chapter. The final chapter includes suggestions for ongoing growth and development at the levels of the individual manager, work teams, and the organization as a whole. There are more chapters, shorter in length than in the second edition, to make the book well suited for a one-semester course.

Acknowledgments

My first appreciations must go to Judith Lewis and Michael Lewis for bringing me on as coauthor. I also thank Susan Cowen, who connected me with Mike Lewis to get this started. Our editors at Brooks/Cole, an imprint of Wadsworth, Julie Martinez and Eileen Murphy, and their staff have been very supportive to a rookie author. Heidi Marschner and Laura Larson have been very helpful with editing and a pleasure to work with.

Several of my mentors, teachers, and bosses were especially helpful in my development as a manager. John Wedemeyer Jr. first showed me the importance of good management; and Kathleen Armogida, Randy Mecham, and Nancy Smith provided valuable nurturing and guidance. At UCLA, Alex Norman and Nathan Cohen in the School of Social Welfare and Jim Taylor and Lou Davis in the Graduate School of Management were particularly helpful. Rino Patti and Anne Dosher have been valued mentors over the years, and Percil Stanford and the late Jack Stumpf were influential during my MSW education. The staffs I have supervised were incredibly tolerant and supportive and often made me look better than I felt I was. My students of administration have been eager learners and have asked great questions, helping me to sharpen my thinking, teaching, and writing.

I would also like to acknowledge my reviewers, including Roslyn Chernesky, Fordham University; John Cox, MacMurry College; Yosikazu DeRoos, New Mexico State University; Marie Maher, University of Minnesota, Rochester; Raymond Sanchez Mayers, Rutgers University; James Roeder, Northern Kentucky University; and Iris Wilkinson, Washburn University. They provided some very useful feedback and suggestions.

I should also recognize John Coltrane, whose music was playing on the computer when I began this project; Bob Marley, playing when I finished; and other musicians who provided energy and inspiration. John Ledingham arranged for me to use a computer while traveling, which was enormously helpful. Finally, my love and thanks go to my wife, Leslie, and my son, Adam, who were incredibly tolerant of all my time at the computer; to my mother, who allowed me to do some work while visiting; and to my family, who didn't mind my occasional time away from them during our Colorado reunion.

T. P.

Author Biographies

Judith A. Lewis, Ph.D., is a professor in the Division of Health Administration and Human Services at Governors State University, University Park, Illinois. She is 2000–2001 president of the American Counseling Association, as well as past president of the International Association of Marriage and Family Counselors. She has published books on adolescent, family, community, substance abuse, employee assistance, health, and women's counseling. Her current consultation and training efforts focus on diversity initiatives and innovative helping strategies.

Michael D. Lewis, Ph.D., is a professor of counseling and psychology at Governors State University. He has just returned to his home university after a year at the University of Botswana where as a professor he assisted in the development of the M.A. in counseling for this national university. He has consulted with numerous corporations from Nairobi to San Francisco and in countries as diverse as Germany and Namibia.

Thomas Packard, DSW, teaches in the School of Social Work at San Diego State University. For twenty years he has maintained a practice as an organization development consultant, including six and a half years with the City of San Diego's Organization Effectiveness Program, which he managed for one and a half years. He has been the director of two community-based human service organizations.

Federico Souflée Jr., Ph.D., had an outstanding career in social work practice at all levels—local, state, regional, and national for 30 years. He moved into social work education to make important contributions to both social work knowledge and to the lives of hundreds of other social workers before his untimely recent death. An alumnus of the University of Texas, Arlington, doctoral program, he joined the School of Social Work faculty in 1981, after a distinguished career in child welfare. He was an associate professor of administration and community practice.

Contents

CHAPTER 5 _____

Organization Design   102

CHAPTER 7 _____

Building Supervisory Relationships   153

CHAPTER 8 _____

Managing Finances to Meet Program Goals   184

CHAPTER 9 _____

Designing and Using Information Systems   209

CHAPTER 10 _____

Evaluating Human Service Programs   235

CHAPTER 11 _____

Leading and Changing Human Service Organizations   267

CHAPTER 12 _____

Meeting the Challenge
of Organizational Achievement   303

Facing the Challenges of Management

The management of human service programs is a major concern not just for agency directors and supervisors but also for the people who deliver helping services. Human service professionals used to cringe when they heard the term *management*. For many, that word raised the specter of the "pencil-pushing bureaucrat," surrounded by paper and cut off from the lifeblood of day-to-day work with clients. Unfortunately, this stereotype led many human service providers to avoid becoming competent in management for fear that they might somehow be turning their backs on their clients or losing their professional identification as helpers.

In fact, management can be defined rather simply as the process of (1) making a plan to achieve some end, (2) organizing the people and resources needed to carry out the plan, (3) encouraging the helping workers who will be asked to perform the component tasks, and then (4) evaluating the results. This process can be shared by managers and by people who currently and essentially identify themselves as human service professionals.

Today most people recognize that awareness of managerial functions is important in any human service organization. Many professionals find themselves in supervisory roles because such positions in human service agencies and institutions are normally filled by people with training in the helping professions. Even professionals who spend all their time in direct service delivery need to understand how their organizations work, to help improve operations and influence their superiors to make needed changes.

After reviewing some examples of the need for managerial competency in human service organizations, this chapter will present organizational *purpose* as a unifying principle and will outline some of the challenges facing managers and the generic skills needed at each level of management. Next, key management functions will be summarized, followed by a discussion of the human relations and decision-making skills that support those functions. Finally, leadership and change management will be presented as ways of involving all staff in the accomplishment of organizational missions, goals, and objectives and ensuring the ongoing viability of the organization.

This review essentially summarizes the structure of the book. Chapter 2 will describe some of the uniquenesses of human service organizations and important factors in the environment that must be addressed. Subsequent chapters will cover planning, program and organization design, human resource management and supervision, financial management, information systems and monitoring, and program evaluation. After a chapter on leadership and organizational change, prospects for human service organizations in the future and guidelines for ensuring and maintaining the excellence of such organizations and their managers will be addressed.

The Need for Managerial Competency

Everyday incidents tend to remind professional helpers that they must learn how to manage people, programs, and resources, if only to safeguard the humanistic, people-centered orientation that should permeate human services. Many human service workers are being forced to choose either to participate actively in the administration of their own programs or to leave leadership in the hands of others who may have little understanding of the helping process. Many are being forced to manage their programs or to lose them altogether.

The following incidents—all typical of the kinds of conflicts professional helpers face every day—speak for themselves.

Keith Michaels. As soon as he had earned his master's degree, Keith Michaels decided to put all his time and energy into the creation of a center that would serve the youth of his community. Now in the fifth year of its existence, that center has grown from a storefront office in which Keith saw a few walk-in clients into a major community center, complete with recreational facilities, a peer counseling project, an ongoing consultation program, a busy staff of individual and group counselors, and a major role in the local youth advocacy movement. Most of the clients, counselors, and community members involved with the center are convinced that the explanation for this growth lies in the fact that the staff has always been close to the community's young people and responsive to their needs. They feel that Keith, with the help of the energetic staff he has recruited, can realize a dream they all share, and they want his promise that he will stay with the center as director.

Keith is hesitant, for the agency no longer "runs itself" the way it used to. There is a need to departmentalize, to organize staff hiring and training, to lay out appropriate plans for further change. Keith is afraid to place the management of the center solely in the hands of a professional administrator because he fears that the community responsiveness that has been a hallmark of the program might be lost. He wants to continue to have an effect on the center's future, but he knows that he will have to learn how to plan, organize, and budget on a larger scale.

Shirley Lane. Shirley Lane has spent several years working in a community agency for developmentally disabled adults. She has developed an approach for working with her clients that she has found highly effective and knows that her approach might be helpful to others. In fact, it would provide a major innovation in the field if research showed it to be as effective as she thinks it is.

Because her approach is so promising, Shirley has consistently been encouraged to submit a proposal for federal funding. Finally, her proposed project is being funded; she will now have the chance to implement a training and research project that can make a significant contribution to the field. She knows, however, that if the project is to be successful, she must develop effectiveness in planning projects, supervising the trainees who will help carry out the project, maintaining the budget, and evaluating the results of interventions. She can meet this challenge only if she can successfully carry out the required managerial functions.

Bill Okita. As the harried director of a small community mental health project, Bill Okita never has enough time. He spends half his time in direct service, working with individuals and groups, and this is an aspect of his job that he would not want to give up. He finds his work with clients to be a positive part of his workday; it is what keeps him going and makes all his efforts worthwhile.

Bill has a small staff of professional service providers, all of whom are highly competent. Perhaps this high level of competence accounts for the dramatic rise in the number of clients. The project now has a waiting list for appointments, which conflicts with Bill's belief that counseling should be readily accessible for community members. Yet the agency's funding does not allow Bill enough financial resources to hire additional counselors. He has to make do with the present staff members, but they are all stretched too thin as professionals.

Bill has just been approached by a local citizens' organization whose members are interested in serving as unpaid volunteer counselors at the center. If they could participate in this way, Bill's time problems would be solved. He would finally have enough personnel available to provide the immediate service that he thinks counselees should have. With the pressure off, he could still devote some of his time to direct services instead of having to spend all his time dealing with pressing administrative problems and fund-raising.

Bill has no doubt that these volunteers could do an effective job of serving clients if he provided training and supervision. It is his own skill in supervising and coordinating their efforts that he questions. In fact, he recently turned down the opportunity to have doctoral-level psychology students complete internships at the center because he was not sure that he could handle their needs. Now, however, the situation is desperate. He needs the help of these volunteers, but he must be able to train, supervise, and coordinate them. If he performs his managerial functions more effectively, he can spend less time on them.

Lillian Sanchez. Lillian Sanchez began her career as an elementary school teacher. She spent many years working with young children and found the work fantastically rewarding. Yet, when she received training as a counselor, she wanted the chance to experience that side of helping, too. She accepted a position as a high school counselor because her city did not employ school counselors at any other level.

That work, too, has been fulfilling. But Lillian has always wished that she could combine the rewards of working with young children with those of working as a counselor. She feels that elementary school is the place where effective counselors should be working, for only at that level might there be a chance to prevent the personal and educational problems her high school clients all seem to be facing.

Suddenly, Lillian has the opportunity of a lifetime. A new elementary school is being built in her area, and the potential principal, a longtime professional colleague, has asked her to join the staff as the district's first elementary school counselor. She will build her own program in the direction she thinks best and perhaps have the chance to consult with other schools in the development of additional programs. Lillian has no doubt that this position would be a dream come true. She has always wanted to counsel at the elementary school level, and now she can create a truly innovative program based on the concept of prevention.

Still, she hesitates. She knows she can counsel the children effectively, but she does not know whether she can build a program where none existed before. She will need to learn how to plan effectively, how to provide leadership for teachers and parents, how to consult beneficially with other counselors, and how to evaluate her efforts. The only way she can have the opportunity to practice her child-counseling skills is to develop administrative skills at the same time.

David Williams. David Williams is one of a group of human service workers conducting a preventive program under the auspices of a child and family service center. In recent years, the financial situation of the center has changed. The agency Is being forced to cut back services in some areas to maintain adequate funding for other programs.

David and his colleagues have been called into the executive director's office and told that, as much as she appreciates their fine work, their program might be eliminated within the next year or two. The director recognizes that the preventive program is very popular in the community; calls have been coming in constantly from schools, churches, and recreational centers to request assistance from it. Although she knows that the program is doing something right, she does not know just what it is. She does not know how important it is in comparison with the functions being performed by workers providing direct, clinical services to troubled families.

David and his colleagues now have a real challenge before them. They know that they are helping the community; the informal feedback they have been receiving from young people, parents, and community agencies tells them that. They also know that right now they have no way of proving it, no way of showing that the prevention program is accomplishing something important. They have a short time in which to prove themselves, and they know that their only chance is to plan their program on the basis of goals that the administration agrees are important, to coordinate their efforts with those of other programs, and to develop an accurate evaluation method. If they are going to survive, they need to learn how to carry out these tasks. In short, they need to be able to manage.

Keith Michaels, Shirley Lane, Bill Okita, Lillian Sanchez, and David Williams are all typical human service professionals. They are not interested in changing their professional identities or in moving up some administrative ladder. They are interested in improving and enhancing their human service delivery systems. It could be argued that they should not make the professional move they are contemplating. Perhaps Keith should turn over the management of his counseling center to someone whose original training was in business administration. Possibly Lillian should stay at the high school level, where she can spend all her time on direct service, and wait until the program is fully established by someone else before moving into an elementary school situation. Conceivably, David and his fellow human service workers should seek employment at an agency where preventive programs are already appreciated and where they would have no pressure to prove themselves or to sell their program.

If they do make these decisions, however, they should make them freely, based on their evaluation of all the possible options and their values, priorities, and professional judgment. They should not be in the position of having to choose inaction just because they lack the skills needed to bring about change either in their careers or in their programs. This book is intended to provide human service workers and students with basic management knowledge that may help them in their current jobs or prepare them to take on managerial work. Human service organizations will be presented as complex, purposeful organizations with the potential of bettering social conditions and enriching the lives of employees, clients, and community members.

The Purposes of Human Service Programs _____

Human service programs deal with the personal and social development of individuals, families, and communities. Sometimes they enhance this development through the provision of direct services such as education, training, counseling, therapy, or casework. Often they work indirectly, through consultation, advocacy, referral, information dissemination, community development, or social action. The ultimate purpose of these programs, regardless of methods used, is to enhance the well-being of clients or consumers. In one study (Harvey, 1998) addressing excellence in human service organizations (HSOs), purpose "was the dimension of excellence mentioned most by participants. Having a very clear sense of purpose, direction, mission, or vision, and a focus on its accomplishments is necessary to achieve excellence in an HSO" (p. 37).

Taylor and Felten (1993) have defined an organization's purpose as the "business mission of the system and its philosophy of human values" (p. 39). They see an organization as having four interactive and interdependent elements (see Figure 1-1). First, an organization is a *transforming agency,* which produces outcomes of value. In the case of human service organizations, people (clients or customers) are typically transformed, from individuals, groups, families, or communities with needs or problems to those with needs met or problems ameliorated. Second, an organization is an *economic agency,* which either produces a profit or, in the case of governmental or not-for-profit agencies, maintains a balanced budget or surplus. Third, an organization is a *minisociety,* with norms and a culture that guide members' behavior and indirectly impact organizational effectiveness. Finally, an organization is a *collection of individuals,* who all come with unique values, beliefs, needs, motivational profiles, expectations, and skills.

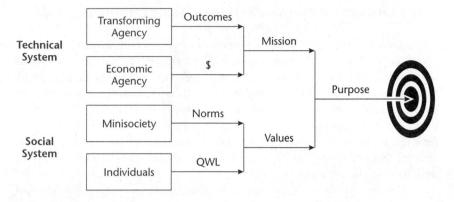

FIGURE 1-1
The Components of Organizational Purpose
SOURCE: *PERFORMANCE BY DESIGN: Sociotechnical Systems in North America* by Taylor & Felton, ©1993. Reprinted by permission of Prentice-Hall, Inc., Upper Saddle River, NJ.

The first two elements, concerning performance and fiscal health, comprise an organization's mission: its distinct competencies and reason for existence. The second two elements address organizational norms and member quality of working life (QWL) and shape the organization's philosophy and values. Purpose, then, is the combination of mission and values: it tells its employees, clients, community, and larger environment why it exists, what it will focus on, and how it intends to treat its staff, clients, and community. Purpose in this sense, when fully articulated and regularly enacted, provides direction, energy, and vision for the organization's employees, who are engaged in a cooperative endeavor to enhance individual and community well-being in some way.

Managers, as leaders of an organization and stewards of its resources, must always maintain focus on purpose, designing systems and behaving in ways consistent with it. *Management* is a set of systems and processes designed to help employees accomplish organizational and individual goals. Rapp and Poertner (1992, pp. 277–278) have gone so far as to invert the traditional hierarchy, putting clients and direct service workers at the top and the director at the bottom. This setup suggests that the manager's job is to help workers get the job done, by clarifying expectations, providing necessary resources, and removing obstacles. In the business sector, this approach has been framed as the "manager as servant" (Greenleaf, 1970). In the demanding day-to-day life of a manager, it is important to keep this perspective and to resist the temptation to focus only on procedure or management needs rather than on organizational results. Management processes and leadership are both essential and should be jointly well executed, and this is a manager's contribution to the success of the organization.

The Domains of Human Service Organizations _____

The value of remaining focused on purpose is represented in the challenge managers face in addressing the multiple interests of those above them and outside the organization and those below them in the hierarchy, providing direct services. Over twenty years ago, Kouzes and Mico (1979) asserted that human service organizations are based on a paradigm that is not common to all types of organizations. Although this point is less true than it may have been then, the model is nevertheless useful for showing the multiple demands placed on managers and the differing perspective of the various stakeholders (those who have an interest or stake in what the organization does).

Kouzes and Mico suggest that each of the domains uses a different set of guiding principles and measures of success that are incongruent across the domains. The *Policy Domain* focuses on governance and includes the board of directors or, in the case of governmental organizations, elected officials and the electorate. The *Management Domain* ranges from executive to first-line managers and historically has focused on control and coordination. The *Service Domain* is composed of service delivery staff. Kouzes and Mico suggest that "discordance, disjunction, and conflicts" occur between each pair of domains. Managers have to contend in the policy domain with laws and regulations coming from various units of government; in the case of not-for-profit or for-profit human service organizations, they need to manage relations with their boards of directors. At the other end, managers need to work effectively with the direct service workers, who emphasize professional autonomy and are concerned with "quality of care" and "professional standards." While the concerns at all levels are important and legitimate, it is a challenge for management to manage uncertainty and differing priorities, developing alignment among the three domains. This balance happens primarily through managerial leadership.

Administrative Expertise

The Managerial Domain can be subdivided further into the institutional, managerial, and technical levels, as described in a classic *Harvard Business Review* article (Katz, 1974) and later applied to the human services by Wilson (1980). Katz outlines three skill areas of managers (see Figure 1-2). *Technical skills* are those related to accomplishing the agency's core activities: counseling, casework, and other services to clients or the community (for example, program design and monitoring). *People skills* involve interpersonal effectiveness such as oral communication, listening, conflict management, leading, and motivating. *Conceptual skills* enable one to use the "big picture" to manage relations with external forces, analyze and understand organizational dynamics and how things fit together, attend to how different functions and processes interact, and solve problems.

As Figure 1-2 shows, technical skills are more important at the supervisor level. For middle managers, these become less important as conceptual skills are

Management Levels	Skills Needed

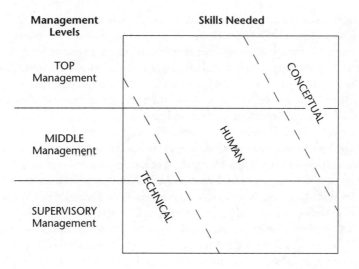

FIGURE 1-2
Types of Management Skills
SOURCE: Hersey, P., & Blanchard, K. (1988). *Management of organizational behavior: Utilizing human resources* (5th ed., p. 8). Upper Saddle River, NJ: Prentice Hall. Reprinted with permission.

more required. At upper management levels, executives need enough basic knowledge of the program's service delivery technologies to make informed managerial decisions, but conceptual skills are more necessary to aid in managing all aspects of the organization. People skills are essential and equally important at all levels. Thus, managers need highly developed interpersonal skills to manage and lead effectively. This reality of organizational life contradicts the axiom that those who are not "good with clients" should "go into administration." This notion is the human service version of the equally misguided axiom from the music field: "If you can't be a musician, be a conductor." While, of course, many examples of this view can be found in the human services, music, and probably all professions, it is more true than ever that managers need very high levels of interpersonal skills to function as leaders, negotiators, coordinators, and motivators.

The need for technical skills even at the upper management levels raises another issue in the human service field and, in fact, in all professions that operate in organizations. In the human services, particularly in midsized and small agencies, managers commonly have been drawn from the ranks from direct services. In fact, often the best direct services workers were promoted based on their professional and technical expertise, only to become ineffective managers because they did not have similar expertise in management skills. An opposite dynamic was noted some years ago with the Peter Principle (Peter, 1969): managers are promoted to the level of their incompetence. Both of these dynamics suggest the need for well-trained managers. This issue in the human service field is concerned with the professional training of these skilled managers.

In reaction to managerial problems noted when human service workers became managers, many organizations began to hire professional managers with business, rather than human service, degrees. In many cases, different problems emerged: the managers could handle finances and information systems but often made bad decisions in the areas of programming and strategy development, relying on their quantitative analytical skills and not properly considering issues of service delivery and professional ethics and values.

Unfortunately, in spite of an increased emphasis in offering management courses in human service master's degree programs such as the MSW, some writers have tentatively concluded that given current graduate education programs, an MBA or MPA degree would probably be more desirable than an MSW for upper-level management (Cupaiuolo, Loavenbruck, & Kiely, 1995). This is partly based on a study of human service executives in Chicago (Hoefer, 1993), in which the MBA or MPA degree was preferred over the MSW for executive-level positions. However, the same study noted that the MSW was favored for entry-level and middle management positions. The implication here is that professional human service degree programs such as the MSW should offer specialized training in management to prepare skilled managers who have both knowledge and experience in service delivery and a professional value base as well as state-of-the art management skills in areas ranging from financial management to leadership.

Functions of Human Service Management

Currently, most human service programs are based either in public organizations, such as departments of social services and schools, or in nonprofit agencies that have been created to meet specific community needs. (Increasingly, for-profit organizations are entering this field, presenting new challenges to existing agencies to clearly achieve desired outcomes in a cost-effective manner while remaining true to professional standards, values, and ethics.) Whether programs provide direct or indirect services and whether they are housed in public or private agencies, they tend to share similar managerial functions. The management of human service programs includes the following major components:

- **Planning**—Developing visions for the future, developing strategy, setting goals and objectives for attaining them, and selecting program models

- **Designing**—Structuring and coordinating the work that needs to be done to carry out plans

- **Developing human resources**—Mobilizing the people needed to make the program work and taking steps to enhance their productivity

- **Supervising**—Enhancing the skills and motivation of service providers

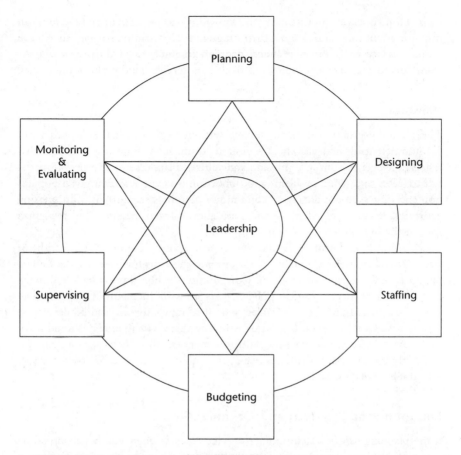

FIGURE 1-3
A Conceptual Framework for Human Service Management

- **Managing finances**—Planning the use of financial resources for reaching goals and controlling expenditures

- **Monitoring**—Tracking progress on program objectives and activities

- **Evaluating**—Comparing program accomplishments with the standards set at the planning stages; using the results as the basis for change

The force that binds together and energizes these processes is leadership: working with employees to articulate a vision, manage the external environment, oversee the design of organizational processes, link elements of the system together, create a supportive organizational culture, and manage change. This model is represented in Figure 1-3.

Human service professionals who know how to perform these functions can play important roles in managing their programs. They can make plans to achieve human service goals, organize the people and resources needed to carry out the plans, encourage and assist individuals delivering services, and evaluate the results.

Planning

The planning process in human service settings begins with the assessment of community needs and visions of a desired future state, from a perspective that reflects the agency's purpose (mission and values). Planners use a variety of methods to determine what problems and opportunities exist within a given population and, just as important, what community members see as their most pressing priorities. If currently offered services are also analyzed, planners can recognize gaps in the human service system.

This assessment of needs and the identification of community strengths or assets (Kretzmann & McKnight, 1996) provide the basis for selecting the potential goals of the agency or program. Community members, potential consumers, and service providers, as well as policymakers, must all be involved in setting service goals. Actual programs, or collections of related activities, can be developed on the basis of these goals. Instead of assuming that a given activity should form the heart of a human service program, planners examine alternate methods for achieving the objectives that have been set. Only then can specific plans for service implementation be laid.

Designing the Program and Organization

If the planning function helps human service workers determine what should be accomplished, the designing function helps them carry out the plan. Designing is done at three levels: the organization as a whole, the program, and individual jobs. There are two aspects of design. First, structure is the element traditionally associated with the "organizing" function: what functions are in the various units and how the chain of command is set up. Second, design includes organizational processes such as communication and decision-making mechanisms. These are not apparent on the organization chart but are key to effective functioning.

Furthermore, as will be explained in Chapter 5, *design* is both a noun and a verb. As a noun, it describes structure and processes; as a verb, it is the process for creating the organization—deciding what needs to be done and determining the best structures and processes. Organization design flows from the result of the planning phase: mission, goals, objectives, and overall strategies.

A design, or, as is more often the case, a redesign, of the organization results in the structure and processes that allow all people and units involved to understand what part they are to play in the organization, how ongoing communication and coordination of effort are to occur, and what the lines of authority and responsibility are expected to be.

Within these parameters, the types of structure possible vary tremendously, depending on the goals, needs, resources, size, and environment of the organization. They also vary in accordance with the values, philosophy, and theoretical approaches of the designers. These will be discussed in Chapter 4.

Developing Human Resources

An organization's plans and design are put into operation by people: human service programs are labor-intensive. A major part of each budget goes toward salaries and benefits for service deliverers and support personnel. The success of services depends on the manager's ability to mobilize valuable human resources so that the immediate and long-term needs of the organization and its clients are met. Especially in times of retrenchment, when financial resources dwindle, human service managers must plan carefully both to bring needed people into the organization and to enhance their development once they have begun to provide services.

The development of human resources involves the use of the unique contributions that all of the workers of the human service enterprise can make. Special attention needs to be paid to the knowledge and skills that women and people of color bring to the organization (Asamoah, 1995; Bailey, 1995; Healy, Havens, & Pine, 1995). Feminist and transcultural perspectives, as represented by a diverse workforce, enhance the capabilities of human service programs to provide relevant and compatible services to diverse client populations.

Careful recruitment, selection, training, and appraisal processes should be used for both paid employees and volunteers. Hiring practices normally take into account the abilities, experiences, and characteristics of potential human service workers, but managers sometimes forget to consider the organization's unique needs. Job responsibilities and priorities should be defined precisely even before vacancies are advertised. This analysis should then form the basis for screening applicants and for hiring those candidates whose qualities best fit the actual jobs to be performed. After hiring, the new employee should be fully oriented to the agency in areas ranging from the governance structure and policies and procedures to agency history and organizational culture.

The environment and program activities of human service organizations change so rapidly that ongoing development of staff is essential. The function formerly known as "personnel and training" has recently been reconceptualized as "strategic human resource management," reflecting the principle that training and development should be guided by the key strategies, priorities, and programmatic needs of the agency. When an agency implements a new program or adopts improved service delivery methods, staff will need appropriate training. As will be discussed later, treating agencies as learning organizations (Senge, 1990) and encouraging lifelong learning on the part of staff are becoming increasingly common principles of staff and organization development. Beginning and advanced training in computer usage will become more necessary as agencies increasingly tap the potentials of the Internet, database management, and other software.

Once people have been hired, performance appraisals should occur regularly. They should be based on objective analyses of the tasks and behaviors that lead to successful job performance. Fair, objective performance appraisals serve dual purposes. They can be used for evaluating individuals and also for identifying areas of needed development in the individual or in the organization. Performance appraisals can point the way toward new behaviors that should be learned and practiced, allowing services to keep pace with client needs.

One way to expand an agency's human resources is to encourage volunteer participation. This approach works as long as recruitment and assignment of volunteer service providers are planned as carefully as is the hiring of professional employees. Volunteers can add significantly to a program's thrust because they provide fresh ideas and strong links to their communities. Community members' participation increases the agency's service delivery capacity, but only if these contributions are respected as highly as those of paid personnel.

Supervising

Supervision involves helping a subordinate maximize his or her effectiveness in service delivery by providing support and encouragement, helping build skills and competencies, and overseeing the supervisee's work. The nature of the supervisory relationship depends on the supervisor's leadership style, the supervisee's motivation, and the organization's needs.

The human service manager performs a number of interrelated functions attached to the supervisory role. Central to the role is the leadership function inherent in the position of supervisor, which ascribes formal authority to guide others in the attainment of organizational goals. As a supervisor, the human service manager is accorded by the organization certain powers of reward and coercion. More important to many subordinates are expert power and referent power (being admired and respected) (Kadushin, 1985, p. 93).

The human service supervisor also fulfills a management, or administrative, function. As such, the supervisor must possess knowledge and skills relevant to the day-to-day direction and control of unit operations—for example, assigning and delegating work, coordinating workers' activities, planning unit goals and objectives, and so on. In addition, the supervisor must have knowledge and skills relevant to broader organizational and administrative concerns, including strategic and tactical planning, structure, staffing, fund-raising and budgeting, and program evaluation.

A third function of the human service supervisor involves mediating relationships between the supervisor's unit and other levels and parts of the organization and between the supervisory unit and the environment (Kadushin, 1985; Shulman, 1993).

Finally, the supervisor's role entails an educational function, sometimes referred to as "clinical supervision" (Kadushin, 1985). In fulfilling all of the functions of the supervisory role, the human service manager provides, as a leader, emotional and psychological support to his or her staff as a means of preventing worker burnout and enhancing motivation and job satisfaction. Educational supervision, in addition, addresses workers' needs for professional growth and development in the provision of job-related services designed to improve client outcomes (Shulman, 1993).

Managing Finances

Human service professionals can understand their own programs only if they know how they are budgeted. When they are directing specially funded projects, full-time service providers control the allocation of limited financial resources. Even when their programs make up only parts of total agency structures, human service workers should try to gain access to and understand the financial reports that affect them.

The process of setting and controlling the budget is closely related to planning and evaluation. In fact, a budget is fundamentally a program in fiscal terms. The more closely related the budget is to goals of people who hold a stake in the agency's success, the more effectively it is likely to work.

A budget must be seen as the concrete documentation of the planning process, bringing ideals into reality. An annual budget does not have to be based simply on a slight increment over the previous year's figures. Instead, it can be based on a recognition of program goals and the costs of activities expected to attain those goals. For instance, zero-based budgeting requires that each set of activities be justified in its entirety before resources are allocated. Program budgeting places accountability on programs by allocating resources for the attainment of specific objectives rather than simply to "line items" such as personnel costs or supplies.

Budget making is thus a decision-making process through which allocations are made to one service rather than another. If it is to be closely related to the program development process, human service providers should be involved. At the very least, they need to be aware of how the planning process has been translated into financial terms.

Even when traditional line item budgets are used, planners can ensure that the budget reflects program priorities by following careful procedures for allocating resources to specific activities. The objectives that have been set as part of the initial plan can be analyzed in terms of the activities that need to be performed before the objectives have been met. Each activity can then be broken down in terms of time span, personnel costs, and nonpersonnel costs until a total cost for the activity has been determined. The costs for these activities can be either budgeted according to program or placed in the context of a line item budget. In either case, the budget that finally sees the light of day is one that has been derived not from assumptions about what items should always be included in a budget but from analyses of program goals and priorities.

Once an effective annual budget is in place, ongoing financial reports help determine whether expenditures and income are as expected or whether significant deviations from what was planned have developed. The human service worker who understands the budget does not need to give it a great deal of attention after the initial stages. Managers, of course, need to pay attention to money matters when there are variances that need to be accounted for or acted on.

Closely related to budgeting is the whole question of funding mechanisms. Public agencies depend for their funding on legislative appropriations as well as other possible sources of revenue. Private, nonprofit agencies tend to depend on some combination of grants, contracts, contributions, and fees paid for services, either by clients or by third parties. For-profit companies operating in the human service field typically are funded by contracts and fees (often paid by third parties) and have the added benefit of using their own capital. The brand of funding can have a major effect on an agency's programs because funding sources vary in terms of long-range predictability and the services they tend to encourage. Program planners and budget makers need to be aware of the agency's major focus and should not lose sight of program goals when new funding possibilities appear. The integrity of agency goals is especially difficult to maintain in times of resource scarcity. At such times, it is most important to recall that budgeting and fundraising should remain subsidiary to planning.

Monitoring and Evaluating

A program must have information systems to enable all staff to keep track of what is being done and accomplished. Such a system is variously referred to as "documentation," "keeping stats," or a "management information system." Such a system should keep track of not only program activities but also the ultimate outcomes, or results, as they relate to clients. Information systems are used both to track organizational activities and progress and to provide data for evaluation. Evaluating a program involves comparing program accomplishments with criteria and standards set at the planning stage. Evaluation is not necessarily a specialized activity carried on only at special times by outside experts descending on an organization. It should be seen as an ongoing self-assessment process in which all human service workers participate.

The agency's information system allows for a constant monitoring of agency activities and provides data for evaluation—an assessment of the effects of services on clients. Human service professionals need to know whether the services being carried out are in accordance with what was planned within a certain time and budget. They also need to know whether the program is meeting its objectives in terms of client change.

When criteria and standards are clear, evaluators can identify the data needed to measure the degree to which objectives have been attained. The next step becomes identifying the source of the data and designing a system for obtaining and reporting information.

If an ongoing information system is in place, evaluations of effort and effectiveness can be implemented either by external consultants or by agency workers. Once evaluation results have been reported, needed program changes can be identified and implemented.

It is difficult to separate evaluation from planning because an effective plan must include an evaluation component, but an effective evaluation must be based on the goals and objectives identified as part of a plan. Most important, human service professionals must be aware of the need to gather appropriate data as part of normal, ongoing program operation. Only then can evaluation gain its rightful place in the management and coordination of all activities. When this takes place, human service workers who already "know" that their services are effective will be able to prove it to others.

Human Relations Skills

Management is never a solo performance. It involves the orchestration of complex human elements into a whole that is characterized by harmony rather than discord. In any organization, managers must be able to work effectively with individuals and groups. They must encourage communication, build personal motivation, and form cooperative problem-solving groups. These interpersonal skills are as important in planning and budgeting as in direct supervision.

Effective application of all of the management functions just described requires polished interpersonal skills. If a plan is to be a living document, its formation must involve active participation of the people who will be affected by it, including potential service consumers as well as policymakers, board members, funding sources, managers, and agency employees. The human service professional who is involved in developing any program plan or innovation must be able to encourage and work closely with a variety of individuals and groups, each of whom might have a special priority in mind.

Budgeting requires far greater skill with people than with dollars and cents. Although the budget is closely involved with the planning process, it invariably attracts more conflict than any other planning component. Allocation of scarce resources means that funds are distributed to some programs, services, or individuals at the expense of others. Even when the most rational possible procedures are used to make the necessary decisions, both the processes and the results need to be sold to participants. When more traditional budgeting approaches are used, political processes and the balancing of conflicting interests come to the fore and need to be accepted as realities. No one can build a budget without being in close touch with the needs of funding sources, consumers, and workers.

The balancing of human and organizational needs is also important in creating an agency's structure. Organizing involves dividing and coordinating the efforts of individuals and departments. These tasks can be done successfully only if the manager is sensitive to the needs of the people contributing to the work effort. The degree of centralization or decentralization, of specialization or generalization, of control or independence built into the organization's structure is a function of the needs being met. These needs include both those dictated by the tasks to be performed and those dictated by the human characteristics of the people performing them. Like a plan or a budget, an organizational structure depends as much on interpersonal dynamics as on technical concerns.

Human relations skills interact even more directly and clearly with leadership functions. A key to management is that tasks are performed not just by the manager but by and through the efforts of other people. Motivating, affecting, and supporting others' behaviors require strong interpersonal competency, whether the object of the leadership activity is a supervisee or a local citizen, an individual staff member or a group participating in a problem-solving meeting.

Finally, human relations skills affect the human service manager's ability to carry out evaluation processes. Not surprisingly, many workers find evaluation threatening. Yet the active participation of all agency employees, at least in data gathering, is necessary to carrying out the evaluation function. If evaluations are to be accurate and if their results are really going to be used as a basis for managerial decisions, cooperative efforts are essential.

The skill of working effectively with individuals and groups runs through the performance of every managerial function, and human service professionals may well find their backgrounds more useful than expected. Professional training can also enhance the development of skills in individual or joint decision making.

Decision-Making Skills

Management is, in a very basic sense, a process of making decisions. From deciding whether to spin off a new agency to choosing the location of a water cooler, from selecting a new staff member to considering alternate data forms, the manager is in the position of constantly choosing among alternatives. Deciding, along with communicating, is what a manager actually does with his or her time.

Decision making involves identifying and weighing alternate means for reaching desired ends. In human service settings, the selection of the best means for achieving an objective is often far from clear. Because of the high degree of uncertainty that will always be present in dealing with human needs, completely rational decision making is impossible. Basic values, desired goals, and the wishes of sometimes opposing factions need to be taken into account. In this context, decision-making skill requires sensitivity as much as rationality.

When carrying out the planning function, human service professionals need to decide what approaches to use in assessing needs, how to involve community members and other stakeholders in the goal-setting process, and what reasonable objectives for a program might be. These decisions actually precede the real decision-making challenge: choosing the most effective combination of services to meet the specified objectives. No one administrator or service deliverer makes these decisions alone. Involvement in cooperative decision making, however, is, if anything, more complex than choosing alternatives on the basis of one person's judgment.

Budgeting is also a decision-making activity. Whether working alone or as a member of a planning group, the human service professional must help decide how resources are to be allocated. Especially in times of economic stress, each positive choice can bring with it the need to make a negative decision somewhere else. Choosing to fund one activity means choosing not to fund another.

The decisions that are made as part of designing programs and structuring the organization also have far-reaching implications. In organizing, the manager must weigh the benefits of varying methods of dividing tasks among individuals and departments. The choices made invariably have major effects on the behaviors and productivity of all members of the service delivery team.

In providing leadership for this team, the manager continues to choose among alternate interventions, methods, and targets for change. Each decision affects both the immediate situation and the life of the agency as a whole. Ultimately, evaluation completes the administrative cycle by measuring the effects of past decisions and laying the groundwork for new choices.

Leadership and Change Management: Keeping the Organization Responsive and Vibrant _____

The managerial functions previously described need to be implemented in order for programs to be effectively maintained. Fortunately for human service managers, the practical, human skills that underlie managerial functions are closely allied with the skills of helping. Social work and counseling degree programs in particular emphasize effective communication skills such as active listening, giving and receiving feedback, group dynamics and facilitation, and positive regard for all individuals. All these skills are important for managers as they design systems and lead staff in accomplishing organizational goals.

In an era of accountability and limited resources, human service professionals cannot afford the luxury of attending to their own customary activities in isolation from general agency goals and operations. Service providers must know how their activities relate to programs and how these programs, in turn, relate to agency and community priorities. Human service professionals, like everyone with a stake in an agency's continued existence, must be aware of managerial processes that enable them to function on a daily basis (how their check is paid, why they need to keep good client records, why evaluations need to occur). Conveying this information and helping staff come to appreciate the importance of it is a task requiring leadership.

As Figure 1-3 illustrates, leadership is the unifying factor for all management processes. Agency executives and, in fact, managers at all levels need to be leaders who help keep the organization and all staff focused on key organizational outcomes and processes necessary to get there; provide energy, confidence, and optimism regarding meeting the challenges facing human service organizations; and oversee the agency's constant evolution and change so that it remains responsive to community needs and concerns. In briefly revisiting Figure 1-1 on organizational purpose, both the technical and leadership functions of management can be seen. The manager addresses the technical system functions through overseeing organizational processes including planning, program and organization design, human resources management and supervision, financial management, and monitoring and evaluation. The manager addresses the social system by providing leadership and vision, articulating key values and ethical standards, ensuring a vibrant organizational culture and high quality of working life, and overseeing constant organizational learning and change.

Change management is a major responsibility for leaders. Chapter 2 will outline some of the powerful external forces affecting human service organizations, pointing for the need for ongoing adaptation and change. As will be seen in Chapter 11, nearly every viable contemporary leadership approach includes change management. Leaders are not always the drivers of change, however, and even when they desire change they sometimes need expertise from an outside source. Organization development, business process reengineering, total quality management, and other change processes are increasingly being used in human service organizations, with both good and disappointing results. Finally, there are techniques for lower-level employees to identify change opportunities and make proposals for improving agency operations. Leadership and change management are the ways that organizational processes and systems are kept up-to-date and responsive so that the agency can be maximally effective and thrive in an increasingly challenging environment.

Summary

Human service organizations exist to accomplish socially desirable purposes. Good management is an essential element in making agencies able to accomplish desired goals. This chapter has reviewed the management processes that are essential to organizational effectiveness. The following chapters will address these areas in greater detail. Chapter 2 will review the uniquenesses of human service organizations and factors in the environment that need attention. Some methods for managing the environment will be described. Chapter 3 will show how strategic planning can be used to respond to the environment. Subsequent chapters will discuss how to design programs based on plans and then how to staff, fund, monitor, and evaluate them. After a chapter on leading and changing organizations, the final chapter will offer perspectives on how today's manager of human service programs can rise to the challenge of attaining organizational excellence.

Discussion Questions _____

1. What do you perceive as the main differences between managing a human service organization and managing a business? Would the same skills, attitudes, and body of knowledge be appropriate for each?

2. Think about a human service organization with which you are familiar. Is it well managed? How could its effectiveness be improved? Which managerial functions are being performed most effectively?

3. What skills would you need to develop to manage a human service program?

Group Exercise _____

Work in groups of six to eight people. Brainstorm as many answers as you can generate to the question "What are the characteristics of an effective professional helper?" Be sure to write down any ideas that anyone in the group suggests.

After completing this list, use a brainstorming approach again, this time to answer the question "What are the characteristics of an effective human service manager?"

Compare the two lists, discussing the following questions:

1. How great are the differences between effective helpers and good managers?

2. To what degree are our ideas about human service managers affected by our own stereotypes of business managers?

CASE 1 _____

Transitions into Management

Review the situations of the individuals profiled at the beginning of this chapter. Choose one with which you can identify in some way and answer these questions from their perspective.

1. What prospective changes in role are facing this person?

2. If you were in this situation, what factors would you consider in assessing your career goals and the kinds of activities you would like at work?

3. If you moved further into management, what additional skills and training would you need?

References

Asamoah, Y. (1995). Managing the new multicultural workforce. In L. Ginsberg & P. Keys (Eds.), *New management in human services* (2nd ed., pp. 115–127). Washington, DC: NASW Press.

Bailey, D. (1995). Management: Diverse workplaces. In R. Edwards (Ed.), *Encyclopedia of social work* (19th ed., pp. 1659–1663). Washington, DC: NASW Press.

Cupaiuolo, A., Loavenbruck, G., & Kiely, K. (1995). MBA, MPA, MSW: Is there a degree of choice for human services management? In L. Ginsberg & P. Keys (Eds.), *New management in human services* (2nd ed., pp. 45–46). Washington, DC: NASW Press.

Greenleaf, R. (1970). *The servant as leader.* Indianapolis: Robert K. Greenleaf Center for Servant-Leadership.

Harvey, C. (1998). Defining excellence in human service organizations. *Administration in Social Work, 22*(1), 33–45.

Healy, L., Havens, C., & Pine, B. (1995). Women and social work management. In L. Ginsberg & P. Keys (Eds.), *New management in human services* (2nd ed., pp. 128–150). Washington, DC: NASW Press.

Hoefer, R. (1993). A matter of degree: Job skills for human service administrators. *Administration in Social Work, 17*(3), 1–20.

Kadushin, A. (1985). *Supervision in social work* (2nd ed.). New York: Columbia University Press.

Katz, R. (1974). Skills of an effective administrator. *Harvard Business Review, 52*(5), 90–102.

Kouzes, J., & Mico, P. (1979). Domain theory: An introduction to organizational behavior in human service organizations. *Journal of Applied Behavioral Sciences, 15*(4), 449–469.

Kretzmann, J., & McKnight, J. (1996). Assets-based community development. *National Civic Review, 85*(4), 23–27.

Peter, L., with Hull, R. (1969). *The Peter principle.* New York: Bantam.

Rapp, C., & Poertner, J. (1992). *Social administration: A client-centered approach.* New York: Longman.

Senge, P. (1990). *The fifth discipline.* New York: Doubleday Currency.

Shulman, L. (1993). *Interactional supervision.* Washington, DC: NASW Press.

Taylor, J., & Felten, D. (1993). *Performance by design.* Upper Saddle River, NJ: Prentice Hall.

Wilson, S. (1980). Values and technology: Foundations for practice. In F. Perlmutter & S. Slavin (Eds.), *Leadership in social administration: Perspectives for the 1980s* (pp. 105–122). Philadelphia: Temple University Press.

2

The Environments of Human Service Organizations

In this chapter, we will first note some of the ways in which human service organizations are different from typical for-profit businesses, identifying some of the unique challenges facing human service managers. Next, we will assess the environmental context of human service organizations and suggest the importance of effective management in responding to social needs. A review of key trends and issues in the environment will provide some context for the managerial processes of human service organizations. As we noted in the previous chapter, organizations are purposeful entities that respond to needs and trends in the environment. The ability to scan and understand an agency's current and future environments appropriately will enable staff proactively to deal with and anticipate changing conditions and, ideally, influence the environment to make it more responsive and hospitable to clients and communities.

Agencies must accurately and comprehensively assess their changing environments on an ongoing basis if they are to be successful in appropriately responding to community needs and visions. Historically, the most common technique for this has been the needs assessment. This valuable tool has been augmented in recent years by techniques such as strength-based approaches (such as asset mapping).

This chapter concludes with a review of some other processes that enable the organization to respond effectively to its environment and not only survive but thrive. A general term for this is *boundary spanning* or *boundary management*. One example of this is environmental scanning: a process of identifying trends and issues such as those discussed earlier. Environmental scanning is a key step in strategic planning, presented in the next chapter. Agency staff also manage environmental relations through their managers' and staffs' involvement in community collaboratives, interdisciplinary teams, service linkage agreements, coalitions, and memberships in coalitions and professional associations. Finally, the functions of public relations and marketing, sometimes viewed with skepticism or disgust by line staff, can be very important in helping the agency deliver services in the most responsive ways.

Uniquenesses of Human Service Organizations _____

Management in human service settings is a highly challenging task, primarily because the factors that differentiate nonprofit organizations from profit-making firms are the very factors that tend to make management difficult. Some of these problems are so common that they might be considered inherent in the nature of human services, although in recent years advances in administrative practice have begun to mitigate each of them to some extent. In fact, there are now probably more similarities than differences between human service and business organizations. Nevertheless, several aspects of human service organizations make their management particularly challenging, and some are listed here.

1. Human service organizations have unclear, "fuzzy" goals. Traditionally, the goals guiding human services have tended to be less clearly stated than those of their profit-making counterparts. In some instances, goal statements are too general to have a great deal of meaning either to consumers or to service deliverers. This situation has been changing in recent years, with the realization that process and output measures common in human services (number of counseling sessions, referrals made, nights of lodging) do not tell the community or policymakers much about what is actually being accomplished. While workers in particular may see this as a threat or at least an annoyance, the trend toward identifying measurable objectives or outcomes should actually be seen as an opportunity to demonstrate more effectively the value of human services. For the time being, the problem of vague or conflicting goals will continue to occupy managers' attention.

2. There are conflicts in values and expectations among the groups involved in human service delivery. In some HSOs, goals are not accepted unanimously by all stakeholders in the agency's work. This situation causes obvious managerial difficulty because those charged with the responsibility for delivering services might actually be working at cross-purposes. Citizens, consumers, service providers, managers, funding sources, and policymakers may have differing ideas about service priorities. Hasenfeld (1992) describes human services as "moral work" (p. 5) to illustrate this dilemma. The 1996 welfare reform law is a good example. For many conservatives, the goal, implied or explicit, was to get people off welfare. If they remained poor, that was not a concern for some, who expect the poor to take care of themselves. For some moderates, the goal was to enhance self-sufficiency. Conflicting policy priorities often result in conflicting mandates and regulations for human service agencies, which are left to respond to the satisfaction of all stakeholders, often without the necessary resources.

The problems are made even more complex by the fact that human service agencies tend to employ many professionals. These workers sometimes have conflicting loyalties between their professional training, which focuses on quality services to all clients, and their responsibility to implement agency policies, which may be driven by cost considerations. Even when different groups of professionals are equally committed to client services, conflict may emerge based on differing treatment philosophies. A dually diagnosed client may be seen very differently by a twelve-step-oriented substance abuse provider and a mental health professional who sees medication as the main way to control behavior.

3. Human service agencies have historically demonstrated more concern for means than for ends. Because of the difficulty in specifying effective service methods and outcomes, human service providers have concentrated more on the nature of the services than on ultimate outcomes. Familiar methods are often used long after changes in community needs or agency mission or practice research suggesting the ineffectiveness of certain treatment approaches. The result can be a lack of connection between the agency's avowed purposes and its employees' activities. As is the case with human service program goals discussed earlier, this situation is improving.

4. Measuring the outcomes of human service programs is difficult. It is easier to count the number of job-training sessions an unemployed client receives than to document having an individual employed in a living-wage job for a particular length of time. Because the results of human service programs are often intangible, administrators are hard-pressed to ensure accountability either on the part of the agency as a whole or on the part of individual employees. This problem, too, is being addressed through the move to outcomes-based program designs, objectives, and budgets.

5. Human service organizations often serve involuntary, "undesirable," or multiproblem clients. Hasenfeld (1992) uses the term *client reactivity* to describe the complexity of the relationship between clients, often with multiple problems, and the service delivery process. This is complicated by the many actors (family members, the legal system, other agencies, and so forth) who may be interested in the case. In an allegation of child abuse, for example, the interests of the child, the parent, other family members, and the community intertwine in complex ways, making service delivery complicated. The "market model" of client satisfaction has less meaning for involuntary clients such as sex offenders or persons with severe mental disabilities. Society sometimes has low regard for some human service clients and therefore inadequately supports programs to serve them, with the early stages of the AIDS epidemic being a vivid example.

But human service agencies are not necessarily doomed to a future of mismanagement and inefficiency. Many of the problems that plague them can be solved or at least cut down to manageable size through more effective planning, which includes proactive attention to key factors in the human service environment. Next, we will review some ways to assess the environment of human service organizations and some of the current major trends.

Stakeholder Expectations

The key actors in the human service organization's environment having the most influence on the organization (now commonly referred to *stakeholders*—individuals or groups with a stake in what the organization does and how it operates) are its funding sources, its regulatory bodies, the legal system, other human service organizations, and the organization's clients and constituency groups. Since "environment" does not necessarily refer to an agency's immediate geographic area, a funding source could be a federal bureau in Washington, DC, the governor's office at the state capitol, a private foundation located in another state, or the local United Way. Or, for agencies having diversified funding sources, it could be a combination of all of these funding agencies, each with its own set of funding conditions, reporting procedures, and accountability standards. Thus, in terms of funding sources alone, an agency's environment can acquire complex proportions. Managed care, privatization of government services, and the recent focus on documenting outcomes of service are all reflections of the political context of human service organizations that are requiring major adjustments.

Regulatory bodies such as accrediting councils can also exert considerable external influence on an organization's structure, including its policies and procedures, hiring practices, technology, and so on. Although membership in these standard-setting associations is voluntary, nonaffiliation can depreciate an organization's status and power, whereas membership in good standing can increase an organization's prestige and image. Also, the effect of the legal system on organizational practices is a common contemporary phenomenon. Lawsuits and countersuits often result in changes in agency policies.

In addition to these external sources of influence, the human service organization is subject as well to environmental influences from other organizations, especially those competing for political or financial resources; from client groups in need of additional services or dissatisfied with current ones; and from interest groups seeking to impose their own agendas on organizational goals and services.

Finally, expectations for improved customer service are challenging agencies to make improvements in service delivery philosophies and methods. Patients' rights initiatives in mental health and disability services exemplify trends that should improve service delivery.

Managers need both depth perception and peripheral vision when looking at the environment. They need to know what is relevant from the past and need to look ahead into the future. In the present, they need to look "sideways" beyond the daily arena of service delivery programs. For example, the business section of the newspaper may show important trends in finance that an astute manager could turn into an opportunity. The "society" section typically covers local fund-raising events that may give a manager ideas on new places to look for support. Generally, the higher one goes in management, the broader and longer-term the vision needs to be. Even at the service delivery level, however, staff need to be looking at the environment to identify emerging needs and new programs, and to find similar organizations using "best practices" (see Chapter 11) that may be adapted in one's own program.

Analysis of Environmental Trends

Garner (1989, p. 27) notes the importance of seeing not only current trends but the underlying deep, strong "currents" and then responding to them by developing strategies and programs. With that in mind, factors mentioned here should in fact be major trends rather than "surface" trends that are likely to become less important in a matter of a year or two.

In his book on strategic planing, Bryson (1995) uses the acronym *PEST* to organize trends in the environment: political, economic, social, and technological factors. Some of these will be reviewed here, with the caveat that this list is incomplete and inevitably out-of-date. Doing your own PEST analysis will be covered in Chapter 3 as part of strategic planning.

Political Trends

The "devolution revolution" (Cooke, Reid, & Edwards, 1997) has resulted in heretofore federal responsibilities being shifted to state and local government, also leading to great increases in contracting and other forms of privatization, with increased expectations for innovation and cost savings. Welfare reform and block grants are prominent examples. This has led to increased interaction across the sectors (government, business, not-for-profit) and new forms of interagency collaboration.

Accountability has been an important word in the human services since the 1970s, when the War on Poverty and other social programs were questioned by the Nixon administration and other conservatives. Recently, the reinventing government movement (Osborne & Gaebler, 1992), welfare reform, and managed care have put renewed emphasis on performance measurement (Martin & Kettner, 1997). There is an increasing emphasis on outcomes, sometimes known as performance- or outcomes-based accountability (Cooke et al., 1997). Human service programs are now expected to measure and document outcomes, not just units of services provided (Mullen & Magnabosco, 1997). Borrowing parlance from business, agencies need to show how their services *add value,* for funders, clients, or the public at large.

Another political trend has been toward increases in individualism, personal responsibility, and civic republicanism (Bryson, 1995, p. 89). The welfare reform act of 1996 is a good example: rugged individualism replaced the government entitlement philosophy that had been in effect since the New Deal. Conservatives now expect the philanthropic sector and the faith communities to move in to help the poor and disadvantaged as government support decreases or ends.

Economic Trends

In spite of the United States' current healthy economy, we can continue to expect limited public sector resources and growth, suggesting the need for continued productivity improvement and creative service delivery arrangements. Economic development and entrepreneurialism are becoming more prominent than traditional "services" strategies to empower residents of the inner city and others at lower income levels. In spite of these efforts, inequality is increasing, further bifurcating U.S. society.

The increased "marketization" of human services—"the reliance in public policy on natural trade exchange practices (for example, competition, privatization, commercialization, decentralization, and entrepreneurialism)" (Cooke et al., 1997, p. 230)—may exacerbate the trend toward increasing inequality. Managed care is another economic force affecting human services, in terms of both quality of service and access to care.

Another economic trend, the increasing globalization of the economy, benefits many of the wealthy but will continue to cause stress and dislocations for residents and workers in the United States. Well-paying blue-collar jobs in the United States are being eliminated in favor of paying lower wages to workers, sometimes including children, in undeveloped countries. Difficult economic conditions in many developing countries add to increased immigration to the United States. With many immigrants able to acquire only unskilled work, often without health benefits, health and social service systems experience strain.

Social Trends

Social and organizational complexity is likely to increase, and chaos theory, adapted from the sciences, is being used to make sense of this (Warren, Franklin, & Streeter, 1997). With increases in immigrants from virtually any part of the world, diversity of the workforce, clients, families, and the citizenry will increase. Baby boomers are aging, leading to a search for new ways for the elderly to contribute to society. Young people entering the workforce, in human services and elsewhere, bring with them new values and priorities. They, and in fact all workers, are likely to experience more career changes than in past generations, leading to more job retraining and a greater use of consultants and part-time and contract employees. This situation has implications for agency salary and benefit structures, working environments, and other considerations for the quality of working life.

Technological Trends

In the human services, *technology* is almost always assumed to mean "computers." A broader definition is used here: the work rules, tools, equipment, information used to transform inputs into outputs (goods or services) (Taylor & Felten, 1993, p. 54). The service delivery methods and processes we use to help change people (for example, casework, psychotherapy, and community organizing) are our technologies. While this topic will be discussed later in the context of program design, it is mentioned here because HSOs are increasingly pressured to change or adopt technologies. For example, managed care policies typically require providers to use short-term models rather than open-ended, long-term treatments, and welfare-to-work programs are precipitating the development of new ways to bring the poor into the workforce.

Technological change in agency operations will continue, using techniques such as business process reengineering and total quality management. Further reductions in the ranks of midmanagement will affect career development prospects for lower-level workers, while at the same time empowering them in their current jobs. Systems redesign, including services integration and the various forms of interagency collaboration, are also affecting the ways agencies deliver services (O'Looney, 1996).

Finally, of course, information technology and computer use will continue to advance. Human service workers have been slow to embrace this trend, in spite of the opportunities to reduce mundane work and have quicker access to more work-related knowledge.

From the World to the Neighborhood: "Thinking Globally and Acting Locally"

The trends we have just reviewed have taken us from the evolving world economy, the World Wide Web, and national political trends to the effects of larger trends at the level of community functioning and agency operations. The wise human service worker or administrator will, to function effectively and purposefully, think globally and act locally.

Based on lessons from both business and the not-for-profit sector, organizations that do a better job of assessing and responding to the environment will, other factors being equal, be more likely to thrive. Techniques for doing this include environmental scanning (a component of strategic planning discussed in the next chapter), data collection techniques such as needs assessments and asset mapping, interagency and community collaborations, and managers assuming "boundary-spanning" roles as part of their jobs. Other management processes that help an agency manage its environment include marketing, public relations, coalitions, professional associations, and networks. We move now to techniques for keeping up-to-date on what is happening in the agency's immediate environment.

Needs Assessment

Human service agencies can be effective only if they allocate resources and respond to expectations based on clear and comprehensive goals. These goals must be responsive to the realities of the given community. Because the services being delivered must be the services that community members require and want, a needs assessment is a common method to inform program selection and design. In this context, a *need* is defined as "the gap between what is viewed as a necessary level or condition by those responsible for this determination and what actually exists" (Siegel, Attkisson, & Carson, 1995, p. 11). According to Stewart (1978), "a comprehensive needs assessment is an activity through which one identifies community problems and resources to meet the problems, develops priorities concerning problems and services, and [begins the process] of program planning and development of new or altered services" (p. 294).

The needs assessment might be a broadly based attempt to measure and evaluate the general problems and needs of a total community, as in the instance of a community mental health center or a health agency beginning operation. It might involve a specific measurement of the needs of a narrowly defined target population, as in the case of an existing agency or institution deciding on the efficacy of an innovative service. In either situation, the needs assessment should be comprehensive in the sense that an attempt is made to identify problems, to measure relevant community characteristics, to analyze consumer perceptions of problems and goals, and to determine whether needs are being met by current programs and services.

Needs assessments are typically conducted by a planning organization (for example, the local United Way) or by an agency or coalition of agencies. Tropman (1995) has noted that the role of the assessor should be consciously considered. The person or group may range from a "neutral" outside observer to an advocate who is perhaps looking for a particular need, and Tropman warns that the assessor must ensure that the data gathered are valid. He adds that it is important to provide community participation through, for example, a local oversight group.

A needs assessment describes the target population or community, including demographic characteristics, the extent of relevant problems or issues of concern, and current services. This is often followed by a discussion of gaps between existing services and unmet needs. Data collection methods include the use of demographic data, social indicators (for example, rates of homelessness), surveys of agencies and community members, interviews of key informants (such as service providers and local leaders), and community forums. Detailed information on needs assessments is available in most social work macro practice textbooks (see Hardcastle, Wenocur, & Powers, 1997; Siegel et al., 1995; Tropman, 1995).

Asset Mapping

As useful as the needs assessment technique is, it has a serious limitation when used in isolation. By definition, it focuses on problems or deficiencies in a community or population and does not consider important factors such as community strengths and assets. As Kretzmann and McKnight (1996) put it, needs assessments "often convey part of the truth about the actual conditions of a troubled community. But they are not regarded as part of the truth; they are regarded as the whole truth" (p. 23).

More recently, a new technique has been developed—"assets-based community development" (Kretzmann & McKnight, 1996)—to provide a broader perspective. According to O'Looney (1996), the mapping of community strengths and capacities is a "first step in learning to build the support structures for self-help, mutual aid, and informal economic development" (p. 248). This provides "a common and comprehensive base of information on which to make decisions" (p. 248), such as where to locate resources and services.

One product of asset mapping can be a database of residents' skills, talents, and willingness to volunteer. Civic associations, families with skills and knowledge to share with others, and goods and services to provide to neighbors can all be identified. Asset mapping must promote a search for multiple resources within the community; meet the needs of diverse social, ethnic, cultural, and interest groups; focus on the grassroots level to uncover hidden resources; involve community residents in the design and implementation of the survey; and "illuminate and enhance the potential for mutual exchange of skills and services" (O'Looney, 1996, pp. 257–258).

The asset-based approach to community development increases the focus on the community, although not to the exclusion of relevant external forces, and this facilitates the development of relationships among community residents and organizations. This approach to combined assessment is well linked with another emerging technology: the community collaboration.

Community Collaborations

While service integration and interagency collaboration have a long history in social work, going back at least to the charity organization societies of the nineteenth century, recent attempts at collaboration reach for deeper and more fundamental ways for service providers and community members to interact. Evidence indicates that interagency collaborations can indeed be successful for all involved, but this type of collaboration must be learned and takes time and effort (Mulroy & Shay, 1998). To acknowledge a strengths-based perspective in this context, Bailey and Koney (1996) assert that "all organizational members must recognize and continually acknowledge the valuable resources each brings to the system" (p. 606).

Models of collaboration are continually evolving in the current dynamic environment. Some basic definitions, examples, and guidelines are offered here to enable the human service manager to assess an agency's local collaboration activities and make decisions regarding how to work within them. Abramson and Rosenthal (1995, p. 1479) offer the following definitions. *Collaboration* is "a fluid process through which a group of diverse, autonomous actors (organizations or individuals) undertakes a joint initiative, solves shared problems, or otherwise achieves common goals." *Interdisciplinary collaboration* "describes the process by which the expertise of different categories of professionals is shared and coordinated to resolve the problems of clients." An *interorganizational collaboration* "is a group of independent organizations who are committed to working together for specific purposes and tangible outcomes while maintaining their own autonomy; they terminate their collaboration or transform themselves into other forms of organization when that purpose is met." Examples of this type of collaboration include coalitions, networks, strategic alliances, task forces, or partnerships. An even more advanced form of collaboration involves formal merging of funds and staff, sometimes into new organizational entities. This has become known as a "community collaborative" or, as we describe it later, organizationally centered services integration. Collaboration can occur at the service delivery or policy levels.

O'Looney (1996) distinguishes between the "soft," informal process that may be seen as the "spirit" of collaboration, which includes the sharing of goals, values, ideas of fairness, and the experience of joint activity; and the "hard," formal process that he calls *service integration*. He sees the latter as representing the "fruits of the collaborative social dynamics," which include cross-training and cross-authorization of staff, pooled funds, colocation of services, shared transportation, and job descriptions that include collaboration as a performance requirement (p. 15). O'Looney asserts that collaborations should be undergirded by basic principles or shared values, suggesting that such services be community based, prevention/early intervention oriented, family focused, and culturally sensitive.

Abramson and Rosenthal (1995) note some of the common obstacles to collaboration, including the unequal balance of power among representatives (based on disciplines or the size or status of the organizations); inequities based on differences in color, gender, or culture (for example, male dominance); role competition or turf issues (fighting over limited funds or competition among professional groups); differing value bases; unclear definitions of roles and responsibilities; and inadequate conflict management processes. If these issues are addressed early and explicitly, in a climate of goodwill, collaborations are likely to be successful.

Abramson and Rosenthal suggest key tasks at the different developmental stages of a collaboration to help ensure success. At the *formation* stage, establishing a common mission, a shared view of problems and tasks, and clear operating ground rules are important. At the *implementation* stage, it is important to deal with communication difficulties, group dynamics, and interpersonal problems that get in the way of completing products such as a community assessment or a strategic plan. At the *maintenance stage,* issues or tensions may arise regarding power, leadership, goals, strategies, and follow-through on agreements. Existing norms and ground rules, agreed to upon formation, may be returned to as aids in resolving these problems.

In particular, Abramson and Rosenthal suggest several key roles for leaders, who have particular responsibility for "setting the tone, assessing and managing the group process, keeping the activity on target, and handling administrative details" (p. 1485). Leaders may rotate, or there may be a central core of leaders, but regardless of the formal structure, all leaders must act in the best interests of all participants. Leaders should help develop a positive climate where all can be

ard, differences are openly discussed, conflict is proactively managed, and a
.. ew of hope and optimism predominates.

Boundary Management: Coalitions, Professional Associations, and Networks

In addition to all of their other responsibilities, managerial leaders, especially
those at the upper echelons, need to assume "boundary-spanning" roles that require them to interface with those elements of their organization's task environment, or suprasystem, that have a direct bearing on the organization's growth,
survival, efficiency, and effectiveness. Knowledge of the environments in which
human service organizations are embedded and of the skills required to negotiate
balanced exchanges of tangible and intangible goods and services between the organization and its task environment becomes an essential component of the managerial leader's professional armamentarium.

Many direct service staff rarely see their agency executives and wonder
where they are during the day. In fact, an effective manager needs to spend much
of her or his time actively engaged with aspects of the agency's environments.
This includes reading literature on current developments in the field, increasingly
via the Internet. Even with these resources, a manager needs to spend a good deal
of time outside the agency, in face-to-face meetings with other service providers,
funders, community members, advocacy groups, and the news media. A manager
may not enjoy traveling to the state capital to meet with legislators or their staff,
but such trips, as well as attendance at worthwhile national conferences or meetings of professional associations, can pay off in the future for the agency.

Not only can state-of-the-art information be acquired about successful
model programs, new funding sources, or pending legislation, but personal relationships are built that will be valuable in later collaboration or problem solving.
A human service manager should become aware of relevant organizations in his
or her field of service and participate in them as appropriate.

Marketing

A human service worker may view the subjects of marketing and public relations
with resentment, puzzlement, bemusement, or indifference. In fact, according to
Hardcastle et al. (1991), "a market orientation is compatible with the social work
values and ethics of client self-determination and empowerment" (p. 316). Managers should understand the value of these tools and use them appropriately for
the good of the agency and its clients. Public relations and marketing will be covered briefly here because they are ways of interacting with the environment. For

a more detailed discussion, see Chapter 11 of Hardcastle et al. (1997). We are jumping ahead a bit, because planning, covered in the next chapter, would occur before engaging in marketing or public relations efforts.

Many people equate marketing with sales, when in fact they are very different processes, particularly in the human services. Some human service organizations, particularly for-profit ones or not-for-profit agencies on fee for service contracts, actively solicit clients, but of course many programs serve involuntary or hostile clients. Marketing takes on a different flavor when designing programs for substance abusers or domestic violence perpetrators, but the principles can be valuable nevertheless.

Lauffer (1984) summarizes the key components of marketing using five *P*s: publics, product, place, price, and promotion.

Publics

Input publics consist of those who provide resources, primarily funding sources, *throughput publics* are staff, and *output publics* are clients. All of these need to be treated as important stakeholders, and agency services and processes should be designed in ways that respond to their key concerns or expectations. This matter becomes particularly complicated, of course, in the case of involuntary clients. In a child abuse situation, protection of the child and perhaps the mother and other family members will be of utmost importance, but attention will also need to be paid to the abuser and relevant funding, policy, or legislative expectations, such as family reunification.

Product

The second *P*, products, are the program's services. From a marketing perspective, it is important that services are in fact seen as a valuable product—something that clients, funders, or referring agencies will want to use. A useful marketing concept in this regard is the notion of the market segment or niche. As will be seen in the next chapter, an agency should design and offer programs based on its unique skills and competencies. An agency will determine a niche (for example, an area of unmet need or an opportunity for a new service) in a community and design a program to fill it. For example, a community may have several programs for sex offenders but none for juvenile sex offenders. After a needs assessment, it may be determined that a program in this niche would be a valuable addition to the spectrum of services in a community. As another example, an agency may see an opportunity for home-based services for mothers coming off welfare, which would become a niche that the agency would try to stake out for itself.

Determining a program's niche can be aided by using a competition analysis (Yankey, Koury, & Young, 1985). The word *competition* may spur skepticism; in fact, *other service providers* may be a better term in some cases. In any case, it is important for a program to assess what service gaps exist and offer services that will truly respond to important unmet needs. A competition analysis involves developing a list of programs within a defined target area that provides similar services or different services to the same clients as the agency doing the analysis. For each agency, additional lists are developed, often put in the form of a matrix, with each agency occupying a separate row. The lists, displayed in columns, describe for each program its primary services related to the service area being assessed (for example, support services for seniors), the program, staff characteristics (master's, bachelor's, and so forth), geographic location, and fees, if any. Additional columns list the market share (the percentage of eligible clients being served) and the market segment (the specific characteristics of clients served) for each program. This is then used to identify service gaps: the percentage of the market share and the segment that is not being served. Gaps can become niches to be filled by a new or expanded program.

Place

The third *P,* place, is relevant in the competition analysis. An agency may see from the analysis that services are missing in a particular geographic area. Strategically, the agency needs to decide what the geographic scope of its new, expanded, or reconfigured program should be. This feature may be defined from a funder's perspective, using identified geographic areas or responding to a request for proposals for programs in a certain area. Place also considers the location of services with respect to client accessibility and convenience. Public transportation routes, parking, and other factors of access need to be considered. Another aspect of place involves days and hours of operation of the program, which should be set based on when clients need the services to be available (for example, evenings or weekends).

Price

Price is of course relevant in terms of the cost to clients for service, which may range from nothing to sliding-scale fees to reimbursements from funders or insurance companies. There are also psychic costs to clients: will there be embarrassment or inconvenience factors to overcome? A client decision to come to an agency may be based partly on the client's weighing of the benefits and the costs. Price is also relevant in the context of grant or contract amounts. Unit costs for services may need to be outlined in the agency's funding proposal. It will be increasingly necessary for an agency to be "competitive," offering funders or clients a valued service at the best cost. The challenge for the agency when negotiating the grant or contract funding amount and scope of services will be to ensure that quality services and desired outcomes can be delivered for the agreed-on cost. Sometimes donations to the agency or foundation funds are used to offset other agency costs to keep service delivery costs to clients or government funders as low as possible.

Promotion

Finally, promotion involves putting all the other *P*s together and "selling" the program's services to its various publics. First, focus is placed on the identified market segment, which may have been chosen based on geography, specific type of service, or client demographics. Market "positioning" then involves orchestrating the way the program or services are presented to the various publics. This is partly public relations: shaping the agency's or program's image through media relations, advertising, brochures, networking, or other public relations activities. More fundamentally, however, the concern should be for addressing the real needs of the various publics, making sure that the services will add value to the lives of clients and the community, will respond to funder and referring agency staff expectations, and will ensure a high quality of working life for agency staff.

Marketing and Collaboration

We will end this discussion of marketing by referring again to collaboration. While some of marketing focuses on competing or otherwise acting independently in the service delivery arena, an agency may engage in marketing through collaboration with other agencies. They may decide jointly to design their promotions to fill complementary niches, based, for example, on each agency providing the same services in a different geographic area. Agencies may form collaboratives that offer a seamless package of services colocated and delivered by interdisciplinary and even interagency teams. The emphasis should always be on responding appropriately to clearly identified community concerns and needs, to the improvement of the quality of life of its members.

Public Relations

In addition to marketing, public relations in general and media relations in particular are important aspects of an agency's interaction with the environment. At the most local level, an agency, especially one providing services that some consider to be controversial or that involve "undesirable" clients, may need to pay extra attention to relationships with local residents and other organizations. Ideally, the agency would have begun to develop relationships with the local community before opening a program there. Sometimes concerns regarding, for example, having ex-offenders or people in recovery living in a neighborhood can be addressed by meeting with residents and introducing the staff and program model.

There may be ways to adapt the program or add new services to build community acceptance. Having good relationships with local politicians, community leaders, and relevant local government staff such as zoning administrators should make it easier to solve problems.

On a slightly broader scale, the agency should have a well-thought-out strategy for media relations on an ongoing basis. Cohen (1998) has provided useful suggestions for connecting with local reporters and editors. The agency should learn which editors and reporters handle human service issues and arrange a meeting to be introduced and provide background on the agency and its services. Reporters will then know people to contact when they are preparing a story.

The agency can make available to the media information on new or modified programs and human interest stories illustrating what a program does and what positive effects it has had on the community. News releases, letters to the editor, guest editorials on television or radio, and op-ed articles are effective ways to reach large numbers of citizens.

Summary

The context for effective human service management has now been established: in a complex, dynamic, and even chaotic environment, managers must note and effectively deal with the current limitations facing human service agencies, such as the difficulties in clearly defining service outcomes, and engage the community and other stakeholders in identifying needs, strengths, and opportunities. Administrators must serve as boundary managers for their agencies, participating in various forms of community collaboration as well as working with professional and special interest organizations. They also develop plans for marketing and promoting their services after creating strategic plans for the future of the agency, discussed in the next chapter.

Discussion Questions

1. Think of a human service organization with which you are familiar.
   a. What are the key forces in its environments (local, state, national) that it should be paying attention to? How well is the agency managing these forces?
   b. How does the agency identify needs and opportunities for new services it may provide? How does it involve the community in the process?

2. What do you think about the uses of marketing and public relations in human service organizations? How should they be adapted to enable HSOs to better deliver services?

CASE 2 _____

Meeting the Needs of Battered Women

Marcia Butler, Angela Ortiz, and Pam Collins worked together at the Department of Human Services (DHS) in a fairly large city. Because they were the only female professionals in their particular branch, they tended to be the ones assigned to work with battered women, and they had all dealt with a number of these situations.

Pam, the youngest and least experienced of the three professionals, often asked Marcia and Angela for advice and support when dealing with difficult problems. One such situation had just presented itself. Pam's client, a very young mother of two who had been severely beaten by her husband on many occasions, had just been referred to DHS for the third time. Each time Pam worked with her, the same thing happened. Immediate, stopgap measures were taken, wounds were healed and promises made, and the young client returned to the same situation. There was no potential for change as long as this client saw herself as without resources for self-sufficiency. She could not support herself and her children economically, her self-esteem was as battered as her body, and she felt she had no future except with her husband.

Marcia and Angela sympathized with Pam's difficulty in helping this client, but they did not have any answers. Each of them had seen similar situations time and again. Yet, as much as they tried to help, they could see no way out, primarily because of the way services were organized.

Battered women could go to a shelter that had been organized by a nonprofit, private agency, but the shelter provided only short-term (two weeks' or less) refuge for women and their children. No long-term services were offered. Women could receive vocational counseling and training through the employment service and personal counseling through the mental health center. Either of these, however, required that the women enter long-term programs before being able to make drastic life changes. In light of their relationships, most women did not feel safe using such programs within the context of their home situations.

Marcia, Angela, and Pam recognized the need for a more comprehensive program to deal with the needs of battered women in their locality. To be effective, a program would have to combine physical refuge, medical services, personal and family therapy, and vocational counseling. The purpose of such a program would not necessarily be to remove all battered women from their current homes but to work with whole family systems and to ensure that women developed more options for their lives.

Although the general manager of DHS recognized the need for such a program when it was presented to him, he did not see how it could fit into the agency's current plans and appropriations. He made it clear that he did sympathize with the aims of the program and that he would be glad to consider it further if he could see a carefully developed proposal. The proposal would need to include hard data concerning needs as well as specific suggestions concerning program activities and funding.

He would not consider reallocating funds currently being used by other programs that were already hard-pressed to serve the number of clients needing assistance.

Similarly, community agencies, such as the women's shelter, shared their philosophical support for a more comprehensive program. None of the currently operating programs, however, seemed ready or able to take on the burden of providing additional services.

Marcia, Angela, and Pam began to recognize that they could not help develop this sorely needed program just by mentioning it to others. They would need to become more involved themselves. The program might be brought into being in any of a number of ways, including creation of an alternative community-based agency, application for a grant that might be awarded either to the Department of Human Services or to the women's shelter, or development of a coalition of existing agencies and services. The possibilities needed to be spelled out, and if Marcia, Angela, and Pam did not take the initiative on this, no one else would.

1. If you were in the situation faced by these human service professionals, would you become involved in seeking a solution? To what extent?

2. What approach to solving the problem seems most promising, given the human service network that exists in the community being discussed here?

3. What steps should Marcia, Angela, and Pam take in developing, and possibly implementing, a comprehensive program?

References

Abramson, J., & Rosenthal, B. (1995). Interdisciplinary and interorganizational collaboration. In R. Edwards (Ed.), *The encyclopedia of social work* (19th ed., pp. 1479–1489). Washington, DC: NASW Press.

Bailey, D., & Koney, K. (1996). Interorganizational community-based collaboratives: A strategic response to shape the social work agenda. *Social Work, 41*(6), 602–611.

Bryson, J. (1995). *Strategic planning for public and nonprofit organizations* (rev. ed.). San Francisco: Jossey-Bass.

Cohen, T. (1998). Media relationships and marketing. In R. Edwards, J. Yankey, & M. Altpeter (Eds.), *Skills for effective management of nonprofit organizations* (pp. 98–114). Washington, DC: NASW Press.

Cooke, P., Reid, P., & Edwards, R. (1997) Management: New developments and directions. In R. Edwards (Ed.), *Encyclopedia of social work supplement 1997* (pp. 229–242). Washington, DC: NASW Press.

Garner, L., Jr. (1989). *Leadership in human services.* San Francisco: Jossey-Bass.

Hardcastle, D., Wenocur, S., & Powers, P. (1997). *Community practice: Theories and skills for social workers.* New York: Oxford University Press.

Hasenfeld, Y. (1992). The nature of human service organizations. In Y. Hasenfeld (Ed.), *Human services as complex organizations* (pp. 3–23). Newbury Park, CA: Sage.

Kretzmann, J., & McKnight, J. (1996). Assets-based community development. *National Civic Review, 85*(4), 23–27.

Lauffer, A. (1984). *Strategic marketing for not-for-profit organizations: Program and resource development.* New York: Free Press.

Martin, L., & Kettner, P. (1997). Performance measurement: The new accountability. *Administration in Social Work, 21*(1), 17–29.

Mullen, E., & Magnabosco, J. (1997). *Outcomes measurement in the human services.* Washington, DC: NASW Press.

Mulroy, E., & Shay, S. (1998). Motivation and reward in nonprofit interorganizational collaboration in low-income neighborhoods. *Administration in Social Work, 22*(4), 1–17.

O'Looney, J. (1996). *Redesigning the work of human services.* Westport, CT: Quorum.

Osborne, D., & Gaebler, T. (1992). *Reinventing government: How the entrepreneurial spirit is transforming the public sector.* Reading, MA: Addison-Wesley.

Siegel, L., Attkisson, C., & Carson, L. (1995). Need identification and program planning in the community context. In J. Tropman, J. Erlich, & J. Rothman (Eds.), *Tactics and techniques of community intervention* (3rd ed., pp. 10–34). Itasca, IL: Peacock.

Stewart, R. (1978). The nature of needs assessment in community mental health. *Community Mental Health Journal, 15,* 287–294.

Taylor, J., & Felten, D. (1993). *Performance by design.* Upper Saddle River, NJ: Prentice Hall.

Tropman, J. (1995). Community needs assessment. In R. Edwards (Ed.), *The encyclopedia of social work* (19th ed., pp. 563–569). Washington, DC: NASW Press.

Warren, K., Franklin, C., & Streeter, C. (1997). Chaos theory and complexity theory. In R. Edwards (Ed.), *Encyclopedia of social work supplement 1997* (pp. 59–68). Washington, DC: NASW Press.

Yankey, J., Koury, N., & Young, D. (1985). Utilizing a marketing audit in developing a new service. In W. Winston (Ed.), *Marketing strategies for human and social service agencies* (pp. 37–50). New York: Haworth.

3

Planning and Program Design

CHAPTER OUTLINE _____

Organizational Vision as a Guiding Principle

Strategic Planning

Selection of Goals: Operational or Tactical Planning

Specification of Objectives

Management by Objectives

Program Design
Identifying and Selecting Alternatives, Conceptualizing the
Program, Developing an Implementation Plan, Developing an
Evaluation Plan

Summary

Discussion Questions

Group Exercise

CASE 3: The Model College Counseling Center

References

All of the problems related to the uniquenesses of human service organizations reviewed in the previous chapter are cited again and again as factors that make many human service organizations ineffective in meeting consumer needs. Yet these characteristics are not inherent in human service organizations; they are inherent in organizations that have not engaged in meaningful planning processes.

The questions that need to be answered as part of the planning process include the following:

- Who should be involved in planning?

- How can we determine what potential clients' needs really are?

- What outcomes are most important for the clients who will be affected by the program?

- What resources are available to help in the efforts to reach program goals?

- What constraints should be taken into account?

- Given available resources and constraints, what program objectives would be realistic, clear, and measurable?

- What alternate methods could be used to meet the objectives?

- What are the best methods for meeting program objectives?

- What steps need to be carried out to meet each objective?

- How can program success be evaluated?

Agencies that plan develop viable strategies and clear goals based on assessment of community needs and visions, input from a variety of stakeholders, and consideration of their core competencies. They attempt to reach a broadly based consensus concerning the efficacy of these goals. They translate their mission and strategies into achievable and measurable objectives, and then they use these objectives as the bases for program design, resource allocation, and program evaluation. In short, the planning process meets head-on the problems that plague human service administrators, service providers, and community members. It enables an agency to respond consciously and proactively to its environment by developing visions of a preferred future and working collaboratively to develop responsive strategies and programs to improve the quality of life in the community.

Of course, as anyone knows who has worked in a formal organization—from a fast-food operation to the federal government—things are not totally rational. The complications of unexpected events, personality factors, and organizational politics can keep any process from remaining rational. This situation is not necessarily a problem, however. Intuition, insight, creativity, and the adroit management of chaos are valuable aspects of planning and may make crucial differences in outcomes. A well-designed planning process provides participants with a sense of order, control, and focus and can also allow for creativity and adaptation to unforeseen circumstances. And, as Bryson (1995) has asserted, precisely because strategic planning focuses on resolving strategic issues, it goes beyond rational planning and is able to accept and accommodate political decision making.

Another important point is that, according to many strategic thinkers, the planning process used is more important than the actual plan that results, especially if the plan is quickly ignored after being proudly introduced to the agency's board or funders. The planning process enables those involved to develop a shared view of the agency's present, past, and ideal future, which can guide its decision making regardless of the details of a formal plan. Ultimately, both the planning and the plan can be valuable, especially if they augment each other, with the plan providing direction and the process guiding actual implementation.

This chapter will begin by discussing the power of an organizational vision of a desired future, which can help develop a sense shared commitment to the organization and its services and provide a foundation for further planning. Next, we will review a common strategic planning process that has been adapted for governmental and not-for-profit organizations. Strategic planning deals with long-term trends in the environment, important issues facing the organization, and visions for where the organization should be in the future. After developing strategies for the organization to pursue, operational, or tactical, planning occurs: specific programs or projects are developed or modified. This is done by setting goals and then developing specific objectives to achieve them. Management by objectives, a venerable management technique, will be presented as a useful way to identify desired outcomes. Next, alternative ways of accomplishing objectives will be considered, with the best method selected. Often this involves designing something new, and will be presented here as the process of program design: choosing an appropriate service delivery technology. Finally, implementation and evaluation planning will be reviewed.

Organizational Vision as a Guiding Principle

A powerful way for planners to frame the agency's mission, strategies, goals, and objectives is to develop a vision for the future. Later we will review methods for developing organizational visions and ensuring that the team members' visions are aligned with those of the organization.

Peter Senge (1990, pp. 223–224), in his classic *The Fifth Discipline*, introduced the notion of "governing ideas" for an organization. These include *mission,* which answers the question "Why do we exist?" *Core values* respond to "How do we want to act?" Finally, *vision* answers the question "What do we want the organization to be?" The first two of these were introduced in Chapter 1 as the elements of organizational purpose. Vision is added as the element that enables staff to describe the ideal future for the organization and themselves. It is presented here as the foundation of planning processes including strategic planning, setting goals and objectives, and designing programs.

Senge (1990) describes an organizational vision this way:

> A shared vision is not an idea. It is not even an important idea such as freedom. It is, rather, a force in people's hearts, a force of impressive power. It may be inspired by an idea, but once it goes further—if it is compelling enough to acquire the support of more than one person—then it is no longer an abstraction. It is palpable. People begin to see it as if it exists. Few, if any, forces in human affairs are as powerful as shared vision. (p. 209)

According to Senge, shared visions for the future of the organization are based on the personal visions of the members of the organization. In this sense, they cannot be developed and announced from "on high"; they must be developed collaboratively by intensive dialogue of all employees. It is not productive to try to "sell" others on the vision. The best someone can do is to "be enrolled yourself," not inflate the benefits of the vision or deny problems, and let the other person choose her or his attitude toward the vision (p. 222).

According to Bryson (1995, pp. 157, 163), an organizational vision should inspire staff, promise that the organization will support members in the pursuit of the vision, be widely circulated, and be used to inform major and minor decisions and actions. It communicates enthusiasm; kindles excitement; fosters commitment and dedication; focuses on a better future; encourages hopes, dreams, and noble ambitions; and clarifies purpose and direction. A vision is typically a relatively short statement and can be communicated not only in words but also in pictures, images, and metaphors.

The Institute for Cultural Affairs (ICA), a consulting firm concerned with organization, community, and world development, has developed an effective process for the development of an organizational vision (Spencer, 1989, pp. 98–100). According to the ICA, a clear vision can help focus strategy (discussed later), and such a vision should be concrete and specific; bold, challenging, and exciting; and attainable.

The visioning process typically occurs in an off-site workshop setting and can include any number of people, from a team to the whole organization. Weisbord and his colleagues (1992) coined the term *future search* for a process of involving entire organizations or communities in developing shared visions. For a vision to be useful, it must be developed in a highly participatory process, so that everyone's personal visions are reflected in it. Senge (1990) notes that there needs to be *alignment* between individual visions and the organizational vision to keep all focused and working in the same direction.

Yankey (1995) suggests the following questions to provide structure to an organizational vision:

- What will the future business of the organization be?
- What will the board composition and structure be?
- How large will the organization be?
- What programs will be conducted by the organization?
- What staff will be required?
- What volunteers will be required?
- What internal management structures will be required?
- What will the funding mix of the organization be?
- What facilities will the organization have?
- How will success be measured? (p. 2323)

A vision statement should also have aspects that are more inspirational, and, if we can say so without becoming tautological, "visionary." These questions focus more on technical issues, some of which cannot be answered fully until a strategic planning process is completed. The "inspirational" aspects of the vision can thus serve as a foundation or preamble for subsequent planning activities, starting with the review of the organization's environment and mission, which we discuss next.

Strategic Planning

Strategic planning achieved cliché status in the human services during the 1990s just as other management innovations such as management by objectives, zero-based budgeting, and quality circles were embraced by government and the human services in previous decades. The fact that these processes were sometimes treated only as passing fads should not lead one to conclude that they are without value. Although the allure of strategic planning in the business sector had faded by the 1990s (Micklethwait & Wooldridge, 1997, chap. 7), the value of true strategic *thinking* was not seriously challenged. While any management technique or principle can be inadequately or improperly used, they all can add value if used in the appropriate way in an appropriate situation (Eadie, 1998; Steiner, Gross, Ruffolo, & Murray, 1994; Yankey, 1995).

Strategic planning should be used with serious attention to its limitations and pitfalls. A sobering finding from one study (Webster & Wylie, 1988) was that many agencies only engaged in strategic planning because their funders required it. From another perspective, O'Looney (1996, pp. 76–78) asserts that strategic planning has been ineffective in the human service field and "frustrating" for public sector managers because local governments can use tactical planning to improve "at the margins" but don't have the discretion to truly choose different strategies. According to O'Looney, "successful strategic planning implies at least a moderate amount of organizational autonomy and the ability to take action in the larger environment," conditions that do not apply in government. He further asserts, "There is little strategy in the human service environment because there is little or no interorganizational war in the human services." However, the environmental conditions outlined in the previous chapter clearly require strategic thinking and response by any human service organization wanting to thrive in the early years of the twenty-first century.

Even in government the need for strategic thinking has become apparent in the wake of increased pressures from Congress for accountability, responsiveness, and efficiency. The reinventing government movement (Osborne & Gaebler, 1992; Osborne & Plastrik, 1997) has affected state houses and city halls across the country, and initiatives such as privatization have radically affected both governmental and not-for-profit organizations. With for-profit firms entering the human services in increasing numbers, with the pace quickening since the 1996 welfare reform legislation, there is, in fact, more competition facing human service organizations, and greater pressure exists to deliver specific outcomes at low cost (Boehm, 1996). Bryson (1995) and Menefee (1997) have provided further evidence for the necessity of strategic planning; indeed, its use in the human services is increasing (Eadie, 1998). Bryson has added, however, that there are "bad" times to do strategic planning. If an organization is in the middle of a large crisis such as a huge funding cut, or if an organization does not have basic managerial skills or the commitment of key decision makers to proceed, these situations should be remedied before engaging in strategic planning.

The following discussion is based largely on the work of John Bryson (1995), a model used successfully in both governmental and not-for-profit organizations. Also useful are a companion workbook (Bryson & Alston, 1996) and a book focused specifically on not-for-profit organizations (Allison & Kaye, 1997). Bryson defines *strategic planning* as "a disciplined effort to produce fundamental decisions and actions that shape and guide what an organization is, what it does, and why it does it" (pp. 4–5). Many managers think of strategic planning as something that the board and executive managers do in a one- or two-day annual retreat. In fact, strategic planning is an ongoing process, reflected in *strategic management:* strategic thinking and strategic acting.

The strategic planning model presented here, adapted slightly from Bryson, consists of eleven stages:

1. Initiate and agree on a strategic planning process.

2. Identify organizational mandates.

3. Identify the organization's stakeholders and their needs and concerns.

4. Clarify organizational mission and values.

5. Assess the organization's external environment to identify opportunities and threats.

6. Assess the organization's internal environment to determine strengths and weaknesses.

7. Identify the strategic issues facing the organization.

8. Formulate strategies to manage these issues.

9. Review and adopt the strategic plan or plans.

10. Develop an effective implementation process.

11. Monitor and update the plan on a regular basis.

This process is typically done at an agency-wide level and ideally is then replicated at a smaller scale within each program, with program strategic plans then shared upward with refinements made as necessary to ensure alignment throughout the organization.

1. Initiating and agreeing on a strategic planning process. For strategic planning to be successful, several conditions need to be met. First, the organization should have competent leadership, which includes a basic level of overall management competence throughout the organization. If there are weak areas in management functioning, these are likely, in fact, to be strategic issues, because they are likely to be related to the ongoing survival of the organization. Therefore, management weaknesses should be addressed through the use of a consultant to develop both staff's management skills and the agency's management processes. Strategic planning can also serve as a way to further develop an organization's managerial competence.

Before embarking on such a major initiative, all decision makers should thoughtfully consider whether the organization is willing to make the commitment not only to develop a plan but also to ensure that it is implemented. A final important implication is that the strategic plan may require the organization to break out of "business as usual" and do both new things and do the ongoing work of the organization in a new way. Decision makers should understand this point and expect that a new organizational culture, perhaps more dynamic and participative, may evolve.

2. Identifying organizational mandates. Any human service organization has both formal and informal mandates. Formal mandates for government organizations are usually easy to identify. Different units of government are responsible for functions such as the protection of children, treatment for the indigent mentally ill, and provision of government benefits such as Temporary Assistance to Needy Families (TANF) and Social Security; these are reflected in legislation, regulations, administrative guidelines, and sometimes court orders. Not-for-profit organizations have formal mandates reflected in their government or foundation grants and contracts and any statements of purpose reflected in the organization's bylaws or charter.

Informal mandates are sometimes harder to discover but may be found by looking at the expectations that the members of the organization's governance bodies bring to their role. For example, elected officials may believe they bring a mandate to make government more accountable or to privatize government services. Agency board members may feel that they need to get the organization to either change or maintain its focus and purpose. Examples would include the use of a feminist philosophy in a battered women's shelter, debates over medical or social models of substance abuse, the nature of services to persons with HIV/AIDS, or the treatment of the poor coming off TANF.

The strategic planning team should work to identify all key mandates, formal and informal, and also consider whether and how easily they could be changed if necessary. Mandates are then taken as "givens": expectations from outside forces that a strategic plan will need to accommodate. Paradoxically, the identification of mandates can be liberating. A strategic planning team may be surprised at how few or constraining the existing mandates actually are, providing great latitude once the limiting parameters are defined. Sometimes moving into the next step, stakeholder analysis, can provide further detail on what key outsiders expect from the organization.

3. Identifying the organization's stakeholders and their needs and concerns. As its name implies, a *stakeholder* is an individual, role, group, or organization with a stake in what the agency does. Usually a stakeholder has specific expectations of an organization and standards, at least implied, about how it judges how well the organization is doing. Some stakeholders are very powerful, such as funding sources and regulators, while others such as clients and community groups may be important but lacking in formal power. Identifying every stakeholder is neither possible nor necessary, but key stakeholders need to be identified so that their interests and concerns can be addressed by the strategic plan.

The criteria by which each stakeholder assesses the agency should be identified and viewed from the point of view of the stakeholder, not the agency. Once the criteria are clear, assess how well the organization is currently meeting them. This may result in sobering insights, especially if it is determined that the agency is not doing well at meeting the needs of particular stakeholders. This is nevertheless a solid place to begin, so that strategies may be developed to improve stakeholder relations and the agency is under no illusions regarding how well it is doing.

4. Clarifying organizational mission and values. Human service organizations are inherently purpose driven and often put significant emphasis on the organization's mission and values (recall the conceptual model in Chapter 1). Developing mission statements was another management fad of the 1980s and 1990s for human service organizations, so most agencies probably have an official mission statement that is publicized to some extent. Initiating a strategic planning process is a good time to reassess and update an organization's mission statement to ensure that it is current, relevant, and useful.

A good mission statement should answer these questions:

- Who are we?

- What basic social needs do we address?

- What we do?

- What makes us unique? What is our niche?

A statement of organizational values typically consists of a limited number of tight statements describing desired principles of behavior. In this sense values serve as guidelines for behavior or decision making. They can also serve as criteria for designing the organization or its programs. It should contain no unreal expectations, and management should be willing to publicize the statement. In some agencies, values are displayed along with mission statements in lobbies and offices. For example, a homeless shelter used a collaborative process to identify as core values compassion, respect, empathy, empowerment, and dignity (Packard, 2000). They were widely publicized and addressed in hiring interviews, new employee orientation, staff meetings, and case conferences.

The draft mission and values statements should be widely circulated throughout the organization for further dialogue, input, and refinement. Through this process, the product's quality should improve with the application of more minds to the task, and those involved will feel a sense of ownership over the result and be more committed to using the mission and values statements to guide their daily work. The new mission and values should be shared widely and regularly, even before the strategic planning process has been completed. They may be reviewed at agency training events, workshops, or even regular meetings such as case discussions. In this way, they can guide both the strategic planning process and everyday staff behavior in the organization.

5. Assessing the organization's external environment to identify opportunities and threats. Doing an *environmental scan* is a useful way to identify opportunities and threats in the environment. These will, of course, vary from agency to agency, but many items, some of which were mentioned in Chapter 2 as factors affecting human service organizations, will be common to many agencies, at least in general terms. Since boards of directors are likely to have more wide-ranging exposure to current environmental forces than staff who operate in a more limited day-to-day environment, it is especially important to involve the board in this process. This may be done with the whole board or a representative group that is part of the strategic planning team.

Bryson (1995) suggests three categories for the environmental analysis: forces and trends in the environment, key resource controllers for the organization, and competitors or collaborators. A useful place to begin the environmental analysis is to conduct a *PEST analysis* of environmental forces and trends. (*PEST* refers to political, economic, social, and environmental forces or trends.) The planning team can begin by brainstorming factors in each of the categories and then review the organization's key resource controllers, including funders, regulators, and clients. The agency's competitors and collaborators, real and possible, should also be reviewed. Much of this can be accomplished by revisiting the stakeholder analysis and the market analysis discussed in Chapter 2.

The group should discuss the significance and meaning of each opportunity or threat. Possible priorities or suggested action steps can be noted (for example, determining which elements need immediate action, which need monitoring or incorporation into the strategic plan, and which can safely be ignored for the time being). Consistent with the axiom that strategic thinking and management are more important than strategic planning, managers should ensure that the environmental scanning process becomes an ongoing activity for the agency.

6. Assessing the organization's internal environment to identify strengths and weaknesses. After the environmental scan, attention should be focused internally, on factors that will eventually be identified as the agency's strengths and weaknesses. As the cliché goes, the agency's greatest resource is its people, so the analysis can begin by looking at the current staff: their knowledge and skills with reference to current programmatic demands and role expectations. Questions here include the following: Do we have staff with the proper competencies or qualifications in all positions? Have our staffing needs changed? Are people properly trained? Are levels of turnover and sick leave within acceptable limits? What is the quality of working life as perceived by employees? Economic resources can then be reviewed. What is the status of current funding? Are program expenditures within the budget? When will grants and contracts end, and what will happen to the programs then? For government agencies, what are the prospects for changes in the next budget cycle? Are foundation funds and donations at expected levels? Have audits been done on schedule, and are identified problems being addressed? Information resources can be assessed by reviewing the management information system to see whether it is providing the data needed to manage and improve program operations. Harder to assess is the organization's culture. Sometimes employee attitude surveys, covered later in the chapter on organizational change, are used to assess the state of the organization's culture.

Even if the organization has never done strategic planning, it is, in fact, guided by strategy, either explicitly or implicitly. If a current strategic plan is not in effect, the organization's present strategies should be articulated so that they can be assessed. Strategy implementation should then be reviewed to see whether activities are on target and what adjustments may be needed, at the levels of both the organization as a whole and individual departments.

Finally, current performance of the organization should be assessed. One discovery here may be that existing information systems do not allow the team to determine what objectives or outcomes are actually being achieved, and this matter may immediately become a strategic issue. Using whatever data or measures exist, the organization's performance over time should be reviewed. Are more or fewer units of service being provided in each program? If effectiveness or efficiency can be measured, how are these figures changing over time?

The internal analysis should conclude with the same type of assessment used for the environmental scan: with a discussion of the significance and meaning of each strength and weakness and preliminary thoughts on possible priorities or action steps.

7. Identifying the strategic issues facing the organization. Strategic issues are identified using a *SWOT analysis:* assessing how internal strengths and weaknesses interact with environmental opportunities and threats. Strategic issues can be differentiated from tactical issues with reference to several dimensions. While determining whether an issue is strategic or tactical, or operational, is by no means an exact science, the following criteria, again adapted from Bryson (1995), offer some guidance. Strategic issues tend to be part of the consciousness of the board and executive staff, have long-term implications, affect the entire organization or at least multiple departments, involve significant financial stakes, are likely to require new or modified programs and changes in resource allocations, are sensitive to community or political concerns, and have no obvious way for being addressed. According to Bryson (1995, p. 105), there are three kinds of strategic issues: (1) those for which no action is needed at present and merely need to be monitored, (2) those that can be handled as part of the regular strategic planning cycle, and (3) those that need to be handled immediately. Issues should be framed something the organization can and should do something about and for which more than one solution is possible.

When an opportunity in the environment can be connected with a strength of the agency, proactive strategies for new programs or initiatives can be developed. The issue is framed as "What should we do to respond to this opportunity?" If a threat in the environment corresponds with a weakness in the agency, defensive strategies will have to be developed to protect the agency. If there is an opportunity in the environment for which the agency has no distinctive competence (for example, a request for proposals for welfare-to-work programs that is assessed by a child abuse agency), the agency should ignore it or, if it is within the agency's mission, develop the competencies to respond. Finally, environmental threats in areas where the agency is strong can in some cases be ignored, at least for the time being, but probably should be monitored for later action if conditions change.

8. Formulating strategies to manage the issues. General responses to the strategic issues identified are to build on strengths, overcome weaknesses, exploit opportunities, and block threats (Nutt & Backoff, 1992). Bryson (1995) defines a strategy as "a pattern of purposes, policies, programs, actions, decisions, and/or resource allocations that defines what an organization is, what it does, and why it does it" (p. 130). Every agency has strategies. For most agencies, these are implicit: continue growing, get new funding sources, keep providing certain services, and so forth. Strategic planning is intended to make strategies both more explicit and, because a thoughtful process is used, more effective.

Strategies can be developed at the overall agency level, at the program level, or for specific functions or processes. There should be a strategy for each strategic issue. Bryson has suggested a five-step process, adapted from the Institute for Cultural Affairs model (Spencer, 1989). The following questions are asked:

1. What are the practical alternatives, dreams, or visions we might pursue to address this strategic issue? . . .

2. What are the barriers to the realization of these alternatives, dreams, or visions?

3. What major proposals might we pursue to achieve these alternatives, dreams, or visions directly or to overcome the barriers to their realization?

4. What major actions (with existing staff and within existing job descriptions) must be taken within the next year (or two) to implement the major proposals?

5. What specific steps must be taken within the next six months to implement the major proposals, and who is responsible? (Bryson, 1995, p. 139)

After these questions are answered, choices are made from the various options and strategies are selected for action. The team should also consider whether any strategies contradict each other and whether any strategies can be combined or need to be coordinated or sequenced together. Strategies can immediately be turned into action plans, with time lines and responsible people, or a full strategic plan can be prepared. A strategic plan can be valuable because it serves as the history of the thinking and analysis that led to the strategies and may be consulted later for background and insight regarding why particular alternatives were chosen. A plan is also useful to newcomers to the agency or to staff who may not have been involved with the entire planning process. The plan itself should include the results of each step of the process:

- The background and rationale for doing the plan

- The process used to develop and adopt the plan, including a list of participants

- The organization's mandates

- Key stakeholders and their needs and concerns

- The organization's mission and values

- The environmental analysis

- The organization's analysis of strengths and weaknesses

- The strategic issues identified for action

- Strategies to manage each issue

- The implementation plan

- The plan for monitoring and updating the plan

9. Reviewing and adopting the strategic plan. The plan should then be shared as widely as possible throughout the organization, ideally at briefing sessions where it can be discussed and the process celebrated. Some organizations may want to send it out for review in draft form for a final round of feedback. The plan in general should not be "news" because employee representatives from all parts of the organization would have been involved in the process, keeping their constituencies informed and getting their reactions and input through the process. Someone should be put in charge of monitoring implementation and ensuring that responsible persons report on their process on a regular, predetermined basis.

10. Developing an effective implementation process. The keys to successful implementation of the plan are the commitment of all key internal stakeholders and, in fact, to some extent all staff and board members, a detailed action plan that is clear to all and for which responsible persons are assigned, necessary resource commitments (primarily staff time and funding), and clear connections between strategies and daily operations. An agency may want to appoint a strategy implementation team, including some members from the strategic planning team, to oversee implementation and ensure that the process gets the necessary attention and support.

Strategies often involve goal setting and designing new programs, which will be covered next; obtaining new funding, covered in Chapter 8; or developing or redesigning organizational systems. Examples of the latter would be moving to performance-based budgeting, developing an integrated computerized management information system, or implementing a management development program.

11. Monitoring and updating the plan on a regular basis. Bryson (1995, pp. 200–202) offers useful suggestions for monitoring strategy implementation. First, he reminds us to stay focused on what is important: the mission and mandates of the organization. The pressures of day-to-day operations often pull staff into focusing on just following procedures or, at the other extreme, aggressively pushing the plan as an end in itself. Indicators of success or failure should be chosen early, and these should be watched for on an ongoing basis so that adjustments can be made where necessary. The strategy implementation team mentioned earlier can serve as a "review group" to identify strategies or action plans that may need to be modified. The review group and the organization's formal and informal leaders will have to show strong support for the action plans and encourage strategic thinking and management as part of daily work.

Selection of Goals: Operational or Tactical Planning ———

Whereas strategic planning is concerned with the agency as a whole, operational planning focuses on individual programs. The heart of the planning process is selecting program goals on which the work of the agency will be based. Goals provide the direct link between strategies based on consumer needs and other environmental factors and agency services, which are operationalized through program design. Given a specific set of objectives concerning desirable client outcomes, we can select from a number of alternate interventions and build a program with a reasonable chance for success.

Planning processes in human service agencies can be made more effective only if goal setting is a high priority. If goals are to lead the way toward successful program development, they should be characterized by their responsiveness to the expectations of key stakeholders and by their ability to be translated into measurable objectives. The people who have a stake in the outcomes of human services should have an opportunity to have input into the decision-making processes concerning organizational goals. It is also important that service providers share in the process of setting the goals that their work will help meet. Only when they have been active participants in setting agency or program goals can service providers see their own work objectives in the context of the work of the agency as a whole.

Common commitment to agency goals is important because the individuals involved can have negative or positive effects on goal attainment through their behaviors. Just as important is the clarity of goals selected. If goals are not clearly stated, the benefits of wide agreement are lost. Stakeholders' commitment to the attainment of specific goals must be based on a clear understanding of what those goals really are. Vagueness brings with it a pervasive sense of confusion as individuals find that their perceptions of agency mission differ from those of other people.

Goals also fail to serve their real purpose if they are not realistic and cannot be operationalized. The function of goals in the planning process is to provide the basis for all decisions regarding programs and services. When goals are clear, objectives designed to attain them can more readily be specified.

Specification of Objectives _____

Whereas goals are broad statements of the outcomes sought by an agency or program, objectives are more specific and measurable statements regarding outcomes. Sometimes the words *goal* and *objective* are used interchangeably. For present purposes, they are semantically differentiated. Objectives identify the accomplishments that relate to a particular goal so that, ideally, if all of the objectives have been reached, the goal will automatically have been attained. Goals are general statements of desired end states. Objectives specify how those end states are to be attained. Objectives are by definition statements of measurable outcomes with a designated time frame.

The importance of goal clarity and objective specification cannot be overstressed. Not only are program activities in a sound plan predicated on selected goals and objectives, but program evaluation—that part of the planning process that informs stakeholders of a program's success or failure—usually takes the form of assessing whether program goals and objectives were met. Since program goals, by virtue of their value-laden declaration of desired end states, are difficult to measure objectively, program evaluators rely on the goals' corresponding objectives to provide the data and information they need to make informed assessments of program efficiency and effectiveness. (The relevance of goals and objectives to the evaluation process is reiterated in Chapter 10.)

Objectives can be categorized into three general types: (1) organizational, (2) activity, and (3) outcome. *Organizational objectives* are related to targets for organizational development or improvement. For example, "to raise $500,000 by September 1, 2002, for capital improvement" is an organizational objective. So is the following: "to increase the ethnic minority representation on the board of directors from six to twelve by the end of the fiscal year." *Activity objectives,* by contrast, pertain to program activities to be performed and/or number and types of services to be delivered—for example: "to provide outreach services to two hundred youth in our geographic area during the program year"; "to provide counseling to twenty families per week during the first year of the project." *Outcome objectives* refer to the expected *impact* of program intervention on the recipients of service. As such, outcome objectives make a connection between program efforts and program results and therefore provide a measure of program *effectiveness.* One example of an outcome objective is the following: "By the end of the program year, 65 percent of the youth dropouts served by the program will have returned to regular school or will have enrolled in an alternative accredited educational program." Another might read, "At least 60 percent of the couples engaged in marital counseling for six sessions will experience improvement in marital satisfaction, as measured by the Index of Marital Satisfaction."

Of the three types of objectives, the one most revealing of agency effectiveness is the outcome objective. This objective justifies the agency's reason for being, its purported relevance to social needs and problems and to their resolution. Today's manager of human service programs can hardly depend on luck to meet program goals or on testimonials to "prove" their attainment. Moreover, it is no longer sufficient for accountability purposes to cite the number of clients served and the cost per client per year. Such bottom-line measures of economic efficiency may be necessary, but they are certainly not sufficient indicators of a program's value to the community.

For outcome objectives to have the utmost utility, they should be stated so that they are

- **behavioral**—clear, concrete, specific, operational;

- **measurable**—subject to observable verification;

- **realistic**—not set too high, and capable of being accomplished with available resources;

- **worthwhile**—not set too low, not petty or meaningless;

- **adequate**—substantial translations of the mission of the system and relevant to real needs and wants. (Egan & Cowan, 1979, p. 126)

Moreover, they should answer the following questions:

- *What* is the desired outcome? What behavior, condition, or attribute is expected to change as a result of program effort?

- *Who* is the target of program efforts? Who is expected to change as a result of program intervention?

- *How many* of the recipients of service will be expected to achieve desired outcomes? That is, among the target population, what is the degree or extent of positive effect anticipated?

- *When* are desired outcomes expected? By the end of the program year? After three counseling sessions?

Irrespective of how they are worded, outcome objectives must address the what, who, how many, and when dimensions of program activity.

Management by Objectives

Management by objectives (MBO) is a way of both managing the efforts of people in an organization and ensuring active involvement and coherence in the planning process. "Objectives start at the highest level and cascade downward throughout the organization. The idea is that lower-level objectives, when achieved, will contribute to higher-level objectives, and that the upward summation of achievement will equal achievement at the highest level of the overall goals of the organization" (Barton, 1981, p. 231).

The planning process as applied in the MBO approach includes much input into the setting of organization-wide objectives, which are then used as the basis for setting the objectives of each department or program. The objectives to which all stakeholders have agreed are used as the basis for planning the work of each member of the organization. Each individual, in concert with his or her supervisor, decides on the part he or she will play in meeting organizational objectives, and this agreement provides the basis on which the individual's work will be evaluated.

Program Design

With a guiding vision, a well-thought-out strategy, and clear goals and objectives in mind, those responsible for planning services and programs can identify possible alternatives, specify any constraints that affect decision making, and determine the services most likely to be feasible, efficient, and effective for meeting consumer needs. Next, considering relevant theories and existing practice methods, a logic model can be selected to show how client needs or conditions can be addressed by the delivery of particular program services. Implementation activities with designation of those responsible can then be outlined. Finally, an evaluation plan should be designed, anticipating later needs for program evaluation.

Identifying and Selecting Alternatives

Choosing an appropriate service delivery method, or technology, has often been given insufficient attention in the human services. As was noted in Chapter 2, technology does not mean computers, as is commonly assumed in our field. Rather, it refers to the transformation process—in our case, changing people or communities. Kurzweil (1999) offers a simple but profound definition: "one interpretation of technology is the study of crafting, in which crafting refers to the shaping of resources for a practical purpose" (p. 16). Particularly relevant for the human services is the notion that "resources" include people and information. This is in essence the program design process: selecting methods and determining needed staff capabilities to achieve objectives.

In many agencies, staff often start a new program using methods with which they are familiar and that are often inadequately conceptualized (for example, "casework," "short-term counseling"). With increasing pressure for agencies to demonstrate successful outcomes, more attention must be paid to the selection of service methods. Logic models (Alter & Egan, 1997; Alter & Murty,

1997) can be helpful in clearly articulating what specific service activities are intended to address specific problems and achieve desired outcomes. Rapp and Poertner (1992) use the term *theory of helping* to emphasize that any method used should be based on theory and ideally have evidence of effectiveness in the form of research results or promising pilot demonstrations. In its most basic form, the theory of helping looks at what the expectations of the client and worker are in achieving predetermined goals and objectives. This is detailed in the following logic model (Alter & Egan, 1997):

- **Problem/need**—The current situation; what needs changing; "what is"

- **Goal**—The desired state to be achieved; "what should be"

- **Objectives**—Milestones or minigoals that lead to goal achievement

- **Inputs**—Concrete and tangible resources needed to achieve the objectives

- **Methods**—Services and activities that put resources into operations

- **Results**—Short-term impact(s) of applying inputs and methods

- **Outcomes**—Long-term impacts of applying inputs and methods

Any service methods being considered should be described and critiqued using this logic model to help ensure that methods chosen have realistic prospects for being successful.

The consideration of alternatives can begin with staff brainstorming models of which they are aware, from their own experience, other agencies, or the human service literature. In the business sector, the search for *best practices* has become common in the quality movement and reengineering initiatives. In the human services, best practices may be found in presentations at professional conferences, professional newsletter articles, government reports, and scholarly publications. Lisbeth Schorr (1997) has set the standard in the human services in this area through her profiling of successful human service programs. The wise agency and manager will always be searching for new methods that have been proven to be effective or show great promise. Critical analysis needs to be done to ensure that an agency does not simply adopt a method that is merely popular or seems appealing. The effective decision maker generates as many alternatives as possible, considers the potential consequences of each, actively searches for all relevant data, and exhibits openness to new information.

This openness is especially important for human service planning. If this process is to be effective, it must be based on a high degree of acceptance of proven service modalities. Alternatives should be rejected not because they are unfamiliar but because they fail to meet reasonable criteria set by policymakers, service providers, administrators, and consumers.

Broad participation should be involved in selecting the criteria that will be used to assess alternate services. These criteria can involve constraints or set requirements that each feasible alternative must meet. In human services, decision makers do not necessarily have a free rein in choosing services to consider or populations to serve. They are limited by legislation, the policies of larger institutions within which a program might be housed, ethical standards, and a host of other factors, even before limitations of resources are considered. In any case, criteria should focus on a prospective method's demonstrated effectiveness in accomplishing desired objectives.

All these limiting factors (and particularly those related to funding availability) must be considered, and some attempt has to be made to measure the costs of various alternatives, not only in terms of money but in terms of the trade-offs that must be involved if limited resources are earmarked for one service rather than for another. In particular, the qualifications of required staff and their salaries, the other necessary resources (facilities, equipment, staff training), and other program elements with costs attached need to be considered with reference to the amount of service to be provided (for example, numbers of clients) and the funds available. (Financial aspects of this decision-making process will be addressed in detail in Chapter 8.)

Decisions made in human service settings cannot be based solely on rational considerations. Causal relationships are not always clear enough to allow us to say that one approach, and only one, can lead to a desired outcome. Many human factors impinge on the decision-making process. Thus, actually deciding among alternative methods for reaching goals involves balancing a number of factors so that the options selected are both in tune with objectives and realistic in nature.

Depending on the situation and the resources available, the decision-making procedure might be as complex as a cost-effectiveness analysis or as simple as the use of an individual rating system. At its most basic level, decision making includes some procedure for considering alternative solutions in terms of the criteria selected. Whether a simple matrix, with each alternative measured in terms of its feasibility, or a decision tree, with all alternatives considered in terms of their costs and probable outcomes, is used, the outcome of the process should be selection of services that are appropriate to agency objectives, acceptable to stakeholders, and economically feasible. Each alternative should have stood the test of stringent questioning, with both innovations and sacred cows being considered, at minimum, in terms of the following questions:

- Does this service fit agency or program strategy, goals, and priorities?

- Is there documented evidence of the success of the model?

- Are available or potential resources adequate for service provision?

- Can the service be accepted by community members and consumers?

- Can the service be delivered by available or potentially available service providers?

- Does the service meet the policy constraints within which the agency or program must work?

- Do the potential benefits of the service appear to outweigh the estimated costs?

- Can we measure service effectiveness?

- Can we develop an implementation plan?

- Are serious risks involved in implementing the service?

When this decision-making process has been completed, the procedures of program design and planning for actual implementation become reasonably uncomplicated.

Conceptualizing the Program

All of an agency's work is accomplished through programs or sets of service-related activities that meet agency goals. Every program has its own set of goals and objectives that will lead to the accomplishment of the agency's more general mission. Normally, each program has resources that have been allocated at the agency level to lead to the accomplishment of its own objectives.

Once a program or service delivery model has been chosen, conscious attention should be paid to how it will be designed for the specific needs, goals, and objectives of the agency. According to Kettner and Daley (1988):

> program design refers to the way in which a program is conceptualized and its elements arranged in an effort to achieve objectives. It included two phases: (1) making explicit the underlying hypotheses of a program and its theoretical context, and (2) examining and defining each of the elements that, taken together, should result in an effective program. (p. 100)

The elements of a program (Kettner & Daley, 1988; Kettner, Moroney, & Martin, 1990) are as follows:

- **Inputs**—raw materials and resources, including clients, staff, facilities, and equipment

- **Throughput**—the service delivery or "conversion process," or how the client's condition is intended to change; includes service definitions and tasks (activities) and the method of intervention (the technology employed and the ways services are delivered)

- **Output**—the products, such as units of service provided
- **Outcome**—the actual changes in the client's quality of life.

These elements parallel the input, methods, results, and outcomes of the logic model presented earlier.

For example, one of the goals of a hypothetical Youth Center is to decrease youth unemployment. At the program design level, planners would assess local characteristics in terms of the specific variable of employment patterns and then base services on the problems and potentials identified. Realistic goals and objectives would have to take into account both needs assessment results and agency mission as a whole. Planners in this context would recognize that the thrust of services would be directed toward the needs of a broad range of typical youth and would see useful employment as a mechanism for preventing such problems as delinquency. Inputs would include the clients and agency staff and facilities. The throughput would describe the theory of helping: what technology (job training, interview training, and so forth) or activities would be part of the service delivery. The output would be the clients at a new level of training, knowledge, or skills, perhaps linked with employment opportunities. The outcomes may include youth remaining employed in jobs with identified hours, wages, benefits, career prospects, and, at the macrolevel, lower unemployment rates in the target population.

The methods identified would also take into account the existence of other agency programs. It might be decided to use the youth advocacy program as the base for advocating the hiring of young people. The actual direct service program might provide career counseling and placement services for young people contacted through community-wide advertising campaigns. Given the nature of the agency's mission, counseling would be focused on young people's development. Clients requesting psychotherapy would be linked with other agencies. Thus, within the context of broad agency goals, program developers would set in motion a detailed program for the implementation of a career development and placement program that would lend itself to effective evaluation in terms of outcomes for clients.

Developing an Implementation Plan

Once objectives and general methods or services to be used have been identified, the planner must begin to lay out a program of action that can provide for the implementation of new or changed services.

Implementation procedures depend on clarity, and some kind of formal or informal document should be in the hands of those responsible for carrying out any aspect of the plan. Each general goal statement should have its own list of objectives because achieving all objectives will lead to goal attainment. Each objective, in turn, should have a specified method, service, or program that has been selected to meet the objective. Each service or method depends for its achievement on an organized set of implementation activities. In short, there must be a plan for implementing the plan.

Young (1978) suggests that at this stage a set of key decisions must be made, including the following:

1. What are the major activities necessary to implement the methods selected?

2. Who will be responsible for performing each activity?

3. What are the starting and completion dates for major activities?

4. What are the basic resources needed to perform each activity? (p. 16)

The answers provide the basis for an implementation plan that specifies who is to perform what activities, when, and using what resources. The plan should be flexible enough to meet unexpected situations, but it should also provide clear and concrete statements concerning individual responsibilities and time frames for completing actions.

In most human service situations, simple time lines with milestones for task completion are adequate for illustrating projected implementation activities. For example, a program for providing newly designed counseling services to young people recruited from the community could not actually begin until counselors were hired and trained, clients were recruited, and clients and counselors were oriented to the program. The time line would need to specify the number of days or weeks needed for recruiting, interviewing, and selecting counselors; for designing the counselor training program; for implementing the counselor training program; for planning client recruitment; for carrying out client recruitment; for screening potential clients; for implementing an orientation session; and so on. The implementation plan would need to specify exactly what procedures would be carried out and by whom. A typical time-line model based on this example and dealing with the hypothetical agency called the Neighborhood Youth Center is shown in Figure 3-1. This time-line model is similar to a chart developed by H. L. Gantt, a turn-of-the-century business management pioneer; it is called, not surprisingly, the Gantt chart (Lauffer, 1997). The one advantage of the time-line model over the Gantt chart is that the time line identifies individuals responsible for performing specific tasks.

When planning is complex, more sophisticated approaches might be needed. For instance, the program evaluation and review technique (PERT) might be used to specify the events that need to take place for a specific event— in this case, the start of the counseling program—to occur on time. Activities are assigned expected times for completion and are graphically arranged so that it is apparent which events depend on the completion of others. In our current

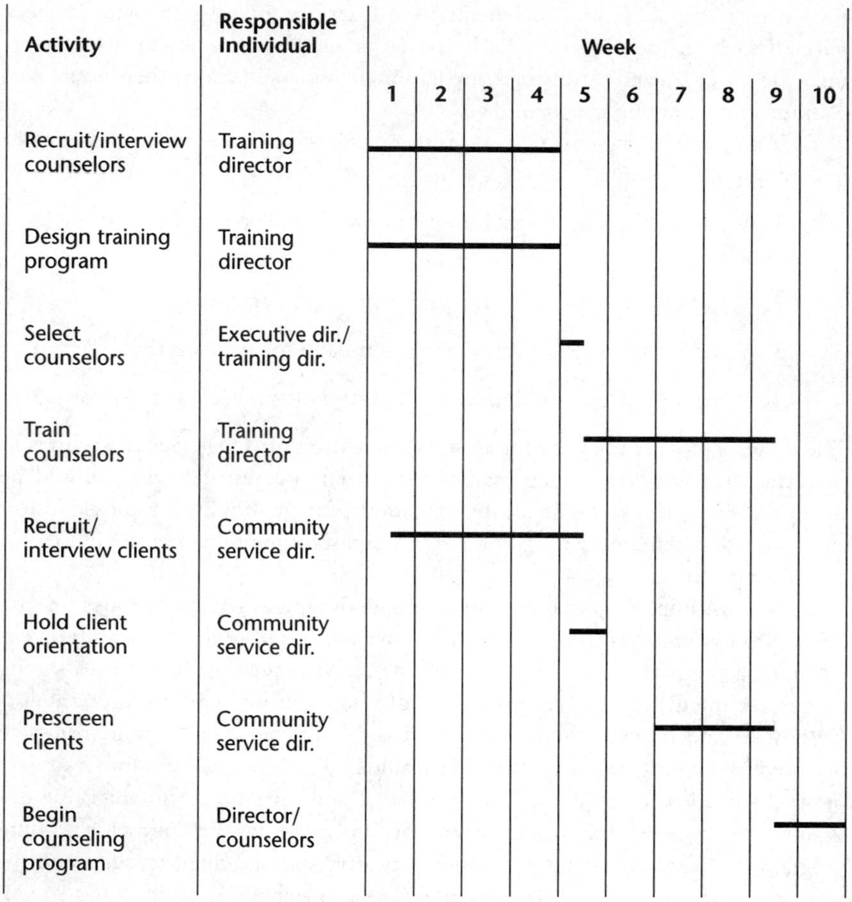

Activity	Responsible Individual	Week									
		1	2	3	4	5	6	7	8	9	10
Recruit/interview counselors	Training director	▬	▬	▬							
Design training program	Training director	▬	▬	▬							
Select counselors	Executive dir./ training dir.				▬						
Train counselors	Training director					▬	▬	▬			
Recruit/ interview clients	Community service dir.		▬	▬							
Hold client orientation	Community service dir.					▬					
Prescreen clients	Community service dir.							▬	▬		
Begin counseling program	Director/ counselors										▬

FIGURE 3-1
Time Line for the Neighborhood Youth Center Career Counseling Project

example (Figure 3-2), Event A (counselors recruited), Event B (training program designed), Event C (counselors selected), and Event D (counselors trained) must all precede the beginning of the counseling program. The clients must also be re-cruited, oriented, and screened before the program can begin. The critical path, however, involves Events A, C, and D. Here there is no slack time. Recruitment and selection of counselors, as well as design of the training program, must take place on time if the program is to begin on schedule.

The charts shown in Figures 3-1 and 3-2 serve as useful implementation guides. Similar formats should be used to determine resource allocations, with budgets based on the planned activities (see Chapter 8).

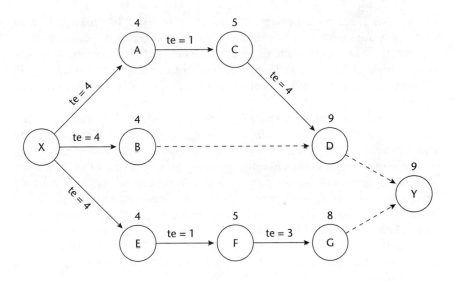

Event X = Project start
Event A = Counselors recruited
Event B = Training program designed
Event C = Counselors selected
Event D = Counselors trained
Event E = Clients recruited
Event F = Clients oriented
Event G = Clients screened
Event Y = Counseling program begun

te = Expected time for activities, in weeks

Digits above each event = Earliest expected
        time, total, in weeks

FIGURE 3-2
PERT: Start-up Time for Neighborhood Youth Center Counseling Project

Developing an Evaluation Plan

At the same time that the initial planning is being implemented, planners should consider the methods that will be used to evaluate the success of the services to be delivered. The objectives identified as part of the planning process also provide the basis for evaluating program outcomes. Thus, evaluation criteria have, at this point, been identified. If the planners also use this opportunity to plan for the gathering of relevant data on an ongoing basis, effective evaluation can become a reality.

One way to ensure that the program will be easy to evaluate is to do an *evaluability assessment,* which basically involves reviewing the program model to see whether it has the necessary elements for evaluation. The main task of an evaluability assessment is to "determine whether a program's objectives are conceptualized and operationalized in a way that would permit a meaningful evaluation" (Gabor & Grinnell, 1994, p. 22). Information systems that document all relevant client characteristics, outcomes, and service processes will also need to be developed.

Considering evaluation throughout the planning process—from needs assessment to goal definition, to decision making, to planning for implementation and evaluation—can prevent many of the problems normally associated with human service organizations. Effective planning lessens the use of unclear, fuzzy goals; brings commonality of purpose and expectation to various concerned groups; focuses concern on ends rather than solely on means; helps specify desired outputs; and attempts to relate resource allocation to goals. This approach provides a basis for planning behaviors, whether the specific task is strategic planning, program development, problem solving, implementation of management by objectives, or innovation. The same basic process is readily adaptable to the needs of each situation.

Summary

In this chapter, we looked at the key role of a vision of a preferred future in focusing energy and commitment. Strategic planning was presented as a way of developing organizational responses to an assessment of the agency's mission and mandates, stakeholder expectations, opportunities and threats in the environment, and internal strengths and weaknesses. Strategies are developed and then operationalized through goals and objectives. Then, a program needs to be designed, using the most appropriate service delivery technologies available. Implementation and evaluation are where the vision comes to life and results are assessed. Before we look at how the multiple programs of an agency are put together, we will review some useful theoretical perspectives that can provide guidance in the design of human service organizations.

Discussion Questions

1. To what extent do you think professionals resist using new service methods? Is it possible to maintain professionalism without placing definite limits on the types of activities an individual is willing to perform?

2. Human service organizations are often accused of having vague and unclear goals. Given the nature of the problems human service organizations address, is it realistic to think that goals can be clear and measurable? Do we have to sacrifice clarity in order to deal with issues of real concern to people?

3. If you were managing a human service program, what steps would you take to ensure that you were responsive to the community?

Group Exercise

Work in small groups of no more than three or four participants. Each group should identify one hypothetical human service organization that the members would like to see in existence. With this fictitious agency in mind, develop an initial plan by writing down answers to the following questions:

1. What is your ideal of what this organization should be like?

2. What do you see as the primary goals toward which the agency should work?

3. Give some examples of specific, measurable objectives that would help meet the goals you have identified.

4. What are some activities or services that would be helpful in meeting objectives?

Give your hypothetical agency a name, and share the results of your work with the other groups. Save your work so that you can use the same hypothetical agency as a basis for later activities.

CASE 3

The Model College Counseling Center

The counseling center of Hillsboro University had been a model of excellence in its early years. It was one of the few such centers offering long-term therapy for students who desired higher degrees of self-awareness. Only in cases of serious psychiatric crisis were students referred to outside agencies. The director of the counseling center prided himself on the fact that, with the highly qualified and credentialed staff of counselors he had hired, Hillsboro students could have all their mental health needs met within the boundaries of their peaceful, tree-lined campus.

In the past several years, however, changes had begun to take place. The number of clients presenting themselves for services at the counseling center had dropped so drastically that the centers staff—all licensed psychologists or clinical social workers—had time to spare. Waiting lists for appointments had never been long, but now the reception area was ominously quiet. This situation was surprising because any indicator that could possibly measure aspects of mental health among students showed that problems did exist. Disciplinary measures for drug and alcohol abuse had increased; the dropout rate at final exam time was as high as ever; and complaints from local police officers and residents showed that students were, indeed, "letting off steam" in the late hours.

In light of the situation, the university's vice president for student affairs, Mary Belmont, initiated a series of discussions with Simon Young, the counseling center director. Vice President Belmont's contention was that the counseling center no longer met the needs of Hillsboro students.

She pointed out, "We simply don't have the kinds of students we used to. The students we have now are not here to find themselves. They're not interested in spending long hours delving into their reason for being. These young people are practical. They want help with immediate decisions, help with time management, help in developing methods for dealing with stress. They are not going to spend long periods of time in a therapist's office. Something has to change."

"But that's exactly my point," Young responded. "These students do have problems, and they're not dealing with them. They think it's not important to delve into their reasons for being, but it is important. They think they can solve their problems with a quick how-to session, but they can't. A good proportion of these students do need therapy—at least as many as needed it five years ago. What we have to do is get those dormitory house parents, student advisers, and professors to start referring students to the center so they can get what they need."

"We're not going to do that, Simon. We don't know what these students need unless we ask them. What I'd like to suggest is that we involve the members of your counseling staff, and then some other members of the university community, and try to implement some planning about what steps should be taken. We can't afford to be paying high salaries for clinicians to be sitting in their offices waiting for someone to remember they're there."

"Now I understand what you're really saying, Mary. It's getting near budget time again. You're not concerned about what these students need. You're concerned about the money being spent on the counseling center, and you're trying to cut costs. I wouldn't mind it so much if you'd just be straight about it. Just remember this: When you hired me as counseling center director, you told me I'd have a free hand to build a quality center. You said that was what you wanted, and that's what you got. If you don't want that anymore, just tell me."

"Simon, I don't want that anymore."

"Then you'll have my resignation on your desk in the morning. I don't know whether the staff will join me or not."

"Simon, just wait a minute. You had some ideas about what kinds of things you wanted to accomplish with young people. You had some goals in mind, and, for a long time, you met them. Now times are changing. Why is it so impossible to consider using different methods to reach students? Why not use decision-making kits that students can use on their own? Why not go into the dorms with life planning workshops? Why not train peer counselors to work with the students who live off campus?"

"Because, Mary, what you're talking about are a bunch of fads. They may save money on professional salaries, but in no way do they accomplish the same ends. These are shortcuts that don't reach the places we're trying to go. What good are they? Maybe I was hasty in talking about my resignation, but I have to tell you that I'm going to support my staff, no matter what it takes. I won't have you firing experienced therapists left and right just to bring in a bunch of kids or pieces of paper that you think can fix people up."

"I'm not suggesting that. What I am suggesting is that the plans you made when you started this counseling center were solid, and your methods worked. But you can't stay married to your methods."

"These aren't my methods, which I just invented. These are the methods that clinicians learn as part of their professional training. They fit accepted professional standards."

"Look, Simon, I understand that. Just give me a commitment that you'll try to explore this further. We won't take any action until we've thought it through."

1. What do you consider to be the most likely outcome of the conflict between Mary Belmont and Simon Young?

2. What are the real issues at stake?

3. Do you see one of these two differing viewpoints as being essentially correct in terms of your own values? Would you be able to present an argument justifying the opposite viewpoint?

4. If you were to be involved in a planning process like the one suggested by the university vice president, what steps would you follow? Who should be involved in the planning process?

5. Is there any way that earlier planning procedures might have prevented the conflict described in this case?

6. To what degree can the planning process be considered rational?

References

Allison, M., & Kaye, J. (1997). *Strategic planning for nonprofit organizations.* New York: Wiley.

Alter, C., & Egan, M. (1997). Logic modeling: A tool for teaching critical thinking in social work practice. *Journal of Education in Social Work, 33*(1), 85–102.

Alter, C., & Murty, S. (1997). Logic modeling: A tool for teaching program evaluation. *Journal of Education in Social Work, 33*(1), 103–117.

Barton, R. F. (1981). An MCDM approach for resolving goal conflict in MBO. *Academy of Management Review, 6,* 231–241.

Boehm, A. (1996). Forces driving competition in human service organizations and positional competitive responses. *Administration in Social Work, 20*(4), 61–78.

Bryson, J. (1995). *Strategic planning for public and nonprofit organizations* (rev. ed.). San Francisco: Jossey-Bass.

Bryson, J., & Alston, F. (1996). *Creating and implementing your strategic plan.* San Francisco: Jossey-Bass.

Eadie, D. (1998). Planning and managing strategically. In R. Edwards, J. Yankey, & M. Altpeter (Eds.), *Skills for effective management of nonprofit organizations* (pp. 453–468). Washington, DC: NASW Press.

Egan, G., & Cowan, M. A. (1979). *People in systems: A model for development in the human service professions and education.* Pacific Grove, CA: Brooks/Cole.

Gabor, P., & Grinnell, R., Jr. (1994). *Evaluation and quality improvement in the human services.* Boston: Allyn & Bacon.

Kettner, P., & Daley, J. (1988). Designing effective programs. *Child Welfare, 77*(2), 99–111.

Kettner, P., Moroney, R., & Martin, L. (1990). *Designing and managing programs.* Newbury Park, CA: Sage.

Kurzweil, R. (1999). *The age of spiritual machines.* New York: Viking.

Lauffer, A. (1997). *Grants, etc.* (2nd ed.). Thousand Oaks, CA: Sage.

Menefee, D. (1997). Strategic administration of nonprofit human service organizations: A model for executive success in turbulent times. *Administration in Social Work, 21*(2), 1–19.

Micklethwait, J., & Wooldridge, A. (1997). *The witch doctors: Making sense of the management gurus.* New York: Times Business.

Nutt, P., & Backoff, R. (1992). *Strategic management for public and third sector organizations: A handbook for leaders.* San Francisco: Jossey-Bass.

O'Looney, J. (1996). *Redesigning the work of human services.* Westport, CT: Quorum.

Osborne, D., & Gaebler, T. (1992). *Reinventing government.* Reading, MA: Addison-Wesley.

Osborne, D., & Plastrik, P. (1997). *Banishing bureaucracy: The five strategies for reinventing government.* Reading, MA: Addison-Wesley.

Packard, T. (2000). *Building commitment through organizational values: The case for a homeless shelter.* Unpublished manuscript, San Diego State University.

Rapp, C., & Poertner, J. (1992). *Social administration: A client-centered approach.* New York: Longman.

Schorr, L. (1997). *Common purpose.* New York: Anchor Books Doubleday.

Senge, P. (1990). *The fifth discipline.* New York: Doubleday Currency.

Spencer, L. (1989). *Winning through participation.* Dubuque, IA: Kendall/Hunt.

Steiner, J., Gross, G., Ruffolo, M., & Murray, J. (1994). Strategic planning in nonprofits: Profit from it. *Administration in Social Work, 18*(2), 87–106.

Webster, S., & Wylie, M. (1988). Strategic planning in competitive environments. *Administration in Social Work, 12*(3), 25–45.

Weisbord, M., & 35 International Coauthors. (1992). *Discovering common ground.* San Francisco: Berrett Koehler.

Yankey, J. (1995). Strategic planning. In R. Edwards (Ed.), *The encyclopedia of social work* (19th ed., pp. 2321–2327). Washington, DC: NASW Press.

Young, K. (1978). *The basic steps of planning.* Charlottesville, NC: Community Collaborators.

4

Organizational Theory for Human Service Organizations

CHAPTER OUTLINE

Classical Theories
Bureaucracy, Scientific Management, Universal Management Principles, Classical Theories in Today's Human Service Organizations

Human Relations Approaches

The Human Resources Model

Open Systems Theory

Contemporary Developments
Professional Bureaucracies, Community-Based Organizations and Feminist Organizations, Japanese Management, Total Quality Management, The Excellence Movement, Business Process Reengineering, Employee Involvement and the Quality of Working Life, Reinventing Government, Learning Organizations

Contingency Theories

Summary

Discussion Questions

CASE 4: The Community Career Center

References

Kurt Lewin, one of the great thinkers in the field of organizational behavior, said, "There's nothing so practical as a good theory" (Weisbord, 1987, p. 70). We all have theories about how things work and which variables affect other variables. Some are ones we have been taught (behaviorism, psychoanalysis, family systems theory); others we have not articulated consciously but guide our behavior (for example, which intervention will work at a given time with a given client). This chapter is intended to provide a core of knowledge of organizational theories currently being articulated and used, so that a manager and those working with managers can consciously and thoughtfully choose the use of an appropriate theory to enhance their effectiveness in an organizational context. These will be particularly relevant in the next chapter, when we discuss the design of organizations.

Few human service workers maintain clear awareness of the practical differences dividing organizational theorists. Although all thinkers in the field of organizational theory seek the "best" answers to the basic questions, they seldom agree about what those best answers really are. The designers of an organization are faced with a myriad of choices. They can build structures that are highly centralized and specialized or systems based on widespread decision-making responsibility and participation. They can departmentalize the organization's activities by joining all the people who perform a specific function, or they can build teams of people with differing but complementary skills. They can use traditional, hierarchical designs or experiment with task forces, committees, or even leaderless groups. The organization's form has major implications for the way its functions will be performed.

Classical Theories

Three prominent classical theories of organization originated in the nineteenth century. Sociologist Max Weber articulated theoretical principles of the ideal *bureaucracy*. Industrial engineer Frederick Taylor developed *scientific management* guidelines for the "best way" to supervise workers in a factory. Henri Fayol developed a set of *management principles* that are still influential today.

Bureaucracy

The earliest major thinker to formulate the concept of an ideal organization was Max Weber, who saw the "rational legal bureaucracy" as the efficient organization in its pure form (Gerth & Mills, 1958). Weber's ideal structure included high degrees of specialization and impersonality, authority based on comprehensive rules rather than on social relationships, clear and centralized hierarchies of authority and responsibility, prescribed systems of rules and procedures, hiring and promotion based solely on technical ability, and extensive use of written documentation.

Weber saw this pure system as a historical trend that would meet the needs posed by the increasing size of organizations and at the same time replace unfairness and uncertainty with rationality and clarity. Perrow (1986) summarizes the key elements of the rational-legal bureaucracy this way:

1. Equal treatment for all employees

2. Reliance on expertise, skills, and experience relevant to the position

3. No extra organizational prerogatives of the position (such as taking dynamite, wallboard, and so forth [workers took such items home in an example cited by Perrow]); that is, the position is seen as belonging to the organization, not the person. The employee cannot use it for personal ends.

4. Specific standards of work and output

5. Extensive record keeping dealing with the work and output

6. Establishment and enforcement of rules and regulations that serve the interests of the organization

7. Recognition that rules and regulations bind managers as well as employees; thus employees can hold management to the terms of the employment contract (p. 3)

Speed, precision, and reduction of friction were associated with the ideal bureaucracy because in this organization everyone would have a clear awareness of both his or her and others' functions. All aspects of the organization's work would be regulated. The repetitiveness of the work would bring with it both steadiness and high quality. Personal enmity and constant questioning would be replaced by rationality and regularity.

One of the most common criticisms of an organization, unit, procedure, or manager is that it or he or she is "too bureaucratic." On the other hand, Perrow (1986) asserts that "many of the 'sins' of bureaucracy really reveal the failure to bureaucratize sufficiently" (p. 5). Other complaints in a bureaucracy are that a person (usually a manager) is not qualified or that someone is receiving preferential treatment—both violations of the principles of bureaucracy. Clearly, one of the failures of modern human service organizations, particularly public sector ones, is that they have sometimes enthusiastically and single-mindedly misapplied bureaucratic thinking, and even Weber was "extremely critical of the way bureaucracy destroys spontaneity" (Gortner, Mahler, & Nicholson, 1997, p. 5).

Ultimately, most would admit that bureaucracy provides useful principles. It is also true that it alone is insufficient to fully guide modern managerial behavior, and the subsequent movements discussed later, starting with the human relations movement, do not replace bureaucracy but add to it. Bureaucratic thinking provides a foundation for personnel practices that all workers appreciate: clear job roles and performance expectations, fair treatment, and due process; but later models would need to add principles recognizing that individuals and situations also must be addressed with consideration of their uniquenesses.

Although Weber's approach was philosophical, the ideals of clearly defined objectives, specialization, hierarchical chains of command, and responsibility commensurate with authority are also basic to the thinking of early management scientists such as Taylor (1911) and practitioners such as Fayol (1949). Taylor in particular has been vilified as much as bureaucracy has, but he also provided principles that are still useful.

Scientific Management

Frederick Taylor, the founder of the *scientific management* school of organizational theory, focused on the assembly line: the core work processes of the organization. As an industrial engineer, Taylor mainly consulted in the steel industry at the turn of the twentieth century. He believed that engineers could study a work process such as loading steel onto railway cars and determine the "one best method" for the task to be done. Workers were then trained on exactly how to do their job and repeated it over and over through their shift. He used time and motion studies to observe workers and identify wasteful steps or movements.

Perhaps his best-known quote describes job requirements for one who loads pig iron (a ninety-two-pound piece of steel): "One of the very first requirements for a man who is fit to handle pig-iron . . . is that he shall be so stupid . . . that he more nearly resembles in his mental make-up the ox than any other type" (1912 hearings, cited in Sashkin, 1981, p. 208). "Taylorism" has come to refer to managers who assume their employees are stupid and need to be told what to do in excruciating detail, assuming that the manager is always right. In fact, Taylor was a complex person who believed that bosses should be "servants of the workmen" (Weisbord, 1987, p. 34) and that workers should share in the profits of the organization.

Taylor's main legacies today are work analysis methods used by industrial engineers (sometimes in human service settings) and profit-sharing plans for workers in industry. As was the case with bureaucracy, some principles such as scientifically analyzing the work to be performed and rewarding workers based on their performance are valuable and can be seen today in the quality movement and organizational reward systems.

Universal Management Principles

The final theorist of the classical school is Henri Fayol, a French contemporary of Weber and Taylor whose views became known as the *universal principles* school.

He conceptualized the five basic functions of management (planning, organizing, commanding, coordinating, and controlling) and developed a set of principles for the design of an organization (Bowditch & Buono, 1997, p. 9):

1. **Division of work**—Specialization of tasks and control of the number of people under each worker or manager improves effectiveness and efficiency.

2. **Authority and responsibility**—The person in authority has the right to give orders and the power to obtain obedience; responsibility emerges directly from authority.

3. **Unity of command**—No person should have more than one boss.

4. **Remuneration**—Pay should be fair and satisfactory to the employer and employee; no one should be under- or overrewarded.

5. **Esprit de corps**—Morale and good feelings about the organization are enhanced by effective face-to-face communication and group cohesiveness.

Another of Fayol's useful principles was the *gangplank,* a figurative bridge that enabled individuals at the same level but in different units or departments to talk directly to each other rather than using the chain of command (Sashkin, 1981).

Classical Theories in Today's Human Service Organizations

With classical management theories still prevalent in so many settings, we need to ask how relevant or useful they are for human service programs and agencies. A human service agency designed on the basis of classical principles would be organized so that all employees, including professionals, paraprofessionals, and clerical workers, perform regular, specialized tasks. A counselor assigned to perform individual counseling with adolescents might spend all of his or her time in this activity; other specialists might conduct group sessions or work with parents. Although the degree of specialization would depend on agency's size and resources, each task would relate to the basic goals of the program as a whole. The activities to be performed in the interests of meeting these goals would have been identified first, and then competent individuals would have been selected and trained to carry them out. It would be understood that the resources and jobs involved in the program would belong not to individuals but to the agency, with replacement of individual workers being possible without disruption in the flow of work. (Agency activities would not change, for example, because a behaviorist was replaced by an Adlerian or because a social worker was replaced by a psychologist.) Each worker would report to one supervisor or director, who would have the authority and responsibility to carry out policies chosen by the ultimate authority (in the case of a human service agency, ultimate authority is usually delegated to an executive director by a board of directors). Each human service professional—like every other worker—would understand the precise limits of his or her function. All similar clients would receive similar services.

The major contribution that classical theories offer to human service programs is in the area of unity of effort, with the idea that all of an organization's activities should relate to its general goals. Human service organizations could benefit from increased rationality in the planning process because one of the weaknesses of human service programs has been the tendency of professionals to perform the functions that are comfortable for them rather than those that can best meet the client-oriented goals of the agency or institution. The idea that a counseling program or agency should have a clearly defined set of objectives that should be met through the coordinated efforts of all workers is one that could enhance the efficiency and effectiveness of helping professionals. Even the bureaucratic ideal of "impersonality" could have something to offer because, as Perrow (1986) points out, it involves the purging of "particularism" and discrimination or favoritism in hiring and service delivery.

The strengths of the classical approach are counteracted by its weaknesses, at least in human service programs. The major problems in applying classical management principles to the helping services lie in the insistence on specialization and centralized hierarchies of authority. Human service professionals tend to see themselves as having responsibility not just to their agencies or institutions but to their clients and professional colleagues as well. They are not easily able to conform to a system that expects them to obey orders that may conflict with their professional standards or their views of their clients' best interests. The use of very specialized, routine work patterns may be of little value in dealing with humans and their unique problems. The worker who gains a "habitual and virtuoso-like mastery" of his or her subject may overlook the differing needs of individuals being served, with the result that agency rules gain in ascendancy while consumer rights are lost.

Human service agencies are beginning to come to grips with the fact that creative approaches are needed to deal with the problem of increasing client needs coinciding with decreasing agency resources. Unfortunately, what bureaucracies may offer in terms of rationality is lost in terms of creativity. Some of these weaknesses are addressed by the proponents of the human relations approach.

Human Relations Approaches

The origins of the human relations approach to organization are usually traced to Elton Mayo (Fischer & Sirianni, 1984) and two of his colleagues, Fritz Roethlisberger and William Dickson (Perrow, 1986), all of whom were involved in Western Electric's Hawthorne plant experiments in the 1920s and 1930s. These studies were undertaken to determine whether changes in the physical work environment affected worker productivity. In essence, they were designed to test some of the postulates of scientific management, specifically those having to do with the effects of illumination, fatigue, and production quotas on worker performance. The underlying purpose of the Hawthorne studies was to find means of increasing organizational efficiency. Small experimental and control groups of workers were identified and placed in separate rooms, where their work was closely observed and recorded by members of the research team. Environmental conditions for the experimental group were altered in both a positive and a negative direction; that is, the lights were turned up and down, rest periods were increased and decreased, and quotas were raised and lowered. Yet the group's productivity continued to increase steadily until it leveled off at a rate unaffected by environmental manipulations (Perrow, 1986).

Finding little support for the hypothesis that variations in environmental conditions (except for the extremely negative, such as almost total darkness) affect productivity, the researchers attributed major experimental results to two social phenomena theretofore given slight importance by theorists: (1) the existence and influence of the informal group within the formal organization and (2) what later became known as the "Hawthorne effect." Both of these findings have implications for today's human service manager. The first has to do with issues of control; the second, with coordination—two important elements of organizational structure.

With respect to the informal group, the Hawthorne researchers found that the relationships formed among the members of the test groups appeared to meet certain social and psychological needs for affiliation that in turn led to enhanced group productivity. Moreover, findings indicated that informal group members established their own production rates based on their collective perception of survival within the organization rather than on quotas imposed by management. That is, the informal group determined at what point underproductivity might lead to being fired and overproductivity might lead to being laid off. Fortunately, and perhaps coincidentally, the Hawthorne subjects established a production rate that was within their managers' zone of acceptance (Perrow, 1986).

The Hawthorne experiments served more to illuminate the importance of the human element in organizational life than to demonstrate the importance of illumination on organizational productivity. Dimensions of worker motivation beyond fear and greed were introduced as valid managerial areas of concern and study.

The human relations approach to organization assumes that the bureaucratic view of human beings is too narrow to be useful in real-life organizations, and it has added immeasurably to views of organizational behavior and management practice. Nevertheless, the human relations school as developed following the Hawthorne studies was later seen to be incomplete as well. This conclusion required further thinking about how to address the human dimension to make organizations more effective.

Before we leave the human relations school, we will visit yet another contemporary of both the classical theorists and the Hawthorne experimenters. Mary Parker Follett was a hugely influential consultant to industry until her death in 1933 and subsequently in her writings (Graham, 1995). Of interest to human service managers, Follett had a twenty-five-year career as a social work manager in Boston before becoming famous as a speaker and writer focusing on the business sector (Syers, 1995, p. 2585). Her thinking predated and influenced such current concepts as participatory management and empowerment, total quality management, conflict management, and leadership (Selber & Austin, 1997). Some of these concepts will be discussed later, but one of her insights is particularly relevant to the transition from the human relations movement begun in the 1920s to a more advanced view articulated by writers including Argyris, McGregor, and Likert.

According to Child (1995), the human relations approach articulated by Mayo and others in fact supported the classical notion of managerial control, whereas Follett believed in substantive worker participation in decision making. In his words, the human relations view "ascribed a privileged rationality to managers that legitimated their authority and was naturally attractive to members of the management movement working on their behalf" (p. 88). The later developments in the human relations school are, in fact, substantively different from the earlier version, and this distinction was made by Miles (1965, 1975) as he assessed different types of employee participation in decision making. He defined his approach as the *human resources* model, which implied more fully using the skills and talents of workers than the *human relations* model of the Hawthorne studies, which has been derisively referred to as "cow sociology": keep the workers contented/happy and they will produce more milk/work.

The Human Resources Model

An early humanistic psychologist, Argyris (1957) pointed out that workers are motivated by many factors other than economics, including desires for growth and independence. To Argyris, the organizational forms mandated by the classical theorists make for immature, dependent, and passive employees with little control over their work and thwart more mature employees capable of autonomy and independence. The purpose of the human resources approach is to develop organizational forms that build on the worker's strength and motivation.

McGregor (1960) distinguished between managers adhering to Theory X and those adhering to Theory Y. He did not say that either of these theories is correct. He did say that each is based on assumptions that, if recognized, would have major implications for organizing activities.

McGregor's Theory X manager assumes that people dislike work, lack interest in organizational objectives, and want to avoid responsibility. The natural result of this situation is that managers must base their organizations on the need to control; to supervise closely; and to use reward, punishment, and active persuasion to force employees to do their jobs. In contrast, the manager who adheres to Theory Y assumes that people enjoy working, desire responsibility, have innate capacities for creativity, and have the potential to work toward organizational objectives with a minimum of direction. The implication of these assumptions is that work can be organized in such a way that personnel at all levels have the opportunity to do creative, self-directed, and responsible jobs.

The organizational implications of McGregor's model are clear. Theory X managers would use high degrees of specialization, clear lines of authority, narrow spans of control, and centralized decision making. Theory Y managers would use less specialization, less control, and more delegation of decision making and responsibility. The organization would be decentralized so that workers' natural creativity could be channeled effectively.

Likert (1967) examined a number of specific organizational variables, including leadership, motivation, communication, decision making, goal setting, and control. He divided organizations into four basic types, based on how they deal with these organizational variables: System 1 (exploitive authoritative), System 2 (benevolent authoritative), System 3 (consultative), and System 4 (participative group). Likert's System 1 organizations are characterized by leaders who distrust their subordinates, decision-making processes that are concentrated at the top of the organizational hierarchy, and communication that is almost exclusively downward, from supervisor to supervisees. Control and power are centralized in top management so that others feel little concern for the organization's overall goals. System 2 organizations also centralize power in the hands of the few at the top of the hierarchy but add an increased degree of communication. More trust is placed in subordinates, but it is condescending in nature. System 3 increases communication; employees have the opportunity to give input, although all major decisions are still made at the top of the management hierarchy. System 4, the opposite of System 1, is characterized by leaders who have complete confidence in workers, motivation that is based on responsibility and participation as well as on economic rewards, communication among all organization members, extensive interaction, decentralized decision making, wide acceptance of organizational goals, and widespread responsibility for control.

Likert (1967, p. 46) said that most managers recognize System 4 as theoretically superior to the others. He pointed out that if clear plans, high goals, and technical competence are present in an organization, System 4 will be superior. The key to its superiority lies in a structure based on group decision making and on the relationship of each group in an organization to every other group through common members or linking pins.

Based on the assumptions of McGregor's Theory Y and Likert's System 4, the human resources model encourages increased subordinate participation in decision making. According to Miles (1965), two models of participatory management exist: the human relations model (of Hawthorne fame) and the human resources model. He asserted that the key element in the human relations approach is its basic objective of making organizational members *feel* useful and important.

> The process is viewed as the means of accomplishing the ultimate goal of building a cooperative and compliant work force. Participation, in this model, is a lubricant which oils away resistance to formal authority. . . . This model does not bring out the fact that participation may be useful for its own sake. (p. 149)

Miles further contended that this model is not very different from the traditional autocratic model insofar as the ultimate goal in both is compliance with managerial authority. The human resources approach differs with the human relations approach in three key areas. In the human resources approach:

1. a basic assumption is that all organizational members are seen as valuable reservoirs of untapped resources,

2. the purpose of participation is to improve decision making and total performance efficiency of the organization rather than to reduce resistance, and

3. improved satisfaction is seen as resulting from improved decision making and performance.

The two models and the classical or traditional model of Weber and Taylor are represented in Table 4-1.

How would an organization based on the thinking of Argyris, McGregor, and Likert differ from a bureaucratic agency? If a human service program were organized in accordance with a human resources approach, it would be characterized by greater freedom of action, both for human service professionals and for their coworkers. Instead of departmentalizing the agency by function, the organization might divide work according to purpose or population being served. An interdisciplinary task force, including various helping professionals, paraprofessionals, community members, and consumers, might work together to solve a specific problem. Such a group might design a program to improve the agency's services to court-referred juveniles or troubled families. It might provide outreach services to displaced homemakers or school-age drug users. It might educate the community concerning mental health or stress management.

The task force itself might be permanent or ad hoc, but this organizational structure would allow each person to participate actively in planning and decision making while decreasing the prevalence of routine, specialized activities. Less attention would be directed toward authority and control, and greater emphasis would be placed on the flow of information from person to person and group to group.

TABLE 4-1
Alternative Theories of Management

Traditional Model	Human Relations Model	Human Resources Model
Assumptions	*Assumptions*	*Assumptions*
1. Work is inherently distasteful to most people.	1. People want to feel useful and important.	1. Work is not inherently distasteful. People want to contribute to meaningful goals that they have helped establish.
2. What workers do is less important than what they earn for doing it.	2. People desire to belong and to be recognized as individuals.	
3. Few want or can handle work that requires creativity, self-direction, or self-control.	3. These needs are more important than money in motivating people to work.	2. Most people can exercise far more creative, responsible self-direction and self-control than their present jobs demand.
Policies	*Policies*	*Policies*
1. The manager's basic task is to closely supervise and control his or her subordinates.	1. The manager's basic task is to make each worker feel useful and important.	1. The manager's basic task is to make use of his or her "untapped" human resources.
2. He or she must break tasks down into simple repetitive, easily learned operations.	2. The manager should keep his or her subordinates informed and listen to their objections to his or her plans.	2. The manager must create an environment in which all members may contribute to the limits of their ability.
3. The manager must establish detailed work routines and procedures and enforce these firmly but fairly.	3. The manager should allow his or her subordinates to exercise some self-direction and self-control on routine matters.	3. The manager must encourage full participation on important matters, continually broadening subordinate self-direction and control.
Expectations	*Expectations*	*Expectations*
1. People can tolerate work if the pay is decent and the boss is fair.	1. Sharing information with subordinates and involving them in routine decisions will satisfy their basic needs to belong and to feel important.	1. Expanding subordinate influence, self-direction, and self-control will lead to direct improvements in operating efficiency.

(continued)

TABLE 4-1
Alternative Theories of Management *(continued)*

Traditional Model	Human Relations Model	Human Resources Model
Expectations	*Expectations*	*Expectations*
2. If tasks are simple enough and people are closely controlled, they will produce up to standard.	2. Satisfying these needs will improve morale and reduce resistance to formal authority—subordinates will "willingly cooperate."	2. Work satisfaction may improve as a "by-product" of subordinates' making full use of their resources.

SOURCE: R. Miles. *Theories of management: Implications for organizational behavior and development.* Copyright ©1975 by McGraw Hill. Reprinted with permission of the publisher.

In the case of a large agency, people would identify with their own projects and feel responsible for their success. In the case of a small agency or a program within a larger institution, all staff members would participate in setting objectives and choosing evaluation methods for the program as a whole. Although a hierarchy of authority might exist, decision-making powers would not be limited to those at the highest levels, and the boundaries between jobs and specializations would not be clear-cut. Structure would be seen as a changing force rather than a constant factor.

A strength of the human resources school for human service agencies is its consistency with the approach of helping professionals. Human service workers tend to favor increasing self-responsibility and options for their clients, and they generally prefer that their supervisors give them high levels of autonomy, as the human resources school prescribes.

The human resources–based organization also has a greater allowance for change than does the bureaucratic structure. Although bureaucracies are efficient for dealing with routine tasks, they do not allow for the creative responses to change that a more fluid environment can make. The human service field needs new approaches to help clients deal with a continually changing world. Professionals who have the opportunity to create and the freedom to innovate might provide better service than their highly specialized colleagues.

Of course, the human resources theories do not provide easy answers. Creating an organization based on concepts of democracy and independence is, if anything, a more complex task than developing a more traditional structure. Although people might have innate capacities for growth and creativity, they have not necessarily had the chance to develop these capacities in schools and work settings that still tend toward Theory X. The Theory Y manager must carefully create structures that can encourage workers to learn how to function without close supervision and at the same time provide effective training and leadership.

A final note is that human service organizations are often closely related to larger systems, and a structure that differs greatly from those used by others is often misunderstood. A System 4 counseling department, for example, within a System 1 school or a System 4 community agency attempting to deal with a System 1 city government faces conflicts that might seem surprising.

Open Systems Theory

Systems can be thought of as sets of elements that interact with one another so that a change in any one of those elements brings about a corresponding alteration in other elements. Open systems take in and export energy through interfaces with the environment so that units within the system are also affected by changes in other systems. Open systems theorists recognize that rationality within organizations is limited by both internal factors, such as organization members' characteristics, and external factors, such as changes in the supply of available people and materials.

Katz and Kahn (1978) spell out the characteristics of the open system as follows:

1. The importation of energy or input—Some kind of energy is brought in from the environment or other organizations to be processed by the system in question. In the case of counseling and human service systems, the input is largely in the form of people.

2. Throughput—Within the system, the energy is processed and changed in some way, such as creating products or providing services.

3. Output—The organization exports products or services to the environment at large and to other systems.

4. Cycles of events—The energy exchange is repetitive so that the export of energy tends to provide the basis for a new import of energy, with the cycle then being repeated continuously.

5. Negative entropy—Organizations try to import more energy than they export. If the reverse takes place—if more energy is exported and less is imported—the system dies.

6. Information input, negative feedback, and the coding process—Systems import information as well as energy. Some kind of coding system is needed to determine which information is useful and which can be ignored. Negative feedback helps the system control outputs because deviations from what is expected can be corrected.

7. Steady state and dynamic homeostasis—When a factor in the environment changes, the organization must change just enough to maintain a steady state and deal with the disruption. The basic character of the organization is maintained through changes in form.

8. Differentiation—Open systems tend to move steadily toward greater differentiation and specialization of the functions performed by units within the organization. Growth is from the simple to the more complex.

9. Integration and coordination—As the organization becomes more differentiated, it also develops process for the various subsystems to work effectively together. This is done through clearly articulated tasks and roles as well as shared norms and values.

10. Equifinality—The same end state can be reached from different initial states and different means. At the same time, different final states can be reached from the same initial states.

SOURCE: List from *The Social Psychology of Organizations,* by D. Katz and R. L. Kahn. Copyright © 1978 by John Wiley & Sons, Inc. Reprinted by permission.

Managers who view their organizations from the systems perspective tend to see the organization more as a process than as a structure. They know that structural changes both affect and are affected by changes in all the other components of the organization. They know, too, that the goals and activities they choose will be influenced by environmental factors that are often beyond their control.

The ideas offered by systems theory might well be more important to human service agencies than to private sector firms because environmental effects on both the program as a whole and individual clients must be considered. Human service professionals using these ideas would develop structures indicating the relationships between the agency and other systems as well as those within the agency. Methods of coordination with community groups, funding sources, government agencies, other helping agencies, educational institutions, professional organizations, and a variety of other systems would need to be identified. In addition, organizational strategies would take into account the progress of individual clients through the system. Methods would be developed for linking clients with various services, following up on clients as they move into other systems, and communicating with referring agencies as new clients are accepted. These methods would be built into the organizational structure, with communication to outside agencies planned as carefully as communication within the program itself.

A major strength of the systems approach is the encouragement it gives to human service professionals to think of themselves as part of a network that, as a totality, can serve the individual client in a coordinated way. This does not mean that human service administrators should allow their programs to be buffeted about by external systems, all making conflicting demands. The other organizational approaches, including the classical management approach, provide some benefits as well, for they can help agencies in their attempts to clarify basic program goals and to find ways to develop unity of effort in reaching those goals.

We will now review some of the organizational theories and principles that have emerged since the human resources models of the 1960s, which operate with the assumption that all formal organizations are in fact open systems that respond to the environments around them and have to devise new ways of addressing emerging community needs and expectations, competition from other organizations, and a workforce with changing expectations regarding the quality of working life.

Contemporary Developments

Since the last major historical period of organizational theory in the 1960s, a proliferation of new practice models and major movements has developed, including the quality movement, the excellence movement, and, in the human services, the advent of community-based organizations. While it may seem odd to refer to the past forty years as "contemporary," these trends are in fact still considered to be recent and are still evolving as they are applied in different ways in different settings. All have relevance for human service organizations.

Professional Bureaucracies

Two particular characteristics of bureaucracy, centralization ("the degree to which decision making authority is confined to the top echelons of the bureau or assigned to the lower echelon offices and officials" [Gortner et al., 1997, p. 95]) and formalization ("the extent to which expectations concerning job activities are standardized and explicit" [Bowditch & Buono, 1997, p. 262]), have caused problems in organizations doing nonroutine work, including human service organizations. Professional employees want decision making to be decentralized and formal rules to be lessened, giving them more autonomy. Employees who have professional training can make all the decisions covered by their professional codes, but they do not necessarily take agency goals, or even changing client needs, into account. On the other hand, a centralized bureaucracy cannot be successfully implemented because the presence of a large number of professionals confounds the hierarchy and eliminates unquestioning subservience to agency wide objectives.

An adaptation of bureaucracy has emerged to deal with these problems: the "professional bureaucracy" (Mintzberg, 1979). Like the traditional bureaucracy, this type of organization depends on the regularity of the tasks to be performed, standardization, and stability. The tasks to be performed in the professional bureaucracy, however, are too technical and complex to be dictated by managers. Instead, authority is based on professional expertise, so the regularity of the bureaucracy is combined with a high degree of decentralization. Each professional worker controls his or her own technology in terms of professional standards and training, even though some of the skills used may be repetitive.

In a professional bureaucracy, conflict can occur between professional judgments and agency policies, especially in a public sector agency with many rules, sometimes from outside the organization based on federal or state laws and regulations. As a principle of organization design, professionals in such settings sometimes need to advocate for the use of decision-making models such as the human resources approach to enable them to use their professional judgment with individual cases. A complication of this model occurs when multiple professions operate within the same organization, such as a hospital, where there may be disagreements among various professionals involved with a case.

Community-Based Organizations and Feminist Organizations

Another reaction to bureaucracies emerged in the human service field in the 1960s with the advent of small, nonbureaucratic, not-for-profit organizations originally known as "street" or "alternative" agencies (Perlmutter, 1988). These agencies developed as an alternative to traditional bureaucracies, which were seen as ignoring or oppressing particular people in need, such as runaways and drug addicts. They were usually started by small groups of committed individuals who ran their programs on very small budgets, initially with little or no government funding and often using donated facilities, furniture, and equipment. According to Perlmutter (1995, pp. 204–205), these programs typically had the following characteristics:

1. They were deeply committed to social change.

2. They were reluctant to acknowledge the reality and legitimacy of formal authority and power.

3. They were designed to meet the needs of special populations not being serviced by existing agencies.

4. Their services were often exploratory or innovative.

5. Staff were deeply committed ideologically to clients, were closely identified with them, or were former clients.

6. Small size of the agency was valued.

7. Agencies were usually in a marginal economic position.

Alternative agency staff believed that runaways and substance abusers, for example, should not be treated as criminals but should be given appropriate social services. They ran their agencies using democratic or consensus decision making, eschewing an all-powerful director.

Over the course of the 1970s, these programs grew, often by becoming more "mainstream" and acquiring government funding, or in some cases remained small and true to their original philosophies, or died. During this period, Holleb and Abrams (1975) suggested that such programs would eventually become bureaucratic, like the agencies they originally reacted against, or would be able to hold onto their original values and principles, a stage they called "consensual democracy." This would involve developing organizational forms in line with these values while somehow accommodating the inevitabilities of growth and becoming more formalized in operations.

Today, it is sometimes hard to see these philosophical origins of community-based organizations with multimillion-dollar budgets, professional staffs, and mainstream facilities. While some agencies are comfortable with their status as more traditional service providers, others work hard to maintain what is special about their original values while adapting to the world of purchase of service contracting. Feminist organizations in fields such as domestic violence have demonstrated some success at maintaining their original ideologies (Gilson, 1997).

Perlmutter (1995) has suggested that administrators of such programs who want to avoid becoming traditional and bureaucratic need to hold firmly to their values and ideology and be comfortable with risk taking, difference and diversity, and periods of economic uncertainty. She adds that such organizations need to be constantly vigilant, focusing on their missions, being alert to environmental challenges, and attending to fund-raising. Administrators need to use nonauthoritarian management styles, develop effective interpersonal skills, and be sensitive to staff issues including possible burnout. Similar practice principles are advocated by those practicing *progressive social work* (Bombyk, 1995).

Japanese Management

By now many Americans are familiar with the story of the advent of the quality movement, traced to the importation from Japan of *quality circles* in the 1980s as the United States had to recognize the dominance of Japan in manufacturing high-quality products at low cost. Ironically, the methods that changed Japan's reputation as a manufacturer of cheap goods to that of a world leader came originally from America, largely through statistician W. E. Deming and others who provided training to Japanese industry after World War II (Schmidt & Finnegan, 1992). With the subsequent problems in the Japanese economy becoming public in the 1990s, many began to question the value of Japanese management methods. Regardless of the state of the Japanese economy, the principles of quality that became popular there are still relevant and important in American organizations, including the human services. Ouchi's (1982) Theory Z provided a good summary of this movement into the early 1980s.

Ouchi developed Theory Z through his study of Japanese corporations. His findings were that Japanese organizations were characterized by lifetime employment, slow evaluation and promotion, nonspecialized career paths, collective decision-making styles, collective responsibility, and an integration of work and social lives. In the increasingly global economy of the 1990s, many of these principles evolved significantly; in fact, some of the weaknesses of them, such as the encouragement of workaholic behavior, have since become evident. Lifetime employment, never a reality for the majority of Japanese companies, became much less common in the economic crisis of the 1990s. The common policy of not laying off employees has changed radically recently, with increasing reports of companies "bullying" employees into quitting so that they will not have to be paid severance pay and retirement benefits (Mangier, 1999).

While the term *Theory Z* is rarely used today, its most valuable principles have been incorporated in other ways in many American organizations. Principles of Japanese management have been summarized for use in the human services by Keys (1995a), who studied their use in Japanese social welfare agencies. These include flexible job descriptions; informal decision-making processes to build consensus before formal decisions are made; training and team building to foster shared values, consensus, and high morale; job reassignment and rotation, in which staff have temporary assignments in other departments or agencies, to foster teamwork and collaboration; and total quality management.

Of these processes and principles, total quality management has received the most attention in American organizations. We will now look at how it has been applied in the human services in the United States.

Total Quality Management

In an organization using total quality management (TQM), "the organization's culture is defined by and supports the constant attainment of customer satisfaction through an integrated system of tools, techniques, and training" (Sashkin & Kiser, cited in Keys, 1995b, p. 2019). The seven primary tenets of TQM have been summarized by Swiss (in Keys, 1995b) this way:

1. First and foremost, the customer is the ultimate determiner of quality.

2. Quality should be built into the product [or service] early in the production (upstream) rather than being added on at the end (downstream).

3. Preventing variability is the key to producing high quality.

4. Quality results from people working within systems, not individual efforts.

5. Quality requires continuous improvement of inputs and processes.

6. Quality improvement requires strong worker participation.

7. Quality requires total organizational commitment. (p. 2020)

Keys (1995b) notes that teams (cross-functional improvement teams, quality circles, and process improvement teams) are an "essential component of TQM" (p. 2021). Other basic TQM tools are used for data collection and analysis of work processes, including statistical process charts and flow charts, Pareto charts, and cause-effect diagrams. Another term that has become part of the process improvement vernacular is *benchmarking,* which involves surveys of other organizations to identify the best practices for accomplishing a particular procedure and setting these as standards (Ammons, 1998). TQM techniques are described in more detail by Hawkins and Gunther (1998) and Gummer and McCallion (1995).

The Excellence Movement

With their publication of *In Search of Excellence,* Peters and Waterman (1982) called attention to the ingredients of successful megacorporations in our society. In almost evangelical tones, they summarize their studies of excelling organizations as follows:

> The findings from the excellent companies amount to an upbeat message. There is good news from America. Good management today is not resident only in Japan. But, more important, the good news comes from treating people decently and asking them to shine, and from producing things that work. Scale efficiencies give way to small units with turned-on people. Precisely planned R & D efforts aimed at big bang products are replaced by armies of dedicated champions. A numbing focus on cost gives way to an enhancing focus on quality. Hierarchy and three-piece suits give way to first names, shirt sleeves, hoopla, and project-based flexibility. Working according to fat rule books is replaced by everyone's contributing. (p. xxv)

Structure, Peters and Waterman conclude, is only "a small part of the total issue of management effectiveness" (p. 9). Among the several other variables identified by these authors in their examination of organizational achievement is "shared values," or organizational culture. This focus has been adopted by several other studies on organizational culture, including those by Cooke and Rousseau (1988), Schein (1992), and Trice and Beyer (1993). (Findings and implications from the "cultural school" of organizational theory are more fully discussed in Chapter 11, which deals with organizational change.)

The research of Peters and Waterman was criticized shortly after their book was published, as it was noted that some of the companies they profiled did not do well in subsequent years (Micklethwait & Wooldridge, 1997, pp. 14–15). However, their general principles have continued to be relevant, if not treated as universal prescriptions. These have been adapted to governmental organizations by Bryson (1995, p. 294):

Local Government Excellence Criteria	Peters and Waterman Criteria
Action orientation: quickly identify and fix problems	A bias for action
Listen to citizens and strive to meet their needs	Close to the customer
Encourage autonomy and entrepreneurship through innovation and risk taking	Autonomy and entrepreneurship
Employee orientation: trust and respect them	Productivity through people
Articulate and act based on values	Hands-on, value driven
Focus on the organization's unique mission, goals, and competence	Stick to the "knitting" (that is, do not provide services outside the organization's distinctive areas of competence)
Simplify structures	Simple form, lean staff
Maintain supportive and effective political relationships	Simultaneous loose-tight properties

There have also been some applications of excellence principles in human service agencies specifically (Harvey, 1998; National Assembly of National Voluntary Health and Social Welfare Organizations, 1989).

Peters and Waterman each published subsequent books, and Peters in particular has become even more evangelical in showcasing additional "excellent" organizations and leaders. Since he uses case studies and generally has not clearly outlined his research methods, it is difficult to isolate specifically the key success factors of the organizations that he profiles. The complexity and contradictions in his work have been profiled by Micklethwait and Wooldridge (1997), who give him premier "management guru" status. The greatest value of Peters and other "paradigm busters" may be not in the substance of their recommendations but the way they encourage managers to question their assumptions and try to do better.

Business Process Reengineering

Quality improvement processes began to be applied at an organization-wide level with the advent of *business process reengineering* (BPR) (Hammer & Champy, 1993), also known as *business process improvement*. BPR has been defined as "a fundamental rethinking and radical redesign of business processes to achieve dramatic improvements in critical contemporary measures of performance such as cost, quality service, and speed" (Hammer & Champy, 1993, p. 32). Whereas TQM focuses on the line-level organizational processes, reengineering focuses on the whole organization, with particular attention to the "silo mentality" in which different functions operate in separate silos without communicating with each other, and on eliminating all organizational processes that do not add value to the product or service for the customer. It quickly became known as a rationale or excuse for downsizing (euphemistically known as "rightsizing") and other cost-cutting initiatives.

Managers and stockholders became so infatuated with these developments that a new term, *corporate anorexia,* entered the management vocabulary: organizations had cut so many staff that they no longer had the institutional memory and brain power to respond effectively to subsequent environmental changes. Rehiring began as the economy improved, although in many cases new hires were contract or temporary employees. Reengineering also received a more critical look at this time when studies showed that 70 to 85 percent of reengineering efforts failed (Zell, 1997, p. 23). In the scientific management tradition, BPR focused on the technical and rational aspects of the organization, ignoring everything that had been learned about human resources approaches. Micklethwait and Wooldridge (1997), who devote a whole chapter to BPR as the "fad in progress" in their critique of management gurus, document its weaknesses and failures, concluding that is does have appropriate, if limited, uses and that it is most effective when used in a "holistic" way, with attention to human factors and employee involvement. Useful design criteria based on reengineering principles and that are relevant to human service organizations will be reviewed in the next chapter.

Employee Involvement and the Quality of Working Life

Employee involvement as a management technology was based on human resources theories and the model of quality circles developed in Japan. It was refined and recontextualized through the *quality of working life* (QWL) movement, which reached prominence in the 1970s and is most fundamentally concerned with more fully involving subordinates in key organizational decisions. Its applications in the human services, most commonly referred to as *participative decision making,* will be covered in Chapter 7 as part of the supervision process. It is mentioned here at the organizational level because it has implications for the macrolevel design of the organization.

The QWL movement was important because it went beyond earlier conceptions of human relations and job satisfaction, on the one hand, and analytical approaches such as scientific management, on the other, by looking holistically at both technical processes such as how the work got done and social processes such as how decisions were made. According to Taylor and Felten (1993):

Quality of working life is more than merely wages, hours, and working conditions; it is more than dignity and respect, social support, prospects for advancement, and challenging work. Employees (management and nonmanagement alike) have an opportunity to experience higher QWL through (a) a sense of importance or relevance of their product to the larger community, (b) through the understanding of their place or direct role in creating the product, and (c) through the opportunity to become competent in dealing with those activities most central to the effective creation of the product. (p. 127)

In an old but still relevant overview, Walton (1975) groups QWL factors into eight areas: adequate and fair compensation, safe and healthy working conditions, immediate opportunity to use and develop human capacities (such as autonomy and multiple skills), opportunity for continued growth and security, social integration in the work organization (egalitarianism, freedom from prejudice), constitutionalism in the work organization, work and the total life space (a balanced role of work: time for family and leisure), and the social relevance of work life (the organization's social responsibility).

QWL principles align well with the expectations that typical professionals would have for human service work, but because of bureaucratic processes and other conditions, they are not always present. QWL "programs" were popular in the 1970s, but more recently QWL is used as a set of underlying principles for employee involvement to enhance organizational effectiveness, most prominently in sociotechnical systems design, which will be covered in Chapter 5 as a model for organization redesign. The concept is also used for assessing organizational conditions in need of change. This is often done using employee attitude surveys, an organizational change strategy reviewed in Chapter 12. QWL principles, as given here or as developed for a particular organization, can be very useful as design criteria for changing an organization's structure and processes.

Reinventing Government

In a groundbreaking book, Osborne and Gaebler (1992) profile dynamic governmental organizations that exemplify a new "entrepreneurial spirit" in government bureaucracies. *Reinvention* is defined as "the fundamental transformation of public systems and organizations to create dramatic increases in their effectiveness, efficiency, adaptability, and capacity to innovate" (Osborne & Plastrik, 1997, p. 13). As summarized by Bryson (1995), Osborne and Gaebler suggest that governments should have the following qualities:

- **Catalytic**—They should focus on steering rather than rowing. Government should decide what should be done but does not have to do it itself.

- **Community-owned**—The programs that work best are the ones that are community owned, capacity building, and empowering rather than delivered by bureaucracies to clients.

- **Competitive**—Competition is to be preferred to monopoly provision of service since competition is more likely to lead to better, more innovative, and less expensive service.

- **Mission-driven**—Government should be animated by mission and vision rather than driven by rules.

- **Results-oriented**—Funding should be based on outcomes, not inputs.

- **Customer-driven**—Government should meet the needs of the customer and citizen, not the bureaucracy.

- **Enterprising**—Entrepreneurship and earning money should be rewarded more than spending money.

- **Anticipatory**—The focus of attention should be on preventing rather than curing problems.

- **Decentralized**—Participation and teamwork should be emphasized more than hierarchy.

- **Market-oriented**—Governments should think creatively about how to use markets to achieve public purposes. (p. 295)

Micklethwait and Wooldridge (1997), who earlier offered thoughtful criticism of reengineering, encourage government managers to be guarded in their adoption of management "fads" such as reinvention. They conclude, however, that "management theory has clearly brought more good than harm to the public sector" (p. 316) and suggest that managers take thoughtful reforms even further. As was the case for the study of excellent organizations, reinventing government principles should not be taken as models to apply exactly but as guidelines for creative thinking and selective adoption based on unique organizational circumstances.

Learning Organizations

In 1990, Peter Senge published *The Fifth Discipline: The Art and Practice of the Learning Organization*. It became a modern classic and was followed by two guidebooks (Senge, Kleiner, Roberts, Ross, Roth, & Smith, 1999; Senge, Roberts, Ross, Smith, & Kleiner, 1994) that describe how to create and nurture learning organizations. The five disciplines discussed by Senge are personal mastery (personal growth and learning), mental models (deeply held images about how the world works), shared vision (alignment of personal visions), team learning (using dialogue to address difficult issues), and systems thinking (a conceptual framework for observing patterns and seeing how to change them).

Becoming a learning organization in the sense described by Senge is a very difficult and time-consuming process that, if approached with energy and diligence, can be very rewarding. Reports of learning organization applications in the human services have been rare (Cohen & Austin, 1994; Kurtz, 1998), which perhaps indicates the difficulty of applying such principles. Learning organization concepts seem compatible with human service principles such as the use of teams and dialogue, and they represent opportunities for growth in human service organizations.

Contingency Theories

The preceding review of classic and current theories and models offers a rich menu from which to choose promising innovations for management practice. No one form of organization is appropriate for all types of settings. In fact, principles from many or all of the theories discussed here may be useful in a given human service organization. Several researchers have indicated that organizational technologies (tasks), environments, and even sizes affect strategy, which should help determine structure. Different organizations bring with them the needs for different structures. Determination of the most efficient and productive type of structure in a given situation depends on the specific contingencies being faced.

The contingency theories—unlike the traditional, human relations, and human resources approaches—recognize that there is no "one best way" to structure all organizations. Rather, a number of "contingency" factors have differential effects on organizations and should be considered in designing structure.

Contingency theories are, in effect, systems theories in the sense that they recognize the effect of the organization's external environment on its internal structure. The contingency perspective, in other words, accounts for the importance of the interaction between the organization and the outside world—a world that provides it with the sanctions (legitimacy, societal acceptance, political support), energy (money, technological advances, human resources), and raw materials (microchips, steel, human beings) to meet its goals. Just as individuals are affected by their environment—its climatic fluctuations, the quality of its atmosphere—so are organizations subject to their environments. Adaptation to new environmental conditions is accomplished, as was reviewed in Chapter 3, through the design and implementation of new programs. Organizational adaptation at a larger scale is accomplished through designing or, more typically, redesigning the organization. This reflects Chandler's (1962) principle that structure follows strategy: once members of the organization decide where they want to go, the best structure and organizational processes are developed to enable the organization as a system to implement its programs and thrive in a complex environment.

The work of Lawrence and Lorsch (1967) provides particular insight into organizational needs in varying situations. Lawrence and Lorsch identify four organizational features that vary with the degree of environmental certainty: (1) reliance on formal rules and communication, (2) time horizon, (3) diffuse or concentrated goals, and (4) relationship- or task-oriented interpersonal styles. They stress that effective organizations have a good "fit" with their environment. An organization with a stable environment can use formal rules, a short time horizon, traditional communication channels, and task-oriented management. An organization with an unstable environment needs more points of contact with the external world so that changes can be recognized promptly. Such an organization also requires a longer time orientation and a more complex communication pattern. Formal rules and hierarchies would interfere with the needed information flow, so it would be inappropriate to rely on them.

Burns and Stalker (1994) distinguish between what they term *mechanistic* and *organic* forms of organization. The mechanistic form, comparable to the classical type of structure, depends on formal authority, specialization, and structured channels of communication. The organic form is highly flexible and informal, with communication channels based not on the hierarchical chain of command but on the need to solve immediate problems by consulting the person with the needed data. In studying a number of British firms, Burns and Stalker found that the organic style seems most appropriate for firms such as electronics companies facing rapid technological change and the need to solve novel problems. The mechanistic form is productive for firms needing efficiency in dealing with very stable conditions.

The contingency theorists make clear that an effective organization can run the gamut from a traditional bureaucracy to a highly organic, constantly changing structure. Which structure is appropriate depends on the organization's needs. At its most basic level the contingency approach offers administrators a method for clarifying their ideas about organization.

If human service professionals were to use contingency theory to determine the best ways to structure the work of their programs or agencies, they would, as a first step, identify the most salient characteristics of their services and settings. Human service workers who view themselves as technicians offering consistent services to a wide range of clients might be able to use mechanistic organizational structures, but such designs would be inappropriate for professionals attempting to deliver multifaceted services based on community needs assessments. Helpers would also need to determine whether their environments were characterized more by rapid change or by stability over time, recognizing that agencies dealing with shifting populations or subject to changes in funding could not afford to use slow-moving, unwieldy organizational structures.

Summary

A rich history of theory of organizations has guided organizational behavior in a wide range of settings. The classical models of bureaucracy, scientific management, and human relations as well as more current approaches such as the human resources models of Likert, McGregor, and Argyris and systems theory all have relevance today. New developments such as Japanese management, the excellence movement, and reinventing government initiatives have all affected the human services. Human service managers do use theory, consciously or unconsciously, and they are likely to be more effective if they consciously apply appropriate theories: the *contingency theory* approach. Being aware of a variety of theoretical frameworks helps human service professionals know that, as they seek to organize their programs, they do have choices. The theories discussed here should offer guidance to those who are designing or redesigning an agency so that all the various components will work effectively and efficiently together. We will now look at how organizations may be designed, based on thoughtful use of organizational theories.

Discussion Questions

Chapter 4 discussed several approaches to organizational design, including (1) classical, bureaucratic theories, (2) human resources approaches, (3) contingency theories, (4) open systems theory, (5) Japanese management, and (6) newer models including excellence and reengineering.

1. Do you find some of these theories more helpful than others?

2. What theories do you see being used, explicitly or implicitly, in an organization with which you are familiar? Are these the appropriate theories to be used? If not, which ones would be better?

3. If you were designing a human service organization, which theories would you be most likely to use?

CASE 4

The Community Career Center

The Community Career Center (CCC) had been initiated several years ago by a group of professionals who became impatient with the impersonality and red tape that overwhelmed their work in public agencies. All four of the center's founders had previously worked for departments of human resources or vocational rehabilitation, and their experiences had led them to think that there must be better ways to deal with clients' career development needs.

A few basic concepts had been part of the center's orientation since it had first begun operation under Department of Labor and fee-based funding. First, the founders felt that one counselor should work with the total scope of a client's career needs, linking him or her with training programs, with educational institutions, with other needed services, and, finally, with jobs. They also believed in using training formats to deal with the kinds of needs many clients shared. From its unassuming start, the center had provided training programs dealing with midlife career change, retirement planning, job-hunting skills, self-assessment, and a variety of other topics. These programs were offered to members of the general public, such as women reentering the job market, and to local institutions and businesses.

At first, the founders of the center provided most of the services themselves. If they felt that a particular training format had exciting possibilities or if they were invited to design something special for a local group, they would provide workshops and group sessions. In the meantime, each of the four also carried a caseload of clients to whom they were dedicated. They saw themselves as counselors, advocates, and placement specialists for their own clients, and their success exceeded even their own idealistic expectations.

Last year, the center's management had begun to get out of hand. Its size had mushroomed, and so had its funding. Local businesses had proven so supportive, especially in contracting training programs, that the initial Department of Labor contract provided only a small percentage of the agency's total funding. Each

training program was self-supporting, and the number of individual clients kept growing. To keep pace, the center had had to hire additional staff members to provide services, so there were now a number of trainers and counselors who had not been in on the original planning. Little by little, the original four founders had become frustrated. Instead of spending all their time with clients and trainees, they were becoming involved in keeping books, planning repetitive services, and supervising staff members. This supervision especially bothered them. New staff members somehow did not understand the concept of being dedicated to their clients. These counselors did their work, but they were not bubbling over with creativity. They were not seeking new challenges, coming up with new ideas, or making that extra effort that made the difference. The original founders, who did have that urge for creativity, were unable to use it. They had become managers, and they did not like it.

The solution they had found last year was to bring in a business manager, a recent MBA, who knew how to organize and control a growing firm. The center's founders breathed a collective sigh of relief when management concerns were taken out of their hands. They gave their new manager a free hand and were pleased with the way he took control of the budgets and financial reports. The new organizational structure that he created also seemed to make sense. He divided the center into departments, including the training department, where programs were designed and implemented; the marketing department, which had responsibility for selling the training programs to industrial and other organizations; the counseling department, which provided direct services to clients; the job development department, which canvassed the community for placement possibilities for clients; and the business department, which took care of administrative concerns, including personnel.

This approach seemed to work for a while. The newer staff members, in particular, seemed pleased with the increased clarity of their job descriptions. They were no longer badgered with instructions to "be creative." They knew what their responsibilities were and could carry them out. The center's founders—still the board of directors of the agency—were pleased to have management responsibilities taken out of their hands. Now they could be creative again.

Yet that sense of renewed creativity had not taken hold. Somehow the agency's new organization did not allow for it. Now in its fifth year of existence, the Community Career Center was in jeopardy, not because it had failed but because it had succeeded. Two of the four board members wanted to resign and spin off a new smaller, more responsive agency. Monica Shannon and Paul Ramirez did not really want to make this move, but they could see no way to carry out what they believed to be their mission through an organization as unwieldy as the CCC had become.

At the most volatile meeting ever held at the center, the board of directors cleared the air. Shannon, one of the two original members who had decided to leave, spoke first.

"Look," she exclaimed, "our original idea was to have an agency that would be responsive to our clients' career needs. We would stick with an individual, be an om-

budsman, help meet all this one client's needs. Now we have a department for counseling and another department for finding jobs. What happened to the idea that got us started in the first place?"

"And what about the training component?" Ramirez chimed in. "The idea was to meet community needs by designing special sessions, not to keep repeating the same program all the time to make it easier for the marketing department. Everything we do lately is to please the marketers, to make it easier for them to sell. But what have they got to sell? We've got the tail wagging the dog."

"Now, wait a minute," Mark Morgenstein responded. "We've got a big organization here. We can't expect everything to be the same as it was. Growth and change was supposed to be one of our big aims, too."

"And you were the ones who got the most excited about bringing in a manager to take the business responsibilities out of your hands," Colleen Morgan pointed out. "You can't have everything."

"I'll tell you one thing," Shannon said. "We may be a large organization now, but we accomplished more in a day when the four of us began than that whole gang of bureaucrats we've got here now accomplishes in a month. That's what we've got here now: a bureaucracy. Why did we ever bother leaving the Department of Human Resources? We've got a duplication right here."

1. Would you describe the Community Career Center's current organization as a bureaucracy? How does it compare with the structure that the agency had at first?

2. The agency grew in size over the years. What organizational theories should guide the organization at this stage?

3. At this point, do you think Monica Shannon and Paul Ramirez are right in wanting to leave the organization? What options do they have?

References

Ammons, D. (1998). Benchmarking performance. In S. Condrey (Ed.), *Handbook of human resource management in government* (pp. 391–409). San Francisco: Jossey-Bass.

Argyris, C. (1957). *Personality and organization.* New York: Harper & Row.

Bombyk, M. (1995). Progressive social work. In R. Edwards (Ed.), *Encyclopedia of social work* (19th ed., pp. 1933–1942). Washington, DC: NASW Press.

Bowditch, J., & Buono, A. (1997). *A primer on organizational behavior.* New York: Wiley.

Bryson, J. (1995). *Strategic planning for public and nonprofit organizations.* San Francisco: Jossey-Bass.

Burns, T., & Stalker, G. (1994). *The management of innovation* (rev. ed.). New York: Oxford University Press.

Chandler, A. (1962). *Strategy and structure: Chapters in the history of the industrial enterprise.* Cambridge, MA: MIT Press.

Child, J. (1995). Follett: Constructive conflict. In P. Graham (Ed.), *Mary Parker Follett: Prophet of management* (pp. 87–95). Boston: Harvard Business School Press.

Cohen, B., & Austin, M. (1994). Organizational learning and change in a public child welfare agency. *Administration in Social Work, 18*(1), 1–18.

Cooke, R. A., & Rousseau, D. M. (1988). Behavioral norms and expectations: A quantitative approach to the assessment of organizational culture. *Group and Organization Studies, 13*(3), 245–273.

Fayol, H. (1949). *General and industrial management.* London: Sir Isaac Pitman.

Fischer, F., & Sirianni, C. (1984). Organization and bureaucracy: A critical introduction. In F. Fischer & C. Sirianni (Eds.), *Critical studies in organization and bureaucracy* (pp. 3–20). Philadelphia: Temple University Press.

Gerth, H. H., & Mills, C. W. (Eds.). (1958). *From Max Weber: Essays in sociology.* New York: Oxford University Press.

Gilson, S. (1997). The YWCA women's advocacy program: A case study of domestic violence and sexual assault services. *Journal of Community Practice, 4*(4), 1–26.

Gortner, H., Mahler, J., & Nicholson, J. (1997). *Organization theory: A public perspective* (2nd ed.). Fort Worth, TX: Harcourt Brace College Publishers.

Graham, P. (Ed.). (1995). *Mary Parker Follett: Prophet of management.* Boston: Harvard Business School Press.

Gummer, B., & McCallion, P. (Eds.). (1995). *Total quality management.* Albany, NY: Professional Development Program of Rockefeller College.

Hammer, M., & Champy, J. (1993). *Reengineering the corporation.* New York: HarperBusiness.

Hawkins, F., & Gunther, J. (1998). Managing for quality. In R. Edwards, J. Yankey, & M. Altpeter (Eds.), *Skills for effective management of nonprofit organizations* (pp. 525–554). Washington, DC: NASW Press.

Harvey, C. (1998). Defining excellence in human service organizations. *Administration in Social Work, 22*(1), 33–45.

Holleb, G., & Abrams, W. (1975). *Alternatives in community mental health.* Boston: Beacon.

Katz, D., & Kahn, R. L. (1978). *The social psychology of organizations* (2nd ed.). New York: Wiley.

Keys, P. (1995a). Japanese quality management techniques. In L. Ginsberg & P. Keys (Eds.), *New management in human services* (2nd ed., pp. 162–170). Washington, DC: NASW Press.

Keys, P. (1995b). Quality management. In R. Edwards (Ed.), *The encyclopedia of social work* (19th ed., pp. 2019–2025). Washington, DC: NASW Press.

Kurtz, P. (1998). A case study of a network as a learning organization. *Administration in Social Work, 22*(2), 57–73.

Lawrence, P. R., & Lorsch, J. (1967). *Organization and environment.* Cambridge, MA: Harvard University Press.

Likert, R. (1967). *The human organization: Its management and value.* New York: McGraw-Hill.

Mangier, M. (1999, July 24). Japanese firms use bullying to thin their ranks. *Los Angeles Times,* Section 1, pp. 1, 11.

McGregor, D. (1960). *The human side of enterprise.* New York: McGraw-Hill.

Micklethwait, J., & Wooldridge, A. (1997). *The witch doctors: Making sense of the management gurus.* New York: Times Books.

Miles, R. (1965). Human relations or human resources? *Harvard Business Review, 9*(43), 148–152.

Miles, R. (1975). *Theories of management: Implications for organizational behavior and development.* New York: McGraw Hill.

Mintzberg, H. (1979). *The structuring of organizations.* Upper Saddle River, NJ: Prentice Hall.

National Assembly of National Voluntary Health and Social Welfare Organizations. (1989). *A study in excellence: Management in the nonprofit human services.* Washington, DC: Author.

Osborne, D., & Gaebler, T. (1992). *Reinventing government: How the entrepreneurial spirit is transforming the public sector.* Reading, MA: Addison-Wesley.

Osborne, D., & Plastrik, P. (1997). *Banishing bureaucracy: The five strategies for reinventing government.* Reading, MA: Addison-Wesley.

Ouchi, W. G. (1982). *Theory Z: How American business can meet the Japanese challenge.* New York: Avon.

Perlmutter, F. (Ed.). (1988). *Alternative social agencies: Administrative strategies.* New York: Haworth.

Perlmutter, F. (1995). Administering alternative social programs. In L. Ginsberg & P. Keys (Eds.), *New management in human services* (2nd ed., pp. 203–218). Washington, DC: NASW Press.

Perrow, C. (1986). *Complex organizations: A critical essay* (3rd ed.). New York: Random House.

Peters, T. J., & Waterman, R. H., Jr. (1982). *In search of excellence.* New York: Harper & Row.

Sashkin, M. (1981). An overview of ten organizational and management theorists. In J. Jones & W. Pfeiffer (Eds.), *The 1981 annual handbook for group facilitators* (pp. 206–221). San Diego, CA: University Associates.

Schein, E. (1992). *Organizational culture and leadership* (2nd ed.). San Francisco: Jossey-Bass.

Schmidt, W., & Finnegan, J. (1992). *The race without a finish line: America's quest for total quality.* San Francisco: Jossey-Bass.

Selber, K., & Austin, D. (1997). Mary Parker Follett: Epilogue to or return of a social work management pioneer? *Administration in Social Work, 21*(1), 1–15.

Senge, P. (1990). *The fifth discipline: The art and practice of the learning organization.* New York: Doubleday Currency.

Senge, P., Kleiner, A., Roberts, C., Ross, R., Roth, G., & Smith, B. (1999). *The dance of change.* New York: Doubleday.

Senge, P., Roberts, C., Ross, R., Smith, B., & Kleiner, A. (1994). *The fifth discipline fieldbook.* New York: Currency Doubleday.

Syers, M. (1995). Follett, Mary Parker (1868–1933). In R. Edwards (Ed.), *The encyclopedia of social work* (19th ed., p. 2585). Washington, DC: NASW Press.

Taylor, F. W. (1911). *Principles of scientific management.* New York: Harper & Row.

Taylor, J., & Felten, D. (1993). *Performance by design.* Upper Saddle River, NJ: Prentice Hall.

Trice, H. M., & Beyer, J. M. (1993). *The cultures of work organizations.* Upper Saddle River, NJ: Prentice Hall.

Walton, R. (1975). Criteria for quality of working life. In L. Davis & A. Cherns (Eds.), *The quality of working life: Volume 1: Problems, prospects, and the state of the art* (pp. 91–118). New York: Free Press.

Weisbord, M. (1987). *Productive workplaces.* San Francisco: Jossey-Bass.

Zell, D. (1997). *Changing by design: Organizational innovation at Hewlett-Packard.* Ithaca, NY: ILR Press.

Organization Design

Human service professionals do not often think of themselves as the designers of organizations. Yet that is precisely the role they play when they engage in such activities as deciding whether service providers in an agency should be divided according to specialization or choosing whether to departmentalize an agency's services according to type of client served (the youth center, the senior citizen center) or according to type of activity performed (counseling, group work, consultation, education). As was noted in Chapter 3, planning involves an agency assessing its environment, developing strategies, and setting goals and objectives. Programs are then designed to enable the accomplishment of goals and objectives. Next, the agency must figure out how all the programs and functions should fit together and operate, and this step is the province of organization design.

Now that we have reviewed some of the most influential organizational theories as they apply to the design and functioning of organizations, we will outline criteria for the design of an effective organization. We will discuss the various ways of describing organizational structure and will end with guidelines on designing, or redesigning, an organization: choosing the best structures and communication mechanisms.

Dimensions of Organization Design

Senge (1990, p. 341) notes the importance of design using the analogy of a ship. Managers as leaders often see their role as the captain. He has found that other managers see themselves as the navigator (setting direction), helmsman (controlling direction), engineer (providing energy in the bowels of the organization), or social director (making sure everyone is involved). Senge's point is that the role of design is both crucial (what if a ship is designed to turn only one way?) and ignored. Design takes place before a program is started, and the effects of design are subtle (compared, for example, to supervision or the setting of salaries) but very important.

Organization design has two components: structure and process. Jackson and Morgan (1982) define *structure* as "the relatively enduring allocation of work roles and administrative mechanisms that creates a pattern of interrelated work activities and allows the organization to conduct, coordinate, and control its work activities" (p. 81). Organizational structure is what people usually think of when describing an organization: how bureaucratic it is, who reports to whom, and how departments are organized. Organizational *processes* can be defined simply as "activities that go on within the structure over some time period" (Robey, 1991, p. 16). Key processes include coordination among functions, organizational communication processes, control systems, and decision making. After both of these components are reviewed, a process for designing the organization will be presented.

Organization design is both a noun and a verb. As a noun, it describes the structure and key processes (such as communication and decision making) of the organization. As a verb, it is the process used to select the most appropriate structures and processes for the organization, given its environment, size, programs, and strategies. Once initial planning has been completed, an organizational structure is needed to carry out the strategies, goals, objectives, and programs that have been selected. This involves seeking the best possible answers to the following questions:

- What activities need to be performed to implement the programs that have been selected as part of the planning process?

- How can the necessary activities be divided so that individuals or groups can be assigned responsibility for performing them?

- Once activities have been grouped into specific jobs, what kind of authority and responsibility should be assigned to each position?

- How should the different programs and units of the agency be organized with reference to each other?

- How and by whom should decisions be made?

- How specialized should roles and jobs be?

- Who should control the nature and quality of the work being performed?

- How can communication and coordination among members of the organization be facilitated?

- How can coordination and communication with the external social environment be facilitated?

The answers to these questions bring with them the ability to describe and chart interlocking roles that in turn form a structure and processes for communication, coordination, and decision making. The result of the entire process is the creation of an *organization,* or a social unit that has been purposefully designed to meet a set of goals through a regular series of planned and coordinated activities.

The nature of the design that is finally chosen varies tremendously, based on the goals, needs, size, environment, technology, age, and resources of the organization, as well as on the theoretical orientations of the people engaged in the design process, as discussed in Chapter 4.

Criteria for the Design of an Organization

The human service professional's philosophical approach toward organization design will affect every decision that he or she makes as a structure is developed. Regardless of theoretical orientation, however, each designer must decide how to identify key processes and individual roles within the organization, how to divide activities among groups or departments, and how to coordinate efforts both within the organization and at interfaces with the environment.

In many human service organizations, organization redesign is often approached simply as restructuring: moving around boxes on the organizational chart without thoughtful consideration of strategy, technology parameters and options, and effects on processes such as decision making. This restructuring is typically done by the agency's top managers, occasionally with consultant help and more rarely with the input of other managers. According to Mohr (1989), traditional approaches to organization redesign rarely deliver promised improvements because they:

> are not based on a detailed operational analysis of actual, current work practices,
>
> have not meaningfully involved those persons closest to the operational process (i.e., workers and line managers),
>
> focus on solving only today's—or even yesterday's—problems rather than creating an organization capable of flexibly responding to tomorrow's challenges,
>
> do not have the necessary commitment and support of those at lower levels, which are required for successful implementation,
>
> are based on the false assumption that modifying only authority/reporting relationships will be sufficient for obtaining intended results,
>
> use analytic perspectives that make the "designers" prisoners of their own histories, cultures, and traditions, and
>
> stem from a constraint orientation emphasizing all that *cannot* be changed, rather than from an inventive/creative orientation central to effective organizational change. (p. 208)

These problems have been addressed in current models of organization redesign that use an explicit analysis and design process and that have high involvement of workers from all levels of the hierarchy. One such model, sociotechnical systems redesign, will be briefly reviewed as a model for human service organizations. This process actually begins with the development of a strategic plan that considers environmental trends and internal organizational strengths and weaknesses, and then the design of programs to implement strategies, as outlined in Chapter 3.

Any design or redesign process needs top-level sanction and support, known as *sponsorship,* and a *champion* responsible for making things happen on a daily basis. Often two groups are set up to do the design (more typically, a redesign of an existing organization). A *steering committee,* consisting of representatives of key stakeholder groups including executive and middle management, supervisors and line staff from different programs, support staff, and representatives from employee organizations, provides overall guidance and policy direction for the effort. A *design team,* similarly constituted with a representative group, focusing more on the lower levels of the organization, will do the detailed analysis and make recommendations for a new design to the steering committee. Ultimately, final decisions are usually made by the organization's executive management and governing board, although if the process is well done, recommendations should be mostly approved as submitted. Other process criteria that have been proven to be helpful include these (Cherns, 1987, cited in Zell, 1997, pp. 27–28):

1. Compatibility—The design process should be compatible with its objectives; for example, an organization intending to be participative in philosophy should be designed in a participative manner. The use of a design team, mentioned in the preceding paragraph, will make the process more participative. If staff who will be implementing the new system are involved in its development, they will be able to design in factors that will enable the work to be done most effectively and efficiently. After all, they know the client circumstances the best. They will also implement the design with greater clarity and commitment because they know its underlying principles and, because "their fingerprints are on the knife," they will feel more responsible for the results. Having nonservice providers on the design team will add a useful outside perspective to ensure that line staff properly consider all important factors.

2. Minimal critical specifications—Only the basic, required parameters of a new design (for example, funds, state and federal requirements) should be given to the design team, and they should be free to design anything that meets these specifications. This is sometimes referred to as "constraint-free design," so that the team doesn't feel limited by current or past thinking and assumptions regarding what is possible.

3. Variance control—Variances (unintended variations in the process, such as a client doing something unexpected) should be controlled as close as possible to their point of origin. In other words, workers should be able to make decisions on handling unique circumstances without necessarily involving managers.

4. Boundary location—Boundaries between functions should not be drawn in a way that impedes communication.

5. Information flow—Information should first be available to those who will need to act on it: workers should get feedback and client information promptly. As O'Looney (1996) has suggested, workers who enter data should have access to all relevant databases needed to make case and programmatic decisions.

6. Power and authority—Workers and managers should have access to the resources they need to do their work and be able to make prudent decisions about their use.

7. The multifunctional principle—Staff should have varied skills, to be able to respond to differing circumstances and needs.

8. Support congruence—Social support systems (for example, rewards) should support desired behaviors such as collaboration and risk taking.

9. Design and human values—Relevant quality of working life criteria (see Chapter 4) should be built into jobs and structures.

10. Transitional organization—Bear in mind the complexities in moving to a new type of organization, and support the design team and others in these challenges.

11. Incompletion—Redesign is in fact an ongoing process in which the organization will always be adapting to new conditions.

In a related vein, listed next are some additional design criteria to suggest how an effective organization should operate. Criteria 1 to 5 are based on Hammer's principles of reengineering and adapted for human service organizations by O'Looney (1996, pp. 148–162).

1. Organize around outcomes, not tasks. Have one person perform as many steps in a process as possible, or have this done by a team who works closely together.

2. Have those who use the output perform the process. For example, staff may be given the authority to directly purchase supplies needed in their work (such as clothing allowances for foster children).

3. Treat geographically dispersed resources as though they were centralized. Use computer networks so that centralized databases can facilitate decentralized decision making on purchasing, other budget expenditures, and allocation of resources.

4. Link parallel activities instead of integrating their results. This approach has become more common with recent renewed efforts at service integration and collaboration. All individuals working on a case should be able to interact with each other in real time to make joint decisions and action plans.

5. Capture information once and at the source. Ensure that different workers do not have to gather the same information from clients. This problem became most vivid when it was noted that child victims of sexual abuse had to tell their story multiple times to multiple individuals, and efforts were initiated to eliminate this through techniques such as videotaping. If workers have access to complete client records in one database, less time will be wasted in data collection and compilation.

6. Keep in mind the client's perspective. How will the client experience the organization? Clients should have as simple an experience as possible. If a client needs multiple services within the agency, have a case manager who can coordinate the work of different staff who will be involved and be certain that the client does not "fall between the cracks."

7. Ensure clarity of individual roles within the organization. Because it is difficult within human service organizations to identify the decision-making centers and to distinguish between agency and professional roles, it is particularly important that individuals have a clear idea of expectations. This does not mean that a bureaucratic structure must be followed. Even in a strongly decentralized decision-making structure such as Likert's System 4, participants do know what role they can expect to play, what kind of decision-making power they have, and how subsystems interact within the organization.

8. Maximize the ability of staff to act autonomously, within broad policy guidelines. If agency staff are trained professionals, they will not normally need close supervision and should be able to operate with a minimum amount of bureaucratic oversight. Minimize the number of layers in the hierarchy so that several managers will not need to get involved in decisions that line staff can make.

9. Ensure that the various functions coordinate and communicate well with each other and outside agencies. The effective human service organization needs to emphasize coordination, both within the agency and between the agency and its environment. It is an open system, and it can maintain its life only when this factor is recognized. The fact that agencies are interdependent with other systems can be seen as a problem, but it can just as accurately be viewed as an opportunity for growth and for efficient use of resources.

10. Build a structure that allows for responsiveness to the need for change. Both classical bureaucracies and their professional counterparts seem too unwieldy to lend themselves to change. Human service agencies need to combine some degree of clarity of structure, communication, and decision making with the kind of flexibility that can bring needed adaptations to changing client needs. One key to dealing with this issue is the management philosophy used by leaders. Participative styles such as System 4 enable an organization to respond quickly to new needs and situations.

Design criteria such as those just discussed will ultimately result in organizational structures of units, roles, and responsibilities as well as decision-making and communication processes. The final sections of this chapter will review common models that can be considered and adapted by organization designers.

The design criteria reviewed here can be applied using the following design process (based on Taylor & Felten, 1993). Both the steering committee and design team would be involved, with the bulk of the day-to-day tasks performed by the design team.

1. Review the organization's purpose and strategic directions. Consult the agency's strategic plan for answers to such questions as: What needs

and opportunities need to be addressed? What are the overall strategies and goals? What specific objectives need to be accomplished?

2. Determine the best service delivery technology.

3. Allocate staff roles and determine the most appropriate decision-making and communication processes.

4. Determine the most appropriate organizational structure.

5. Jointly optimize the service delivery model with the structure, staff roles, and organizational processes.

Organizational Structures

Organizational structures can range from a *simple* structure in a very small agency in which one supervisor can oversee all activities to complex forms such as a *matrix* in which workers may have more than one supervisor. The most common structures are the *functional* and *divisional* forms.

Functional Structures

Functional structures are very common, particularly in bureaucratic agencies. Functional departmentation involves grouping together all personnel who share common functions or procedures, such as personnel, finance, information systems, administrative support, and so forth. Functions may also be based on policy area or program. For example, a child protective services division may have units for court intervention, permanency planning, and adoptions. Sometimes these divisions are made based on funding requirements that originate in the laws or regulations that created the programs.

This type of departmentation is usually considered efficient because functions are routinized and duplication of effort is avoided. The weakness of the functional form is that individuals tend to be so aware of their own departments that they lose sight of the common purpose of the organization as a whole. Power and authority become overly centralized in the hands of the few top managers who are able to see the "big picture." A major disadvantage of the functional model is that it often treats a client in a fragmented way: client needs may span multiple programs, requiring a transfer of a client to a new worker at each stage in the service delivery process.

Divisional Structures

The problem of fragmentation can be mitigated to some extent by a divisional structure. In this model, the agency is organized by *client, geographic area,* or, in industrial terms, *product. Product departmentation* involves grouping together all the people contributing to the development of a given product or service. For example, a product would be a welfare recipient becoming gainfully employed or a formerly institutionalized person living independently. *Customer* or *client departmentation* involves all the workers dealing with a specific category or segment of the public being grouped together. *Geographic departmentation* is highly appropriate for human service settings. This approach involves decentralizing operations so that smaller organizations are duplicated in each of several geographic areas. Its strength is that individual workers can closely identify with the outcome of their work in terms of the creation of goods or services rather than becoming involved strictly in means or methods. When agencies divide by geographic location, using small, community-based agencies rather than centralized offices, they tend to increase the active participation of both service deliverers and consumers. Effective coordination and sharing of resources among such outreach branches are important because duplication of effort is as uneconomical in the human service agency as it is in the production-oriented firm. For small organizations, however, the duplication of effort involved in re-creating functions across divisional lines can be costly.

An example of functional and divisional structures in local government is a redesign through a merger of a department of social services and a department of health services. Social Services had divisions organized by functions, including Income Maintenance, Employment and Training Services, and Child Protective Services. Health Services included Mental Health, Drug and Alcohol Services, and Community Health. Since many clients received services from more than one division, it was decided to move to a divisional structure based on geography. In the new model, there were regional managers in all sections of the county who each had responsibility for all programs in the region. Every client was to have a case manager who would facilitate the client's receiving services from other professionals. A welfare client needing job development, income maintenance, child protective services, and substance abuse treatment, for example, would be treated in a comprehensive manner so that she would not need to drive to multiple locations to meet with different workers for each need.

Matrix Structures

The most complex structure is the *matrix,* which can be seen as a compromise between the functional and divisional forms. Organizations using this structure are functionally divided but use temporary task forces for projects that require the work of several specialists. Each project has its own manager, and personnel receive temporary assignments to work with special projects. The strength of this structure is that it uses the positive aspects of both of the other types of departmentation. It tends to be complex and require strong human relations skills on the part of managers who must share authority with others, but it allows for rapid reorganization in response to immediate needs for change.

The matrix has been used in human service organizations, primarily in health care. After its successful development in complex business sectors such as aerospace, many managers in other fields including the human services became infatuated with it, leading to its inappropriate application. Experience has shown that this structure is very complicated and costly to implement well, and it should only be used where it is clearly necessary (Gortner, Mahler, & Nicholson, 1997, p. 100).

Linking and Coordinating Mechanisms _____._____

The matrix was developed to address problems noted in Chapter 4 by Lawrence and Lorsch (1967): a complex organization will have several functions that, because of their unique needs, are differentiated from each other. In social service settings, agencies are often divided between counseling services and income maintenance services, and differing organizational structures might be appropriate for each. Recognition of this factor might lead to creative attempts to integrate divergent departments and eliminate some of the rancor that often accompanies such units' attempts to reform each other. Similarly, counseling departments housed within traditional academic institutions might develop methods of coordinating efforts that previously had been seen to have little in common. Functions need to be integrated so that the organization as a whole can function well.

The matrix is the most complex and formal way to ensure high levels of integration. The simplest integrating mechanisms are bureaucratic: a *hierarchical command and communication system* (direct supervision) and the use of *rules, regulations, plans,* and *schedules* (Gortner et al., 1997, p. 97). Other formal integrating mechanisms include *staff meetings, task forces,* and *memos.* A valuable integrating mechanism is an *integrator role,* which may be formal, such as a liaison position, or informal, in which an individual can serve as an internal *boundary spanner,* communicating with different groups in the organization to ensure that they work well together. Finally, *project organizations* have *multifunctional teams* as in a matrix but are more temporary (for example, a project team formed to start an agency facility in a new community). *Team-based organizations* (such as multidisciplinary mental health teams) are more permanent than project organizations.

Managers also need to ensure that the organization has mechanisms for coordinating with its environment. The concepts of networking and linkage are especially useful for the coordination function. *Networking* involves a recognition that human services are part of a helping network that includes mental health facilities, educational institutions, rehabilitation settings, and a wide variety of specialized agencies. In the interests of efficient use of resources as well as effective delivery of services, the efforts of these services should be coordinated.

Networking combines the creativity and flexibility of the small, organic agency with the efficient utilization of resources found in the larger, more mechanistic organization. As a coordinating technique, networking is appropriate both for coalitions of small, independent agencies and for subdivisions of large, complex service organizations.

Closely related to the concept of networking is the idea of *linkage*. Effective coordination requires that consumers, as well as providers, of services recognize the connections among departments and among separate agencies. Organizing for linkage involves developing procedures that overcome fragmentation in service delivery so that individual clients do not become lost in a tangle of agencies and programs. Linkage efforts can include special coordinating departments, interface task forces among agencies, or client advocates.

Structural arrangements are represented visually using organizational charts, which we will now review. They do not tell the whole story, however. They do not show how decisions get made or how different roles and units communicate with each other. These *process* aspects will follow the discussion of organizational charts and the definitions of line and staff roles.

Organizational Charts

Traditional, mechanistic organizations depend on organizational charts to clarify the chain of command and to illustrate the expected flow of communication. Organic structures place less stress on charts but still use them to clarify roles. Organizational charts alone do not explain functions in great detail but must be combined with written job descriptions that provide additional information. They fail to show the degree to which decision-making responsibilities are delegated or the emphasis placed on interpersonal communication within an organization.

A traditional structure might look like that shown in Figure 5-1. The organizational chart shows that the executive director is the chief executive officer of the agency, reporting to a board of directors either directly or through a committee structure. The assistant directors handle whatever matters the director delegates. The remainder of the duties to be performed by the agency are handled by staff members, who are assigned duties, or by volunteers, who are supervised by their director.

If this very small but traditionally structured agency should grow in size, organizational changes would involve the addition both of more vertical levels and of more horizontal specializations. Vertically, growth would bring the placement of directors in charge of smaller departments, with supervisory levels added between directors and staff members. Horizontally, specialties such as training director and personnel director might be added, and the professional services department would be divided into smaller sections based on type of service offered. Another major by-product of growth in a mechanistically structured agency would be the beginnings of differentiation between line and staff positions.

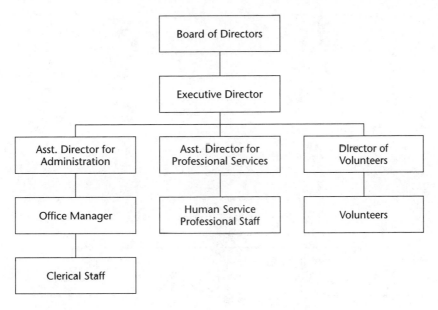

FIGURE 5-1
Organizational Chart for a Traditional Human Service Agency

Line and Staff

Many large organizations divide their personnel into the two categories of line and staff. *Line managers* have responsibilities in carrying out the major purposes of the organization and have the authority to direct others in carrying out these purposes. In a bureaucratic structure, they are part of the chain of command that links all levels of the managerial hierarchy. *Staff personnel* do not have the same kinds of authority relationships. Instead, they act in advisory capacities to line managers, either as personal staff or as experts able to give advice in specific fields. The agency illustrated in Figure 5-1 might add personal staff, perhaps in the form of an assistant to the director, or specialized staff, perhaps in the form of a research and evaluation department. The personnel department might be considered a staff, rather than a line, department.

  In community agencies delivering counseling or social services, human service providers are considered line personnel because the services they perform are directed toward the major purpose of the organization. Sometimes, however, human service functions are parts of larger organizations. Then it becomes very important to determine whether service providers are considered line or staff personnel. For instance, in many school situations, counselors are not certain

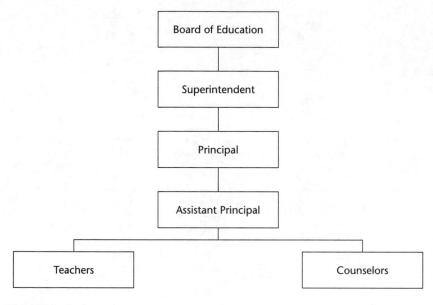

FIGURE 5-2
Counselors as Line Personnel

whether they are to be considered line or staff. Major conflicts between administrators and counselors arise because that distinction has never been clarified. Consider the major differences in the counselor role as it would be perceived by the principal in Figure 5-2, as compared with the way it would be perceived by the principal in Figure 5-3.

In Figure 5-2, counselors, along with teachers, are line personnel. They report to the principal through the assistant principal and are charged with carrying out one aspect of the educational process.

In Figure 5-3, counselors are seen as staff personnel. Their function in this school is to help line personnel—teachers, the assistant principal, and the principal—carry out their duties. The counselors assist through their specialization and ability to advise on such matters as individual differences among students.

Neither of these approaches is necessarily correct, but it is vital that the counselor's view of his or her place in the organization be consistent with the administrator's view. Counselors who are considered line personnel should not be surprised when the assistant principal tries to give them orders, and counselors who are considered staff should not expect to be "promoted" to assistant principals.

This kind of issue is always apparent in school settings. It also appears in a number of other human service agencies because the dual hierarchy is almost always a factor when human service professionals are employed. It is as important

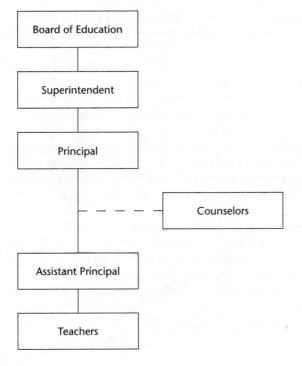

FIGURE 5-3
Counselors as Staff Personnel

to determine whether those professionals are considered line or staff as it is to determine their place within the agency's system of departmentalization.

Key Organizational Processes: Decision Making and Communications _____

An organizational chart cannot show how decisions are made or how communications occur. These factors deserve at least as much attention as do structural considerations, which often dominate discussions of "reorganization."

Decision-making processes at the broadest level can be grounded in management theories discussed earlier. In a highly centralized organization, most decisions will be made at the top, as proposed in scientific management or as reflected in McGregor's Theory X or Likert's System 1. In decentralized, professional organizations, human resources models such as Theory Y and System 4 are more appropriate. In such a system, a worker has a large amount of autonomy to make decisions in her or his area of responsibility, whether it be regarding services to clients or management of a program. Of course, contingency theory suggests that there is no one best way, but individual supervisors and their subordinates or teams should discuss explicitly which decisions should be made by which roles in the organization. This matter will be covered in more detail in the chapter on supervision, in which models of participative decision making will be discussed.

Perhaps the most commonly cited problem in organizations is "poor communication." Because communication is so fundamental, communication processes and mechanisms in organizations, paradoxically, are often neglected. We will review here some communication mechanisms that should receive specific attention when designing an organization. These range from the grapevine and rumors at the informal level, to communication roles, to, at the formal level, newsletters and memos.

The grapevine and rumors should be recognized, both because some studies have shown that the grapevine is up to 75 percent accurate (Bowditch & Buono, 1997, p. 133) and because rumors often begin because accurate and timely information has not been forthcoming from reliable formal sources. This situation points to the importance of effectively using formal mechanisms such as newsletters, videos, Web sites, memos, and meetings to keep employees informed. The use of rituals and ceremonies, which will be discussed later in the context of organizational culture, are powerful ways for leaders to communicate using symbolism as well as facts.

An untapped resource for communication is the use of staff in *communication roles*. *Liaisons* were mentioned briefly earlier as integrating functions in the organization. Their main responsibility is to serve as links between different groups and coordinate their joint work. Liaisons need to have the same characteristics as gatekeepers and also to be able to generate respect and trust from the different groups they are working with. The linking pin role identified by Likert is an example of a formal liaison: an individual who has membership in two or more groups and serves as a communication link between them. *Boundary spanners* are liaisons who interact with the environment. They may be upper-level managers who meet with external groups as part of their jobs, intake workers or others who interact with other agencies as part of their job, or employees who serve as members of external task forces or coalitions. Liaisons and boundary spanners are key roles, and individuals who can fill them should be identified and sanctioned by the organization.

Informal communication roles such as gatekeepers and opinion leaders should also be acknowledged when assessing organizational communication patterns. *Gatekeepers* are individuals who control the flow of information as part of their job (Bowditch & Buono, 1997, p. 135). They are often secretaries or administrative assistants who have access to large amounts of information and can decide what information to pass on to whom. An effective gatekeeper needs to be aware of managers' information needs, know when information is needed, and assess the quality of information being shared. *Opinion leaders* are able to informally influence other members of the organization. They are usually influential only in specified areas. Managers can share information with opinion leaders to get initial feedback and reactions before making formal announcements and can attempt to influence opinion leaders to share particular information or preferences with others in the organization.

Summary

We began this discussion by noting the importance of design in creating an effective organization. *Organization design* can be a noun or a verb. As a verb, staff can engage in a process to determine how the parts of an organization should be organized and operate together. An organization should be designed, or, more commonly, redesigned, based on contingencies such as the nature of the clients and services, the environment, and the organization's size. A process that involves staff will be more likely to result in a design that will both respond effectively to client needs and provide a high quality of working life for staff.

The result of this process is *organization design* as a noun: a description of the structures and processes such as decision making and communication in use. In recent years, the more common functional structures are often being replaced with divisional structures oriented to client or geographic considerations. Of course, a structure means very little until people are inserted into it. We will now look at the various human resources functions necessary for an agency to hire, train, evaluate, and develop its staff.

Discussion Questions

1. Think of an agency or organization that you found particularly effective in meeting the needs of its clients or members. In general terms, how was that organization structured? To what degree did the design seem to affect the organization's accomplishments?

2. What is the best way to departmentalize human service organizations—by function, geography, client, product, or use of a matrix design? What factors would you take into account in deciding this?

Group Exercise

In small groups of three or four, design a hypothetical agency to meet a range of community needs. Design an organizational structure to make the agency operational. Begin this process by writing down your group's answers to the following questions:

1. How should the organization's work be departmentalized?

2. How should work be divided among departments and individuals? Draw an organizational chart that you would use to describe the agency's design.

3. How would you make sure that the work of various individuals and groups was effectively coordinated?

Share your organizational chart with the other groups. Have most of the groups designed similar organizations, or are there major differences among them? What seems to account for the difference?

CASE 5 _____

The Umbrella Organization

The roots of the Atlantis Community Mental Health Center (ACMHC) were in its inpatient, outpatient, and emergency services. Although, in keeping with the federal mandate, consultation and education services had always been included, emphasis had never been placed on preventive, community-based interventions until a recent major upheaval.

In response to an evaluation report showing that many groups within its highly diverse geographic area were not being reached through traditional services, the board and administrative staff of the ACMHC decided to add several new service components. The new programs were to include an outreach program for families, a drug and alcoholism program, a crisis intervention team, and several storefront outposts that would encourage using the service by members of the minority community.

The ACMHC's funding sources were uniformly in favor of this approach but would provide funding only if a major organizational change were made. The funding sources recognized that many of the proposed services were already being offered on a smaller scale by tiny, community-based agencies scattered throughout the area. Each of these small agencies had worked independently for years, often with unknowing duplication of the services of other organizations. This new thrust of the ACMHC was recognized as a possible vehicle for a more efficient approach to human services than had been possible before. It was suggested that the human service network of Atlantis develop more effective linkages, with each agency maintaining a degree of autonomy but with the organizations joining for the sharing of resources. The mental health center would act as the umbrella organization, offering community outreach services through existing local agencies rather than duplicating these services with the development of new programs.

Because of the obvious financial benefits to be gained through this cooperative endeavor, the mental health center and a number of community agencies made the commitment to developing a new organizational structure. A subcommittee, including a number of agency and center service deliverers, as well as funders and community members, was charged with the responsibility of drafting a suggested structure, to which the various member agencies could respond. Of course, representatives of differing organizations brought divergent viewpoints to the meeting.

Hilary Johnson, the ACMHC's program officer, represented a major source of funding for the organization. Her primary concern was that services be effectively delivered at Atlantis without needless duplication of effort and without the usual endless competition among agencies for limited funds. She knew that all of the agencies involved provided greatly needed services, but she also knew that these services could be provided more efficiently through greater coordination. She thought it would be possible to centralize the work of these agencies to accomplish common goals and to divide resources equitably among programs.

Caroline Brown, Juan Casel, and Evelyn Mays were all staff members of small, community-based agencies. Each of them brought to the meeting a high degree of concern for maintaining the nature of his or her own agency. They knew that their agencies' strengths lay in their responsiveness to local needs and in the fact that their programs had been developed by community members. They had always resisted pressures to expand, recognizing that the smaller agency can sometimes maintain a degree of responsiveness and

flexibility that a large organization cannot duplicate. They knew that fiscal realities meant they had to become part of a larger entity, but they also realized that there would be dangers involved in losing their own identities. They could not duplicate the center's lack of accessibility; they understood that if that happened, they would go under.

Similarly, Nick Chan and Sally Allen, representing local citizens' groups, recognized that maintaining accessibility would be important. They knew that many of their neighbors resisted using the services of the center but felt more comfortable in their dealings with the smaller agencies in their immediate neighborhoods. They knew that the creative and open atmosphere of the small agencies needed to be maintained. Chan and Allen also realized, however, that the service consumers would be the losers if more efficient use of funds did not begin to take place.

Nelson Richards, director of the ACMHC, was most interested in the degree of centralization that could be accomplished. Although he would have preferred unilateral expansion of services on the part of the center, he recognized that some major benefits could be gained from using the center as an umbrella organization. He could see great possibilities for the sharing of resources. For instance, each agency could become part of the management information system so that the flow of clients from agency to agency would be enhanced. Common budgeting could mean a significant increase in the funding available for the center as a whole. Such activities as staff training, personnel, and purchasing could be centralized, so each agency would gain greatly in efficiency. Planning could be broadly based, and purchases could be made in money-saving quantities. Looking at it from a more humanistic standpoint, services to consumers would be improved, and no client would ever again be able to "fall between the cracks" because of lack of information or lack of comprehensiveness.

Melvin Hammond was also in favor of a high degree of centralization but for a different reason. As a human service consultant called in by the state funding agency, he knew that the best resource utilization would involve having one central agency to act as fiscal agent for funds. He recognized, however, that the direction this agency would take would depend to a great extent on the kind of organizational structure they developed. One possibility would be to departmentalize the new, enlarged organization by type of service, with all direct service providers in one department, all outreach specialists in another, and all community organizers in still another. A different alternative would be to divide the organization according to population served, with all drug abuse program personnel working in one department, all family service professionals in another, and so on. To Ham-

mond, the important aspect of the organization was that workers should identify themselves with Atlantis rather than with their former agencies.

Each of these individuals had organizational priorities that differed. Yet the committee would need to decide on an organizational structure that would please everyone, at least to a degree, and that would work.

1. What are the major organizational issues involved here?

2. What do you see as the primary alternatives for the organizational structure?

3. If you were asked to give input to the committee, what organizational structure would you suggest? Why?

4. What would be the implications of varying approaches to departmentalization?

5. How centralized do you think the organization should be?

References

Bowditch, J., & Buono, A. (1997). *A primer on organizational behavior.* New York: Wiley.

Gortner, H., Mahler, J., & Nicholson, J. (1997). *Organization theory: A public perspective* (2nd ed.). Fort Worth, TX: Harcourt Brace College Publishers.

Jackson, J. H., & Morgan, C. P. (1982). *Organization theory: A macro perspective for management* (2nd ed., pp. 449–469). Upper Saddle River, NJ: Prentice Hall.

Lawrence, P. R., & Lorsch, J. (1967). *Organization and environment.* Cambridge, MA: Harvard University Press.

Mohr, B. (1989). High-performing organizations from an open sociotechnical systems perspective. In W. Sikes, A. Drexler, & J. Gant (Eds.), *The emerging practice of organization development* (pp. 199–211). Alexandria, VA: NTL Institute.

O'Looney, J. (1996). *Redesigning the work of human services.* Westport, CT: Quorum.

Robey, D. (1991). *Designing organizations* (3rd ed.). Homewood, IL: Irwin.

Senge, P. (1990). *The fifth discipline: The art and practice of the learning organization.* New York: Doubleday Currency.

Taylor, J., & Felten, D. (1993). *Performance by design.* Upper Saddle River, NJ: Prentice Hall.

Zell, D. (1997). *Changing by design: Organizational innovation at Hewlett-Packard.* Ithaca, NY: ILR Press.

6

Developing and Managing Human Resources

CHAPTER OUTLINE

Job Design

Hiring Practices
Recruitment, Selection, Orientation, Promotion

Staff Training
Assessing Training and Development Needs, Developing
Training Objectives, Designing the Training Program,
Implementing the Training Program, Evaluating Training

Performance Appraisal

Appraisal Mechanisms
Behaviorally Anchored Rating Scales, Management by
Objectives, Critical Incident Techniques

Valuing Diversity

Federal Legislation*
Enforcement of Federal Legislation, Affirmative Action

Diversity Implications for Human Resource Development

Encouraging Volunteer Participation

Burnout
Causes of Burnout, Preventing Burnout

Employee Assistance Programs

Summary

Discussion Questions

Group Exercise

CASE 6: Director of Training

References

After the environment has been assessed, strategies have been developed, programs have been designed, and an overall structure is chosen, the purposes of the agency are operationalized by staff delivering services. Human service agencies are labor-intensive organizations. A sizable portion of each budget goes toward salaries and the other costs of maintaining human, rather than just material, resources. The way these human resources are to be used and enhanced must be carefully decided.

The concept of *human resource development* provides a context for a broad vision, encompassing the needs of the organization as a whole. It also uses a long-term perspective in planning, attempting to deal with both immediate needs and future requirements.

> Human resource development (HRD) is a planned approach to enhance the development and growth of employee skills, abilities, judgment, and maturity to better meet overall organizational and individual employee goals. HRD programs are implemented to develop employee capabilities to carry out job functions more effectively and to meet projected staffing needs. (Craft, 1979, p. 103)

To meet their human resource needs in the new millennium, human service managers must deal effectively with a number of related issues:

- They must design jobs that will enable program objectives to be accomplished and workers to use all of their training, knowledge, skills, and creativity.

- They must develop effective and efficient methods for hiring, appraising, and rewarding agency employees.

- They must provide training and development to enhance the staff's effectiveness.

- They must make greater advances in making their workforces more inclusive and diverse.

- They must maintain their commitment to equal employment opportunity, even in the face of cutbacks.

- They must expand human resources by encouraging the participation of volunteers.

- They must protect valuable human resources by taking steps to prevent burnout and improve the quality of working life.

Each of these steps plays an important part in the effective development of human resources and will be addressed in this chapter.

Job Design

Program design, covered in Chapter 3, results in a clearly articulated *theory of helping:* a set of activities to be performed by staff to accomplish objectives. The next step is to design the specific jobs (staff roles) that fit into the program design. Two considerations are implicit here: the job needs to allow for the accomplishment of program objectives and the satisfaction of the expectations of key stakeholders, including clients, and the job should have built into it elements that will provide a high-quality working life for the employee.

The first consideration is addressed initially through a program design with clear expectations for the provision of particular services. This should result in a general set of staff positions needed to implement the program: direct service staff, supervisors, managers, support staff. Specifics of each position are developed by conducting for each a *job analysis:* "a purposeful, systematic process that provides descriptive, important job-related information that distinguishes the job being analyzed from other jobs" (Foster, 1998, pp. 322–323). This analysis can be done by interviewing and analyzing individuals currently performing the job and reviewing related documents or by constructing it "from scratch" based on the treatment or service delivery model being used in the new program. This process can provide the following information: work activities, equipment needed, standards of job performance and time required for tasks, the job context (physical environment, schedule, organizational environment), and personnel requirements (knowledge and skills, training, work experience, aptitudes, and so forth) (McCormick, cited in Foster, 1998, p. 323). Note that this is *not* the same thing as a job description, which is a summary of the job analysis.

A key component of the job analysis is a *task analysis* (Rapp & Poertner, 1992): a set of task statements that clearly state the expectations of a position. According to Rapp and Poertner (p. 152), task statements need to be written in jargon-free language and collectively developed by managers and staff, and they should lead to desired performance (that is, they will enable program objectives to be accomplished).

The second aspect of job design is concerned with the employee's *quality of working life,* covered in Chapter 4 as a current trend in organizational thinking. Relevant for our purpose here is the criterion (Walton, 1975) of "immediate opportunity to use and develop human capacities." This concept is well represented by the *Job Characteristics Model* (Hackman & Oldham, 1980), which suggests that positive outcomes, including high satisfaction and better performance, are affected by three aspects of the work experience: the employee feeling that the work is meaningful, experiencing responsibility for the end result, and receiving feedback on results. These task elements are influenced by five job characteristics (Hackman & Oldham, 1980):

> **Skill variety:** the degree to which a job requires a variety of different activities in carrying out the work, involving the use of a number of different skills and talents of the person . . .
>
> **Task identity:** the degree to which a job requires completion of a "whole" and identifiable piece of work—that is, doing a job from beginning to end with a visible outcome . . .
>
> **Task significance:** the degree to which the job has a substantial impact on the lives of other people, whether those people are in the immediate organization or in the world at large . . .
>
> **Autonomy:** the degree to which the job provides substantial freedom, independence, and discretion to the individual in scheduling the work and determining the procedures to be used in carrying it out . . .
>
> **Job feedback:** the degree to which carrying out the work activities required by the job provides the individual with direct and clear information about the effectiveness of his or her performance (pp. 78–80)

It is also important to note that there are three "moderating" factors that may influence the effects of job characteristics on performance. First, the worker needs a basic level of *knowledge and skill* to increase the likelihood that, for example, autonomy will lead to good outcomes. Second, employee *growth need strength* varies from worker to worker: some prefer high levels of the characteristics listed here; others may be happy with low levels. Finally, *contextual satisfaction* is relevant: if other aspects of the job such as pay and working conditions are bad, an enriched job may not make a difference. This model is represented in Figure 6-1.

Hackman and Oldham have suggested several strategies for job redesign to improve job outcomes. *Combining tasks* is perhaps a bigger innovation in factories than in human services work, in which professional workers often perform a variety of tasks. Nevertheless, this concept would suggest that, for example, child protective service bureaus allow one worker to follow a case from intake to resolution, not "handing off" the case when it moves from one stage to another (for example, intake to court intervention). *Forming natural work units* is also common in the human services and involves grouping workers into teams that have total

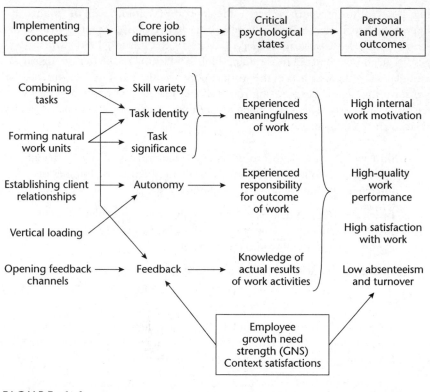

FIGURE 6-1
Job Characteristic Model
SOURCE: Copyright ©1975, by The Regents of the University of California. Reprinted from the *California Management Review,* Vol. 17, No. 4. By permission of The Regents.

responsibility for a case or function. *Establishing client relationships* occurs naturally in human services work, as opposed to factories, in which workers rarely if ever see those who use their product. *Vertically loading the job* involves allowing the worker more responsibility and authority to make decisions and solve problems. This strategy is often described as enhancing employee participation in decision making (discussed in detail in Chapter 7). *Opening feedback channels* would include ensuring that the worker received clear and direct feedback on the results of work performed. Sager (1995) discusses in more detail the applications of these principles in the human services.

The implication for the design of a job is to incorporate as much of these characteristics as possible. For example, an enriched and motivating job for a human services worker would allow that employee to perform a variety of tasks, work with the client holistically, see that the work is important to the client and

society, have the freedom to make professional decisions without excessive bureaucratic control, and see the results (outcomes) of work with the client.

Hiring Practices

Hiring consists of recruitment and selection. Recruitment "is concerned with
providing the organization with an adequate number of qualified applicants. Selection is concerned with reviewing and assessing the qualifications of job applicants to decide who should be offered the position" (Pecora, 1998, p. 155).

Recruitment

The first step of recruitment should already be done: defining the job through
the job description, which should include necessary *KSAs*: knowledge, skills, and
abilities. These are typically listed using the job title, classification, and description of duties, with minimum requirements in terms of educational degrees, any
licensing or certification, and years of related job experience included. Work
hours, location, and any particular requirements (such as a driver's license and
availability of a personal car to use for field visits) should also be clearly noted.
There must be a clearly demonstrated connection between each requirement and
the work to be performed. The salary range, employment benefits, and the
agency's equal employment and diversity values and policy should be included as
well. The starting date, application procedures, and closing date for applications
should be listed.

Selection

In the spirit of team management and to bring a wide range of screening and
assessment expertise to the hiring process, others beyond the supervisor of
the position should be involved. For example, a committee may be used in a
strictly advisory capacity or by having the committee rank-order or select candidates. Staff can be involved in all phases of the process, from developing criteria
to hiring.

Selection processes work most effectively when information about job
openings is widely disseminated. Wide dissemination helps ensure fairness for potential applicants, but it also assists the agency by expanding the pool of available
individuals. In addition to newspapers, employment agencies, employee referrals,
recruiting firms, professional journals and association newsletters, also beneficial
are university departments and placement centers, local community organizations,
and special interest newspapers and newsletters. Tapping into these resources can
enhance the diversity of the applicant pool by reaching people who may not be
contacted by some traditional sources. Remember that recruitment is also a form

of public relations (Pecora, 1998). Announcements for jobs tell the community your agency is hiring and is particularly interested in hiring its members. This approach may demonstrate an interest in becoming more inclusive of segments of the community historically underrepresented in particular jobs or fields.

You may use an application form or résumés for screening. Pecora (1998, pp. 162–163) has provided a screening grid and checklist to organize key information on candidates. The grid has columns for candidate names and key criteria from the job announcement (qualifications, education, specific prior experience). Each candidate's information is summarized in a separate row, so that the person's background may be screened (meets/does not meet criterion) or ranked. A more specific checklist may be used to provide detail, such as ratings for not meeting, meeting, or exceeding expectations. After screening, the best candidates are identified for further processing.

Although tests are often used for civil service positions, they are not common in not-for-profits. Interviews are the most common assessment method, and growing evidence indicates their value in predicting job performance (Pecora, 1998). Assessment centers are sometimes used for hiring decisions, particularly for promotion to managerial positions in larger agencies. They are also sometimes used to assess the management potential of current employees and are particularly valuable in identifying development needs for employees individually and as groups. They will be presented here in the latter context and for that reason will be covered later in the section on training.

Pecora (1998) lists four phases for an interview. In the *opening phase,* the interview panel introduces themselves and establishes a "comfortable, confidential, supportive, and non-threatening atmosphere" and summarizes the plan for the interview (p. 166). In the *information-gathering phase,* a structured set of job-related questions are asked in the same way to all candidates. Questions should be open-ended and followed by probes as needed. They should enable an applicant to describe relevant qualifications and how she or he has performed relevant duties or handled situations in the past or would do so in a work situation. Role plays can be used to see how a candidate may respond to a case or a management team problem. If a role play is used, it should be done in the same way for all candidates. (For a detailed example of the use of role-play simulation tests in staff selection, see Kaman & Bentson, 1988.) In the third phase, which Pecora calls *responding to applicant questions,* the applicant is given the opportunity to ask any questions he or she may have. With regard to Phases 2 and 3, Pecora adds that "it is also important to assess the degree of match between the applicant's career goals and the organization's mission" (p. 166). In the *closing phase,* the interviewee is thanked and the time line for next steps is reviewed. This phase may also include a tour of the facility and the opportunity to meet other staff.

Written materials on the agency (program descriptions, annual report, brochures, and so forth) may be provided to the candidates to give them a more complete picture of the agency. References (preferably at least three) should also be checked. Have your questions prepared in advance, and be sure to ask whether the reference would rehire the applicant (Jensen, 1981, cited in Pecora, 1998, p. 170).

After all interviews have been completed, the team must systematically assess all relevant information about the candidates, from the résumés and screening forms to interview notes and feedback from all staff who met all the candidates. Hiring decisions should be made quickly. This process is another aspect of public relations. Good candidates can be lost because of delays in the decision-making process. The person accepted should receive a letter of confirmation with relevant details. After the offer is accepted, applicants who are passed over deserve the courtesy of being notified and thanked for their interest. Hutton (1984) suggests that the agency stay in touch with the new hire during the period between acceptance of the offer and start date to cement the relationship between her or him and the organization.

Orientation

Make sure that everything is ready for the person to begin working on the first day, from a clean and well-stocked office to all relevant paperwork ready to be filled out. On the employee's first day, take care to make sure she or he feels welcomed into the organization. Reintroduce the new hire to those met during interviewing, and introduce her or him to other staff. Have relevant materials (for example, program descriptions, strategic plans, funded grant or contract proposals, the most recent annual report, information system forms, policies and procedures) ready to be read. In particular, the agency's performance appraisal system and instruments (discussed later) should be shared with the employee. Getting the new hire acquainted with the organization's culture will also be important. This process will happen naturally over time, but the supervisor and colleagues can expedite it by describing the culture and telling some of the organization's "stories" (see Chapter 11).

Promotion

Many of the principles already discussed can be used or easily adapted for promotion decisions. Assessment centers, discussed in the next section, may also be used as part of the evaluation process. In many governmental organizations, promotional opportunities (except at the executive level) are typically available only to current employees. In most not-for-profit agencies, promotional opportunities are treated as new hiring opportunities with the exception that the organization's current employees may apply.

Promotion from within has obvious benefits in offering career growth opportunities to employees, and more is known about candidates with a work history at the agency. One perceived disadvantage is that if a current employee is not

selected, the hiring staff will need to provide very specific feedback regarding reasons for his or her not being selected and perhaps deal with feelings about this decision that may affect future performance. If criteria are clear to and accepted by
all applicants, this possible outcome may not be a problem.

A new hire into a supervisory position has the advantage of bringing a fresh
perspective and new ideas and will be less susceptible to the "that's the way we
have always done it" syndrome. A disadvantage is created, however, if the new
hire has brought her or his own "that's the way we've always done it" view from
the previous setting. Any transition issues can be handled through discussions with
one's supervisor (see the next chapter) and team members.

Staff Training

Effective use of limited human resources requires that human service workers receive ongoing training to meet the changing needs of community and clients.
The basic steps to be followed in implementing training programs are the same
whether the focus is on an individual or a group, on immediate needs or long-
term plans.

Assessing Training and Development Needs

For the sake of both appropriate use of resources and participant motivation,
training programs must be based on careful assessment of real needs. The assessment might be based on new programs or organizational strategies, existing problems in service delivery, suggestions of employees or supervisors, or on the results
of an assessment center.

At the most comprehensive level, Van Wart (1998, p. 279) has suggested the
use of an *organizational needs analysis* consisting of seven elements:

- *ethics assessments* or *audits* look for gaps between stated values and
  organizational performance;

- *mission, values, vision,* and *planning statement reviews* use formal documents
  to identify possible gaps and needs;

- *customer* and *citizen assessments* provide data on emerging needs;

- *employee assessments* reveal employee opinions and values;

- *performance assessments* identify gaps between stated and actual
  performance;

- *benchmarking* involves looking for best practices elsewhere and using
  them as standards; and

- *quality assessments* review "customer satisfaction, employee involvement and development, continual learning and improvement, prevention over inspection, and supplier partnerships."

These steps are not normally all done at once. An organization should focus on those areas that seem to need attention. Van Wart (1998, pp. 280–281) provides a checklist to focus this analysis.

The second level of assessment is a *departmental needs analysis,* for which two approaches are available: the performance gap approach and the comprehensive approach (Van Wart, 1998, pp. 281–285). The performance gap approach works best when there is an obvious need area and typically begins with a "preanalysis," during which a training advisory group considers whether training will be the right answer. In the data collection phase, focus groups, interviews, questionnaires, or surveys can be used to get feedback on training needs and options. Assessment centers, described later, are another data collection tool, particularly regarding management skill needs. The analysis phase involves looking at the gap between the needs of the job and current skills, knowledge, and abilities of employees. It should be noted that a gap may be based on factors beyond the employee (poor management, excessive job demands, and the like), and training may not be the answer. The comprehensive approach involves a much more detailed analysis of individual job tasks and skills, looking at their "importance, frequency, level of proficiency required, criticality, and degree of responsibility required" (Van Wart, 1998, p. 284). In either approach, recommendations for training or other interventions are made to administrative decision makers. A third level of analysis—individual training needs—can also be done as a part of supervision and performance appraisal.

The assessment center concept was pioneered by industries attempting to assess potential managers or executives. It is both a process (a set of activities) and a place (typically an off-site setting such as a hotel or community center with conference rooms) (Swanson, 1998). A group of middle-management personnel might be brought together in an assessment center to examine their skills in leadership, organizing, decision making, human relations, or other factors considered relevant for managerial performance. Behavior samples are gleaned from a combination of in-basket exercises, leaderless group discussions, simulations, individual presentations, objective tests, management-style instruments, and interviews (Swanson, 1998).

Assessment requires a job analysis to ensure that the center will focus on job-relevant behaviors (Swanson, 1998). Centers use multiple methods of assessment and multiple assessors, each of whom has been trained to make judgments based on observations of performance. Assessors' independent evaluations are combined to make final assessments of participants using pooled data. Assessment center methods can be adapted to the needs of human service agencies and used to assess service deliverers as well as managers. When such analyses have been completed, even small agencies can use some of the assessment center ideas by building opportunities for objective behavioral appraisals into the selection process and performance appraisal system.

Once learning needs are identified, they need to be prioritized by the training advisory committee, managers, supervisors, and the learners themselves so that the most pressingly felt needs can be imminently addressed. Without an adequate assessment effort, subsequent training/development programs may miss their mark, affecting agency performance.

Developing Training Objectives

All of these approaches to staff development and training lead to the same point. Once learning needs have been clearly identified, they can be stated in terms of objectives. In some way, it is expected that trainees will be different after the educational intervention. Their behavior will be changed because they will have developed new skills, gained new knowledge, or learned new attitudes. The specific nature of the desired change should be clearly stated before the training program is designed.

Designing the Training Program

The design of the training program depends on the objectives being met and the resources available. In most work settings, training can run the gamut from on-the-job instruction and coaching to specially designed workshops for groups, ongoing classroom teaching, individualized programmed instruction, use of audiovisual media, laboratory training, and conferences. Within the confines of the workshop format, which is used very commonly in human service settings, methods can involve lectures or panel discussions, case conferences, demonstrations, use of media, discussions, structured experiences, role playing, exercises, or simulations. The nature of the activity selected must take into account the availability of both human and inanimate resources, and the program design must be based on the learning objectives that have been set. Knowledge acquisition objectives can sometimes be met through essentially passive learning, such as reading, watching videos, listening to lectures, or using programmed materials.

Either skill acquisition or attitude change, however, depends on learners' active involvement and should use principles of adult learning such as emphasizing immediate usefulness, responding to learners' concerns, building on experience, using media to match learners' styles, offering immediate feedback, and providing opportunities for reflection (Rapp & Poertner, 1992). And, of course, the interventions selected must suit the objectives that have been developed and at the same time meet the needs and orientations of trainers and trainees.

Implementing the Training Program

If the training methods selected are appropriate to the objectives that have been set, the likelihood for effectiveness is enhanced. It is still important to remember, however, that intervention methods should be appropriate to adult learners' needs. Their motivation depends on their ability to recognize the importance of the training program to their own work effectiveness. They must have been actively involved in selecting training goals. At the same time, they should be assured that the skills and knowledge they are gaining will be recognized and reinforced in the context of their posttraining work. The training program to avoid is one that has little connection with the ongoing work of the agency and its employees. The one to use extensively is the type that seems a natural outgrowth of the needs that have been identified through the appraisal process and are recognized by all involved.

Evaluating Training

Evaluation of training is useful in several ways: it shows the ultimate effects on job performance, it identifies additional training or development needs, and it provides feedback on the usefulness of various training activities and methods. Many terms used in program evaluation (see Chapter 10) are relevant to training evaluation, including outcome-process and formative-summative distinctions.

Criteria for training evaluation exist on several levels (Goldstein, 1993). The *reaction* level assesses what trainees thought of the program. Measuring *learning* involves looking at what principles, facts, techniques, or attitudes were learned. *Behavior* measures regard changes in job performance. Finally, *results* criteria assess effects on organizational objectives such as costs, turnover, error rates, and morale. Unfortunately, the criteria of most interest—behavior and results—are the hardest to measure. Trainee reactions are commonly measured with an anonymous questionnaire. Learning can often be measured with an instrument (for example, reactions to a case that are subjected to content analysis), ideally in a pretest-posttest format. Behavior on the job can be measured by observation by an evaluator or the supervisor, and results can sometimes be assessed using the agency's management information system. Care must be taken to ensure that results are related to the training and not other variables. At a minimum, training events should be evaluated with reaction forms, and ideally results (based on training objectives) should be assessed.

Performance Appraisal

Every organization has some kind of performance appraisal system. Whether the system is formal or informal, explicit or implicit, objective or subjective, the organization uses some method to evaluate the way employees do their jobs. This process can have a major influence on the effectiveness of the organization as a whole.

The performance appraisal should not be looked at in isolation and thought about only a few weeks before the employee's hiring anniversary date, when most policy and procedures manuals say the review should be done. Performance appraisal flows logically from a clearly defined job with clear standards and expectations and is based on the supervisor having worked closely with the subordinate over the previous rating period (see the next chapter). According to Millar (1998), "a good performance evaluation system should meet three criteria: it should be valid, reliable, and practical" (p. 222). This means that it should measure what it is supposed to measure, give consistent appraisals to all individuals, be acceptable to all staff, and be relatively easy to use.

Despite their limitations, performance appraisals serve several functions, each of which is important to the management of human resources. These functions boil down to two major purposes, which might seem to be in opposition to each other: *judgmental* and *developmental* (Daley, 1998, p. 369). Both are concerned with the employee's performance, but whereas developmental purposes focus on the growth of the employee and enhancing her or his skills, judgmental purposes focus on compliance with organizational expectations and often on related rewards or punishments. One way of addressing this dilemma is to have *multiple appraisals* (Meyer, 1991, cited in Daley, 1998, p. 370)—having separate appraisals for judgment and development at different times.

Another way to mitigate the inherent dilemmas of performance appraisals is to ensure that it is clearly based on the job itself: the job analysis discussed earlier (Daley, 1998, p. 376). The assessment should be concerned only with two factors: behavior and results (Daley, 1998, pp. 371–372), or what the employee has done with reference to job criteria and what the employee has accomplished with reference to stated objectives over the course of the rating period.

A further strategy to ensure that the appraisal process is seen as both fair and useful is to involve the subordinate in both the development of performance criteria and the appraisal process. (Criteria development will be addressed later in the sections on behaviorally anchored rating scales and management by objectives.) Involving the subordinate in the appraisal process is a notable advance over the traditional approach of having the supervisor doing all the assessing and rating. Supervisors and other staff who will be asked to implement the appraisal program need to receive ongoing training so that they can use rating mechanisms fairly and confidently. If supervisors and employees agree that the strengths and weaknesses being measured are the ones that matter, appraisal can provide guidelines for meeting the training and development needs of human service workers.

Millar (1998) suggests that

the ideal performance evaluation system should:

- emphasize managerial expectations as well as self-development and professional growth on each dimension by use of a benchmark (expected level of performance)

- include both generic (core [applicable to all employees]) and job-specific (á la carte [based on a particular job]) dimensions

- not be associated with pay or increments (annual raises)

- describe and be anchored in real events

- be responsive to both development and diminution in ability over time

- have a goal orientation step as part of closure

- fit all staff

- be able to grow and change with the organization. (p. 223. Adapted with permission.)

More technical/legal requirements, based on current case law, are these (Burchett & DeMeuse, cited in Daley, 1998, p. 376):

1. An up-to-date *job analysis* should be the foundation of the appraisal, so that expectations for performance are clear.

2. *Job-specific work behaviors* are the basis of the evaluation.

3. Clear *communication* is necessary so that all employees know the standards and process and receive feedback on their performance.

4. *Supervisory training* is necessary to ensure that supervisors have skills in using the instruments and handling the sessions.

5. *Documentation* is required not only to respond to possible appeals or lawsuits but also to ensure that all involved have the same knowledge about what was discussed and agreed to.

6. *Monitoring* will ensure that all aspects of the system are up-to-date and that procedures are being followed.

As was mentioned earlier, the process should be participative: the agency's system should be designed by a representative group of employees, and criteria for a specific job should be developed by the subordinate, the supervisor, and ideally others who know the subordinate's work. Generally an appraisal is done annually, and the best time seems to be the anniversary of the employee's beginning employment, if timely information on the employee's accomplishments and all relevant behaviors is available.

After the instrument (the appraisal mechanism, discussed next) is designed, it should be completed by evaluators in advance of the performance appraisal session. Results should be reviewed at the session, with a focus on development for the future, collaboration, mutual support, and fairness. The session should end with a joint assessment of the subordinate's strengths and accomplishments for the year and specific action plans for correcting problem areas and advancing further growth and development.

Appraisal Mechanisms _____

Any appraisal system depends on the use of some kind of mechanism to form the basis of rating employee performance. The best appraisal mechanisms come closest to evaluating the behaviors that actually distinguish between successful and unsuccessful job performance. Any mechanisms used should be based on objective criteria that have been established through analysis of the jobs being performed. Although this point may seem obvious, arbitrary and subjective performance measures are still too frequently used in human service organizations. The nature of many commonly used evaluation techniques makes unreliability and rater bias common. For example, every human service worker has used evaluation systems based on rating scales. Usually, a list of characteristics is presented, and the assessor is asked to rate the employee on each quality listed. Ratings are usually on three-, four-, or five-point scales, from "excellent" to "poor" or "needs improvement," with gradations in between. Such ratings are usually vague, subjective, unreliable, and ultimately not helpful in improving employee performance. Another historically common system, rating and comparing employees, has similar weaknesses. Performance tests (for example, rating videotapes of worker performance) have been less common but equally limited. Assessment centers, mentioned earlier, can be useful here if they are well designed.

The most objective approaches are *behaviorally anchored rating scales* (BARS) and the uses of *management by objectives* (MBO). These should therefore be the key elements of a rating system. The final form used should have the employee's role, the time period, all job standards, BARS and MBO factors and ratings, narrative by the supervisor, and any action plans for further development. Overall ratings should be based on a compilation from all raters, weighted if necessary using a formula agreed to in advance. Both the employee and supervisor should sign the form, which is typically reviewed and signed by the supervisor's supervisor and filed to be referred to during the next rating period if necessary.

Behaviorally Anchored Rating Scales

Five major steps are used in developing behaviorally anchored rating scales, or BARS. First, people who are familiar with the job list specific kinds of incidents that would illustrate effective or ineffective performance, referring to all dimensions of the job articulated in the job analysis. These incidents are then clustered into groups or performance dimensions. For each performance dimension, five to seven behaviors are developed to represent performance levels ranging from clearly deficient to outstanding. Typically the midpoint is the basic expectation for the position. Once incidents and performance dimensions have been selected, the incidents are scaled and a final instrument is developed. The incidents that have been selected now serve as "behavioral anchors" that translate important performance dimensions into concrete, behavioral, measurable terms. An example can be seen in the following subsection.

BEHAVIORAL DIMENSIONS: IDENTIFYING AND ASSESSING CLIENT PROBLEMS   This dimension considers your ability to identify and assess problems. Are you able to collect information and prioritize the presenting problems? Can you see how these problems interfere with client functioning?

   7—This person has a superior ability to collect data and identify significant client problems. He or she can expertly see how the problems interfere with client functioning.
   6—This person has an excellent ability to collect data and identify client problems. He or she can skillfully see how the problems interfere with client functioning.
   5—This person has advanced ability to collect data and identify significant client problems. He or she can readily see how the problems interfere with client functioning.
   4—This person has ability to collect data and identify significant client problems. He or she can see how the problems interfere with client functioning.
   3—This person has some ability to collect data and identify client problems. He or she can see, to some extent, how the problems interfere with client functioning.
   2—This person has deficiency collecting data and identifying client problems. He or she has difficulty appreciating how the problems interfere with client functioning.
   1—This person is unable to collect data and identify client problems. He or she cannot see how the problems interfere with client functioning.

SOURCE: Copyright 1998, National Association of Social Workers, Inc., *Skills for Effective Management of Nonprofit Organizations.* Reprinted with permission.

The shortcoming of this approach is that many people must spend long hours developing the instrument, and some human service managers might not want to devote a great deal of time and energy to performance appraisal. Once such an instrument has been developed, however, it will save time and effort by streamlining evaluation. In the long run, more time will be wasted by using inaccurate measures that take supervisors' time but do not provide real assistance in decision making.

Management by Objectives

As was noted in Chapter 3, management by objectives (MBO) is a commonly used mechanism to identify outcomes of service activities and other tasks such as special projects. Based on the strategic plan, objectives are set at the program level and then at lower levels, with involvement by those who will be responsible for their accomplishment. MBO is also extremely valuable as an element of performance appraisal (Daley, 1998).

As in the case of BARS, this process is based on the employee's job tasks. At the beginning of the annual cycle (or when new activities need to begin), the employee and supervisor meet to select four to five (up to eight or ten, based on particular employee assignments) major responsibilities for which the employee will be accountable over the year (rating period), and these are written as objectives. Objectives by definition are measurable and have a time frame. Ideally they should be stated in terms of *outcomes:* accomplishments that have clear benefits to clients or the organization (for example, ensuring that a percentage of a worker's clients are living independently by the end of treatment). There may also be *process* objectives, which are activities taken to reach outcomes, such as attending a training event. Standards can be based on historical results from past years or on grant or contract requirements. They should be both challenging, so that the employee will need to stretch, and realistic, so that achievement is possible. It should be agreed to in advance whether 100 percent accomplishment is expected (BARS levels may be used for this, with the basic expectation at the midpoint). All objectives should be reviewed together, with analysis, if necessary, to ensure that they are achievable by the employee in the reporting period with resources available and given existing organizational and environmental conditions. If some objectives are more crucial than others, they may all be weighted.

Critical Incident Techniques

Supervisor logs of important incidents demonstrating employees' strengths or weaknesses provide solid data that can be used to give feedback to employees. Such incidents should refer specifically to job-related criteria and be described specifically enough to enable later recall by the employee and supervisor. Supervisors using this method do need training to be as objective as possible in selecting and recording incidents. A halo effect can occur, with supervisors finding negative or positive incidents that support their overall impressions of certain employees. Critical incident summaries should be used only as an adjunct to more thorough systems such as BARS and MBO.

Valuing Diversity

The dominant formal organizations—business, government, and not-for-profit—in the United States have gone through three broad periods regarding ethnic and gender demographics of employees. In the first period, organizations were owned, managed, and largely staffed by white males. This history of discrimination does not need to be recounted here, except to note that the history of such organizations sometimes still affects aspects of organizational life. The second period dates from the beginnings of the civil rights movement in the 1950s until the affirmative action backlash that began in the 1980s. The third period of paradox and complexity began in the 1980s and is characterized by continuing conflicts over affirmative action, recurring documentation of discrimination in the workplace, greater attention to groups beyond the initial civil rights emphasis on African Americans and other people of color (sexual harassment and the glass ceiling, people with disabilities, gays and lesbians, and aging workers), and the current interest in the value of diverse and inclusive workforces.

In the new millennium, agencies need to go beyond earlier support of affirmative action to a strategic commitment to valuing, creating, and sustaining a diverse workforce because it is consistent with the values and policies of human service professionals such as social workers and because such agencies will, all other things being equal, be more effective and responsive to community needs and visions. *Equal employment opportunity* "is largely viewed as a means to prevent discrimination in the workplace on the basis of race, color, religion, gender, national origin, age, and physical and mental abilities," whereas *affirmative action* "emerged in response to pervasive employment discrimination [and] refers to proactive efforts to diversify the workplace in terms of race, ethnicity, gender, and even [sic] physical disabilities" (Riccucci, 1998, p. 166).

Diversity in this context represents a philosophy of valuing and working to create a workforce that includes qualified and committed workers from all sectors of society. This concept amounts to a change of organizational culture, from one in which homogeneity and conformity may be the norms, to one in which differences are valued and capitalized on, teams are common, and collaboration is a preferred method for dealing with conflict. According to Hyde (1998), this "mainstream" model of diversity makes three assumptions. First, the rationale for diversity is improved organizational performance. In fact, there is increasing evidence for the "business case" for diversity: that a diverse workforce makes better decisions (Guy & Newman, 1998, p. 88). Second, "diversity is conceptualized as all-inclusive, broadened beyond race and gender to encompass national origin, age, disability, sexual orientation, education, marital/parental status, functional specialty, religion, and leadership style as dimensions of diversity" (Hyde, 1998, p. 20). Third, diversity is both a goal and a process to be managed.

Federal Legislation

Diversity and discrimination are also addressed through legislation and executive orders in areas including equal employment opportunity and affirmative action. Efforts to secure equal employment opportunities for minorities and women in the United States can be traced back several decades, notably since World War II. Throughout this period, organized labor has regularly played an important role in the protection and promotion of workers' rights and, sporadically, in the promulgation of legislation supporting the rights of working women and minorities (Lawrence, 1987).

Some of the key pieces of equal employment legislation include *Title VII of the Civil Rights Act of 1964,* the *Equal Employment Opportunity Act of 1972,* the *Americans with Disabilities Act of 1990,* and the *Family and Medical Leave Act of 1993.* Since state laws and case law are changing in this area, a proactive manager keeps up-to-date on relevant laws and government policies in the agency's jurisdiction.

Enforcement of Federal Legislation

The Civil Rights Act of 1964, along with its later amendments, is enforced by the Equal Employment Opportunity Commission (EEOC), which maintains offices in a number of cities. An individual who believes that he or she has been a victim of employment discrimination can file a charge with the EEOC. After an investigation of the charges, the commission can seek a conciliation agreement with the employer. If no settlement is reached and if the EEOC decides that the employer is in violation, a suit can be filed by the commission (if the employer is a private company) or by the U.S. attorney general (if the employer is a public agency). If the EEOC does not bring suit, a "right to sue" letter is provided for the individual, who is then free to sue privately.

If the employer is found to have engaged in discriminatory practices, the company may be required to make up for losses suffered by the employee or applicant, often involving payment of back wages. If systematic discrimination has taken place, the employer might need to develop organization wide remedies, including affirmative action programs.

Affirmative Action

Affirmative action programs are designed to remedy discriminatory patterns that have existed in the past. *Affirmative action plans* (AAPs) "are systematic attempts to enhance employment opportunities for women, minorities, the handicapped, and other groups who have had great difficulty in either obtaining employment or being utilized at levels equal to their qualifications" (Heneman, Schwab, Fossum, & Lee, 1986, p. 54). An organization, recognizing that past inequities have brought about an underrepresentation of women and minorities in the workforce, can develop a set of goals for hiring and promoting groups that have been the victims of past discrimination. It should be emphasized here that goals are not the same thing as quotas. Opponents of affirmative action often criticize the use of quotas, which are in fact rare and are "generally set by courts after a finding of employment discrimination" (Riccucci, 1998, p. 173). *Goals* are flexible indicators of a desired level of employment for certain groups (*protected classes,* usually based on race, ethnicity, gender, disability, or age) and take into account both the specific problems of the organization and the presence of the protected class of workers in the available labor force.

Affirmative action plans are usually based on surveys of the local labor market and the employer's own workforce. If inequities are found, the employer develops goals, usually in terms of time guidelines, and decides on the methods to be used in reaching them. The goals might affect either the percentage of targeted groups in the company's total workforce or the number of women and minorities in managerial or professional positions.

In the 1990s, affirmative action laws were increasingly challenged and repealed. Any human services manager should become familiar with current laws and regulations at the state and federal levels.

Diversity Implications
for Human Resource Development

It is important that human service managers value and work toward achieving a diverse workforce and maintain an awareness of the basic intent of equal employment legislation and affirmative action. The spirit of equal opportunity recognizes that changes in human resource management practices must occur if equity in the workplace is to grow. These changes can take place only if people involved in hiring and appraising employees take time to think through the methods they are using. A great deal of discrimination happens not because decision makers purposely exclude women and minorities but because unexamined practices result in unintentional exclusion. Unfortunately, however, these unexamined practices are often the products of institutionalized sexism, racism, and other forms of discrimination. It is therefore incumbent on human service managers to reassess the organization's employment policies and practices to divest it of any possible vestiges of outmoded perspectives on the place of women and minorities in today's human service enterprise.

Concerns regarding discrimination and diversity can be addressed to a degree through fair and effective personnel policies such as those discussed earlier in this chapter. In addition, human service managers cannot afford to be aloof with respect to the controversies surrounding equal opportunity and affirmative action policies and practices. They must realize that the gains made over the years in equal employment and affirmative action programs have been outcomes of arduous and contentious sociopolitical processes and that maintenance of achievement in these areas also requires sociopolitical strategies and clear commitments on the part of agencies and their managers.

Diversity initiatives are becoming increasingly common as one way to address these issues. In one study of diversity efforts in human service organizations,

Hyde (1998) found that diversity efforts had three interrelated goals: "to create a welcoming place, to develop culturally competent staff, and to formulate critical analyses and take action" (p. 24). Diversity training involved "integrating diversity into the organization's daily activities, relationship-building, and consciousness-raising" (p. 26). In addition to providing cultural awareness training, agencies engaged in outreach and retention activities and in some cases addressed power dynamics in the agency. The fact that numerous barriers were identified suggests that this is an area of great challenge for agencies and will require strong leadership and a major commitment of resources over time.

Although some managers find it difficult to intensify commitments to diversity and inclusion and maintain their commitments to affirmative action in the face of economic adversity, equal employment opportunity must be maintained. In the private sector, fairness in hiring, appraising, and promoting diverse workers is often seen almost entirely as a benefit for the employees themselves. In human service agencies, the presence of diverse service providers and managers is also of major importance for clients. A human service program is limited in its effectiveness if the makeup of its professional staff differs significantly from that of its clientele. A diverse workforce affects the agency's services as much as it benefits the target group of employees.

People involved in making decisions about the allocation of human resources need to understand exactly how the intent and effects of their practices can either make the organization more effective and responsive or perpetuate discrimination against people of color, women, and others. Beyond this, managers and supervisors must be aware of the federal and state legislation and guidelines governing fair employment practices. In human service agencies, which are often too small to maintain separate personnel departments, equal employment opportunity must be understood by everyone with decision-making power.

In addition to serious and proactive efforts at compliance with relevant laws and policies, agency leaders need to be assertive in establishing a new organizational culture of inclusiveness and policies and practices that value diversity and advance it within the organization. An organizational culture that values teams and cross-functional collaboration and that works to avoid competition as a conflict management mode will be more welcoming for diverse employees and also create a better work environment for all. Evaluating and rewarding managers for diversity efforts, redesigning jobs to support team functioning, and mentoring underrepresented employees will help advance diversity goals. Mor-Baran and Chemin (1998) have suggested that the dimension of inclusion-exclusion perceptions of employees can be used to assess how supportive an organization's culture is to diversity. Specific activities for responding to and enhancing diversity are detailed elsewhere for the areas of aging workers (West, 1998), advancement of women as managers (Chernesky, 1998), sexual harassment (Hoyman & Stein, 1998), management of a multicultural workforce (Asamoah 1995), sexual orientation (Appleby, 1998), and general diversity issues (Daly, 1998).

Encouraging Volunteer Participation _____

The use of volunteers in administering and providing social services enjoys a long and fruitful history dating back to the 1880s, when volunteer community leaders served on the boards and as the "friendly visitors" of the Charity Organization Societies and as social advocates in the settlement house movement. The patterns of volunteering have changed, however: volunteers are likely to be involved in more than one cause (Dunn, 1995), and the roles filled by volunteers have been changing. Perlmutter and Cnaan (1993) found that many volunteers were involved not only in direct practice but also in administration, advocacy, and policy. Well-planned and competently administered volunteer programs are well worth the effort to both agency and clients (McCroskey, Brown, & Greene, 1983).

The use of volunteer human service deliverers must be as carefully planned as the hiring of paid employees. Determining the need for and the organization's readiness for volunteers is the first step (Dunn, 1995). Dunn has suggested the following questions as part of this assessment:

- What is to be achieved through a volunteer program?

- Is there a legitimate need for a volunteer staff?

- How committed are the board of directors and upper-level management to establishing and monitoring a volunteer program?

- Can the work be divided into jobs, some of which can be performed by part-time volunteers? (p. 2485)

Other questions that should be asked would ensure that potential volunteers are available, there are resources for training and supervision, and staff would be supportive of a volunteer program. A volunteer program then should be planned as any other program, using processes similar to those for paid staff regarding the development of job descriptions, recruitment, orientation, training, supervision, evaluation, and rewards and recognition (Dunn, 1995).

Burnout _____

The development of human resources must take into account the fact that agency employees are valuable and that steps must be taken to protect them, to the degree possible, from some of the work-related stress that can lead to burnout.

According to Johnson and Stone (1987), *burnout* "refers to a state of physical, emotional, and mental exhaustion resulting from involvement with people in emotionally demanding situations" (p. 67). It was originally identified in human service organizations but has also been found in other high-stress settings

(Maslach & Leiter, 1997). In the most popular conceptualization (Maslach, Jackson, & Leiter, 1996), it has three major factors:

- emotional exhaustion,

- a feeling of low personal accomplishment with clients, and

- a sense of depersonalization (a dehumanizing, uncaring attitude toward clients).

A key factor in burnout is an experienced loss of autonomy—"the sense that one can do as one wants" (Burisch, 1993, p. 83)—and is manifested most vividly in organizations as limited decision latitude (the opposite of participative decision making, discussed in Chapter 4). It includes a tendency to leave behind idealism and personal concern for clients and to move toward more mechanistic behaviors.

The most widely used tool for assessing burnout is the Maslach Burnout Inventory (Maslach et al., 1996). In lieu of using the instrument, managers can assess their organizations and staffs in other ways, from informal sensing to interviews to employee surveys (see Chapter 12). Because human service work is inherently stressful, managers should try to prevent burnout with proactive strategies, some of which are discussed here.

Causes of Burnout

Although the stressful nature of human service jobs has long been recognized, it was not until 1974, when Herbert Freudenberger posited the concept of burnout as an occupational disease, and 1976, when Christina Maslach elaborated on its consequences, that a serious effort was undertaken to elucidate the possible determinants of the syndrome. Since that time, numerous research studies and theoretical perspectives have been presented to describe, explain, and predict the conditions leading to worker burnout (Schaufeli, Maslach, & Marek, 1993).

Whereas researchers tend to agree that burnout has deleterious effects on the worker, clients, and organization, causes vary based on unique organizational conditions. Whereas initial research and conjecture focused on worker's personal deficits—a sort of blaming-the-victim perspective—or nettlesome worker-client interactions (Harvey & Raider, 1984), more recent explorations have concentrated on organizational variables. In an old but comprehensive and still-relevant model, Cherniss (1980) lists possible causes at the individual, organizational, and cultural levels:

- **Individual**—Personality factors (for example, "Type A") or unrealistically high career goals or expectations may predispose individuals to become burned out.

- **Organizational norms**—Bureaucratic rather than flexible management philosophies, lack of feedback, a competitive climate, large amounts of conflict, and low openness and trust can contribute to burnout.

- **Organizational roles**—Burnout may be more likely if an individual is experiencing role conflict (disagreements about expectations), ambiguity (unclear expectations), or overload (too much work); has a job with low motivating potential (see the prior section on job design); or has low autonomy.

- **Supervision and social support**—Supervisors who use participative decision making and are responsive to worker needs and concerns may help minimize burnout.

- **Cultural**—Aspects of the culture at large, including a declining feeling of community, frustrated expectations for the self-actualizing potential of work, and pervasive competition, create a climate conducive to burnout.

More recently, Maslach and Leiter (1997) have summarized these causes into the categories of work overload, a lack of control, insufficient rewards (from money to joy), a breakdown in community, the absence of fairness (trust, openness, and respect), and conflicting values.

Preventing Burnout

Burnout has an adverse impact on worker productivity and therefore on organizational effectiveness. Human service agencies cannot afford the loss in productivity involved when an active, enthusiastic professional burns out. This process can never be completely prevented because individual, as well as organizational, characteristics affect susceptibility. Cherniss (1980) suggests, however, that a number of positive steps can be taken to lessen organizational stress and prevent burnout.

One approach is to change the way jobs are structured. Many human service professionals find it stressful to work continually at a single type of service, often without feedback or collegial interaction. Changes might be as simple as assigning more varied types of clients to each service deliverer or, of course, lowering caseloads. Flextime, part-time work, job sharing, and increased use of volunteers can provide some relief from inherently demanding jobs. Creating opportunities for new program development and new career options for staff can help. Adaptations must depend on the unique problems of a specific organization, but the key factor is to find ways to modify routine patterns and to increase the rewards that participation in human service delivery can provide.

Attention should also be paid to the supervisory relationships that each human service professional has the opportunity to form. New professionals often need support, information, and some degree of structure because they tend to be concerned about their own competence. Supervisors can help human service workers make the transition from newcomers to self-sustaining, confident professionals if they devote energy to establishing strong relationships and if they understand their own importance as role models. Supervisors, too, can burn out, and they need feedback, support, and interaction in their own work lives.

The organization as a whole can also provide a more or less stressful work environment depending on whether all organizational members share a sense of excitement and strong purpose and clear goals and objectives. Human service professionals, paraprofessionals, and volunteers can often withstand very demanding work if they feel they are participating in an effort that will lead to major accomplishments. Clarity of purpose in an agency and a commitment to ongoing learning and development of staff and the organization can help in providing such a supportive climate.

To address the underlying causes of burnout, a participative management philosophy such as the human resources model discussed in Chapter 4 will maximize staff autonomy and allow creative and innovative ideas to flourish. Also in this vein would be strategies for ongoing organizational improvement such as the use of problem-solving groups and other organizational change activities covered in Chapter 11. These organizational strategies for burnout prevention and remediation are a major responsibility of management. Most important here are helping ensure that workers are doing meaningful work (Cherniss, 1995), are not overloaded with impossible demands, and have the decision-making autonomy appropriate for professionals. Such activities can be undergirded by the organization and its managers articulating and acting upon humanistic values (Maslach & Leiter, 1997).

At the individual level, staff development interventions such as in-service training, especially on subjects such as time management, and peer support groups for problem solving and resource exchange can provide symptomatic relief from burnout but do not address underlying causes. This is also true for the provision of counseling for employees that can help meet staffs' emotional needs, usually offered through employee assistance programs, to which we now turn.

Employee Assistance Programs

In any organization, most employees want to be productive. Unfortunately, a number of factors can stand in the way, causing job performance to deteriorate and productivity to decline. These influences—all correlated highly with absenteeism, loss of motivation, and errors—include both job-related stress and personal concerns. Alcoholism, drug dependency, emotional problems, family conflicts, interpersonal difficulties, and legal and financial issues are all personal matters. They become the concern of the organization, however, when they affect on-the-job behavior.

Many organizations provide *employee assistance programs* (EAPs) for workers experiencing such problems (Van Den Bergh, 1995). EAPs typically offer direct services including counseling and referrals as well as crisis management services after incidents such as workplace or client violence. Indirect services include lectures or workshops on subjects to enhance employee well-being, supervisor training, and employee problem-solving task forces.

There is now clear evidence that EAPs can both improve productivity and lower costs (Van Den Bergh, 1995). Human service agencies are faced with increasing challenges along with level or declining resources. They cannot afford to lose the productivity of their most valuable resource: the people who make the programs work. Employee assistance programs and burnout prevention strategies can help mitigate the effects of these pressures, and effective practices in the areas of hiring, training, and appraising staff can have a major effect on creating an environment conducive to effective and satisfying work.

Summary

For programs to function properly, they must have well-designed jobs that allow workers to use their skills and talents fully. Staff need to be carefully selected, and an ongoing training program should be available to ensure that they remain responsive to program and job needs. An agency needs a good performance appraisal system to provide feedback and ensure that staff are meeting expectations. The value of a diverse workforce is becoming more and more clear, and an agency should give deliberate attention to creating a welcoming and inclusive environment for all staff and clients. The use of volunteers, burnout prevention, and employee assistance programs are ways of ensuring that staff can function effectively in the challenging human services environment. A key factor in pulling these processes together is the supervisory relationship, the subject of the next chapter.

Discussion Questions

1. Suppose you were directing an agency that needed to extend its community outreach programs to generate revenues. What would you do if you believed that this direction was right, but the professional service deliverers insisted on staying in their offices and waiting for individual clients to come in? Would you try to change the behaviors of these professionals? What steps would you take to train them for new functions?

2. If you were setting up an assessment center to measure the competencies of current or potential human service workers, what types of measurements might you use? What competencies would you be looking for?

3. We favor equal employment opportunity and affirmative action not just because of their legality but also because of the importance of having diversity among service deliverers. What ways do you see for combating racism, sexism, and other forms of discrimination in human service organizations?

4. Many agencies use volunteers because of their helpfulness in strengthening ties to the community and because of the personnel dollars saved. Although this approach can be very positive, many people have pointed out that using volunteers can cost human service workers their jobs. Should agencies be encouraged to save human resource costs by using volunteers in place of salaried personnel? What do you see as the primary arguments on either side of this question?

Group Exercise

In groups of six to eight people, develop a job description for a human service worker in a hypothetical agency. Use this job description as the basis for role-played employment interviews. Take turns playing the parts of interviewer and job applicant, with the other group members observing. When observing, watch for the effects of the job description that has been developed. Is it clear enough to provide guidelines for the interviewer? Think also about suggestions you can make to the interviewer concerning his or her skills in eliciting needed information.

CASE 6

Director of Training

When the Atlantis Community Mental Health Center became an umbrella organization, the traditional services normally offered by the center were combined, for the first time, with the more nontraditional approaches favored by the small "grass-roots" agencies in the community. ACMHC now included both "the center" and the "neighborhood outposts" that had formerly been independent agencies.

This drastic change in the organization brought with it the need for new approaches to training. Nelson Richards, director of the center, recognized this need. His response was to hire Ellis Shore, a mental health professional with experience in university teaching, to design and implement a comprehensive training program.

Richards's directive to his new training director was clear. The skills of the paraprofessionals in the outposts were to be upgraded. Richards felt that the service deliverers in the community-based agencies lacked the background and education that he would expect of professional helpers. These people were now working under the Atlantis name, so they would have to provide professional-level services. He would leave the methods up to Shore, but the mental health skills of the community agency workers would need to be enhanced.

Shore began this work with great enthusiasm. He created, almost single-handedly, a series of workshops designed to develop trainee competencies in individual, family, and group therapy. He also developed a complex schedule that would allow the workshops to be provided on-site at each of the neighborhood centers. Knowing that he could not provide all the training himself, he involved several mental health professionals who had been employed by the center before the creation of the umbrella organization. He asked these professionals to serve as cotrainers and made sure to include people with varying therapeutic orientations, from psychodynamic to behavioral to existential.

Shore and his cotrainers agreed that the workshops he had designed would upgrade trainees' skills if they became actively involved in the process. Use of the outposts as training sites would mean that participation would be so convenient for agency workers that attendance could be purely voluntary.

With high expectations, the training director and his cotrainers began the first series of workshops. At the first workshop, twenty participants appeared. Although only twelve remained for the whole day, Shore was relatively pleased with the turnout. At the second workshop, only ten paraprofessionals attended. The third drew only six.

Shore, in frustration, confronted Isabel Phillips with this evidence of lack of motivation among agency workers. Phillips, who had administered one of the more successful of the city's community-based agencies and who was now coordinator of the outreach program, was in touch with the paraprofessionals in the neighborhood centers. She would know how to get these service providers more actively involved.

"Isabel, I've been given the authority to make these workshops compulsory," Shore pointed out, "but I really don't want to do that if I can avoid it. How can I light a fire under these people? You know them. Why aren't they motivated?"

"As a matter of fact, you're right," Phillips responded. "I do know these people, and what I know about them is that they're the most motivated people you're ever going to see in your life. Every one of them has put in more hours in a week than you can imagine for pay that hardly puts them over the poverty level. They do it because they believe in what they're doing and because they know how much they're needed. When you say they're not 'motivated,' I have a hard time picturing what you're talking about."

"Well, what I'm talking about is the fact that they're not showing up for these workshops, which they know are encouraged by the director, which they know they have released time for, and which they don't even have to step outside doors of their agencies to get to. Now, if these folks are so concerned about their work, something just doesn't fit."

"You're right, Ellis. Something doesn't fit, but the thing that doesn't fit is your training program. What makes you think they need upgrading in their therapeutic skills?"

"Isabel, are you kidding? That's what I was hired to do. When Richards gave me the job, he told me that he didn't care what methods I used, but that the skills of the paraprofessionals in the outreach programs had to be upgraded. That was the word he used: *upgraded.*"

"Well, let me tell you something about Richards. He's completely out of touch with the community. He's always been out of touch. He doesn't know what the people need from the agencies, and he doesn't know what kind of training the workers need. They don't do therapy in those agencies. They don't have the luxury of sitting in their offices dealing with one person at a time for months on end. They're out there in the streets, getting people organized and helping them deal with real, concrete problems. In fact, has it ever occurred to you that you just might be designing all

these beautiful training interventions for the wrong people? The folks in my agencies know what they're doing. It's the people in the center who need training. They don't know how to do anything but therapy, and the community isn't buying it. If you want to make a training contribution, why don't you hire yourself some paraprofessionals as cotrainers, go up to the center, and provide some on-site training on how to close the gap between the center and its so-called consumers? From what I hear, business isn't exactly booming in that big granite building uptown."

1. If you were Ellis Shore, what steps might you take to develop a more comprehensive and appropriate training program?

2. What special leadership issues might be involved in a decentralized agency such as the ACMHC?

References

Appleby, G. (1998). Social work practice with gay men and lesbians within organizations. In G. Mallon (Ed.), *Foundations of social work practice with gay and lesbian persons.* New York: Harrington Park.

Asamoah, Y. (1995). Managing the new multicultural workplace. In L. Ginsberg & P. Keys (Eds.), *New management in human services* (2nd ed., pp. 115–127). Washington, DC: NASW Press.

Burisch, M. (1993). In search of theory: Some ruminations on the nature and etiology of burnout. In W. Schaufeli, C. Maslach, & T. Marek (Eds.), *Professional burnout: Recent developments in theory and research* (pp. 75–93). Washington, DC: Taylor & Francis.

Chernesky, R. (1998). Advancing women in the managerial ranks. In R. Edwards, J. Yankey, & M. Altpeter (Eds.), *Skills for effective management of nonprofit organizations* (pp. 200–218). Washington, DC: NASW Press.

Cherniss, C. (1980). *Professional burnout in human service organizations.* New York: Praeger.

Cherniss, C. (1995). *Beyond burnout.* New York: Routledge.

Craft, J. A. (1979). Managing human resources. In G. Zaltman (Ed.), *Management principles for nonprofit agencies and organizations* (pp. 71–119). New York: AMACOM/ American Management Association.

Daly, A. (Ed.). (1998). *Workplace diversity issues and perspectives.* Washington, DC: NASW Press.

Daley, D. (1998). Designing effective performance appraisal systems. In S. Condrey (Ed.), *Handbook of human resource management in government* (pp. 368–385). San Francisco: Jossey-Bass.

Dunn, P. (1995). Volunteer management. In R. Edwards (Ed.), *The encyclopedia of social work* (19th ed., pp. 2483–2490). Washington, DC: NASW Press.

Foster, M. (1998). Effective job analysis methods. In S. Condrey (Ed.), *Handbook of human resource management in government* (pp. 322–348). San Francisco: Jossey-Bass.

Goldstein, I. (1993). *Training in organizations.* Pacific Grove, CA: Brooks/Cole.

Guy, M., & Newman, M. (1998). Toward diversity in the workplace. In S. Condrey (Ed.), *Handbook of human resource management in government* (pp. 75–92). San Francisco: Jossey-Bass.

Hackman, J., & Oldham, G. (1980). *Work redesign.* Reading, MA: Addison-Wesley.

Harvey, S. H., & Raider, M. C. (1984). Administrator burnout. *Administration in Social Work, 8*(2), 81–89.

Heneman, H. G., Schwab, D. P., Fossum, J. A., & Lee, D. D. (1986). *Personnel/human resource management.* Homewood, IL: Irwin.

Hoyman, M., & Stein, L. (1998). Sexual harassment in the workplace. In S. Condrey (Ed.), *Handbook of human resource management in government* (pp. 183–198). San Francisco: Jossey-Bass.

Hutton, T. J. (1984). How to recruit successfully. *Journal of Systems Management, 33*(12), 14–16.

Hyde, C. (1998). A model for diversity training in human service agencies. *Administration in Social Work, 22*(4), 19–33.

Johnson, M., & Stone, G. L. (1987). Social workers and burnout: A psychological description. *Journal of Social Science Research, 10*(1), 67–80.

Kaman, V. S., & Bentson, C. (1988). Roleplay simulations for employee selection: Design and implementation. *Public Personnel Management Journal, 17*(1), 1–8.

Lawrence, S. (1987, September). Has the push for workers' rights shaped social change? *Personnel Journal,* pp. 74–91.

Maslach, C., Jackson, S., & Leiter, M. (1996). *The Maslach Burnout Inventory manual* (3rd ed.). Palo Alto, CA: Consulting Psychologists Press.

Maslach, C., & Leiter, M. (1997). *The truth about burnout: How organizations cause personal stress and how to get out of it.* San Francisco: Jossey-Bass.

McCroskey, J., Brown, C., & Greene, S. R. (1983, Winter). Are volunteers worth the effort? *Public Welfare, 41,* 5–8.

Millar, K. (1998). Evaluating employee performance. In R. Edwards, J. Yankey, & M. Altpeter (Eds.), *Skills for effective management of nonprofit organizations* (pp. 219–243). Washington, DC: NASW Press.

Mor-Baran, M., & Chemin, D. (1998). A tool to expand organizational understanding of workforce diversity: Exploring a measure of inclusion-exclusion. *Administration in Social Work, 22*(1), 47–64.

Pecora, P. (1998). Recruiting and selecting effective employees. In R. Edwards, J. Yankey, & M. Altpeter (Eds.), *Skills for effective management of nonprofit organizations* (pp. 155–184). Washington, DC: NASW Press.

Perlmutter, F., & Cnaan, R. (1993). Challenging human service organizations to redefine volunteer roles. *Administration in Social Work, 17*(4), 77–95.

Rapp, C., & Poertner, J. (1992). *Social administration: A client-centered approach.* New York: Longman.

Riccucci, N. (1998). A practical guide to affirmative action. In S. Condrey (Ed.), *Handbook of human resource management in government* (pp. 165–182). San Francisco: Jossey-Bass.

Sager, J. (1995). Change levers for improving organizational performance and staff morale. In J. Rothman, J. Erlich, J. Tropman, & F. Cox (Eds.), *Strategies of community intervention* (5th ed., pp. 401–415). Itasca, IL: Peacock.

Schaufeli, W., Maslach, C., & Marek, T. (1993). *Professional burnout: Recent developments in theory and research.* Washington, DC: Taylor & Francis.

Swanson, C. (1998). A practical guide to conducting assessment centers. In S. Condrey (Ed.), *Handbook of human resource management in government* (pp. 349–367). San Francisco: Jossey-Bass.

Van Den Bergh, N. (1995). Employee assistance programs. In R. Edwards (Ed.), *The encyclopedia of social work* (19th ed., pp. 842–849). Washington, DC: NASW Press.

Van Wart, M. (1998). Organizational investment in employee development. In S. Condrey (Ed.), *Handbook of human resource management in government* (pp. 276–297). San Francisco: Jossey-Bass.

Walton, R. (1975). Criteria for quality of working life. In *The quality of working life: Vol. 1. Problems, prospects, and the state of the art* (pp. 91–118). New York: Free Press.

West, J. (1998). Managing an aging workforce: Trends, issues, and strategies. In S. Condrey (Ed.), *Handbook of human resource management in government* (pp. 93–115). San Francisco: Jossey-Bass.

CHAPTER 7

Building Supervisory Relationships

CHAPTER OUTLINE _____

The supervisor, who oversees the work of other staff, is a key link between organizational expectations and the provision of services. Most human service professionals find themselves playing at least limited supervisory roles throughout their careers. Some act as managerial supervisors, with responsibility and authority for overseeing the work of other supervisors, but most supervisors work with direct service staff.

The distinction between managerial and professional supervision may be less important to supervisory effectiveness than is the quality of the relationships that the individual supervisor is able to create. A model for supervision should be broad enough to accommodate the subtle role differences within the supervisory relationship. Such an all-encompassing model must take into account issues related to the supervisee's motivation, the supervisor's leadership style, the relevance of power and authority, and the special problems inherent in human service settings. Once again, a contingency perspective will be used: there is no one best approach for supervising a human service worker.

In this chapter, we will first discuss the role of the supervisor, the supervision process, and the dynamics of supervision. Then, we will review some models of motivation and the related issues of rewards and power and examine leadership styles as they apply to supervision. We will give particular attention to democratic supervision and participative decision making, which are commonly preferred approaches in supervising professionals. The chapter concludes with a review of some of the challenges of supervision, including discipline and termination.

Supervisory Roles

Today's human service supervisor must fulfill several roles and functions to ensure efficient and effective services to clients. First and foremost, the supervisor, by virtue of the position, is an organizational leader. As such, the supervisor, through positional authority, is charged with the legitimate use of power in mobilizing and directing supervisees' motivation and activity toward the accomplishment of organizational goals and objectives. This general purpose of supervision is accomplished through the assumption by the supervisor of three corollary roles and functions: *manager, mediator,* and *mentor.* Together with and anchored by the leadership component, these other dimensions of supervision in human services comprise a dynamic model of supervision.

As a *manager,* the human service supervisor must develop knowledge and skills in the areas of planning, budgeting, organizing, developing human resources, and evaluating programs. In today's world of organizational accountability, the administrative, or managerial, function of supervision has attained significant importance (Kadushin, 1985). The supervisor is responsible not only for his or her own performance but ultimately for the performance of his or her supervisees as well. In fact, supervisory performance is usually measured in terms of the performance of the supervisor's unit or team of supervisees. Moreover, the supervisor not only is accountable to the employing human service organization but becomes "part of the ethical means for assuring competent and accountable practice with and for clients" (Akin & Weil, 1981, p. 472).

As a *mediator,* the human service supervisor is at the nexus between the two primary technologies found in the human service organization: the technologies of administration and direct practice. It is where the two technologies meet that service goals are operationalized into functional service objectives. It is the responsibility of the supervisor to mediate between and articulate the two technologies in a manner that satisfies the requirements of both in the efficient and effective delivery of services. As a mediator, the supervisor is the link between administration and direct services, between policy formulation and policy implementation. A critical function of the mediator role involves the integration of vertical and horizontal interactions and interdependencies between the supervisor's staff and other levels and units of the organization. When necessary, the supervisor serves also as the mediator between supervisees and the organization's environment, including clients and other service providers. This role requires considerable skills in decision making and conflict management and a sensitivity to the needs of clients, staff, and the organization. It also leads to feelings on the part of the supervisor of being "caught in the middle."

In addition to fulfilling the roles and executing the functions of leader, manager, and mediator, the human service supervisor also assumes the role and function of *mentor* to his or her supervisees. As leader, the supervisor is concerned with the morale, productivity, and job satisfaction of subordinates, including their integration into the agency and their identification with agency mission, goals, and objectives. As manager, the supervisor must deal with the day-to-day administrative tasks of work planning, work assignment and delegation, and work coordination and evaluation (Kadushin, 1985). As mediator, the supervisor attends to the negotiation of relationships among staff members and between staff and other internal and external organizational units. As mentor, the supervisor's main responsibility is the professional growth and development of his or her supervisees.

It is in the mentor role that the supervisor has the best opportunity to provide individual emotional and psychological support to subordinates as well as to impart knowledge and help develop skills to enhance service delivery. This important role and function reflects the supervisor's commitment to professional values and ethics in service to clients and to the assurance that those values and ethics are reflected in the supervisees' practice. In this capacity, the supervisor differentially socializes the supervisees to such professional norms as fostering client self-determination, being nonjudgmental and objective, and protecting the confidentiality of case information. As mentor, the supervisor also helps workers develop self-awareness in terms of their own feelings and responses to clients and the various issues that clients present.

To execute faithfully the educational functions of the mentor role, the supervisor must have mastery of the direct service technology being employed by the supervisees. Although specifically addressing social work practice, Kadushin's

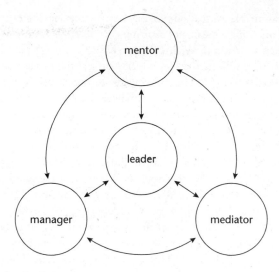

FIGURE 7-1
A Model of Human Service Supervision

(1985) comments on the educational component of supervision have relevance to other therapeutic technologies: "Educational supervision is sometimes termed clinical supervision. It is concerned with teaching the knowledge, skills, and attitudes for the performance of clinical social work tasks through the detailed analysis of the worker's interaction with the client" (p. 139).

This model of supervision places the leadership function and role in the center of the supervisory configuration of responsibilities, as depicted in Figure 7-1. It does not distinguish between managerial and professional supervision. It conceives of the supervisory role as a professional one involving managerial, mediating, and mentorship functions, all carried out through the medium of leadership within the context of professional supervisor-supervisee relationships. It takes into account issues related to the supervisor, the supervisees, and the human service agency. As such, it is a dynamic model, the interaction of whose parts are, ideally, always aimed at the enhancement of services to clients.

The Supervisory Dyad

The process of supervision has several complementary goals. The supervisor's responsibilities include the following:

- Providing encouragement and support for the supervisee
- Building motivation

- Increasing the mutuality of individual and organizational goals
- Enhancing the supervisee's competency in service delivery

Kadushin (1985) lists three other functions of supervision that, taken together, can accomplish the goals of the supervision process. *Administrative supervision* includes selecting and orienting the worker; planning, assigning, and evaluating work; communicating up and down the chain of command; and serving as an administrative buffer. *Educational supervision,* a staff development function, includes training and teaching and often occurs through client case discussions in individual or group session. Here Kadushin emphasizes the importance of giving effective and useful feedback to workers, offering these guidelines:

1. Feedback should be given as soon as possible after the performance. . . .

2. Feedback should be specific. One should be able to point to a specific intervention, act, or comment that needs praise or correction. . . .

3. Feedback should be objectifiable. One should be able to point to the concrete behavior which illustrates a deficiency in performance. . . .

4. Feedback should be descriptive rather than judgmental. . . .

5. Feedback should be focused on the behavior of the supervisee rather than on the supervisee as a person. . . .

6. Feedback should be offered tentatively for consideration and discussion rather than authoritatively for agreement and acceptance. . . .

7. Try to tie feedback as explicitly as possible to what you want the supervisee to learn. . . .

8. Good feedback involves sharing ideas rather than giving advice, exploring alternatives rather than giving answers. . . .

9. Feedback needs to be selective in terms of the amount that a person can absorb. (pp. 201–202)

SOURCE: Quoted from *Supervision in Social Work,* 2nd Ed., by A. Kadushin. Copyright © 1985 by Columbia University Press. This and all other quotations from this source are reprinted by permission.

Supportive supervision is concerned with helping the worker deal with job-related stressors and includes offering encouragement, reassurance, empathy, affirmation of the worker's strengths, and facilitation of problem solving. It is important that this not enter the realm of providing therapy for the worker, an inappropriate function of supervision.

The nature of the supervisory relationship depends on the specific situation, especially on the supervisee's needs and developmental level. It is unrealistic to think that one supervisor could form the same kind of relationship with each of his or her supervisees. In fact, the relationship with each supervisee changes over time as the supervisee grows in competence and independence.

In the context of the dyadic interaction, the two participants together should select both the objectives toward which the individual is expected to strive in his or her work and the goals of the supervisory process itself. It is important to have clarity concerning both the supervisee's work objectives and the supervisor's role in providing support and assistance.

It is especially helpful to think of the supervisee's needs in terms of the Hersey and Blanchard model of readiness in motivation and ability (Hersey, Blanchard, & Johnson, 1996). The supervision needs of a "high-readiness" supervisee can be expected to differ significantly from those of an individual who needs active assistance either in the development of ability to perform or in the enhancement of willingness to learn.

In human service settings, the equivalent of the less mature worker is simply one who does not have a fully developed set of goals, methods, and motivations for meeting client needs. The major factor is not the supervisee's length of time on the job or years of training but rather his or her readiness to function independently. A specific supervisee may need additional task supervision to gain competence in a new area, or he or she may simply prefer a close working relationship with the supervisor. Whether the level of readiness is defined in terms of abilities or personal needs, the supervisor's goal should be to help the worker move steadily toward higher levels of maturity and thus increased autonomy. A supportive supervisory relationship can form the basis for moving the individual from a stance of dependence to one of independence.

Throughout the supervision process, the supervisor and supervisee work together to specify objectives, clarify the criteria against which progress will be measured, and identify movement from one stage to the next. The supervisor must also specify his or her own contributions to the relationship, ensuring that the degree of personal support and task-oriented training needed will be offered. The supervisory contract involves recognizing both the supervisee's work objectives and the supervisor's contribution toward meeting them. As the worker becomes increasingly competent, the relationship may move away from a high task orientation to a more supportive interaction and, finally, to increased delegation and autonomy.

Skilled supervision is needed in the joint selection of goals in the attempt to find commonality between the supervisee's individual needs and the agency's or program's mission. When dealing with a professionally competent supervisee, the supervisor should place a high priority on seeking a set of goals and objectives that are acceptable to both parties of the supervisory dyad. These goals must be based on a recognition of changing client needs, with both supervisor and supervisee attempting to determine what amount and kinds of services the specific worker can reasonably be expected to provide. The degree to which additional training or support is needed should also be specified. Most important, the supervisor should accept that, once agreement about goals and objectives has been reached, the mature supervisee should be allowed to work in an autonomous fashion.

Yet autonomy does not mean isolation. Throughout the supervisory process, the relationship between supervisor and supervisee remains important. Although the need for active intervention may lessen, the supervisory dyad thrives in an atmosphere of trust and supportiveness. The supervisee in a human service setting is learning not just to perform tasks but to use the self as an instrument for helping others. That process implies a need for continual growth and nondefensiveness. In human service organizations, workers should be, and usually are, motivated by high needs for achievement and effectiveness. Their continued motivation—whether they are professionals, paraprofessionals, or volunteers—depends on the degree to which their jobs can be enriched and the degree of involvement they feel in the ongoing work of the program.

The Supervision Process

Shulman (1993) uses the term *interactional supervision* to emphasize the role of supervision as helping the worker manage interactions with the various systems (for example, agency processes, clients, staff) in the work environment. His model of supervision outlines "phases of work" that occur over the life of a supervisory relationship and within a supervision session: preliminary, beginning, work, and endings and transitions.

The *preliminary phase* occurs before the first meeting of the supervisor and staff. A key skill at this stage is *tuning in:* "trying to develop some preliminary empathy by putting oneself in the place of the other person" (p. 36). It will also help to tune into one's own feelings, assessing one's own "fears and concerns."

The *beginning phase* is concerned with contracting, including clarifying the purposes of the supervision, specifying the supervisor's role (for example, giving direction or facilitating regarding cases), and resolving questions of supervisory authority. In addition to sharing one's sense of purpose as a supervisor and discussing one's role conception, the supervisor should also solicit feedback from staff regarding their perceptions and "discussing the mutual obligations and expectations related to the supervisor's authority" (p. 41). Shulman notes a common mistake of new supervisors: the "hired-gun syndrome" (p. 52), in which the new supervisor feels the need to "lay down the law," using an authoritarian management style to attempt to show one's boss that things are changing. A more proactive approach would be to spend a large amount of time listening to one's new subordinates; validating their positions, ideas, and concerns; and mutually agreeing on a contract for working together to accomplish organizational goals.

Shulman's middle phase, or *work phase,* of supervision is organized around using groups of relevant skills. *Sessional tuning-in skills* include anticipating feelings or issues that are likely to come up during the session. While this is useful preparation, the supervisor should be prepared to quickly abandon preliminary expectations and adapt to the reality of what is actually presented for discussion. *Sessional contracting skills* enable the supervisor to plan with workers the agenda for the session. *Elaborating skills* are used after an issue is raised for discussion and include moving from the general to the specific (getting details on a situation to focus discussion), containment (holding back one's impulse to quickly jump in and answer a question prematurely), focused listening, questioning, and responding to silence by trying to draw out its meaning with questions. *Empathic skills* are useful in helping workers share frustration and deal with job stress. *Skills in sharing one's feelings* help the staff see the supervisor as a human being who is not always in control and on top of things. Related to this is *showing vulnerability,* which can both model appropriate self-disclosure and allow a "clearing" of one's feelings so that empathy can begin. *Showing anger* can be a useful skill, acknowledging that it is a normal emotion that can lead to dysfunctions such as apathy if it is suppressed. Showing vulnerability and anger may make it easier to express more positive feelings such as warmth and caring. Finally, *skills in making a demand for work* are essential for moving beyond the discussion of feelings and issues to helping staff develop an action plan, for dealing with a client or staff or for self-development.

Shulman uses the term *facilitative confrontation* to represent the skill involved in being both demanding and supportive. *Partializing* is a useful way to begin problem solving: breaking problems down into more manageable parts for action. An additional technique is *rehearsing:* helping staff practice the handling of a difficult situation through role playing. Other tactics regarding the demand for work are keeping the worker focused on the problem at hand and "challenging the illusion of work": confronting the worker(s) and even oneself when there is much discussion with little meaning. *Skills in pointing out obstacles* can help here: creating a climate in which discussion of "taboo" areas is possible or allowing discussion of authority issues. *Skills in sharing data* are important: the supervisor should be alert to the right time to share her or his knowledge on an issue, sharing opinions in a way that they do not have to be automatically accepted. *Sessional ending skills* including summarizing, generalizing from the case to larger principles, and identifying next steps to help ensure proper closure to a session. Finally, if a pattern of "doorknob communications" (raising a huge problem when reaching for the door at the end of the session) develops, the supervisor will need to confront this with demands for work earlier in the session.

These skills are relevant whether supervision is done individually or in a group. They may be particularly valuable when dealing with difficult issues such as a client's death, death of or an attack on a worker, public criticism of a unit or agency, cutbacks or reorganizations, or a social trauma such as large-scale social unrest in the community. Skills of tuning in, empathy, sharing feelings, and demands for work can be especially useful in helping staff deal with such issues.

Shulman also notes that the supervisor may on occasion have to help staff deal with difficult aspects of the agency as a system such as huge caseloads, political dynamics in the agency, and autocratic upper management. It is important that the same processes are used: allow the sharing of feelings, but do not let this degenerate into nonfocused complaining; rather, focus on the demand for work: changing what can be changed within the team and proactively developing ways to address larger issues as is possible.

The *ending and transition phase* of the supervisory relationship may involve a promotion, a new job, voluntary resignation, a layoff due to funding cutbacks or a grant ending, or a termination. Shulman identifies some common themes needing attention regardless of the ending circumstances. There may be denial, with little discussion of staff feelings; a sense of urgency to wrap up unfinished business; feelings of guilt regarding opportunities to do more that were not taken. Supervisors can deal with endings proactively with the work team by announcing the ending date; addressing dynamics regarding issues such as denial; sharing one's own feelings (positive and negative); and allowing staff to share their feelings, celebrate the contributions of the worker, say good-bye, and reach closure. Individually with the worker, the supervisor can help strategize wrapping up with clients and can facilitate a mutual evaluation of the supervision, to highlight learnings. Some agencies also have a formal *exit interview* process, conducted by the supervisor or human resources manager, that allows the worker to provide feedback to the agency that may be useful for improving organizational processes.

Making the Transition to the Supervisory Role

Many new supervisors find the transition from independent practitioner to manager and motivator of others difficult to make. Managerial functions can be carried out effectively by human service professionals if their clinical training is supplemented by the development of leadership skills.

Yet the transition from service provider to synthesizer is by no means easy. The professional must move from the position of being nonjudgmental with clients to one of being an evaluator of workers, from a stance of encouraging clients to take total responsibility for their own goals to one of motivating other human service workers to strive toward the meeting of mutually accepted objectives. These sometimes subtle differences often lead to ineffective supervision, with the individual either placing total focus on relationship behavior at the expense of the tasks to be performed or, recognizing that accustomed behaviors are not workable in this new situation, focusing total attention on the task in an authoritarian style. These difficulties in finding a comfortable leadership style are exacerbated by the problems inherent in human service organizations: the facts that appraisal of the quality of work is difficult and that those being supervised are often professionals who themselves have little interest in conforming to organizationally defined expectations.

A number of other transitional issues are involved in moving from direct practitioner to supervisor, not the least of which is the shift in both position and occupation, requiring new sets of skills and knowledge and involving greater responsibilities and authority. According to Kadushin (1985), the supervisor "has responsibility to the supervisees for administration, education, and support, and ultimate responsibility for service to the client." Additionally, he or she "assumes greater responsibility for policy formulation in the agency and community-agency relationships," and, "instead of being responsible for a caseload, the supervisor is now responsible for a number of caseloads" (p. 299).

Adaptation to the exercise of authority is another issue facing the new supervisor. The principle of client self-determination, so protected and promoted in direct practice, does not enjoy the same prominence in the supervisor-supervisee relationship. As an employee of the agency, the worker is subject to the organization's policies and procedures and its administrative directives, commonly implemented by the supervisor. The worker's freedom of choice is usually limited to complying with those policies, procedures, and directives or selecting to work elsewhere. By the same token, the supervisor has no choice but to enforce administrative dicta if the supervisor wishes to remain in that position. This is not to say that workers cannot and should not be allowed to participate in decision making. What it does mean is that not in all cases will all workers accept administrative decisions and that it is the supervisor's responsibility to exercise the authority inherent in the position to ensure that these decisions are carried out. The new supervisor must therefore learn to live with the consequences of sometimes enforcing unpopular decisions.

Another transitional issue is one of either partially or completely giving up the satisfaction of direct therapeutic contact with clients in favor of nontherapeutic contact with supervisees. In his or her new role and occupation, the supervisor learns to derive satisfaction from serving clients through others and from helping workers grow and develop professionally.

The shift from worker to supervisor thus entails several changes in perspectives and behaviors, in allegiances and responsibilities.

> In accepting the transition, the new supervisors face the complex processes of developing a clear conception of what the new position entails behaviorally and attitudinally; they have to divest themselves of old behaviors and attitudes appropriate to the direct service worker's position and learn and commit themselves to behavior and attitudes appropriate to the new position; they have to emotionally accept a changed image of themselves and a changed relationship with former peers and newly acquired colleagues. (Kadushin, 1985, p. 306)

Transition involves change, and change can be painful. Change, however, can also offer the opportunity for personal development and self-actualization, and it is in this latter dimension that the neophyte supervisor can find solace and encouragement.

Theories of Motivation

Supervision requires an understanding of the complex needs that affect individual performance. These needs have been categorized and explained in a number of ways. At the broadest level, motivation theories are grouped as *content theories,* which have specific motivating factors, and *process theories,* which are content-free and describe the ways in which needs, behaviors, and rewards may interact. We will first review the three most common content theories of motivation, followed by a discussion of the most popular process theory: expectancy theory.

Content Theories

MASLOW'S HIERARCHY OF NEEDS   Maslow's (1954) hierarchy of needs is familiar to human service professionals in the context of personality theory. This concept is also important in the study of motivation in the workplace.

According to Maslow, human needs can be identified in terms of a hierarchy, with higher needs coming to the fore after lower needs have been met. The hierarchy of needs includes, from lowest to highest, (1) physiological needs, at the level of basic survival; (2) needs for safety and security; (3) needs for belonging, love, and social interaction; (4) esteem and status needs; and (5) self-actualization needs. Maslow's notion is that the lower needs dominate until they have been reasonably satisfied. When the lower needs have been met, the human being becomes increasingly motivated to satisfy higher needs. Finally, the search for self-actualization, or the realization of individual potential, can begin.

This idea has strong implications for work-related motivation because leadership must involve the identification of those needs that will form the basis for employee performance. Traditionally, attempts to motivate workers were oriented toward the use of economic rewards and the giving or withholding of job security. This process recognized only the lower-order needs.

Maslow's theory makes it clear that once these lower-order needs have been met, they no longer serve as motivators. When economic needs have been met and when some degree of security has been achieved, workers will tend to seek ways to meet higher-level needs through their work. When that point has been reached, the supervisee can best be motivated if some method is used to help him or her strive toward self-actualization. The worker at this level can be motivated only if the job itself allows for some degree of creativity, autonomy, and growth toward increased competence. It should also be remembered that if an agency is going through funding cuts or if there are real threats to security such as possibilities of client violence, higher-order needs will be replaced in prominence by lower-level ones until concerns related to basic needs are resolved.

HERZBERG'S MOTIVATOR-HYGIENE THEORY   The notion of differing sets of motivating needs is enhanced in the work of Herzberg (1975), who makes a clear distinction between the factors related to job dissatisfaction and those involved in producing job satisfaction and motivation. The factors that relate to job dissatisfaction, what Herzberg calls *maintenance factors,* involve such aspects of the work environment as the fairness of company policies, the quality of supervision, relationships with supervisors and coworkers, salary, job security, and working conditions. These are not motivating factors; their presence or absence determines whether the worker will be dissatisfied with the work setting. The *motivator factors* relate to the job itself and involve the ability of the specific job to offer the worker opportunities to accomplish something significant, receive recognition for accomplishments, grow and develop, gain increased responsibility, and advance.

According to Herzberg, the maintenance factors simply trigger the worker's pain avoidance behavior, and the motivator factors relate to the need for growth and advancement. These growth factors are intrinsic to the nature of the job and relate to job satisfaction. Attention to hygiene factors is insufficient to motivate workers. The only way supervisees can be effectively motivated is through attention to the degree to which their work provides chances for growth, development, and increased responsibility. Herzberg's notion is to use the concept of job enrichment, building into each job the maximum opportunity for challenge and advancement (see the discussion of job design in Chapter 6).

McCLELLAND'S NEEDS THEORY   McClelland (1965) suggests that three distinct motivators can impel individuals in the work setting: the need for achievement, the need for power, and the need for affiliation. Although workers may possess all these needs to some degree, each individual is most strongly motivated by one. Thus, the achievement-motivated person values personal success and views it in terms of his or her ability to achieve measurable accomplishments. The individual who is motivated by achievement needs sets individual goals that are ambitious but clearly attainable and seeks frequent feedback concerning his or her competence and success. The person motivated by affiliation needs is most concerned with interpersonal relationships and is most effective in a setting offering supportiveness and opportunities for positive interactions. The power-motivated worker, being primarily concerned with influencing others, is most highly motivated in a setting giving him or her the opportunity to meet this need.

McClelland also makes an important distinction between two types of power. *Personalized power* involves the worker acting to enhance her or his own power and influence without regard to larger organizational goals, and it is generally seen as dysfunctional. *Socialized power* is manifested through an attempt to influence others for the good of the organization as a whole; it is seen as a legitimate and valuable motivator.

This approach to motivation has several implications for supervision. First, it makes clear that people with differing motivational sets have contrasting supervision needs. The affiliation-motivated worker is likely to respond to a relationship-oriented style, but an achievement-motivated person can be most effective when he or she has been delegated tasks that allow for individual performance. A power-oriented worker can be put in a position of leadership such as chairing a task force, in which this person will have opportunities to influence others to accomplish desired tasks.

A second implication for supervision is that achievement motivation, which may be closely related to high performance on the job, can be developed. In many work settings, training modalities and job redesign have been used to increase individuals' achievement motivation, and this approach might work in human service settings. In fields such as counseling and social work, an emphasis has historically been placed on affiliation—building relationships—with less attention to achievement. In counseling, for example, the client is seen as responsible for achieving change and the worker acting as a catalyst. Power dynamics in the past were typically seen as distasteful, with some exceptions in family therapy and radical therapy approaches articulated beginning in the 1970s. McClelland's model offers an opportunity for workers and supervisors to give greater attention to achievement of results, ranging from more adaptive behavior by a person with a mental illness to a welfare recipient getting a job. This model can also validate the appropriate use of power or influence to help create change.

Process Theories

EXPECTANCY THEORY   Expectancy theory is a general model of motivation developed by Vroom (1964). Bowditch and Buono (1997) have summarized its key elements:

> (1) an effort-performance expectation that increased effort will lead to good performance (*expectancy*); (2) a performance-outcome perception that good performance will lead to certain outcomes or rewards (*instrumentality*); and (3) the value or attractiveness of a given reward or outcome to an individual (*valence*). (p. 95)

An employee's effort is affected by the perceived value of the reward, the likelihood that effort will lead to the reward, and organizational factors such as the job context. Effort does not automatically lead to performance, however. It is moderated by the employee's abilities and traits and her or his role perceptions: work may not be performed if the employee feels an activity "is not my job." Performance may result in intrinsic rewards such as a feeling of accomplishment and extrinsic rewards such as praise or perhaps an extra day off (*lack* of performance may ultimately lead to no rewards, such as being fired).

The implications for supervisors are several. First, the supervisor should understand the *employee's* perceptions and abilities: what rewards are valued, what the employee's role conception is and views regarding equity, and whether effort does lead to rewards. The manager can then intervene by showing how effort leads to results and that results will in fact be rewarded in ways the employee appreciates.

The employee's role can be clarified, and additional training can be provided to enhance abilities if needed. As a *process* theory, this model allows for vast individual differences in terms of motivating factors: particular *content* (rewards) can be applied based on individual employee needs and values.

Applying Theories of Motivation

We will now review some supervision techniques that can be used to apply motivation theories toward worker performance. These include management by objectives, presented earlier as a tool in planning and performance appraisal, organizational behavior modification, reward systems, and the use of power and influence.

Management by Objectives as a Motivator

Although MBO may be thought of primarily as a planning and a performance appraisal tool (see Chapters 3 and 6), it also has strong implications for individual motivation. When an organization uses MBO, overall goals are developed through the agency's planning process. Objectives are then set so that each department or work unit has a set of objectives designed to work toward the general goals of the organization. Individuals participate with their immediate supervisors in setting objectives for their own participation in the overall design. These objectives then form the basis on which their performance is evaluated, using MBO as discussed in Chapter 6.

The use of MBO has been questioned, but it can improve productivity; in fact, the way in which it is implemented, rather than the technique itself, is usually the source of problems (Bowditch & Buono, 1997, pp. 99, 100). Several principles should be applied to maximize the effectiveness of the process. First, objectives should be developed *mutually* by the worker and supervisor, not imposed from above. If a worker feels pressured to set particular objectives, she or he is likely to comply only as much as possible to avoid negative consequences. Also, according to Bowditch and Buono (1997):

> If it is to be successful, MBO should be characterized by (1) an active give-and-take between managers [or supervisors] and their subordinates; (2) a high level of face-to-face communication; (3) top management support and involvement; (4) flexibility in setting goals; (5) attention to implementation details (e.g., communication of its importance; MBO-related training; sufficient time frame; monitoring); (6) a high degree of fit with the specific needs of the organization; and (7) an organizational culture and climate that supports openness and sharing. (p. 100)

The agreement that forms the basis of MBO can be broadened to involve a mutual understanding of the kinds of outcome rewards that might be attached to successful meeting of objectives, as well as the degree of support needed to "clear the path" to success.

Organizational Behavior Modification

Behavior modification has been viewed with skepticism or aversion by many in the human services. In fact, however, even a Rogerian therapist nodding earnestly and saying, "Tell me more," is using behavior modification. As is the case of many techniques, behavior modification is not inherently bad or good, effective or ineffective. Organizational behavior modification (OBM) is, of course, not universally necessary, but it can be a useful element of some supervisory relationships. Even if the organization does not comprehensively apply the model, OBM principles may be useful to a supervisor and worker as they discuss, for example, how the worker can best be rewarded.

Luthans and Kreitner (1975) suggest that OBM can provide a system through which positive reinforcement, or reward, is made contingent on improvements in work-related performance. The supervisor and supervisee would work together to define specific target behaviors. The individual's interests, concerns, and abilities would be taken into account as reinforcers for specific behaviors were selected. As the individual's work effectiveness improved, he or she would receive positive reinforcers. The supervisor would also try to make the work environment favorable for skill development. Ideally, as the supervisee became more effective and confident, he or she would have complete control over the reinforcement schedule, with little outside help needed. The behavior modification approach might be used more directly with new or inexperienced workers or with those grappling with a specific difficulty. Experienced professionals can more easily monitor and reward their own behavior.

Once again, Bowditch and Buono (1997) offer useful guidance. They suggest that in successful OBM programs,

> managers (1) reward people with what they value; (2) explicitly link the reward with the desired behavior; (3) appropriately fit the magnitude of the reward with the magnitude of the behavior; (4) are able to reward better performers more than average performer; and (5) give feedback and the reward after the performance. (p. 102)

Reward Systems

Rewards are a key element of all models of motivation. We will review here examples of the types of rewards available to supervisors. The broadest categories of rewards are *intrinsic* and *extrinsic*. Extrinsic rewards include direct compensation (basic salary, overtime and holiday premiums, and performance bonuses), indirect compensation (health, pension, and other benefits), and nonfinancial compensation (desirable work assignments and office furnishings such as a computer). Intrinsic rewards are those at the higher levels of Maslow's hierarchy and are almost unlimited, including opportunities for participation in decision making or personal growth, interesting work, autonomy, and a feeling of accomplishment.

Because supervisors often have no control over some rewards, such as pay levels or intrinsic feelings of satisfaction felt by the employee, they must work with the subordinate to discuss what available rewards are desirable and how and under what conditions they may be given. For example, the supervisor may be able to recommend that the employee be moved up a step in pay grade or receive a bonus for exceptional work on a special project. The supervisor may also have some control over assignment of office space or equipment such as computers and accessories. The supervisor can usually provide rewards in the form of interesting work assignments or training opportunities, and, of course, recognition in the form of praise and symbolic rewards such as token gifts is possible. If an agency has employee- or team-of-the-month awards, a supervisor can nominate staff. Supervisors should remain up-to-date on what an employee would feel rewarded by and be alert for opportunities to reward whenever appropriate.

Some rewards such as praise may be given independent of agency systems; many rewards should be an explicit part of the agency's personnel policies. This would include pay scales, criteria and standards for advancement, the use of merit pay or bonuses, and perhaps employee-of-the-month awards. Any effective reward system should meet these requirements (Orsburn, 1994):

1. They must be visible and understandable to the people.

2. They must be perceived as being consistent and fair.

3. They must be aimed at the appropriate target (individual or team).

4. They must dispense a valued reinforcer (money, praise, status, etc.).

Recent developments in formal reward systems, including merit pay (Gabris, 1998) and team-based rewards (Orsburn, Moran, Musselwhite, & Zenger, 1990), may be options for some organizations. Administrators designing such systems will need to consult specialized sources (see, for example, Siegel, 1998) for guidance to ensure that any system chosen is appropriate and well designed. Even within limited or traditional agency systems, an individual supervisor can use dialogue and creativity with a subordinate to develop meaningful and useful rewards.

Power and Influence

Power (the ability to control others), influence (the ability to persuade others), authority (formalized power or influence), and their uses are sometimes viewed with distaste or ambivalence by helping professionals, but it must be admitted that human service workers do use power and influence in their work, in enforcing requirements of clients or trying to persuade coworkers (Gummer, 1990). It therefore behooves human service workers to be comfortable with the appropriate use of power and influence and to use power tactics to enhance organizational performance.

The use of power in the supervisory relationship is an example. Fortunately, if a subordinate wants to succeed in a job or profession, the supervisor does have the power to influence behavior. In fact, some supervisors are more influential than others, depending on the kind and amount of power they hold in the organizational context. The interactions among power, authority, and leadership are complex, and they can have significant effects on the supervisory process.

An individual's power to direct or influence others comes from a variety of sources. Most observers of power relationships still find useful the categories suggested by French and Raven (1959): coercive power; legitimate, or positional, power; expert power; reward power; and referent power. Hersey and Blanchard (Hersey et al., 1996) add to this list information power and connection power. In a supervisory situation, the use of *coercive* power is based on the supervisor's ability to control punishments, such as poor job assignments, low compensation, or disciplinary action. *Legitimate,* or *positional,* power involves acceptance of the supervisor's right to influence the supervisee's work by virtue of his or her official position in a hierarchical organization. *Expert* power depends on the supervisees respect for the expertise and knowledge that the specific supervisor brings to the work setting. *Reward* power finds its source in the supervisor's ability to provide positive rewards as incentives for defined behaviors. *Referent* power depends not on the external trappings of power but on the personal relationship between supervisor and supervisee and on the degree to which the supervisee respects and identifies with the supervisor. *Information* power draws on the supervisor's access to valuable information: a supervisor who has "inside information" or knowledge of upcoming developments before others may be more highly valued by staff. *Connection* power becomes a reality when the supervisor is perceived as having close contact with other influential people.

A supervisor's power must be perceived as real by the supervisee if the relationship itself is to prove influential. Some supervisees will respond to position power alone, however, and others will respond only to other types of power such as expertise. Supervisors do want to influence supervisees' behavior, attitudes, and effectiveness, and the supervisory relationship is the vehicle through which this process takes place. The form of the relationship must take into account the source of supervisory power. If supervisees are inexperienced, insecure, or at the beginning of the training process, they might at first respond to supervisors who clearly control the rewards and punishments that the system has to offer. More experienced and professional human service workers tend to gain only from supervisory relationships based on their respect for the expertise of a supervisor who is willing to maintain an egalitarian affiliation. Ideally, the supervisory relationship can develop and change over time, as the supervisee is actively encouraged to take increasing control over his or her learning.

In human service settings, issues of power are often especially difficult because supervisors tend to be wary of overcontrolling others' efforts. Professionals want to be mentors but might feel uncomfortable about evaluating and influencing other workers' progress toward effectiveness. The supervisory relationship must recognize the existence of power while taking into account the unique aspects of the human service environment.

All of the models and principles of motivation discussed earlier can be applied by supervisors in their roles as leaders of workers and work units. We will now review some basic models of leadership, many of which are based on human resources theories of management covered in Chapter 4.

Leadership Models in Supervision

Leadership at the organizational level will be addressed in Chapter 11, but since *leadership* is defined as the process of influencing human behaviors in the interest of achieving particular goals, it is a key factor in supervision. The supervisor is clearly interested in influencing the supervisee's behavior, so some kind of "leadership event" must take place.

Two ways of looking at supervisory leadership will be presented here: Blake and McCanse's *leadership grid* (originally known as the *managerial grid,* developed by Blake and Mouton [1985]) and *situational leadership* as developed by Hersey and Blanchard.

Blake and McCanse's Leadership Grid

Blake and McCanse (1991) propose a two-axis model to make a distinction between *concern for people* and *concern for production or results.* On the grid, point 9 indicates maximum concern, whereas point 1 denotes minimum concern. The leadership grid pictures graphically the management styles of leaders, who are identified not necessarily by their behaviors but by their attitudes. Managers who are concerned primarily with output, or task, and are less concerned with people are considered 9,1–oriented managers. Those more concerned with people and who have little concern for production are considered 1,9–oriented managers. It is also possible to be a 1,1–oriented manager or a 9,9–oriented manager. The two axes are independent, so more concern for one factor does not necessitate less concern for the other, as is shown in Figure 7-2.

Thus, the 1,1 management style is one in which the manager displays little concern for either people or results. Often called an "impoverished" style, it implies a withdrawal from leadership functions. The 9,1–oriented manager, whose

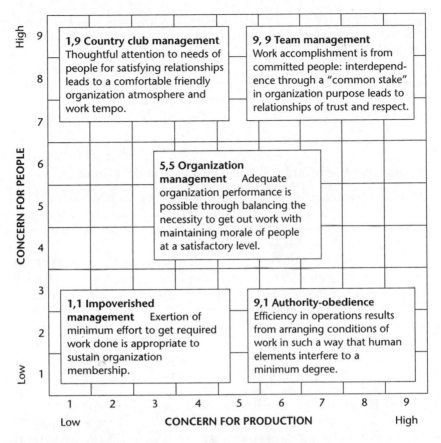

FIGURE 7-2
The Leadership Grid
SOURCE: From *Leadership Dilemmas—Grid Solutions,* by R. Blake and A. McCanse. Houston: Gulf
Publishing Company. Copyright © 1991. Reprinted by permission.

concern for production or results clearly overrides a concern for people, is a task
leader whose leadership depends on strong authority. The 1,9-oriented manager,
or "country club" leader, shows high concern for employees, providing protection and morale-building support at the expense of the tasks that need to be performed. The 5,5 orientation indicates a compromise, with the leader feeling that
concerns for production and for people are mutually exclusive and continually
trying to maintain balance. The 9,9-oriented manager sees concern for people and
concern for production as complementary. This team-oriented leader sees people
as potentially productive and enhances this productivity by building commitment
and mutual responsibility. New additions to the model are *opportunistic management,* in which managers use any style to enhance personal gain, and *paternalism/
maternalism,* in which rewards are based on loyalty and obedience.

According to the leadership grid, the 9,9 management style is seen as the ideal and one toward which managers can and should strive. While research on this theory has been inconclusive (Bowditch & Buono, 1997, p. 199), the model is based on well-developed leadership principles and offers useful intuitive guidance, suggesting that any leader or supervisor should be *concerned* about both people and results. According to contingency theory, however, leaders can be concerned about both factors and behave focusing on different combinations of them, as illustrated in situational leadership.

Hersey and Blanchard's Situational Leadership Model

Hersey and Blanchard (Hersey et al., 1996) suggest that the effectiveness of leadership styles depends to a great extent on the situation. Their model is unique in its attention to the variable of follower readiness (formerly maturity) level, which they see as the most important situational factor.

Hersey and Blanchard's situational model distinguishes between task behavior and relationship behavior on the part of the leader (see Figure 7-3). They contend that either high-relationship or high-task orientations can be appropriate, depending on the readiness level (ability and willingness to accomplish a specific task) of the follower or followers. In this model, ability is associated with relevant knowledge, experience, and skill; and willingness with the confidence, commitment, and motivation that one brings to the situation. The followers' readiness is measured in terms of the specific task to be performed; a given follower might be ready in one setting and not ready in another.

The bottom of the figure illustrates differing levels of follower readiness in terms of ability and willingness. The follower at the lowest level of readiness (R1) is both unable and unwilling to perform the task at hand. The follower at the R2 level is willing but unable. At the next level of readiness, the follower has the necessary ability to perform but not the appropriate level of motivation or confidence for working independently. At the highest readiness level, the follower combines both the ability and the willingness to perform the task with a minimum of assistance.

According to the situational leadership model, the leader should adapt his or her style to the followers' needs. A leader dealing with individuals who are at low readiness in terms of the task in question should use a high degree of structure or task orientation (either a "telling" or "selling" style). As the follower's maturity level increases, less structure and increasing attention to relationships become appropriate ("participating," such as in human resources models covered in Chapter 4). Finally, when followers have reached a high degree of maturity, the leader can decrease both supportiveness and structure ("delegating," also a use of human resources models such as Likert's System 4).

This model can be especially helpful to supervisors in human service settings, in which supervisees may vary greatly in terms of their readiness levels. Although a person new to an agency might require a high degree of structure, at

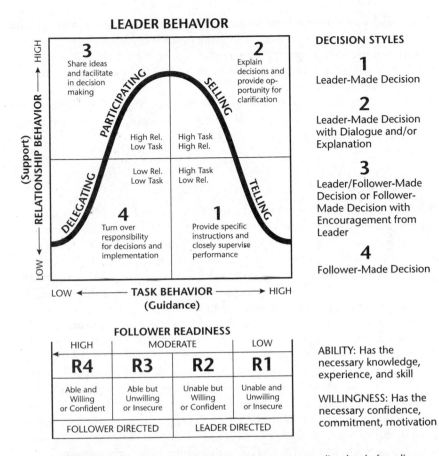

LEADER BEHAVIOR

DECISION STYLES

1
Leader-Made Decision

2
Leader-Made Decision with Dialogue and/or Explanation

3
Leader/Follower-Made Decision or Follower-Made Decision with Encouragement from Leader

4
Follower-Made Decision

(from the chart)
HIGH RELATIONSHIP BEHAVIOR (Support) LOW

3 Share ideas and facilitate in decision making — PARTICIPATING — High Rel. Low Task

2 Explain decisions and provide opportunity for clarification — SELLING — High Task High Rel.

DELEGATING — Low Rel. Low Task

TELLING — High Task Low Rel.

4 Turn over responsibility for decisions and implementation

1 Provide specific instructions and closely supervise performance

LOW ← TASK BEHAVIOR → HIGH
(Guidance)

FOLLOWER READINESS

HIGH	MODERATE		LOW
R4	**R3**	**R2**	**R1**
Able and Willing or Confident	Able but Unwilling or Insecure	Unable but Willing or Confident	Unable and Unwilling or Insecure
FOLLOWER DIRECTED		LEADER DIRECTED	

ABILITY: Has the necessary knowledge, experience, and skill

WILLINGNESS: Has the necessary confidence, commitment, motivation

When a Leader Behavior is used appropriately with its corresponding level of readiness, it is termed a High Probability Match. The following are descriptors that can be useful when using Situational Leadership for specific applications:

S4	**S3**	**S2**	**S1**
Delegating	Participating	Selling	Telling
Observing	Encouraging	Explaining	Guiding
Monitoring	Collaborating	Clarifying	Directing
Fulfilling	Committing	Persuading	Establishing

- -

TASK BEHAVIOR   The extent to which the leader engages in defining roles telling what, how, when, where, and, if more than one person, who is to do what in: goal setting, organizing, establishing time lines, directing, and controlling.

RELATIONSHIP BEHAVIOR   The extent to which a leader engages in two-way (multi-way) communication, listening, facilitating behaviors, socioemotional support. Includes giving support, communicating, facilitating interactions, active listening, and providing feedback.

FIGURE 7-3
Situational Leadership®

SOURCE: Situational Leadership® is a registered trademark of the Center for Leadership Studies, Escondido, CA. Used with permission. All rights reserved.

least temporarily, a seasoned professional might be comfortable only with the kind of independence allowed in the fourth quadrant (delegating). It is especially important that the human service professional recognize the individualized nature of motivation and make distinctions between both individual followers and stages in one supervisee's development.

Situational leadership offers perhaps the most direct guidance regarding contingency factors in leadership behavior. In the next section, we will review some additional principles of contingency theory.

Contingency Theory

The idea that varying leadership styles may be appropriate in different situations was studied in depth by Fiedler (1967). While his own theory has mostly been studied only by his students and associates, and although the model's specific elements have not been proven to be the key ones, his articulation of the contingency perspective has been extremely valuable. Effective leadership is generally seen as a function of the subordinate, the supervisor, and the situation. Subordinate factors are addressed thorough motivation theory. Leadership theory provides guidance with respect to both the worker and the supervisor. Situational factors are relevant particularly when time is critical or a crisis is occurring. A participative manager may become very directive during a crisis and workers normally preferring a democratic style will comfortably respond to such an approach under those conditions. We will apply contingency theory here with reference to the models of motivation already discussed and the use of leadership styles.

Morse and Lorsch (1975) adapted the notion of contingency theory in organizational structure to questions relating to individual motivation. The common factor Morse and Lorsch identify is that of the need for competence:

> All people have a need to feel competent; in this one way they are similar. But in many other dimensions of personality, individuals differ, and these differences will determine how a particular person achieves a sense of competence. . . . We must not only seek a fit between organization and task, but also between task and people and between people and organization. (p. 387)

The competency need, shared by all, can be met in a variety of ways. How it will be met depends both on the individual's other needs, such as the need for affiliation or power, and the organization's other needs, such as the need to adapt structures to environments. The motivational process becomes one of balancing organizational, task, and individual needs so that one worker's tasks both allow for his or her sense of competence and fit the nature of the work to be done by the organization as a whole.

Contingency theory can be used with reference to the content theories of motivation. A worker may have differing needs in each of Maslow's levels, and these may change over time or based on circumstances. As McClelland suggests, individuals have varying needs profiles with respect to achievement, affiliation, and power. In terms of leadership style, some workers function best when supervised in a democratic or participative style, while other individuals prefer more directive approaches. According to Hersey and Blanchard, individuals may respond best to a particular style based on their current job knowledge and motivation. Contingency theory suggests that the effective supervisor will consider all relevant factors in the worker, the situation, and her or his own style preferences and strengths when deciding how to work with a particular subordinate.

Democratic Supervision

Contingency theory usually suggests, for professional workers, a participative, delegative leadership style. This approach is sometimes referred to as *democratic supervision* or *participative decision making*. With these approaches, supervisors find ways to involve workers as a group in planning and problem-solving processes.

Because human service workers are often motivated by idealistic needs, they tend to work most effectively toward goals in which they feel a sense of ownership. Since their work entails personal involvement as well as task completion, they must be committed to what they are doing. The human services, almost by definition, do not lend themselves to mechanistic task performance.

The nature of human service organizations also lends itself to collegial and democratic approaches to management, as represented by human resources approaches such as Theory Y, System 4, and Hersey and Blanchard's Styles 3 and 4 (participating and delegating). The goals toward which human service organizations work are often complex and certainly are subject to a variety of interpretations. At the same time, many possible methods can be used to serve client needs. If an attempt is to be made to work toward client goals rather than to emphasize performance of accustomed services, the ideas of many people are needed. Workers who are very familiar with client needs can help reach innovative solutions to long-standing problems.

In effect, what Blake and McCanse (1991) would call a 9,9 manager is an appropriate participant in the human service scene. Such an individual recognizes that one cannot choose between concern for people and concern for production. Instead, he or she knows that everyone who will be affected by a decision should have a part in making it. All of the people whose commitment will be needed in carrying out a new solution should be involved in the problem-solving process. All of the people whose individual objectives will lead to the meeting of organizational goals should be part of the goal-setting process.

Participative Decision Making as a Supervision Approach

Participative decision making (PDM) and *participative management* have evolved as generic terms for involving employees in greater decision making, based on the human resources theories of Likert, McGregor, and others (see Chapter 4). PDM is defined here as "actual staff involvement, whether formal or informal, direct or indirect, in decision processes regarding issues affecting the structure, funding, staffing, or programming" of the organization (Ramsdell, 1994, p. 58). PDM is not an either/or factor but is on a continuum from no involvement in the decision to "complete control or veto power over the decision" (Ramsdell, 1994, p. 58). In one test of the use of PDM, Packard (1989) found that child protective services units whose supervisors were seen as more participative had higher performance and job satisfaction than those with less PDM. Interestingly, Packard (1993) also discovered that these supervisors felt that workers were capable of much more PDM than they were currently allowed, suggesting that this is an underused approach.

To respond to this opportunity, Shera and Page (1995) suggest strategies for employee empowerment that allow greater PDM: at the organizational level, this can happen through a culture of shared leadership and meeting chairing, team problem solving and decision making, and flexible job designs. Effective communication, rewarding employee initiative, mutual (two-way) feedback, and employee development can enhance empowerment. Shera and Page add that the agency's service delivery technology (for example, focusing on client outcomes) and information sharing through computers can be empowering. Bowditch and Buono (1997) list these four keys to effective empowerment:

1. employees need to know organizational performance expectations and actual outcomes,

2. employees must be rewarded for their contribution to organizational performance,

3. team members need the knowledge and skills necessary for them to understand and contribute to organizational performance, and

4. individuals must be given the power to make decisions which impact work processes and performance. (p. 216)

The facts that human service workers are likely to want more PDM, that supervisors and managers believe they are capable of more PDM (Packard, 1993), and that there is growing evidence of the effectiveness of PDM with skilled and motivated workers (Bowditch & Buono, 1997, p. 216; Pine, Warsh, & Maluccio, 1998) suggest that supervisors should look for opportunities to increase their use of PDM.

Group Dynamics and Supervision _____

PDM is often used in group settings, such as a team of a supervisor and her or his subordinates. Human service professionals are often very familiar with principles of group dynamics, but they may have difficulty applying them when they serve in supervisory capacities in their own agency settings. A few basic guidelines can help in the process.

First, when a group of colleagues is expected to make a decision, develop a plan, or solve a problem, be sure to clarify beforehand what constraints might be present. Groups in human service settings often spend endless hours developing novel solutions only to learn later that their ideas cannot be implemented because of budgetary constraints, little-known federal regulations, specifics in the agency's bylaws, or opposition of a powerful board member. After this happens several times, workers' commitment to involve themselves in agency governance lessens, and a low degree of energy is available to the task.

Second, clarify the purpose of a meeting or task force. Sometimes there is misunderstanding concerning the purpose of a procedure, whether it involves a face-to-face meeting, a series of task force projects, or individual interviews and questionnaires. The people who are asked to give input need to know whether the process they are involved in is meant to provide useful advice to a problem solver or whether they, as a group, will be asked to solve the problem or submit the plan of action. A meeting, like an agency plan, must be seen as a means to some specific end.

Third, clarify the procedures to be used. Just as participants must be aware of the goals toward which they are working, they must also be privy to the process being used. Clarity concerning procedural questions is especially important in human service settings, in which clear-cut guidelines are often lacking and participants can be expected to be reasonably expert in using a variety of processes. Many human service workers know how to use such approaches as brainstorming and priority setting with clients but fail to use such useful tools in the context of their own meetings.

Fourth, pay attention to process variables. A major concern in democratic supervision is the blending of concern for task with concern for people or relationships. As workers join in a mutual search for effective solutions, they need to stop and check the process of their own interactions. This awareness of human interactions is an important part of the leadership process and one that cannot be left to chance.

Fifth, choose carefully who is to be involved in each problem-solving process. The human service professional as leader often makes the error of involving too many or too few people in a problem-solving or planning process. It is well worth the time spent to identify, as specifically as possible, who will be affected by a particular decision and then to involve all the people listed in the decision-making process. At the same time, there is a need to recognize the differences between major and minor problems and to use human resources wisely. A large number of people, including volunteers, should be involved in setting broad agency goals; a small number of people should strive to set the specific objectives of one individual or work unit. A large number of people should be involved in seeking the solution to a major problem; a small number should work actively on the elimination of a minor annoyance.

In the long run, it is up to the supervisor to recognize that human service workers bring a variety of needs and motivations to the work setting and that they can meet those needs most effectively if they are actively involved in controlling the quality of their own work lives.

Challenges in Supervision

Inevitable problems and challenges in supervising staff can typically be handled using techniques already discussed. However, even though a supervisor does everything "right," sometimes disciplinary action is necessary. Weinbach (1998) outlines a useful *progressive discipline* process through which a problem may be addressed as early as possible, using the appropriate level of intervention. The agency should have a fair and clearly outlined progressive discipline procedure in its personnel manual, and the supervisor should ensure that the worker is aware of the process and that it is followed precisely if it is needed.

If work performance is below expectations, the worker should hear this as soon as possible, using feedback guidelines listed earlier. This approach plus Shulman's use of tuning in, empathy, and demands for work will often be enough to get performance on track again. If the employee does not respond to such efforts, a verbal *reprimand* may be necessary: "a direct, one-to-one, private, and confidential communication of employee shortcomings" (Weinbach, 1998, p. 194). A common occurrence in organizations should be avoided: giving a group reprimand at a staff meeting when only one worker is at fault. Comments such as "Staff should stop being rude to clients" leave all wondering whether they are doing anything wrong and inevitably lower morale. If verbal reprimands are not effective, a written reprimand, with a copy for the employee's personnel file, may be needed. This should list specific behaviors that need to be changed, the expected behavior, and a time line. At this point, and before all subsequent steps, the supervisor's manager should be informed and consulted.

Some organizations have additional procedures such as provisions for suspensions without pay or performance contracts that include warnings about imminent termination. Transfers of staff may be warranted in particular circumstances, such as personality or other situational factors, but should not be used to move problem employees with no prospect of a behavior change.

Termination of a worker is the next step and normally occurs only for unsatisfactory performance that has not been corrected despite explicit attempts or for gross misconduct, such as sexual involvement with a client. Termination for gross misconduct can normally occur "on the spot," without using progressive discipline, but agency procedures and standards still need to be followed.

Rivas (1998) and Weinbach (1998) both offer useful guidelines for handling termination. At the termination interview, the supervisor needs to be absolutely clear that the employee is being terminated and that the decision is not negotiable. The reasons for the termination should at this point not be surprises, and they should be stated clearly in behaviorally specific terms. If the agency has an appeal or grievance procedure, the worker should be made aware of it. Of course, the worker should be treated with respect, and support in the form of suggestions for new employment, education, or behavior change may be offered. An exit interview may be offered, in which mutual feedback and a debriefing of the worker's experience at the agency can be reviewed.

Summary

Clear, comprehensive, and fair personnel procedures; creative fulfillment of the various supervisory functions; appropriate leadership of staff; and attention to the motivating and rewarding of employees will contribute greatly to the effectiveness of a program's services by valuing and fully using staff: the agency's most important resources. We will now address another essential agency resource: the acquisition and management of funds for program operations.

Discussion Questions

1. Think about the best and the worst leader or supervisor you can remember. What does leadership theory tell you that helps you understand what went on in each situation?

2. Recall a situation in which you and your coworkers or fellow students were highly motivated and effective. What motivation theories help you account for higher motivation and effectiveness?

3. How would you describe yourself as a leader or supervisor? Which leadership theories most help you understand your own style? Do you tend to supervise the way you like to be supervised, or do you assume that other people have different needs and motivations?

4. What do you see as the most important characteristics of an effective supervisory relationship?

Group Exercise

In a group, take turns role-playing the following situations. The rest of the group should be prepared to discuss alternative ways of dealing with the same situations.

1. The supervisee is a volunteer in a human service agency. Although his or her work with clients is excellent, this supervisee has been undependable. The supervisor counts on this volunteer but never knows whether he or she will show up on a given day as promised.

2. The supervisee is a professional therapist who has been working in an agency for many years. Because of changes in the agency's mission, the supervisor hopes that the supervisee can be encouraged to move toward doing preventive work with families and groups. The supervisee does not want to change.

3. The supervisee is a counselor who has effective helping skills but does not seem to have an overall theory of helping or confidence in his or her work. He or she keeps asking the supervisor to suggest specific techniques that can be used with all clients. The supervisor feels that no single technique works for everyone all the time. He or she hopes that this counselor will develop professionally and clarify his or her goals for client service.

4. Generate some situations from your own experience and role-play the supervisory process.

CASE 7

The Token Economy

Having worked as a therapist for a number of years, Jim Forrest had developed a high level of expertise in dealing with problems related to substance abuse. His work had included jobs in several settings, including a short-term detoxification program in a hospital, a community-based methadone treatment center, and a community mental health outpatient program.

Although his work with clients had always been satisfying, two things continued to trouble him. One major issue for Forrest was that his experience had convinced him that his clients' milieu was more important than any other aspect of treatment. Although one-to-one counseling could be helpful, it was always less important than the reinforcement clients got for various behaviors in their immediate social environments.

The other aspect of his work that tended to trouble him was the question of management. As a professional therapist, he had grown impatient with the pressure on him to stick to specific time lines and methods regardless of his clients' needs. In each agency, managers tended to create methods of operation based more on business principles and treatment costs than on the effects of various treatment modalities. Forrest felt that given the chance to do what he felt was best for his clients, he could work both effectively and efficiently.

Forrest finally had the chance to try out his ideas when he was invited by a former colleague to take on a job as head of a newly funded detoxification program being set up in one wing of the local community mental health center. The program had been funded to provide short-term services, and two of the therapists from the previous, smaller program were to remain on staff. With this exception, Jim would be free to develop the program in whatever way he saw fit. Funding was sufficient to provide for the hiring of a staff of four more professional therapists and eight paraprofessionals.

Forrest began interviewing potential employees, telling each of them the same thing. The program would be based on use of a token economy, meaning that clients would receive concrete and specific reinforcements for behaviors that were consistent with responsible, adult conduct. Every staff member would need to be involved in recording and reinforcing appropriate client behaviors, for only then would the clients begin to learn new ways of dealing with their environment. Beyond this "bottom line" of commitment to the token economy as a treatment modality, professionals would be free to set their own hours and work with clients according to their best interests. Newcomers would be more closely supervised at first. Later they, too, might have the kind of freedom already granted to the experienced professionals.

Most of the new workers started in at their tasks with a high degree of enthusiasm. It was like a dream come true, and after a few weeks, Forrest began to think that he was already seeing results in terms of client change. A few problems, however, were beginning to surface.

First, Hugh Schmidt, one of the two therapists who had already been employed at the center, began to complain to anyone who would listen about the idea of the token economy. Schmidt believed that long-term therapy, insight, and intrapsychic change were the only ways to deal with substance abusers. Changes in behavior could not get at the root cause of the problem, and the token economy could change only concrete behavior, not attitudes. He continued to work with clients in the same way he always had, but the token economy was constantly being sabotaged.

Another member of the professional staff was troubled not by the token economy but by the freedom Forrest allowed for the employees. Carol Cooke pointed out that although the staff members had been enthusiastic at first, they would not maintain a high level of commitment unless they were aware of the rules and regulations governing their own behaviors. Forrest scoffed at these concerns until one Friday afternoon when he had to make a presentation at an out-of-town conference. When he realized he had forgotten something, he called the office. Not one of the professional staff members was there.

The problems Forrest had begun to face were minor, but they started to make him think. Could he maintain a central focus in the program if every member of the professional staff were not necessarily committed to it? Could he trust the professional staff in the way he had always wished to be trusted? The challenges began to seem a little more difficult than he had expected.

1. What do you think of Jim Forrest's approach to program administrations What are his strengths and weaknesses in dealing with his new leadership position?

2. If you were Forrest, what would you do about the problem posed by Hugh Schmidt's attitude? Is it necessary for the staff to work as a closely knit team, or is there room for a great deal of variation?

3. What would you do about the problem posed by Carol Cooke? Do employees—even trained professionals—need clearer behavioral guidelines than Forrest provided?

4. Do you think Forrest has the potential to be more effective than the business-oriented professional managers he had encountered before?

References

Akin, G., & Weil, M. (1981, October). The prior question: How do supervisors learn to supervise? *Social Casework, 62,* 472–479.

Blake, R., & McCanse, A. (1991). *Leadership dilemmas—grid solutions.* Houston: Gulf.

Blake, R., & Mouton, J. (1985). *The managerial grid III.* Houston: Gulf.

Bowditch, J., & Buono, A. (1997). *A primer on organizational behavior.* New York: Wiley.

Fiedler, F. E. (1967). *A theory of leadership effectiveness.* New York: McGraw-Hill.

French, J. R. P., & Raven, B. (1959). The bases of social power. In D. Cartwright (Ed.), *Studies in social power.* Ann Arbor: University of Michigan Press.

Gabris, G. (1998). Merit pay mania. In S. Condrey (Ed.), *Handbook of human resource management in government* (pp. 627–657). San Francisco: Jossey-Bass.

Gummer, B. (1990). *The politics of social administration.* Upper Saddle River, NJ: Prentice Hall.

Hersey, P., Blanchard, K., & Johnson, D. (1996). *Management of organizational behavior: Utilizing human resources* (7th ed.). Upper Saddle River, NJ: Prentice Hall.

Herzberg, F. (1975). One more time: How do you motivate employees? In Harvard Business Review (Ed.), *On management.* New York: Harper & Row.

Kadushin, A. (1985). *Supervision in social work* (2nd ed.). New York: Columbia University Press.

Luthans, F., & Kreitner, R. (1975). *Organizational behavior modification.* Glenview, IL: Scott, Foresman.

Maslow, A. H. (1954). *Motivation and personality.* New York: Harper & Row.

McClelland, D. (1965). Achievement motivation can be developed. *Harvard Business Review, 43,* 6–24.

Morse, J. J., & Lorsch, J. W. (1975). Beyond Theory Y. In Harvard Business Review (Ed.), *On management*. New York: Harper & Row.

Orsburn, J. (1994). *Recommendations regarding a competency-based reward system.* Unpublished manuscript.

Orsburn, J., Moran, L., Musselwhite, E., & Zenger, J. (1990). *Self-directed work teams: The new American challenge.* Homewood, IL: Business One Irwin.

Packard, T. (1989). Participation in decision making, performance, and job satisfaction in a social work bureaucracy. *Administration in Social Work, 13*(1), 59–73.

Packard, T. (1993). Managers' and workers' views of the dimensions of participation in organizational decision making. *Administration in Social Work, 13*(1), 59–73.

Pine, B., Warsh, R., & Maluccio, A. (1998). Participatory management in a public child welfare agency: A key to effective change. *Administration in Social Work, 22*(1), 19–32.

Ramsdell, P. (1994). Staff participation in organizational decision-making: An empirical study. *Administration in Social Work, 18*(4), 51–71.

Rivas, R. (1998). Dismissing problem employees. In R. Edwards, J. Yankey, & M. Altpeter (Eds.), *Skills for effective management of nonprofit organizations* (pp. 262–278). Washington, DC: NASW Press.

Shera, W., & Page, J. (1995). Creating more effective human service organizations through strategies of empowerment. *Administration in Social Work, 19*(4), 1–15.

Shulman, L. (1993). *Interactional supervision.* Washington, DC: NASW Press.

Siegel, G. (1998). Designing and creating an effective compensation plan. In S. Condrey (Ed.), *Handbook of human resource management in government* (pp. 608–629). San Francisco: Jossey-Bass.

Vroom, V. H. (1964). *Work and motivation.* New York: Wiley.

Weinbach, R. (1998). *The social worker as manager: A practical guide to success* (3rd ed.). Boston: Allyn & Bacon.

8

Managing Finances to Meet Program Goals

CHAPTER OUTLINE _____

The process of budgeting is inextricably attached to that of planning. A program exists to meet needs or address social problems, which, as we saw in Chapter 3, are identified through the needs assessment and addressed through strategies that ultimately are reflected in the design of a program. A budget is fundamentally a program reflected in fiscal terms. Just as the previous two chapters showed the importance of people—the staff who work with clients and the community and those who support direct service providers—this chapter highlights the importance of other resources such as facilities, supplies, and equipment that are reflected in the budget.

The budget itself is simply a projection of operational plans, usually for a one-year time span, with the plans stated in terms of the allocation of dollars for varying functions or activities. Whether the budget helps or hinders the agency's efforts to set and meet its goals depends on the degree to which it is placed in perspective as a tool at the service of program planners. The budget, then, should be the servant, rather than the master, of planning. As a decision-making tool, it helps transform goals into service realities. Proficient use of this tool requires expertise on the part of the human service manager not only in budgeting but in other aspects of financial management as well.

While the human service administrator does not need to be an accountant, he or she is responsible for the total management and operations of the agency. Other agency staff, such as program and project directors and supervisors, are often called on to write a budget for their program or unit or to serve on a budgeting committee. Therefore, it is incumbent on the administrator, supervisor, or project leader to have some working knowledge of financial management.

Any manager or staff member in a human service program that receives government funds, foundation grants, or charitable contributions is a steward of the resources of others. This stewardship implies the best possible use of these scarce resources. Having a well-thought-out strategic plan to respond to pressing social and community needs; using well-designed and proven service delivery methods; and having trained, competent, and motivated staff are part of this stewardship, as is the responsible use of funds. This includes thorough planning on how to allocate the funds (budgeting), and making the expenditures as planned (reflected in ongoing financial reports). In this chapter, we will cover these core processes as well as fund-raising, writing proposals, and using financial reports and controls.

Steps in the Budgeting Process

Flynn (1995) outlines four stages in the budget process. The first stage, defining the problem and target groups to be addressed, setting goals and objectives, and determining that program models or interventions are actually accomplished, occurs through the planning process discussed in Chapter 3. In the second stage, revenues and expenditures are estimated. Revenue estimates are based on available funds (for example, grant or contract amounts or other funds raised, as discussed later in this chapter), and expenditures are determined using the processes discussed in the next section. The third and fourth stages occur after program implementation: monitoring expenditures and revenues and making necessary revisions.

Determining the Program Model

A recent budget innovation, *budgeting for results* (O'Looney, 1996, p. 202; Schick, 1990), attempts to make a more direct connection between mission, goals, and objectives on the one hand and detailed revenue and expenditure estimates on the other. It is a descendant of earlier reforms not heard of much today: *performance-based budgeting* was proposed by the Truman administration to connect funds to specific activities, functions, and units of work; and the *planning, programming, budgeting system* of the Johnson administration allowed for cost comparisons of different program options (Flynn, 1995). Budgeting for results (BFR) incorporates elements of these earlier innovations and is based on three main principles (Cothran, 1993, cited in O'Looney 1996, p. 203): specification of goals from the top (for example, the strategic plan), choices on means of accomplishing goals and objectives determined at the program level, and accountability and incentives for results. The program model (intervention method or technology) chosen earlier based on its efficacy is now detailed by listing expenditures that will be necessary to accomplish results (objectives).

BFR is based on several assumptions, which in reality are expectations that must be met for the model to work (O'Looney, 1996, pp. 206–211). First, there need to be clear and measurable objectives, and responsibility for their achievement needs to be clearly assigned to programs, units, or individuals. More specifically, targets need to be established: the changes in client behavior or condition, numbers of clients or services to be delivered, and a time frame. Another important assumption is that "results are a function of organizational resources effectively used" (O'Looney, 1996, p. 208). This points to the importance of an appropriate program design: a model with a track record of being effective in the circumstances that are planned by the program. Next, managers and their staffs need to have the authority and responsibility to do what is needed to achieve objectives. This suggests a participative management philosophy in which lower-level staff are entrusted to make decisions on how to accomplish objectives.

According to O'Looney, "BFR says to managers, 'Tell us what you can do with a certain set of resources and if your proposal seems reasonable, we will remove all or most line-item controls, and if you actually are able to do more with these funds, even more resources will be forthcoming'" (p. 204). This is a vivid example of systems theory in organizations: there needs to be a fit, or alignment, among different subsystems—in this case planning, program design, financial management, and managerial philosophy.

Estimating Expenditures

The program model (that is, the services to be provided, staff needed and their qualifications, required facilities, and other resources) and the program objectives (service outcomes expected, numbers and types of clients, projected units of service and activities) become the basis for estimating expenditures. Projected expenditures are first developed using two basic formats: *line item budgeting* and *program budgeting.*

Line item budgeting, the simplest format, involves listing total projected expenditures in functional groupings, typically including such categories as personnel (salary and fringe benefits), consultant costs, equipment, supplies, travel, capital outlay, and other expenses. Each of these categories is a line item in the budget, as represented in Table 8-1 (Thompson, 1999).

A line item budget obviously says nothing about how resources will be specifically applied to the accomplishment of particular objectives, except perhaps on the broadest level. Therefore, line item budgets typically are useful only if they are incorporated into program budgets.

A *program budget* has line items for each expenditure category, but all items are categorized as program areas. A program budget replaces such line items as personnel costs, travel, and postage with groupings such as youth counseling program, educational outreach program, and legal advocacy program. Whereas a typical line item budget might show personnel costs for a whole agency without distinguishing among staff members tied to various programs, the program budget ties resources to specific sets of activities. This approach facilitates the budgeting process being tied closely to planning and evaluation. When resources are related to programs, the programs themselves are considered accountable for achieving objectives that lead to accomplishment of the agency's overall goals. Thus, the program budgeting approach requires that attempts be made to determine which programs are effective in terms of outcomes achieved and efficient in terms of resources consumed in pursuit of objectives.

Further useful detail is provided through a variation of program budgeting known as *functional budgeting.* This format reports allocations and costs by programs (counseling, referral and information, youth services, and so on) and support services (functions such as central administration and fund-raising) by line items, providing a comprehensive picture of total agency expenditures by specific expense categories and functions (Skidmore, 1990). Each function can then be treated as a *cost center:* its costs are detailed by its own line item budget, and it is accountable for specific objectives.

For our purposes here, we will discuss how to develop a line item budget for a specific program. That is, we will determine how many of what kinds of staff will be needed to accomplish program objectives using the designated service delivery method and what nonpersonnel expenditures, from rent and telephones to mileage and training, will be needed as well.

TABLE 8-1
Program Budget, July 1, 2000–June 30, 2001

Line Item	Requested	Match	Total
Personnel			
Professional			
Administrator (0.05 FTE)	2,100		2,100
Coordinator (0.75 FTE)	24,960		24,960
Leaders (1.0 FTE)	21,873	7,247	29,120
Fringe benefits (20% of above)	9,787	1,449	11,236
Personnel total	58,720	8,696	67,416
Nonpersonnel			
Consumable supplies			
Program supplies	5,800		5,800
Office supplies	1,200		1,200
Telephone	800		800
Printing	1,500		1,500
Postage	352		352
Field trips (admission and bus rental)	3,600		3,600
Food (club snacks)	2,000		2,000
Equipment (computer and printer)	3,200		3,200
Advertising	285		285
Staff travel			
Mileage ($0.30 per mile for 3,000 miles)	900		900
Out-of-town conference for 3 staff	2,300		2,300
Evaluation consultant ($40/hour × 80 hours)	3,200		3,200
Evaluation instruments	600		600
Staff training	300		300
Rent	1,100		1,100
Insurance	1,100		1,100
Nonpersonnel total	28,237		28,237
Total direct costs	86,957	8,696	95,652
Indirect costs (15% of total direct)	13,043	1,304	14,348
Total	**100,000**	**10,000**	**110,000**

Budgets need to be developed under two circumstances. First, in the preparation of a proposal for the funding of a new program (discussed later in this chapter), a budget needs to be developed to determine how funds will be spent on
staff, facilities, equipment, training, and other program needs. Second, budgets for
ongoing programs are typically updated every *fiscal year.* The fiscal year for many
human service programs begins on July 1 and ends on June 30, the common cycle
used for government agencies. The major exception to this is that the federal government uses an October 1–September 30 fiscal year. Budget preparation should

begin several months in advance of the start of the new fiscal year, with the specific timetable determined by the deadlines of funders and the agency's board.

We begin with the development of the budget for a new program, such as would be described in a proposal for funding submitted to a governmental or foundation funding source. Even if the program is new, the agency will have established line item formats which can have numbers for the new program inserted into them. The agency will also have job roles with qualifications and salary ranges (see Chapter 6) and knowledge of facilities expenses, travel expense rates, and other nonpersonnel costs to use as starting points and guidelines. Existing agency spread sheet formats will be particularly useful for computations such as fringe benefits.

Creating the Annual Budget

Yet another distinction between types of budgets must be introduced here: *revenue budgets* and *expense budgets*. Both are ways to describe the same program. Revenue budgets list the various sources of revenue (grants, contracts, donations, and so forth) available to the program, and expense budgets list exactly how the funds will be spent. We will first discuss expense budgets, assuming that the new program idea came from the strategic plan and funds are not yet available. Later we will review how to locate a funding source and develop revenue for the program.

Many questions need to be answered as the budget is developed to operationalize the program design. These can be structured based on the line items of the budget. Line item budgets have two major categories: personnel and nonpersonnel. Personnel costs include salaries and benefits for all paid staff. Nonpersonnel costs include everything else, as can be seen in the line item budget in Table 8-1. These are some of the questions that can be asked to determine budget amounts:

- What are the qualifications (and salary rates) of staff needed to deliver services and provide support?

- How many staff of each classification will we need to accomplish program objectives?

- What kind of facility will be needed, where should it be located, and what should the hours of operation be?

- What supplies and equipment will be needed?

- What travel will be required?

- What training will need to be offered to staff?

- What consultants will need to be used (staff development, management information systems, and so on)?

As has been emphasized previously, budget needs depend on the objectives that have been developed as part of the planning process. By closely scrutinizing their implementation plans, budget makers can come close to estimating precisely what the budgetary needs of various activities might be.

It is best to begin with personnel expenditures, because they are the essential component of the service delivery process and because they will in all likelihood be the largest line item. As an example, we will use the sample budget in Table 8-1 for a teenage girls peer support program that includes after-school activities, academic and personal counseling, and peer support.

Staff allocations are listed in *full-time equivalent* (FTE) positions. A staff position allocated for a year at 100 percent time would be 1.0 FTE. This is one of several programs or a larger agency, and the agency's executive director will be assigned to this project for 5 percent of her time (her annual salary is $42,000, and 5 percent of that amount is $2,100, budgeted for this program). There will be a three-fourths-time coordinator (0.75 FTE) and two half-time leaders, totaling 1.0 FTE. The budget planner would also need to take into account other costs of the program, including office and program supplies, printing, postage, and telephone.

With all this taken into account, the financial planner would be able to make a reasonably accurate estimate of the cost of getting the program in motion. These estimated costs could then be integrated into the amounts budgeted for the agency's line item budget as a totality (that is, specifying the total personnel costs for the agency by adding together the salary expenditures for this and all other agency programs). Whether these planning data are used to develop program budgets or to be subsequently translated into line item terms, the same kinds of procedures can be followed. The only major factor involved is that the agency's budget must fit the reality of its planned activities. If plans include carefully designed implementation strategies, the creation of a budget simply means translating activities into monetary terms.

Tremendous variation is possible in the forms that budget documents, once completed, can take. The agency will need to use the formats provided by the funding source. In our example, we have a line item budget for a federally funded project. The agency is asking for $100,000 from the funding source. This includes $86,957 of direct program costs. Additionally, indirect costs, sometimes known as *administrative costs* or *overhead*, are included to help pay the project's share in the total overhead of the agency housing the program. Indirect costs are those not directly related to program operations. A funder may have specific definitions of indirect costs or overhead (that is, what line items are "allowable" for billing to the funder). If guidelines are provided, they should, of course, be followed.

Usually, the budget of all of the agency's central office would be considered an administrative cost. An exception would be if the agency executive spends a percentage of her or his job providing programmatic or clinical supervision to the program, that amount (for instance, the 5 percent FTE of the administrator's salary in our example) can be charged as a program rather than administrative cost. The amount of indirect costs can vary tremendously, depending on the agreements worked out between the agency and the funding source, but it is usually computed as a percentage of total direct (program) costs. In this instance, the government funder has agreed to pay for overhead at 15 percent of the total direct costs.

The form a budget takes and the information included depend on the funder's and the agency's requirements. The agency must meet the guidelines of the funding source. In this example, the requirements are relatively simple. In many instances, agencies are required to provide matching funds (sometimes known as *cost sharing*), either in money or in "in-kind" contributions. Examples of in-kind contributions include office space provided to the program by the agency or volunteer time. Cash matches are usually from the agency's unrestricted funds (for example, donations or fees) that are not paid by another government grant or contract. When adding a match, include another column, showing local contributions, in the budget. In our example, the agency is proposing to match this grant with $10,000 of funds it raises from local foundations.

As is the case with overhead rates, make sure the funder's definitions of acceptable match items are followed. In addition to following all the funder's requirements and definitions, remember that budget format follows need, and the most important factor to consider is whether the items and figures are readily understandable to the people who need to make decisions regarding allocations, expenditures, reports, or accountability. We will now briefly review the use of financial reports as useful monitoring mechanisms.

Financial Reports

Financial reports can serve both monitoring and coordinating functions (Strachan, 1998). *Interim statements* help monitor expenditures, and *annual reports* provide information about the agency's fiscal condition to funding sources, policymakers, and concerned citizens. *Audits* are periodic examinations of agency financial reports and their supporting documents, conducted by independent accountants not affiliated with the agency. Audits are done to determine whether financial statements were prepared in accordance with generally accepted accounting principles. Financial reports such as operating statements and balance sheets assist in coordination by providing an agency-wide picture of how programs are performing.

Program managers typically are required to develop, implement, and monitor budgets but will not be heavily involved with other financial reports. Agency executives will need to be more familiar with these systems, while program managers can rely on agency accountants for expertise. Nevertheless, because annual audits are such an important aspect of agency management, program managers should at least be aware of this process.

Audits

On completion of the audit, normally done annually, the accountant will submit to the agency's governing body an "opinion" or report as to whether the agency's financial statements fairly represent its financial position. Based on the auditor's report, the agency can then take whatever action is necessary, ranging from "Let's keep up the good work" to "We need to take corrective action." The periodic financial audit can be as anxiety provoking to fiscal managers as the program evaluation is to service providers, but if a system is well designed and properly used, no major surprises but only identified opportunities for minor improvements or adjustments should emerge. We will now look at how both audit results and changing program conditions can lead to budget changes.

Updating the Annual Budget for an Ongoing Program

The continuation of an ongoing program involves not only an audit but also the yearly submission of a proposed budget to the manager, board, funder, or governing body controlling resource allocation. The same type of routine tends to be followed whether the budget maker is a project director appealing for funds from a funding agency, a program manager vying with other departments for a share in an agency's total budget, a nonprofit agency executive presenting a proposal to the board of directors, or a public administrator seeking legislative appropriations of tax dollars.

The budget request is usually formulated in response to notification from the next higher authority that the document is to be developed by a particular deadline. The budget for the current year generally provides the basis for beginning analysis of needs for the following year. Usually, the final results of the current year, in terms of expenditures, need to be estimated. These estimations, along with reports of expenditures to date, help the budget developer determine projections for the coming year. The current year's budget is the building block on which analysis of the next year's need is based.

The decisions in question at this stage of the budgeting cycle tend to be oriented not toward the budget as a whole but toward the difference between the current and the proposed budget. This budgeting approach is termed "incremental" because it normally accepts the current funding level as a base from which to adjust, ideally upward if new funds are available. Applying the incremental approach to the budgeting process suggests that attention is directed to the changes that occur between the existing state and the proposed state. The marginal difference between what is and what is proposed is examined. This process accepts the existing base and examines in detail only the increments that extend the current budgeting program into the future.

Budget adjustments are made not only annually but also routinely during the fiscal year based on new developments. Such adjustments are made within parameters set by funders and the agency board. For example, a funding source may allow moving up to 10 percent of the nonpersonnel budget from one category to another (for example, from Supplies to Mileage) without prior approval, with larger changes requiring advanced approval from the funder. A program manager should be aware of all relevant time lines, parameters, and procedures to manage funds properly throughout the year.

Political processes come into play in regard to these annual or midyear increments, or small changes in resource allocation (Gummer, 1990). Competing programs, projects, and agencies, each with its own accepted base, must share limited resources. The questions asked change from "'What is the appropriate funding level for program X?' to 'Whose appropriation should be cut or whose taxes raised to finance an increase in program X?'" (Skok, 1980, p. 448). Then preferences must be expressed, support bases sought, bargains struck, and agreements reached.

Through these procedures, incrementalism focuses on small, yearly funding increases that are allocated without a great deal of attention to program goals or effectiveness. According to Mayers (1989):

> the incremental approach assumes that the programs and activities in the previous year's budget are essential to the accomplishment of agency goals and should be continued; that they are being performed in an effective, efficient manner, and that they will be cost effective next year. These are assumptions that may not necessarily be valid, and they need to be examined. (p. 28)

SOURCE: Quote from *Financial Management for Nonprofit Human Service Agencies,* by R. S. Mayers. Copyright © 1989 by Charles C. Thomas, Publisher. This and all other quotations from this source are reprinted by permission.

When resources are scarce, attention may need to shift from the idea of providing for steady increases to the notion of creating a *downward-sloping* expenditure line. To deal with declining resources, it may be necessary to use *decremental budgeting:* a "planned response to sustained budgetary contraction" (Flynn, 1995, p. 465). Decremental budgeting uses the same steps as its more growth-oriented predecessor. Now, however, political forces help determine not which programs gain the most but which sets of activities sacrifice the least. When budget imbalances become major, such decremental budgeting is known as *cutback management.*

Cutback Management

Resource scarcity brings with it the need for all stakeholders in human service programs to become involved in the search for program or administrative expenditures that may be cut or the development of more efficient administrative or service delivery processes. When resources decline, policymakers sometimes fall victim to the notion that indiscriminate slashing of funds can solve the problem. In reality, however, such approaches are oversimplifications of highly complex issues. Taubman (1985) cautions against the unquestioned acceptance of budget cuts and the attendant ideology that less is more. "Ideologies," he believes, "are belief and value systems that have always played a role in motivating people toward social change. Like political pressures and cost-benefit analyses, professional ideologies can be used for good or evil" (p. 180). Retrenchment, he suggests, can have the effect of co-opting professional commitment to service.

How can an agency conserve resources without merely punishing the more efficient programs that have already eliminated wasteful practices? Levine (1978) lists five commonly used cutback methods: (1) decisions based on employee seniority, (2) hiring freezes, (3) across-the-board cuts, (4) use of criteria related to program productivity, and (5) some form of zero-based budgeting. Each of these decision-making methods has clear shortcomings, especially in terms of fairness to service deliverers and clients.

If jobs are cut on the basis of the jobholder's seniority, control over the nature of program cuts is lost. Similarly, hiring freezes also leave a great deal to chance, depending on which individuals leave or retire at any given point. Using seniority and hiring freezes provides hardship for both women and minorities, who tend to have been the last hired. Across-the-board cuts are commonly first attempts at problem resolution, but this approach can buy only a small amount of time and thus should be avoided.

Gummer (1990, pp. 62–65) suggests that strategic planning can help make cutback management more rational. For this to be effective, he asserts that the agency needs centralized authority so that top administrators can make difficult decisions for the good of the whole agency, continuity of top management, rapid and accurate feedback on agency operations, budgetary flexibility allowed by funding sources, and incentives for conserving resources.

This recommendation implies an authoritarian management style that normally is demotivating for employees and lessens their commitment. Flynn (1995) offers principles that do not necessarily require authoritarian decision making: "(1) creating an early warning system for detection of adverse trends; (2) seizing the initiative in reacting to impending changes; and (3) implementing a fiscal strategy designed to maintain organizational robustness" (p. 465), adding that "successful budgeting during retrenchment must be predicated on a clear and reasonable, accurate diagnosis of the reasons for decline in resources and an honest estimate of whether the slump is likely to be permanent" (p. 466). She suggests tactics such as figuring out ways to raise productivity, avoiding across-the-board cuts in favor of targeting reductions based on priorities and expected consequences, and, if cuts are necessary, making corresponding cuts in scopes of services and documenting these impacts on the community.

In a related vein, Weatherley (1984) contrasts "technician" and "statesman" (sic) approaches, with the former emphasizing efficiency, cost-effectiveness, and authoritarian management and the latter emphasizing fairness, accountability to clients, and a democratic management style. While the technician can easily recommend cutting staff and services, increasing workloads, or deprofessionalizing services, the statesman must also consider "ethical and professional considerations, assessments of how the various options will affect clients, staff, and the organization itself" (p. 53). A statesman has few options in such circumstances, and prevention is the best way out: "the key to statesmanship is contingency planning and forecasting" (p. 53). Also, staff and clients can sometimes be involved in brainstorming ways of dealing with potential cuts, as long as the limits of participation are clear: staff and clients cannot be forced to make recommendations such as whom to lay off but may be able to suggest cost savings or ways to bring in new resources.

Ultimately, decisions concerning the nature of agency cutbacks must depend on the concerted efforts of individuals willing to share the responsibility for deciding which programs contribute most to the agency's mission and which services must be sacrificed. If the agency is serving a community on the basis of assessment of local needs, community members must be involved in deciding which of their goals and needs have the highest priority. They must also help decide whether cuts in funding will be fought or accepted.

Limitations of Incrementalism

The traditional approach to budgeting, whether used to allocate increases or decreases in expenditures (including, at a larger scale, cutback management), depends on bargaining mechanisms, usually focuses on small changes rather than on total policies, and stresses expenditure rather than results. Over the years, many budget makers and funders have found these methods adequate. Decision making is simplified when attention is paid to modifications in existing practices rather than to reexamination of total programs and policies. Uncertainty concerning means and ends—always a problem in human service delivery systems—is lessened when changes are designed in small increments, for major, irrevocable errors are avoided. In short, decision makers are freed from the responsibility for making major commitments in terms of the value of alternate programs and freed from the need to engage in highly complex calculations.

The inherent weakness in incrementalism lies specifically in its failure to force consideration of major policy questions as part of the budgeting process. Traditional approaches fail to make distinctions between effective and ineffective programs or between necessary and unneeded services. This shortcoming has especially serious consequences when resources are scarce because the method does not help decide what programs or services should be cut, in what order, and to what extent. Of course, budgeting based on the strategic plan and using results of evaluations of any existing programs (see Chapter 10) help address this problem. Zero-based budgeting, cost-benefit analysis, and cost-effectiveness analysis can also be useful in helping make thoughtful budgeting decisions.

Zero-Based Budgeting

Zero-based budgeting provides an alternative to traditional procedures in that it emphasizes the need for each program to justify its very existence as part of the planning process. Instead of comparing a request for funds with the previous year's expenditures, decision makers compare and contrast every proposed program in terms of overall agency goals. Existing programs are, theoretically at least, in equal competition with untried innovations. Through analysis of comparative effectiveness, activities are prioritized so that decision makers can decrease expenditures on ineffective functions and reallocate these resources to programs identified as having higher priority. The process is zero based because each program must start from zero in justifying any commitment of resources.

Mayers (1989) explains the utility of zero-based budgeting in the following terms:

> While incremental budgeting starts with an established base of the previous year's operating levels, and seeks to justify changes in the current year, zero-based budgeting (ZBB) attempts to provide some accountability by starting from a base of zero. In ZBB each proposed expenditure must be justified; this encourages the analysis of competing claims on resources, and reduces the possibility of continuing obsolete, inefficient programs. (p. 29)

Zero-based budgeting is accomplished through the use of decision packages, which describe a set of related activities that lead to the accomplishment of a given goal. Full applications of ZBB have decreased since its brief peak in popularity during the Carter administration, but the general notion of "zero basing" is still sometimes used.

For instance, if a human service goal involved placing one hundred high school students in part-time jobs, decision packages would allow decision makers to analyze the costs and effects of eliminating the program altogether, increasing or decreasing the number of students placed, and using alternative methods (having the service provided by volunteers from the business community, paraprofessionals, or professional human service workers; using mail, telephone, or personal contacts; interviewing students in the schools or in centralized office settings). According to Flynn (1995), "this method serves to highlight the value of each additional dollar added or subtracted to the budget base and gives a clearer picture of program priorities at successive funding levels" (p. 463). All of the choices, including program elimination and program expansion, would be analyzed, with priorities set on the basis of this analysis. The agency's entire budget would then be devised on the basis of rankings, under the assumption that resource allocation would then be tied closely to program goals. Flynn adds that "zero-based budgets also demand that each program be evaluated by its rate of return on investment compared to other proposed programs" (p. 463).

Cost-Benefit Analysis and Cost-Effectiveness Analysis _____

Additional analytical tools that are useful in planning both a program's scope and its expenditures or making decisions when budget adjustments need to be made are *cost-benefit analysis* and *cost-effectiveness analysis*. Both of these attempt to relate costs to program outcomes. Analysis can either begin with a desired level of performance and compare alternative activities in terms of the cost of reaching this level or start with specification of available resources and consider alternatives in terms of the performance level that can be reached with a given amount of funding. In either instance, costs are related to measurable outputs or activities, which are, in turn, related to program outcomes or results.

According to Lohmann and Lohmann (1997), "the idea of cost-benefit analysis is one of the most misused concepts in modern social services management" (p. 221). In cost-benefit analysis, decision makers must translate goals into primarily monetary terms so that programs are evaluated according to their economic (and other) benefits to the community or some specified group. The challenges in actually accomplishing this goal have been demonstrated by Buxbaum (1985), who notes that both costs and benefits need to be identified in three categories: direct, indirect, and intangible. In his example, direct costs of a program include staff, facilities, and supplies. Indirect costs include local property tax revenues foregone because a service is delivered by a not-for-profit organization and client costs such as expenses involved in travel to the agency. Intangible costs could include community fears related to having abusing clients walking through their neighborhood. Direct benefits may include reduced medical costs if child abuse is prevented, and indirect benefits may accrue if a nonabused child contributes to the economy as a working rather than disabled adult. An intangible benefit would be the feeling of well-being in a child no longer abused. Identifying and documenting all the relevant costs and benefits in such a situation can be so time-consuming as to be not worth the effort.

In contrast, cost-effectiveness analysis considers the relationship between costs and outcomes without translating results into monetary values. "Thus, for example, the general cost-effectiveness formula for prevention programs is the full (or contract) cost of the program divided by the number of problems prevented" (Lohmann & Lohmann, 1997, p. 222). While this technique is much more promising in the human services than is cost-benefit analysis, huge challenges remain. Outcomes (effectiveness) in prevention terms are difficult to document, and in any case they may be evident only over a period of years. Direct services may be easier to document. For example, the cost-effectiveness of a program placing a youth in a job may be documented. This would involve allocating precise program costs to that objective distinct from other program objectives and dividing this number by the number of youth placed. Challenges here include, on the cost end, dividing worker, facilities, and other costs by program objective and, on the benefit end, having a clear definition of an outcome (see Chapter 10): Is it full-time employment? At what pay? For how long?

Regardless of the challenges in doing cost-effectiveness analysis, this promises to be an increasingly important and useful technique in program planning and evaluation. Funding sources are increasingly expecting documentation of concrete results, with welfare-to-work programs being a vivid example. For budgeting purposes, this technique is useful in determining the best use of scarce resources as programs are designed or modified.

The decision-making data generated through these methods are potentially helpful for balancing priorities and distinguishing between efficient and inefficient programs. In its ideal form, a rational planning/budgeting approach can reallocate scarce resources so that agency services improve. Innovations can be emphasized, and the end results of programs can receive more attention than they have in more traditional procedures. When resources diminish, such methodologies as zero-based budgeting can provide sorely needed guidelines for change.

Rational analyses have not proven themselves as panaceas for human service delivery systems. In small agencies, the expertise and resources for carrying out highly complex analyses are not typically present. In larger organizations, analyses can be carried out, but an unwelcome side effect has often been that those concerned with programs bow out of the planning process, leaving power concentrated in the hands of technicians concerned more with costs than with effectiveness, more with dollars than with human needs. While some human service workers may be put off by the use of terms such as *value added* and *return on investment,* the reality is that part of being a good steward of public resources is making decisions in favor of the most effective programs that are most likely to have the greatest positive impact on clients and the community, while recognizing that there will never be enough funding to fully meet all identified needs. This illustrates the importance of fund-raising.

Fund-Raising

Human services are funded most commonly through grants, contracts, fees (including third-party payments), contributions, or a combination of two or more sources. The nature of an agency's funding has major implications for the planning and budgeting processes as well as for the way the agency's accountability is perceived. *Fund-raising* is the term used to describe the efforts made by agencies to solicit and acquire resources from their environments to provide needed community services. Funding—that is, the acquisition of funds—is the result of an agency's direct and/or indirect efforts at fund-raising. Examples of direct fund-raising by the agency are proposal writing (applying for grants or contracts through the submission of written proposals to funding sources for the provision of particular human services) and arranging donations through annual funds, capital campaigns, special events, and other sources.

Grants and Contracts

Grants and contracts can come from either public funding sources, such as federal agencies, or private foundations. The differences between grants and contracts are in the degree of control and specificity on the part of the funding agent. A *grant* is a sum of money provided for the achievement of a set of objectives through the recipient's activities. A *contract* is similar but usually lays out the specifics of activities to be performed even before the recipient of the funds is selected. To initiate the process of funding a grant or contract, a funding source will release a *request for proposals* (RFP) that spells out a need and goals to be addressed, preferred or required methodologies, budget limits, and other requirements.

The use of contracting—or, more specifically, *purchase of service contracting*—has increased in recent years, for reasons including increased privatization of government functions and higher demands for accountability that are more easily achieved through contracts than grants. While increased accountability cannot be denied as a legitimate goal, problems have emerged related to this funding mechanism. For example, Kettner and Martin (1996) found that declining resources and increased demand from clients who cannot pay resulted in fewer clients being served and longer waiting lists. More insidious may be increased workloads and declining quality of services as agencies try to cope with "doing more with less." This situation has important implications for agency strategy development and may lead to strategies to stop taking contracts that result in low salaries and service quality. Kettner and Martin add that agencies should look more closely at ways to educate and influence the public regarding the value and true cost of services so that funding may more closely match need or performance expectations.

Elsewhere (Kettner & Martin, 1995), the same authors assess the potentials of an emerging development in contracting known as *performance contracting.* Performance contracting has been defined as "a contract that uses performance specifications and ties at least a portion of a contractor's compensation to their achievement" (Kettner & Martin, 1995, p. 48). Specifications can be based on process (inputs and throughputs, design criteria such as treatment modalities) or performance (service volume, client impact or outcomes). This method has some notable advantages as well as disadvantages such as developing valid measures and potential cash flow problems due to reimbursement procedures (Green, 1998; Kettner & Martin, 1995).

This method is likely to become increasingly common, and managers should become familiar with it. In this regard, Green offers some suggestions: (1) if the agency does not have good cost data from experience or knowledge of other programs, it should be avoided; (2) unit rates should be maximized to avoid a budget shortfall, (3) try to arrange at least some "upfront" payment to avoid cash flow problems, (4) be thoughtful and careful in defining service units and outcome measures, and (5) make sure the program design is well matched with the measures.

Writing Proposals for Grants or Contracts

Any project that is eventually funded must meet priorities set by the funding agency. For instance, in the case of monies funded through federal programs, projects are expected to be helpful in carrying out objectives specified at the level of national policy. Thus, when a human service agency submits a proposal or application for funding to a federal funding agency, the proposal will be considered first in terms of its appropriateness to the funding organization's priorities and guidelines. If the proposal does not fit funding priorities, it will be eliminated without consideration, regardless of its merits. If the proposal does have potential for helping meet the funding program's goals, it will be considered, in most instances, on the basis of the following questions:

- How well does the applicant demonstrate that there is a real need for the proposed project?

- How clear and attainable are the project's objectives?

- Does the proposal spell out a plan of action that suits project goals and objectives?

- Is the applying agency likely to be able to carry out the proposed project and meet the specified goals within the suggested time frame?

- Is the budget clearly thought out and appropriate for the scope of the project?

- Are plans for evaluation and dissemination well documented, feasible, and appropriate?

The questions potential funding agents ask bear obvious similarities to those human service planners ask in the context of budget preparation. Careful planning and goal clarity are valued in the process of awarding grants and contracts. This factor provides one of the major strengths of the project grant as a funding mechanism for human services. There is a potential for tying resource allocation and goal accomplishment together through this type of funding.

Obviously, writing a proposal is not strictly, or even primarily, a financial matter: it involves needs assessments, sound strategy development and program design, consideration of staffing issues, and the development of information systems and evaluation methods. Because it leads, if funded, to an agreement to manage resources, it is included in this discussion of financial management. Excellent guidance on writing proposals is now widely available (see, for example, Henry, 1998; Lauffer, 1997), so only some general guidelines will be offered here.

First, any proposal should be firmly grounded in the agency's strategic plan, which will ensure that the agency has the capacities to implement it if funded and that it fits within the agency's mission. Second, a human service manager should have good, ongoing, and up-to-date knowledge of the range of funding possibilities in the agency's arena, including federal, state, and local government sources; national and local foundations; United Ways and local religious or civic organizations; and perhaps corporate sources.

Proposals typically originate as a concept evolving from a need or opportunity identified in the strategic plan or as a response to an RFP, and our remaining suggestions have to do with responding to an RFP by writing a proposal. The format and requirements in the RFP should be followed precisely (do not be afraid to call the funder's contact for clarification), but the following are common elements of a good proposal.

The proposal often begins with a cover letter and an executive summary or abstract. The narrative section typically includes a statement of need, a description of the organization's capabilities, a budget including staffing patterns and job descriptions, a project time line, and data collection and evaluation plans. In the midst of this is the "heart" of the proposal: the project design and description, including specific goals and objectives to be achieved. Sometimes plans for the future of the program after the grant or contract ends are outlined. Often letters of support, agency forms, organization charts, and time lines are in an appendix.

A number of almost unavoidable problems are associated with grants and contracts when they form the agency's fiscal base. Most immediately apparent is the uncertainty of funding. Grants are designed for the support of short-term projects, and although ongoing support is often possible, it is not built into the official funding process. Contracts, while often renewable, are usually for short time periods such as one year. An agency that depends solely on grants or contracts for its survival is unable to make long-range plans easily because of the lack of a financial base. Any vibrant and dynamic agency should not rely on only grants or contracts for funding. Other sources not only provide "unrestricted" funds that can be used for purposes not funded by grants or contracts but also enhance the agency's relationships with different segments of the community. We will look briefly at a few additional funding sources: fees, planned giving, and other contributions.

Fees

Many human service agencies charge direct fees for services rendered. When these fees are charged to individual clients, they are often based on sliding scales, with individuals paying differing amounts depending on their financial status. Frequently, fees are paid not by consumers themselves but by outside organizations or third parties. Third-party payments can come from insurance companies, Medicare, public agencies purchasing services for clients, or other sources.

Sometimes third parties can have the same effect on agency practices as other funding sources might have. For example, an insurance company might pay for counseling services only if they are provided by licensed therapists, despite the fact that other trained professionals normally provide such services in a particular agency. Such "strings" attached to payments can provide restrictions on an agency's activities. With this exception, however, fees for service tend to have the same effect on budgeting whether they are paid by consumers or outside organizations.

A rarely noted problem faced by agencies that depend on fees for a significant percentage of their fiscal base is the tendency to emphasize direct services at the expense of alternate activities, such as community education, consultation, and advocacy. Although grants or appropriations might provide some support for such indirect services, fees are most closely associated with such traditional treatment modalities as individual counseling or therapy. Fee-based human service agencies have difficulty moving into innovative service areas when their funding depends almost completely on the number of individuals personally served. This is true not only when fees are charged to consumers but also when agencies receive contracts from public organizations to provide treatment for a specific number of clients.

Another implication of the use of fees as a funding base is the inherent difficulty in predicting income. Planners must be able to estimate very accurately the number of clients likely to be served in a given time period, with estimations becoming even more complex if sliding scales mean that not all clients will generate the same amount of revenue. Some agencies can use a flexible form of budgeting, but this works only if service costs are highly variable. (For example, if a training program uses part-time trainers on a consultant basis, hires them only when enough trainees are enrolled, and rents temporary facilities at the same time, then each training implementation can have its own budget.) Normally, however, human service agencies have fixed costs, especially personnel costs, that must be met; so revenues must be predicted with a high degree of accuracy when the yearly budget is developed.

Contributions and Planned Giving

Contributions to an agency's operating budget can run the gamut from $5 donations by individuals to multimillion-dollar endowments. The process of fundraising can mean anything from sending out direct mailings to knocking on the doors of corporate offices to mounting campaigns for special-purpose funds. Agencies that depend on large contributions for their fiscal bases often use the services of professional fund-raising or development specialists as well as encouraging the fund-raising efforts of board members. Regardless of the size of the fund-raising operation, however, human service professionals and administrators are likely to be affected, at least indirectly.

As is the case with proposal writing, many useful resources regarding fund development are available (for example, Benefield & Edwards, 1998; Edwards & Benefield, 1997; Lauffer, 1997; Turner, 1995). In fact, many principles for writing effective proposals apply here as well. Fund development activities should be part of the agency's strategic plan and should be coordinated with the acquisition of funds from other sources (grants, contracts, fees). In fact, the agency's planned giving program should be a major component of the strategic plan.

Fund development involves knowing the environment: identifying a *donor base* and conducting *prospect research*, which can range from clients to national corporations and foundations. The donor may then be conceptualized at the center of the "donor-giving triangle" (Edwards & Benefield, 1997), which consists of motivation, capacity, and opportunity.

Mechanisms for obtaining funds range from capital campaigns (for example, to buy a building for the agency), cultivation of major gifts from wealthy individuals or organizations, annual fund campaigns, to special events such as dinners. A recently emerging strategy in fund-raising is *strategic philanthropy* (Marx, 1996), which is the use of traditional corporate philanthropy to advance a business's strategic objectives. This approach presents great opportunities to not-for-profit human service organizations that may be able to develop partnerships with local or even national corporations for mutual benefit. In fact, all fund-raising tactics have the potential of not only bringing in needed resources but also fostering and furthering relationships with individuals and groups in the community.

Managing Multiple Funding Sources

According to Benefield and Edwards (1998), "a key goal of any good fund-raising program is to identify and cultivate a diverse network of government, individual, foundation, and corporate donors" (p. 61). Agencies should attempt to diversify their funding procedures so that the "drying up" of one funding source does not cause a fiscal crisis in the agency.

This diversity, however, will also demand paying greater attention to coordination and alignment among multiple funding sources. Once again, the agency's strategic plan can provide guidance. If the strategic plan is not adhered to, agency-wide coordination and long-range strategy implementation will be difficult to implement. This factor also makes even the keeping of normally simple reports a complex endeavor. It is often difficult for agencies to consolidate information concerning a number of totally separate funding sources and projects, especially when time lines differ and reporting procedures vary among funding agencies.

Finally, the need for funding often encourages human service planners to take on projects that would not ordinarily fit the scope of their agency, interfering with efforts to maintain the integrity of their mission. Agencies are easily tempted to submit proposals for grants or contracts that look attractive but do not fit the agency's mission, distinct competencies, strategic plan, or market niche. When this happens repeatedly, agency administrators, service providers, and consumers suddenly find that the very nature of the agency's program thrust has inadvertently been changed. Administrators and boards must use good judgment, restraint, and discretion in choosing which grant or contract to respond to. In this context, it is challenging to keep in mind a clear picture of the agency's primary mission.

Although multiple funding makes planning and reporting complex, it also prevents dependence on one source or one mechanism. Separate financial statements are needed for each earmarked fund; yet, in the interests of accountability and control, combined statements should also be available.

Summary

The ability to operationalize a program into fiscal terms with an appropriate and well-developed budget is an essential aspect of human service management. Furthermore, the idea of openness in fiscal matters is one whose time has come. Agencies need to increase their openness in terms of both sharing financial information and seeking input from a variety of sources. This openness can begin to take place when human service professionals, managers, funding sources, and community members accept the fact that budgeting, far from being a mystical force only accountants understand, is merely a method for bringing plans to fruition. We will now turn to another aspect of demonstrating accountability: the use of information systems.

Discussion Questions

1. Suppose that, as director of a human service agency that had always been supported by federal funds, you learned that your funding was going to be cut drastically. Would you concentrate your efforts on fighting against the cutback or on planning for more limited programs? What factors would you take into account in making decisions about program cutbacks?

2. How useful are budgetary processes such as zero-based budgeting for human service agencies?

3. Do you think it is possible for an agency to maintain its commitment to a central mission or purpose when funding patterns change and new types of activities are supported? How would you deal with a situation in which you could get funding only if you changed the basic focus of your agency's programs?

4. If you were coordinating a program in a human service agency, what information would you need concerning income and expenditures?

Group Exercise

Look again at the hypothetical agency you developed as part of the group exercise on planning in Chapter 3. In the same groups of three or four, study the activities you identified as being important for your fictitious agency. Generate a list of possible nontraditional funding sources that might help get your programs into action. What funding sources might have an interest, for whatever reason, in supporting these activities?

Choose one of the activities on your list and try to figure out what its costs might be. Take into account the timing of the activity, the personnel costs for workers who would be involved in carrying it out, any special consultant costs, and nonpersonnel costs such as supplies, equipment, and office space. How much money would you need to carry out this activity for a given period of time?

Each group should share the results of its discussion with the other groups.

CASE 8

The Best-Laid Plans

Katherine Wilson, director of the Allenville Senior Center (ASC), was very much oriented toward planning. In fact, one of the first things she had done after her appointment as director was to set a planning project in motion. A committee made up of employees of the center, community leaders, consumers of the agency's services, and representatives of the American Association of Retired Persons and the Gray Panthers had worked to develop a new strategic plan for the agency.

One of the first things the hardworking committee had done was to survey the center's members to assess their needs and interests. At the same time, an analysis of other human service programs in the community was also completed. A series of community meetings provided a transition from needs assessment to goal setting, and, as a result of all of these procedures, a new set of agency goals had been developed.

The ASC's mission was to bring Allenville's older citizens into the mainstream of community life. Toward this end, the center would provide services such as the following:

1. A foster grandparents program involving the centers members in helping care for young children in the community
2. A consultation project, through which retired members would provide consultation to young businesspeople
3. A placement program assisting retired people to share part-time, paying jobs
4. An educational program, in cooperation with the local college, providing credit courses that would allow members to work toward degrees

Many of the functions the planning committee identified could be carried out under current funding. Some, however, would work more effectively as specially funded projects. The central focus of the program was clear, and Wilson was ready to carry out her promise to the committee and her very supportive board of directors. She would try to obtain the funding needed to carry out community-based programs. In the meantime, some of the activities could begin through allocation of part of the time of currently employed staff members.

Wilson was occupied in completing a tentative budget plan based on the planned activities when she received a call from the chair of ASC's board of directors. With excitement in his voice, Jonas Pratt exclaimed that he had just been contacted by the Rodin Foundation. They were interested in funding a project to build a country retreat for senior citizens. Funding would be very generous, and they would welcome a proposal from ASC.

"Be sure to get on this right away, Katherine," Pratt bubbled. "He said he'd be interested in receiving our proposal, but you know we're not the only ones he called. The write-up had better be good. And be sure you come on strong with the needs assessment."

"But Mr. Pratt, what about the planning document we just did? That was approved by the board, and this project you're talking about doesn't sound as though it has any relationship to it. It sounds as if we'd be going in the opposite direction."

"Well, I know, but this idea is so new we just didn't think of it ourselves. The kind of funding they're talking about could keep us out of trouble for a long time."

"Mr. Pratt, it would also keep us from carrying out the plans for community in-

volvement that we all agreed made sense," Wilson replied. "Our center members don't want to go to the woods on a retreat. They want to be involved in their own community. How can we show a needs assessment supporting a project like this when the needs assessment we really did pointed the other way? Do you think there might be any chance at all that the Rodin Foundation might be interested in funding one of our own projects?"

"Katherine, I just don't think so. They didn't sound as if they were just out shopping for proposals. They had something darned specific in mind. Listen, there's no point in our talking about whether we want this Rodin money when we don't even have the grant. We can always decide whether we want to accept it with the strings attached or not after we've gotten it. In the meantime, let's just put all our efforts into doing the proposal. If we don't get the funding, no problem. If we do, then we can decide."

1. If you were in Katherine Wilson's shoes, what steps would you take next? Would you write a proposal for a country retreat or try to convince the board to stay with the plan that had already been developed? What are the pros and cons of each?

2. If Pratt's point of view does win out, how should Wilson deal with the planning committee?

3. Choose one program idea—one of the four in the organizational plan or the retreat center—and develop goals and objectives for it. Then prepare a line item budget to accomplish the goals and objectives.

References

Benefield, E., & Edwards, R. (1998). Fund-raising. In R. Edwards, J. Yankey, & M. Altpeter (Eds.), *Skills for effective management of nonprofit organizations* (pp. 59–77). Washington, DC: NASW Press.

Buxbaum, C. (1985). Cost-benefit analysis: The mystique versus the reality. In S. Slavin (Ed.), *Managing finances, personnel, and information in the human services* (pp. 61–79). New York: Haworth.

Edwards, R., & Benefield, E. (1997). *Building a strong foundation.* Washington, DC: NASW Press.

Flynn, M. (1995). Budgeting in community organizations: Principles for the '90s. In J. Tropman, J. Erlich, & J. Rothman (Eds.), *Tactics and techniques of community practice* (3rd ed., pp. 450–466). Itasca, IL: Peacock.

Green, R. (1998). Maximizing the use of performance contracts. In R. Edwards, J. Yankey, & M. Altpeter (Eds.), *Skills for effective management of nonprofit organizations* (pp. 78–97). Washington, DC: NASW Press.

Gummer, B. (1990). *The politics of social administration.* Upper Saddle River, NJ: Prentice Hall.

Henry, C. (1998). Effective proposal writing. In R. Edwards, J. Yankey, & M. Altpeter (Eds.), *Skills for effective management of nonprofit organizations* (pp. 45–58). Washington, DC: NASW Press.

Kettner, P., & Martin, L. (1995). Performance contracting in the human services: An initial assessment. *Administration in Social Work, 19*(2), 47–61.

Kettner, P., & Martin, L. (1996). The impact of declining resources and purchase of service contracting on private, nonprofit agencies. *Administration in Social Work, 20*(3), 21–38.

Lauffer, A. (1997). *Grants, etc.* (2nd ed.). Thousand Oaks, CA: Sage.

Levine, C. H. (1978). Organizational decline and cutback management. *Public Administration Review, 38,* 316–325.

Lohmann, R., & Lohmann, N. (1997). Management: Cost measurement. In R. Edwards (Ed.), *Encyclopedia of social work supplement 1997* (pp. 214–228). Washington, DC: NASW Press.

Marx, J. (1996). Strategic philanthropy: An opportunity for partnership between corporations and health/human service. *Administration in Social Work, 29*(3), 57–73.

Mayers, R. S. (1989). *Financial management for nonprofit human service agencies.* Springfield, IL: Thomas.

O'Looney, J. (1996). *Redesigning the work of human services.* Westport, CT: Quorum.

Schick, A. (1990). Budgeting for results: Recent developments in five industrialized countries. *Public Administration Review, 50*(1), 26–34.

Skidmore, R. A. (1990). *Social work administration: Dynamic management and human relationships* (2nd ed.). Upper Saddle River, NJ: Prentice Hall.

Skok, J. E. (1980). Budgetary politics and decision making: Development of an alternative hypothesis for state government. *Administration and Society, 11,* 445–460.

Strachan, J. (1998). Understanding nonprofit financial management. In R. Edwards, J. Yankey, & M. Altpeter (Eds.), *Skills for effective management of nonprofit organizations* (pp. 343–370). Washington, DC: NASW Press.

Taubman, S. (1985). Doing less with less. *Social Work, 30,* 180–182.

Thompson, J. (1999). *Stand by me: Model proposal.* Unpublished manuscript, San Diego State University.

Turner, J. (1995). Fund-raising and philanthropy. In R. Edwards (Ed.), *Encyclopedia of social work* (19th ed., pp. 1038–1044). Washington, DC: NASW Press.

Weatherley, R. (1984). Approaches to cutback management. In F. Perlmutter (Ed.), *Human services at risk* (pp. 39–56). Lexington, MA: Lexington.

9

Designing and Using Information Systems

CHAPTER OUTLINE _____

Just as psychotherapist Fritz Perls defined *responsibility* as the ability to respond, *accountability* may be seen as the ability to account. We have already looked at several important accountabilities of human service organizations. Accountability to the community is addressed through needs assessments, strategic planning, and, in a most encompassing sense, a focus on the agency's mission. Accountability to clients, other service providers, and standards of professional organizations is reflected in the use of the most appropriate and effective service delivery models. Accountability to staff occurs through human resources policies and processes that ensure that staff are well trained, supervised, and evaluated and that enhance the high quality of working life through factors such as fair and equitable treatment by the agency. We just reviewed how financial management systems can help ensure accountability to funders and the community at large and can demonstrate this through financial reports and audits.

We will now look at another important way to account to the community, clients, board, and other stakeholders by documenting the agency's activities and accomplishments. These processes, sometimes looked at by staff with as much annoyance as are references to the budget, are variously referred to as "data collection," "doing stats," "documentation," or the bane of bureaucracy: "paperwork." The most common term is probably *management information system,* or MIS, and it, too, requires some explanation: it is not a system for management to use for some mysterious purpose but for the management of information by all in the agency. Partly because of possible confusion or preconceptions regarding the term *MIS,* we will use a slightly broader term here: *information systems* (IS). This usage is intended to suggest that many types of information are useful and should be gathered, from units of service and client outcomes to staff turnover rates and assessments of employee job satisfaction.

This discussion is based on three important assumptions. First, we assume that pressures for accountability and, more specifically, documentation of results will increase (Martin & Kettner, 1997). Policymakers and the public can legitimately expect to be shown the results of the expenditure of governmental resources, for *any* purpose, including child abuse prevention, mental health treatment, drug-smuggling interdiction, new weapons systems, or corporate welfare. We are concerned here, of course, about the stewardship of government, foundation, and other funds in the human services.

Second, we assume that all employees in human service organizations want to do well: they want to feel that their work is valued and that they are truly helping clients and addressing problems.

Third, we assume that feedback on performance adds value in an organization. As we noted in Chapter 6 in discussing job design, receiving feedback on one's performance enriches the job and may enhance performance. Feedback is also an important component of motivation, with expectancy theory, McClelland's achievement motivation, and organizational behavior modification being vivid examples. Furthermore, regarding one of Peters and Waterman's (1982) characteristics of excellent organizations, "productivity through people," "information and availability and comparison" is seen as an important factor (p. 266). In this context, they note the organizational axiom "what gets measured gets done" (p. 268) as a commonly accepted principle. As Rapp and Poertner (1992) put it, "the collection and feedback of information influences behavior" (p. 89). Information systems, which document results and provide feedback to staff, can be immensely helpful in these areas.

We will begin with a review of the various purposes of information systems. We will then outline a process for designing, or redesigning, an agency's information system and look at common data collection methods and measures. The use of computers and the Internet will receive particular attention, followed by a discussion of other uses of information in areas including organizational learning and the monitoring of employee quality of working life.

One important conceptual distinction should be noted at the outset. When human service workers hear the term *management information systems* or *information systems,* their thoughts usually turn to computers. While computers will be an important or essential part of any modern information system, it is important to note that for the foreseeable future IS will entail nonautomated aspects as well. More important, the system should first be designed conceptually without regard to data management procedures, to keep the focus on organizational purpose and results. It is tempting to gather data that can easily be retrieved and presented using a computer, but these data may be easy to collect but only marginally important. Many know the computer axiom "garbage in, garbage out," which represents this problem. Furthermore, it is a waste of time and resources to automate systems that are ineffective or inefficient, sometimes known as "paving cowpaths." Schoech, Schkade, and Mayers (1984) note that successful computerization depends on agency processes and procedures being in good shape before computerization. We will therefore address the design of the IS first and then review how computers can be used to maximum effect within the system.

Purposes of Information Systems _____

According to Rapp and Poertner (1992, pp. 97–100), information systems can be categorized into three types, each with different purposes. *Housekeeping systems* are used for basic routine processing of information and are the most likely to be automated. These systems are used to "increase the efficiency and accuracy of 'getting out the checks' to clients, staff, and other agencies" (p. 97). In addition to handling finances (accounting, budgeting, personnel), housekeeping systems are used to maintain client records, provider agencies, and other databases.

Decision support systems using technology such as mathematical modeling are much less common in the human services. Because of the nonroutine technologies of human services and the complexity of their environments, existing mathematical models are less relevant, and decision support is most likely to come through processes such as Web searches for relevant databases, agency best practices, program evaluation results, and needs assessment or other demographic data. Decision support systems may become more common at the case level, however. One example is *structured decision making* (SDM), which has been instituted in some California counties to aid decision making on child protective services cases (Freitag, 1999). SDM involves "identifying specific decision points in the life of a case, and providing highly structured assessment tools for each critical decision" regarding the likelihood of future child maltreatment (Freitag, 1999, p. 16).

Performance guidance systems offer the most promise for human service organizations. This system can also be used to use case-level information "to inform decisions by managers, administrators, policy-makers, even legislators and researchers" (Freitag, 1999, p. 16). The goal of a performance guidance system is "to instigate action" (Rapp & Poertner, 1992, p. 99). Based on organizational purpose, goals, and objectives, it provides data that staff can use to adjust their behavior, modify programs, or plan new activities.

This discussion will not address decision support systems, which to date have not been common, or housekeeping systems, which are typically designed by the agency's accounting and human resources experts or consultants and often use specialized software programs. The focus here is on ways of tracking *organizational performance* so that program objectives can be accomplished and agency strategies can be effectively implemented and modified. The design or redesign of an information system is thus based on both a current strategic plan and a solid program design (theory of helping and clearly defined service activities) with well-written goals and objectives.

Regarding the notion of performance management in particular, research and practice have revealed some other principles or characteristics of effective information systems. Perhaps most important, as Rapp and Poertner (1992) assert, "managers must know what constitutes performance" (p. 95). This knowledge is based on agency strategies and program objectives, but actual implementation requires serious thought and discussion on the part of the managers and in fact all employees. It is not enough to say "provide the best service possible to clients"; all staff must be clear on exactly what results are desired in terms of service outcomes and the way they use their time and focus their energy on a daily basis.

As the model of organizational purpose introduced in Chapter 1 showed, organizations and staff need to be consciously *purposeful,* devoting scarce time and resources to service outcomes, responsible management of funds, a supportive organizational culture, and a high quality of working life. There need to be systems to track progress in all of these areas so that staff can celebrate accomplishments and be rewarded and so that adjustments can be made to ensure desired results. Rapp and Poertner (pp. 100–101) also note that real challenges arise in measuring service delivery performance in the human services, but this does not mean that staff should give up on developing valid measures for client outcomes.

Specifically, Rapp and Poertner (1992) list these "principles for using information to enhance performance":

1. The role of information in an organization is to initiate action and influence behavior.

2. The act of collecting information (measurement) generates human energy around the activity being measured.

3. To increase the expenditure of energy for performance, the collection and feedback of information must be systematically linked to explicit goals, standards for performance, and rewards.

4. To insure that information directs human energy toward enhanced performance, data collection and feedback must be used to: (1) foster and reinforce desired behaviors; (2) identify barriers to performance and problem-solve; and (3) set goals for future performance.

5. Feedback directs behavior toward performance when it provides "cues" to workers to identify clear methods for correction, and when it helps workers learn from their performance.

6. Feedback motivates behavior toward performance when it is used to create expectations for external and internal rewards, is linked to realistic standards for performance, and is directed toward the future versus used punitively to evaluate past performance. (p. 90)

The purposes and uses of an agency's information system should always be kept in mind by those designing or changing it. Every form, procedure, measure, data collection task, and data summary should be in direct response to a particular need of the agency. These needs include expectations from funders for reports on accomplishments and the use of resources, but a system should not be driven by these external demands. Staff must know that all the agency's systems are designed by and used by the agency itself and that accountability to funders is only one (albeit an essential one) purpose of the system.

The Challenges of Measuring Performance

The criteria of effective information systems just listed are, of course, not easy to apply fully in human service organizations. As we noted in Chapter 2, two characteristics of HSOs, "fuzzy" goals and the difficulties in measuring outcomes, have in the past caused frustration for both managers who want to demonstrate the good work of their organizations and funders, policymakers, and other stakeholders who want to know what they are getting for their money. It is much easier for a car dealer, for example, to document results in terms of numbers of cars sold, gross income, or profit per car than it is for a human service manager to measure in a valid way the effects of services designed to reduce problems such as child abuse and neglect.

Until recent years, many funders did not demand precise documentation of success, perhaps understanding the complexity of isolating causal factors and measuring what activities made a difference, or at least concluding that the resources required to gather such data would be extensive and better used in simply delivering more services. Regardless of historical factors, pressure to document results and organizational performance is likely to increase even further, and a proactive human service manager devotes considerable attention to this task, not only to answer the questions of funders and others but also to improve performance of the agency's programs to better serve clients. We will review some of these challenges and dilemmas, with the expectation that they can be met and that human service organizations can, in fact, document performance in valid, meaningful, and useful ways.

Partly in response to increasing accountability demands, the most important recent development in human service program information systems has been the growing interest in outcomes measurement (Mullen & Magnabosco, 1997). In the past, funders and agencies have focused primarily on outputs—numbers and types of clients, units of services provided—rather than ultimate outcomes. In addition to the challenges in documenting human services reviewed in Chapter 2, even defining a unit of service can be problematic, particularly when trying to compare unit costs (Lohmann & Lohmann, 1997). Nevertheless, in recent years, the measurement of client outcomes has progressed significantly.

A powerful and influential analysis of this issue by Lisbeth Schorr of the Harvard University Project on Effective Interventions reviews where we are now and where we need to head. Schorr (1997) describes the trend this way: "What counts is no longer confined to whether rules are being complied with. Instead, accountability procedures are beginning to reflect common sense: what matters is whether public purposes are being accomplished" (p. 115). After outlining some of the things that this type of accountability can accomplish and some of the fears of program staff and their supporters, she lists some ways of "minimizing the dangers and maximizing the benefits of an outcomes focus" (p. 122). While focused on macro- or community-wide systems, some of these apply to the agency level as well:

- Choose the right outcomes: "get everyone who has a stake, including skeptics, to agree on a set of outcomes considered important, achievable, and measurable" (p. 122).

- Set ambitious goals for which measurable outcomes may be developed: a goal may be to have all children grow up safe and nurtured; outcomes may include items from increasingly popular "children's report cards"

(McCroskey, 1997) such as violent crime rates, family reunification, or poverty status.

- "Distinguish between outcomes and processes" to avoid "process creep" in which the focus shifts to means or activities rather than end results (p. 125).

- Place outcomes in "a broader accountability context" (p. 126) in which an agency is not held totally responsible for outcomes or conditions partly beyond its control (for example, lack of child care or transportation may affect parents' participation in an employment program).

To develop systems that provide the newer types of data that will be needed, Schorr suggests "human intervention mapping" (p. 130), referred to later in this chapter as *flowcharting,* which enables service providers and decision makers to track client conditions, service activities, and interim and ultimate outcomes and to show the links among them. This strategy presents opportunities not only to assess the effects of particular program interventions but also, on a macrolevel, to educate policymakers regarding the complexity of social and community problems and the activities necessary to address them adequately.

Another way both to educate policymakers and others and to design more comprehensive information systems is to note the multiple measures of effectiveness in the human services. Heffron (1989) has developed a useful typology of approaches for measuring organizational effectiveness:

- **Goal approaches** include setting measurable objectives in areas such as effectiveness and efficiency

- **Internal process approaches** look at documented procedures and units of service—the most common method in the past, now augmented by goal (outcomes) approaches but still relevant in terms of ensuring that funds are being spent according to programmatic guidelines.

- **Political approaches** are not part of a formal system but are important in assessing the extent to which an organization is responding effectively to the needs of key stakeholders.

- **Human resources approaches** measure job satisfaction and morale through employee attitude surveys, assessment of turnover, and absenteeism.

- **Systems approaches** are like political approaches in that they are not typically used explicitly, except, for example, in assessing the organization's growth and adaptiveness as reflected in its ability to maintain funding sources and acquire new ones and to adapt strategically to the environment in other ways.

While the goal approaches will usually be the most important, a human service manager will benefit from assessing the ways in which any of the others may be relevant and require monitoring. The information system can then be designed to meet the multiple information needs of managers, staff, the board, and outside stakeholders such as funding sources.

The importance of multiple measures of organizational effectiveness has also become part of the discussion in the business sector. In a seminal *Harvard Business Review* article, Kaplan and Norton (1992) present the *balanced scorecard* as a method for tracking multiple measures of factors that affect performance. They propose that organizations gather information to answer four basic questions, each representing an important perspective from which to view the organization:

- How do our customers see us? (customer perspective)

- What must we excel at? (internal perspective)

- Can we continue to improve and create value? (innovation and learning perspective)

- How do we look to shareholders? (financial perspective) (p. 72)

Kaplan and Norton recommend that managers not overload themselves and their systems with too much data but rather "focus on the handful of measures that are most critical" (p. 73). In a business, "customers' concerns tend to fall into four categories: time, quality, performance, and service" (p. 73). In a human service organization, adaptations would of course be necessary, such as the inclusion of other important stakeholders. For example, in a child protective services program, "customers" may include a child who may be the victim of abuse or neglect, parents, and other family members, often with conflicting interests and expectations. Law enforcement and the court system are other relevant stakeholders. Measures of customer satisfaction may include response time for initial investigations, actions taken by a social worker, and the quality of a court report. The important principle here is that an organization needs to define key goals, objectives, and criteria for a service and then create measures for them. Most of this, of course, is done at the program design stage. If the program design and methods and the original objectives are clear, developing useful measures will be easier.

Key internal processes should also be measured: the "business processes that have the greatest impact on customer satisfaction—factors that affect cycle time, quality, employee skills, and productivity" and the organization's "core competencies, the critical technologies needed to ensure continued market leadership" (pp. 74–75). Human services have been noted for measuring processes, such as units of services provided, but these are not often directly related to the accomplishment of objectives. Processes measured should be the key ones in getting results. Again, a solid program design based on empirically validated service delivery theories and methods will make it easier to identify key factors to measure. In the human services, staff skill and competence (for example, risk assessment in protective services), relationship building and assessment skills, and efficiency in conducting visits and preparing reports may be relevant. Other internal processes such as employees' understanding of and commitment to the agency's mission and goals, their role clarity, and levels of burnout can be measured through periodic employee surveys (discussed in Chapter 11).

Increasingly, organizations will have to better measure their own adaptive abilities. As Kaplan and Norton put it, "a company's ability to innovate, improve, and learn ties directly to the company's value" (p. 76). In the human services, relevant variables to measure may include the number of new programs initiated, new funding acquired, employee ideas for program innovations, and cost savings related to increased efficiencies. An agency's activities related to becoming a learning organization (see Chapter 4) or organizational change activities (Chapter 11) may be worth tracking. As much as possible, these activities (visioning, educational, or dialogue sessions with staff) should be measured in terms of relevant results, such as action plans for new programs or strategies, and connected as clearly as possible to actual desired organizational outcomes. Documenting the number of organizational visioning sessions will have little meaning or value unless these activities have effects on performance in the near or short term.

The final balanced scorecard measure is the one that has been the most popular in business but perhaps the most neglected in the human services: financial goals. Of course, only for-profit human service organizations will have goals related to profit or shareholder value, but not-for-profit and governmental organizations can and should develop relevant measures of financial success. Balanced budgets, increases in funds from various sources, and financial stability are legitimate measures and should be tracked, but not to the detriment of other goals such as customer satisfaction or program quality. In fact, a major point of the balanced scorecard is that measures in all areas should be assessed from a systems perspective, so that improvements in one area do not happen at the expense of other areas. Kaplan and Norton use as a metaphor "the dials and indicators in an airplane cockpit" (p. 72), all of which must be monitored and responded to.

Once an organization has developed clear and viable program designs with measurable objectives and has articulated conceptually the various key success factors that it will need to monitor, designing an information system becomes much easier.

Design Process Guidelines

Before reviewing the design process itself, we will look at some additional guidelines that will help make things go smoothly (Butterfield, 1995; Weirich, 1980). First, those who initiate the design process should be aware of the dynamics of organizational politics and power in the agency. Staff may feel threatened that a new information system will highlight inadequacies in their work or lead to more unnecessary paperwork. The idea of a new information system should be introduced by staff with a power base sufficient to overcome resistance. Typically a major component of this is top-level support, but equally important is getting the commitment of workers at other levels of the organization. The best way to do this, consistent with human resources management approaches covered in Chapter 4, is to involve staff in the process. Their knowledge and creativity will be invaluable in developing a good system, and their involvement will give them a stake in the outcome, broadening support for the initiative.

Related to this is the issue of resources. Top management support needs to go beyond announcements and meetings to making in advance a sufficient commitment of resources to enable the system to be implemented. Regarding computerization, Butterfield (1995) suggests that a person should be assigned as the computer "champion," and this advice applies to IS development as well. Assigning a person for this initiative both demonstrates management support and helps ensure that the process can proceed as planned.

Ideologically based issues may surface as well. Staff may see an information system as a bureaucratic method to control all staff and stifle worker autonomy and initiative. Staff will need to be shown what the purposes of the system will be and how data from the system will be used (for example, to improve services for clients and to demonstrate the value of the program to current and prospective funders). Concerns regarding confidentiality will also need to be addressed, such as controlling access to files and computerized databases. Staff will also need to believe that a new system will not require a net increase in work on their part (for example, paperwork or data entry). Through training it should become clear how the system will actually be more efficient for workers and will provide valuable information. This does not involve "selling" staff: the system should be designed so that the benefits are real and evident to all.

Another implication of a well-designed information system is that decision making will become more data based and rational. This point may be seen as a threat to staff who are used to making decisions based on gut feel, values, or impressions. It should be emphasized to staff that no decision-making process is fully rational and that staff impressions can in fact help guide decisions but that they should use all the data available to increase the likelihood that the decisions do lead to improved performance.

Finally, an effective way to deal with any resistance is to note the pressures for change. Funding sources are regularly increasing their expectations for accountability and results, and this point can be used to leverage both the organization's commitment in terms of resources and the staff's interest in change: they must all see that a new system will have a concrete payoff for them. All of these dynamics should be considered as plans for introducing an IS design process are developed.

The Design Process _____

Recent experiences in the development of information systems and computerization have provided knowledge regarding the steps that should be taken to ensure that an IS is appropriate, effective, efficient, and valued by staff (Kettner, Moroney, & Martin, 1999; Schoech, 1995; Zimmerman & Broughton, 1998). The following steps are adapted from the process developed by Schoech (1995). This process may be used when updating, refining, or totally redesigning an existing IS or designing a system for a new program or agency. Such a process may also involve computerizing an agency's system, but computerization only occurs after the system is designed or redesigned. Specifics regarding computerization are discussed after the generic design process is covered.

Step 1: Assessment of the Current Situation

According to Schoech (1995, p. 1474), the focus here is on "preparedness and feasibility" on the part of the agency. A decision to update or redesign an IS typically originates with a discussion among agency managers and perhaps other staff, and a good deal of dialogue should occur before making a commitment to proceed. Ideally there would be strategies or other elements in the agency's strategic plan, and perhaps even a strategy addressing this directly, suggesting that IS redesign and/or computerization is necessary. In any case, this idea should be announced to staff, outlining the intended purpose and objectives of the initiative. This may also include a preliminary timetable and list of those involved.

To begin building employee involvement and commitment at the beginning, a steering committee should be formed to complete the assessment process. In large, complex agencies, day-to-day work on the system design may be performed by one or more task forces or a design team, similar to the organization design process outlined in Chapter 5. Such a committee or team should have representatives from all major sectors of the agency: management; supervisors; line staff; office staff; IS staff, if any; and labor organizations, if any. Ideally the initial announcement would solicit volunteers from staff who would like to participate.

A preliminary estimate should be made of necessary resources, including time for staff to attend meetings and work on the project and perhaps costs for a computer consultant. Existing conditions such as staff skills, values, and ideologies; existing equipment and processes; and staff goals and visions should be assessed. The steering committee should comprehensively and honestly review the likely system impacts (such as a higher quality of data in more usable forms, inefficiencies during implementation and training, changes in the way work is done) and the likely effects on key stakeholders (particularly staff who will be using the system). The result of this step is a report for circulation to staff and a decision to proceed or terminate the effort.

Continuing with our example from the previous chapter, the executive team overseeing the teenage girls peer support program (the Girls' Support Club) decided that with the recent growth of the agency, including acquiring two new grants with very explicit expectations for documentation of program results, a total updating of the agency's information system was in order. Their existing system was in reality separate systems: data were collected on each program just to meet the requirements of each grant or contract. The agency could not get an overall picture of clients being served, program outcomes, and measures of efficiency or cost-effectiveness. Computers were used for agency bookkeeping and personnel records and for word processing, but no client database existed. To address this situation, agency executive staff met with all program staff groups and announced plans for addressing this issue through the formation of a steering committee. Volunteers were solicited for involvement in the steering committee and a task force for each program. Staff saw the need for this initiative, but to validate their informal impressions and to ensure that all staff could consider the issue, each task force assessed the needs for and the purposes of a new information system, developed proposed action plans and timetables, and prepared a feasibility report.

The steering committee consisted of the agency associate executive director, directors of two programs, three direct service staff, and the agency's director of administration. This committee was to develop a plan for developing a comprehensive information system including a client database that could be used not only to demonstrate program effectiveness and efficiency to funding sources but also to provide information to aid in program planning and development. Additionally, for the newly funded Girls' Support Club program, a task force was formed to develop the information system for that program specifically, which would be coordinated with the efforts of the steering committee and task forces for other programs to develop the overall system and specific data collection tools for the Support Club. This task force included the new program director, two program staff members, and the program's administrative assistant. Feasibility reports recommending a "go" were submitted to the executive team and the board of directors, and a decision was made to proceed.

Step 2: Analysis of the Existing System

If the agency decides to proceed, the next step is to analyze the existing system. The key to a system's effectiveness is the degree to which it meets the agency's unique planning, management, and evaluation needs. Agency personnel need to identify as specifically as possible the kinds of data needed, the source of these data, and the frequency with which they should be collected and distributed. Beyond this, planning for effective gathering and disseminating of information involves working out the type of system most appropriate for the agency's functions, size, and degree of complexity. The steering committee should bear in mind that the main purpose of an IS is to guide staff performance in accomplishing program objectives: to make a difference in the lives of clients and communities. This analysis should therefore begin by reviewing the program objectives and service delivery models.

An IS must enable staff and other stakeholders to track progress on objectives and provide other information useful to the program. Information needs should be listed here: client demographics, staff tasks and units of service, intermediate and ultimate client outcomes, and so forth. The IS may also be needed to answer questions related to program evaluation or research (for example, what effect does a particular job-training program have on the ultimate employment of selected welfare recipients?).

The information that can be provided by an effectively planned information system includes the following:

- Information related to the community, such as demographic information, data on social and economic characteristics, identification of under served populations, and listings of external services and resources

- Information concerning individual clients, groups of clients, and the client population as a whole, including such data as presenting problem, history, type of service received, length of service, socioeconomic and family characteristics, employment, and measurements of satisfaction and service outcomes

- Service information, including types of service provided by units within the agency, number of clients served, number of admissions and discharges in a given time period, and specification of service-related activities

- Staff information, including time spent in varying activities, number of clients served, volume of services, and differences among separate programs within the agency

- Resource allocation information, including total costs, costs for specific types of services, and data needed for financial reporting

With the exception of the external community information, all these data can be obtained through normal agency operations. Regardless of how complex or expensive the system might be, however, it can store only what planners have selected as useful information.

A helpful technique for detailing the service delivery process so that it may be documented is the *flowchart* (Lauffer, 1984, pp. 213–221). A flowchart is constructed by documenting each step that occurs with a client as she or he is processed through the agency, from an initial contact to the termination of services. Boxes or other figures are used to represent each step in the process (for example, filling out a form; interviewing a client). These steps are organized in sequential order and connected by lines. They indicate what happens to each form or piece of data collected.

Activities occur at each stage that are based on the service delivery model and documented in case files and other records. Typically, at intake a fact sheet is developed, containing basic demographic and other information. There may be a screening or assessment process during which client data are gathered, perhaps using forms or checklists. After problems are identified, a case plan, including objectives, is developed and documented in the client file. Activities at each stage of the service delivery process may be documented as well. Results are assessed at predetermined times, and eventually the case is terminated, with, ideally, follow-up planned. Designers of the IS can use this chart, program objectives, and other information needs of the staff and outside stakeholders to determine what data need to be collected in the new system.

Also at this stage, problems with the existing system can be identified for action. Benchmarking of best practices can be useful: members of the design team can research agencies providing similar services to identify "best practices" in the use of information systems. These processes or ideas may be considered for adoption or adaptation during the design steps outlined later.

Rapp and Poertner (1992, pp. 101–104) provide useful criteria for measures of changes in client status or behavior:

- Measures need to be valid (for example, completion of a substance abuse program does not necessarily mean that a client is no longer using drugs).

- Measures must be observable, replicable, and uniform.

- Measures should be understandable when they are summarized in reports.

- Measures need to be susceptible to change within the period being reported.

- There should not be too many measures.

- Measures need to be efficient (simple and easy to collect and report).

Rapp and Poertner (1992, pp. 106–107) also offer a useful grouping of the basic types of data collection methods: self-administered questionnaires, interviews, observation, and agency record keeping. An information system would probably use several of these, to help compensate for the limitations of single instruments (clients may report in socially desirable ways; interviewers or observers may miss important data).

Kettner and Martin (1993, p. 66) provide a useful typology for describing measures of organizational processes and performance. At the *process* level, data may be collected on *inputs* such as staff, facilities, equipment, funding, and clients and on *throughputs,* which are the tasks performed as part of the service delivery technologies. *Performance* is measured by *outputs* such as measures of service volume or *outcomes:* the impacts on clients. An information system would probably gather data in all of these areas: numbers and types of staff, budget allocations, client characteristics, services provided, and outcomes.

Identification of outcomes is, of course, much easier if program objectives have been written in terms of outcomes rather than outputs. This approach will avoid *endogeneity,* a common problem in human service evaluation in which the program activity is stated as an outcome, such as a goal of recruiting substance abusers into a program (Rossi, 1997).

According to Rapp and Poertner (1992, pp. 108–120), outcomes may be assessed in several categories: affect, knowledge, behavior, status, or environment. Changes in *affect* and attitude are often measured in human service programs (such as satisfaction with services), and they may provide useful feedback to staff but do not necessarily correspond to desired end results. Changes in *knowledge* can be useful as well (for example, regarding methods for birth control or safe sex) but again may not change ultimate behavior (practicing safe sex). *Behavior* changes can be seen in both skills and performance, with the latter usually being the most desirable end result. The use of behaviorally anchored rating scales, discussed in Chapter 6 as a performance appraisal technique, is becoming increasingly common as a method for assessing client change. *Status* changes are often highly desirable, such as when a client can move from a group home for the mentally ill to independent living. The final category described by Rapp and Poertner, changes in the *environment,* are not commonly addressed, although measures of child and family well-being, or quality of life changes, are being increasingly used to track the effects of the 1996 welfare reform law on children and families.

An assessment of the existing system and needs for a new system can point to the types of data needed and ways to collect them, ideally addressing ultimate and desired client outcomes. Results of this step should be summarized in a report by the design team or steering committee, and once again the agency should decide whether to proceed. Measures for assessing outcomes will be reviewed in the next step.

The Support Club Information System Task Force started by reviewing the program design outlined in the funding proposal. They concluded that it would be essential to develop measures for outcomes: the accomplishment of objectives listed in their original grant proposal. They also wanted to measure key outputs such as units of service so they would later be able to correlate amounts and types of services provided with ultimate outcomes. Since this would be a new program, they could start from scratch in developing forms for case records and forms for data compilation and reports. They noted that in other programs in the agency, only outputs were measured, and they had no real way of knowing what the ultimate benefits to clients were. They wanted to avoid this situation in the Support

Club program so that they would have some idea as to what activities really made a difference to clients. The task force prepared a flowchart describing what would happen to a client as she received services and what forms would be needed to capture data for both case management and later evaluation. They met with staff at programs that provided similar services for at-risk girls and found only one offering helpful guidance: a program with a computerized database for client records that kept track of demographic data and services provided. They concluded that they had a huge task in front of them but that they definitely should proceed so that they would be able to clearly show the program's accomplishments.

Step 3: Detailed Design

If the agency commits to continuing this process, changes are made in the existing system based on data gathered at the previous stage. The flowchart is analyzed and unnecessary steps are eliminated, including newly needed data or forms, and the process is adjusted in other ways as needed (for example, making changes related to automation). Once information requirements have been specified, agency personnel need to determine the appropriate sources for these data. Most agencies use forms that identify client characteristics and/or the nature of services delivered. Evaluation data requirements should be taken into account when such forms are designed.

A method for handling evaluation data should be built into the routine agency operations, allowing the collection of evaluation data to become part of the agency's everyday operating procedures. Evaluators can determine what person or functional unit within an agency can most easily record needed information, to whom the information should be reported, and who should be responsible for analyzing the information.

This step involves answering questions about how the data will be used. The system should be easily usable by service delivery staff, of course, and program staff and administrators will use data summaries to track progress for the project as a whole, both as early intelligence regarding needed adjustments such as changing staffing configurations and as annual reviews or evaluations. Decisions can be made regarding which data will be computerized and which will be maintained manually. This approach suggests the types of forms that will be needed in case files and for summaries to be used in monthly and annual reports. Evaluation needs such as correlations among variables should be anticipated so that required statistical manipulations will be easy to perform.

Other parameters such as the frequency of data entry, needs for links with other databases (such as those in other programs in the agency), and confidentiality should be taken into account here. If more than one option is under consideration, each can be evaluated with regard to the criteria chosen and the best design selected for detailing. At this point, software to meet the system needs can be selected, and new hardware can be chosen to match the software and provide necessary staff access and technology (printers and so forth). Specifics regarding automation will be addressed in a later section in this chapter, but one beneficial side effect that may result from computerization will be mentioned here. Oyserman and Benbenishty (1997) found that in the process of designing a computerized MIS in a child welfare setting, the design team discovered problems in the existing practice model (for example, integration of care across practice sites) that could be addressed by problem solving.

Finally, the proposed design, including data that need to be collected, methods for collecting and storing data, data entry, forms for case files, and formats for data collation and analysis, as well as software and hardware needed, can then be prepared for review and decisions. If various task forces have been working on different aspects of the plan, their work is integrated and reviewed, typically by the steering committee and then by agency executive staff and other staff groups who will be using the system. After the design proposal is approved or modified, implementation can begin.

The Support Club Task Force used the flowchart to note service activities at each step of the program and the data that would need to be gathered. At the macrolevel, the agency had data on measures such as juvenile crime, poverty, unemployment, race and ethnicity, child abuse rates, and child health for the county as a whole and the areas served by the schools participating in the program. They planned to gather data on these variables for each client served by the group to help determine representativeness of the girls in the program (the program was funded to serve one hundred girls, only 13 percent of the target population). They designed a face sheet for demographic data such as age, ethnicity, school performance, health indicators, law enforcement contacts, and current involvement with other service providers such as child protective services. This also would include premeasures related to program objectives (self-esteem, knowledge of health issues, and awareness of career opportunities). They knew they would also need forms for the measurement of self-esteem, health issues, and career opportunities. Changes in academic improvement would be gathered from school records, and law enforcement contacts from police and probation. Another form would be used for the case plan, which would outline services to be provided. These could include tutoring, academic assistance, career opportunity exploration, health education, recreation, field trips, and listening to guest speakers. The case plan would have individual case objectives written so that their accomplishment could be easily documented with a yes/no field or a behaviorally anchored rating scale. Demographics, premeasures, and services received would be documented in the case file, using fields that could be used for entry into a computerized database. They would also need an activity report describing all activities that occurred at each participating school each day, including the staff, volunteers, guest speakers, and number of client attendees to be used for monthly, quarterly, and annual reporting. This report would list staff hours, to compare with budgeted figures and to assist in cost-effectiveness analysis. Each form was reviewed to ensure that data could be easily computerized and collated and that correlations and other statistical analyses would be possible. The task force coordinated their work with that of the other task forces and the steering committee to ensure maximum compatibility of formats.

Step 4: System Testing and Agency Preparation

After the design of a new system has been approved, new equipment, or at least software, will probably need to be purchased. This step often will require a lump-sum expenditure for hardware and software as well as initial training of staff. Regular maintenance and upgrading of hardware and software and training for new staff would then become ongoing budget items. The importance of the training of staff and other users of the system (data entry or IS staff) is often not fully appreciated or emphasized. In addition to learning how to use any new software and hardware, development of a new or significantly changed information system, automated or not, represents a significant cultural change for most organizations: staff will need to see and use information in a new way, as a more important component of their work in delivering services to clients and planning or modifying programs. Principles of organizational change, covered in Chapter 11, will need to be applied here.

In terms of the basic training itself, Zimmerman and Broughton (1998) offer some useful suggestions for training staff in computer usage, many of which are also useful guidelines for IS training not necessarily involving automation:

- Train in small groups. . . .
- Train for short periods of time. . . .
- Make sure workers have access to computers and software at their work site before training. . . .
- Make sure workers train on the same software they have on their work computers. . . .
- Do not interrupt training with other work. . . .
- Have workers take classes appropriate for their level of competence. . . .
- Give new computer users time to practice their new skills. . . .
- Use the buddy system for training. . . . (pp. 334–335)

Further emphasizing the importance of training, Schoech (1995) suggests that "a rule of thumb for developing successful information systems is to spend 10 percent of total resources on hardware; 40 percent on software; and 50 percent on development, implementation, and training" (p. 1476).

The new system also has to be built into the agency's policies and procedures. New staff positions, such as an information systems coordinator, may be created, and the job duties of others may change, to include data entry. These changes need to be reflected in modified job descriptions, performance appraisal criteria, and perhaps as new criteria for particular staff positions.

During the testing of the new system, it may become clear that refinements in forms or procedures will be needed, and these changes can be made, with clearance through any relevant task forces or the steering committee to ensure that the overall system will still work.

Step 5: Conversion

Normally a new system is implemented in stages, such as program by program, rather than all at once. If automation is occurring, the new and old systems should both be used for a time, to ensure that nothing is lost in the transition to the new system. After a test period shows that the new system does provide all needed information, the old system may be discontinued. Conversion may also involve reorganizing office locations or space within offices (for example, to create computer workstations).

Step 6: Evaluation

The ultimate test of any organizational system, including an information system, is its performance in accomplishing stated objectives, from improvements in services to clients and increased responsiveness to stakeholders such as funders, to cost savings and increased quality of working life. All who have been involved with the design and implementation of the new system, including the steering committee, any task forces, and all staff who use the system, should have an opportunity to review the original goals, objectives, and expectations for the new system and compare actual results to these. Sometimes there is interest in assessing the effects of the new system on some aspect of performance, such as efficiency or cost savings. Assessing the views of staff, through a survey or focus groups, can identify accomplishments of the system and also emerging issues or potential problems and ideas for addressing them.

Step 7: Operation, Maintenance, and Modification

By this point, the new system and its procedures and forms should be fully operational and functioning as intended. Key factors now include ensuring that the new procedures are in fact followed (or changed as needed based on new experiences) and that mechanisms are in place for ongoing adaptation to new needs and conditions. As was noted in Step 4, principles of change management should be followed: someone should be responsible for ongoing monitoring and ensuring that the system is used as intended and continues to provide needed information. Questions to be asked have to do with the ease of use of the system and the utility of its outputs: do staff use data in their daily work, and do managers use reports in monitoring and adjusting programs and activities?

Any system will also need updating, notably regarding software but also in response to new programmatic needs. Provisions need to be made for not only the training of new staff on use of the system but training for other staff whenever changes are made. The agency should have mechanisms such as periodic focus groups or discussions at staff meetings to monitor staff feelings about and use of the system so that it continues to be seen as valuable to them in their work. Presenting summaries of data gathered by the system can both provide a context for staff's daily data collection activities and show how their work helps lead to valued program outcomes. For example, if patterns or trends become evident regarding changes in client characteristics, amounts or types of services provided, or outcomes, these data can be fed back to staff for analysis and modification of program activity as needed. This is one aspect of program evaluation, which we will address in the next chapter, after a review of some current issues and developments regarding information systems.

The Use of Computers

As noted earlier, information systems are often equated with computers, and while they are not the same thing, they clearly overlap greatly in today's human service organizations. Computers are becoming increasingly prominent in the work life and personal life of human service staff and will become more so in the future. This development can be seen in trends in the literature, including the establishment of the journal *Computers in Human Services* in the 1980s (renamed the *Journal of Technology in Human Services* in 1999) and books on computers (for example, Downing et al., 1991; Leiderman, Guzetta, Struminger, & Monnickendam, 1993; Schoech, 1990) and on the Internet (Butterfield & Schoech, 1997; Karger & Levine, 1999). Here we will review briefly some of the common and emerging uses of computers in the human services.

All human service workers probably have some familiarity with the traditional uses of computers: word processing, spreadsheets, and databases. More specifically, Butterfield (1995, pp. 596–603) suggests that computers can be of use in these areas:

- data collection and assessment (for example, to answer closed-ended questions);

- computerized interviews (Butterfield summarizes research that shows, perhaps surprisingly, that clients were comfortable with computerized interviews, which were also found to be cost-effective);

- computerized therapy (many programs of "dubious value" [p. 598] and still in the experimental stage);

- assistive devices, bulletin boards, and other on-line services for people with disabilities;

- bulletin boards (for messages and transfer of files or databases);

- community-based networks (for example, bulletin boards for resource exchanges);

- modifying worker and agency behavior (such as improving client outcomes by using data on cost and availability of services and client characteristics);

- policy development and advocacy (for instance, mailing lists, newsletters, monitoring legislation, bulletin boards); and

- on-line and CD-ROM databases.

Many agencies, particularly in the public sector, are now on-line, providing staff with access to E-mail and the Internet. Zimmerman and Broughton (1998) note the increasing use of LANs (local area networks, in which computers within an agency are linked), which enable staff to share printers and use *groupware* for tasks such as sharing databases and doing group scheduling.

Regarding the Internet specifically, Butterfield and Schoech (1997) describe more recently emerging advances such as *listservs,* in which E-mail can be sent to groups of subscribers interested in a particular topic. Another type of on-line program is *usenet,* "also called 'Internet news,' 'newsgroups,' or 'News Net.'. . . With News Net, e-mail messages are sent to and stored in a single computer, where anyone who contacts that computer can read the messages" (p. 157). Human service workers are increasingly using Web search tools to locate information on a specific topic by simply typing keywords into a *search engine* available through on-line services. Butterfield and Schoech also discuss the importance of confidentiality considerations, the risk of the transmission of computer viruses, and the importance of *netiquette* to avoid the insults and confusion that can occur with this form of nonverbal communication.

Karger and Levine (1999) provide detailed guidance on getting on-line: using Web browsers, listservs, and newsgroups and developing a Web page. This field is advancing so rapidly that readers of a book may find outdated information and will certainly have to consult journals, newsletters, newspapers, and, of course, on-line sources to remain up-to-date on computer and Internet developments.

Finally, Butterfield (1995) notes some additional significant issues related to computer usage that should be addressed by agencies embarking on automation. An initial infatuation with the potential of computers may lead to a misplaced focus on what a computer can easily measure, ignoring or downplaying important complexities and subtleties in the service delivery process. It is easy to count the number of job-training sessions a welfare recipient attends but harder to identify precisely which factors will lead to successful or unsuccessful entry into the labor market. As we implied earlier, management needs to pay attention to workers' legitimate concerns regarding the new layers of control that are possible with computers, and they must ensure that control mechanisms are used to enhance performance and reward staff for good work. Confidentiality and security of data will, of course, need attention as well.

Organizational Learning and the Quality of Working Life

We will end this discussion of information systems by putting "data" in a larger context. It is easy to get caught up in numbers, performing elaborate statistical manipulations and preparing impressive reports. These may in fact be useful and important tasks, but it should always be remembered that the data are only representations of more important realities. Definitions supplied by Schoech (1995, p. 1473) can illustrate this point. He defines *data* as "the assigned characters that represent facts, entities, or events" and offered "15" as an example, in this case representing age. At the next level, *information* is defined as "data processed to add additional meaning," with "15 percent error rate" as an example. He then defines *knowledge* as "information in the form of descriptions and relationships," illustrated by the relationship that "previous abusive behavior increases the likelihood of subsequent abusive behavior." At the highest level of abstraction, a *concept* is defined as "a generalized idea or model formed on the basis of knowledge or experience," such as child abuse. Program purpose is reflected at each level, and managers may need to remind themselves not to neglect the levels of knowledge and concepts at which meaning is attributed to numbers in a way that they can be used to adjust programs or activities and plan for the future.

This is the level of analysis at which recent discussions of *learning organizations* and *organizational learning* occur. Learning organizations were discussed briefly in Chapter 4 as an important current model for looking at organizational functioning. The concept has been connected to information systems by Rapp and Poertner (1992), who assert that "a learning organization takes periodic readings on its performance and makes adjustments so that performance is improved" (p. 93). This is an important principle for managers, whose job it is to help staff and the organization remain intently focused on the organization's purpose and objectives and on getting and using feedback to improve performance, make adjustments, and reward employees. Framing information systems this way may facilitate staff's commitment to the importance of gathering and using data regularly.

The use of feedback is also a relevant consideration in staff quality of working life, in terms of job design and rewards, both of which add meaning to the work for an employee. In Chapter 6, job feedback was noted as a key component of the Job Characteristics Model of Hackman and Oldham, which, if appropriately addressed, can enhance both the quality of working life and organizational performance.

Summary

A well-designed information system can enhance an organization's effectiveness and responsiveness and raise employees' sense of satisfaction and purpose. Managers should bear these points in mind to avoid having an IS designed only to meet external accountability and evaluation needs and not fully valued or supported by staff. An IS should be designed with careful attention to information needs (related to program outcomes, for example) and should include significant participation by staff who will be using the system. Such a system will probably involve computers, the potentials of which are increasing daily. An IS should meet both internal needs (for example, for feedback, program modification, and employee satisfaction) and external needs related to accountability and program evaluation, to which we now turn.

Discussion Questions

1. Think of a human service organization with which you are familiar. What kinds of outcomes would you hope this organization could bring about? Are there ways to measure the outcomes you have in mind?

2. Continuing to consider the same human service organization, think about the kinds of information decision makers would need to plan and implement programs.

CASE 9

Evaluation Emergency

Mario Rinaldi, director of the Developmental Disabilities Training Project, called an emergency meeting of the project staff.

"You've all been working really hard on the training manual," he said. "I hate to pull this on you right now, but I've got to tell you that I just had word. The feds are sending in their evaluator. He's going

to be here next week, and we've got to be ready."

Amid the groans, Jane Carlin, a staff trainer, spoke up. "What's the big problem?" she asked. "We've been providing a training session every week. We've had workshops on developmental disabilities for the teachers, for citizens; we've had the

TV show, now we've got a manual for parents. It seems to me we're in great shape. So what's the problem?"

"Well, I was kind of putting this part off," Rinaldi answered. "They sent along the new evaluation form so that we can complete the self-study before the evaluator gets here. That's the tough part. We're going to really have to dig to get the information ready."

"What kind of information do we need? Remember, we did that pretest and posttest with all the people at the workshops. We've got a lot of data on the learning effects from the workshop. Of course, it's not that easy to do with the TV program."

"That's the least of our problems, Jane. Remember, this is a training project. What they want is information on all participants in any training workshop. They want the ages of trainees, their sex, their employment, their income—all the demographic stuff. I just didn't think about all that because the form we used last year didn't ask for it. You see, we're using the same kind of evaluation form as continuing ed. programs are. It doesn't make any sense, but I'll bet we can dig up that information somehow."

"Wait a minute!" George Steinberg called out. "I worked my tail off on that TV program, and there's no way in the world I'll ever be able to even guess who watched it. Does that mean the whole thing didn't happen? Does that mean I get a grade of zero? I flunk?"

"Now, George, you know it isn't like that. They just like to have the information so they can put it together with the data from all the other projects they funded. They've got to show results, just as we do."

"That's fine to say, John, but if they're going to evaluate us on how many men, women, and children show up at our sessions, we should do the kind of stuff that can lend itself to what they're looking for. I'm feeling as if my work just isn't going to make the grade."

"I'm starting to feel that way, too," Carlin said. "What's the point of doing one thing if they're evaluating something else?"

"Wait a minute, everybody," Rinaldi responded in frustration. "We're getting way off the track here. These people aren't here to tell us what we should and shouldn't do. They're not going to grade us on what we did. One of the things they ask us about in an open-ended question is the content of the program, the kinds of interventions we did. There's no problem there. The problem is just in putting together the data they want, the demographic characteristics and all that. Now, I've got most of it somewhere. All I need is for somebody to volunteer to help me dig through the files and see what we can find that might relate to some of the questions they're asking. We'll be able to get the sex of participants by looking at their names on those address cards we had them fill out. The ages will be hard. That we'll have to guess at."

1. How might the agency have avoided this "emergency" situation?

2. How might the funding source have helped avoid the situation?

3. What data should the staff have been collecting for this program?

4. How should the staff deal with this immediate situation?

References

Butterfield, W. (1995). Computer utilization. In R. Edwards (Ed.), *Encyclopedia of social work* (19th ed., pp. 594–613). Washington, DC: NASW Press.

Butterfield, W., & Schoech, D. (1997). The Internet: Accessing the world of information. In R. Edwards (Ed.), *Encyclopedia of social work supplement 1997* (19th ed., pp. 151–168). Washington, DC: NASW Press.

Downing, J., Fasano, R., Friedland, P., McCullough, M., Mizrahi, T., & Shapire, J. (Eds.). (1991). *Computers for social change and community organizing.* New York: Haworth.

Freitag, R. (1999). California's child welfare structured decision-making. *NASW California NEWS, 26*(1), 16.

Heffron, F. (1989). *Organization theory and public organizations.* Upper Saddle River, NJ: Prentice Hall.

Kaplan, R., & Norton, D. (1992, January–February). The balanced scorecard—measures that drive performance. *Harvard Business Review,* pp. 71–79.

Karger, H., & Levine, J. (1999). *The Internet and technology for the human services.* New York: Longman.

Kettner, P., & Martin, L. (1993). Performance, accountability, and purchase of service contracting. *Administration in Social Work, 17*(1), 61–79.

Kettner, P., Moroney, R., & Martin, L. (1999). *Designing and managing programs: An effectiveness based approach* (2nd ed.). Thousand Oaks, CA: Sage.

Lauffer, A. (1984). *Strategic marketing for not-for-profit organizations.* New York: Free Press.

Leiderman, M., Guzetta, C., Struminger, L. & Monnickendam, M. (Eds.). (1993). *Technology in people services.* New York: Haworth.

Lohmann, R., & Lohmann, N. (1997). Management: Cost measurement. In R. Edwards (Ed.), *Encyclopedia of social work supplement 1997* (pp. 214–228). Washington, DC: NASW Press.

Martin, L., & Kettner, P. (1997). Performance measurement: The new accountability. *Administration in Social Work, 21*(1), 17–29.

McCroskey, J. (1997). Outcomes measurement for family and children's services: Incremental steps on multiple levels. In E. Mullen & J. Magnabosco (Eds.), *Outcomes measurement in the human services* (pp. 189–197). Washington, DC: NASW Press.

Mullen, E., & Magnabosco, J. (Eds.). (1997). *Outcomes measurement in the human services.* Washington, DC: NASW Press.

Oyserman, D., & Benbenishty, R. (1997). Developing and implementing the integrated information system for foster care and adoption. *Computers in Human Services, 14*(1), 1–20.

Peters, T. J., & Waterman, R. H., Jr. (1982). *In search of excellence.* New York: Harper & Row.

Rapp, C., & Poertner, J. (1992). *Social administration: A client-centered approach*. New York: Longman.

Rossi, P. (1997). Program outcomes: Conceptual and measurement issues. In E. Mullen & J. Magnabosco (Eds.), *Outcomes measurement in the human services* (pp. 20–34). Washington, DC: NASW Press.

Schoech, D. (1990). *Human services computing: Concepts and applications*. Binghamton, NY: Haworth.

Schoech, D. (1995). Information systems. In R. Edwards (Ed.), *Encyclopedia of social work* (19th ed., pp. 1470–1479). Washington, DC: NASW Press.

Schoech, D., Schkade, L., & Mayers, R. (1984). Strategies for information system development. In A. Lurie & G. Rosenberg (Eds.), *Social work administration in health care*. New York: Haworth.

Schorr, L. (1997). *Common purpose*. New York: Anchor Books Doubleday.

Weirich, T. (1980). The design of information systems. In F. Perlmutter & S. Slavin (Eds.), *Leadership in social administration* (pp. 142–156). Philadelphia: Temple University Press.

Zimmerman, L., & Broughton, A. (1998). Assessing, planning, and managing information technology. In R. Edwards, J. Yankey, & M. Altpeter (Eds.), *Skills for effective management of nonprofit organizations* (pp. 325–342). Washington, DC: NASW Press.

CHAPTER 10

Evaluating Human Service Programs

CHAPTER OUTLINE _____

Purposes of Evaluation
Administrative Decision Making, Improvement of Current
Programs, Accountability, Building Increased Support, Acquiring
Knowledge Regarding Service Methods

Producers and Consumers of Evaluations
Professional Evaluators, Funding Sources, Policymakers and
Administrators, Human Service Providers, Consumers and
Community Members

The Scope of Human Service Evaluation
Evaluability Assessment, Process Evaluation, Outcome
Evaluation, Efficiency Evaluation

Implementing the Process Evaluation
Process Evaluation Strategies, Information Gathering, Analysis

Implementing the Outcome Evaluation
Routine Outcome Measurements

Implementing the Efficiency Evaluation

Experimental Design Options

Issues in Human Service Evaluation

Summary

Discussion Questions

Group Exercise

**CASE 10: Evaluating the Consultation
and Education Department**

References

Planning, designing, and implementing human service programs are worth the effort and resources they consume only if the programs prove useful. Ultimately, evaluation is needed to let us know whether services have taken place as expected and whether they have accomplished what they were meant to accomplish. This kind of information can provide the basis for making sensible decisions concerning current or projected programs.

According to Rossi, Freeman, and Lipsey (1999), *program evaluation* is "the use of social research procedures to systematically investigate the effectiveness of social intervention programs that is adapted to their political and organizational environments and designed to inform social action in ways that improve social conditions" (p. 2). This definition highlights the major aspects of program evaluation:

- it is a systematic process: it can't be thrown together or rushed and should be planned for even as the program is being designed;

- it looks at the effectiveness of interventions, so that policy and programmatic decisions can be made about the best use of scarce resources;

- in addition to effectiveness, evaluations can answer questions regarding adequacy (the extent to which an identified need is addressed), efficiency (cost-effectiveness is maximized), process (whether programs and procedures are implemented as planned), and possible unintended effects;

- it is inevitably conducted in a complicated political environment, and the needs of the various stakeholders need to be addressed from design through implementation and report preparation; and

- the internal environment of the organization needs to be considered: staff may be resistant or indifferent to evaluation, and rarely is extra staff time available to be allocated to evaluation activities.

Evaluation is an eminently practical endeavor, designed with as much technical care as possible but oriented toward immediate improvement of program quality. Although research designs can play an important part in this process, program evaluation does differ from research to a certain extent.

Research, in comparison to evaluation, tends to be more theory oriented and discipline bound, exerts greater control over the activity, produces more results that may not be immediately applicable, is more sophisticated in complexity and exactness of design, involves less judgment of the researcher, and is more concerned with explanation and prediction of phenomena. Conversely, evaluation is more mission oriented, may be less subject to control, is more concerned with providing information for decision makers, tends to be less rigorous or sophisticated, and is concerned primarily with explanation of events and their relationship to established goals and objectives (Burck, 1978, p. 179).

Human service evaluation, if it is to be of value, must be seen as an integral part of the management cycle and must be closely involved with the kinds of decisions that are made in agencies every day. Its results must be disseminated to and understood by the people most concerned with program functioning, including community members, funding sources, and service providers, as well as administrators. It can be practical only if it is seen as useful by individuals who influence service planning and delivery.

Purposes of Evaluation

Evaluators may use research techniques, but they apply them to the needs and questions of specific agencies and stakeholders. Evaluation can be used to aid in administrative decision making, improve currently operating programs, provide for accountability, build increased support for effective programs, and add to the knowledge base of the human services.

Administrative Decision Making

Evaluation can provide information about activities being carried out by the agency as well as data describing the effects of these activities on clients. Information about current activities can help decision makers deal with immediate issues concerning resource allocations, staffing patterns, and provision of services to individual clients or target populations. At the same time, data concerning the outcomes of services can lead the way toward more rational decisions about continuation or expansion of effective programs and contraction or elimination of less effective services. Decisions concerning the development of new programs or the selection of alternate forms of service can also be made, not necessarily on the basis of evaluation alone but with evaluative data making a significant contribution.

Improvement of Current Programs

A basic thrust of evaluation is toward the comparison of programs with the standards and criteria developed during the planning and program design stages. Evaluation can serve as a tool to improve program quality if it provides data that help contrast current operations or conditions with objectives. Activities performed as part of an agency's operations can be compared or contrasted with standardized norms, such as professional or legal mandates, or with the agency's own plans, policies, and guidelines. Evaluation of service outcomes means that results can be compared with measured community needs, leading to an assessment of the program's adequacy. Data collection technologies such as employee attitude surveys, management audits, and quality audits can provide information that is very useful in improving program or agency operations. With systematically collected data on hand, agency personnel can make improvements either in the nature of the services or in the ways they are delivered. Although evaluation does not necessarily identify the direction an agency should take, its systematic application does point out discrepancies between current and planned situations. Without it, quality cannot be improved.

Accountability

Most human service programs are required to submit yearly evaluation reports for the scrutiny of funding sources or public agencies, and many specially funded projects are required to spend set percentages of their budgets on evaluation. Beyond this, however, agencies are also accountable to their communities. The "accountability model" described by Windle and Neigher (1978) stresses this component of evaluation. This model takes the position that a program

> should be evaluated by the public and/or those who support it. Such evaluation can have at least three purposes: (1) to let the public or other supporters make wise decisions concerning support, (2) to motivate the public and other supporters to greater program support by involving them in the goals and activities of the program, and (3) to motivate the program staff to greater public service and efficiency by their awareness that their activities are being monitored. (p. 97)

According to Schorr (1997), in the past "outcomes accountability" and evaluation were separate activities, the former the province of administrators and auditors and the latter of social scientists. Now, however, "the accountability world is moving from monitoring processes to monitoring results. The evaluation world is being demystified, its techniques becoming more collaborative, its applicability broadened, and its data no longer closely held as if by a hostile foreign power" (p. 138). Dissemination of evaluation reports describing the agency's activities and their effects can help reinforce program accountability. People concerned with agency performance can gain knowledge about the results of services, and this information undoubtedly increases community members' influence on policies and programs.

Building Increased Support

Closely related to accountability is the "advocacy model" (Windle & Neigher, 1978), which assumes that agencies, in the context of their accountability, must compete for scarce resources. Evaluation can enhance an agency's position by providing the means for demonstrating—even publicizing—an agency's effectiveness.

Evaluation provides information that helps the agency gain political support, along with community involvement. Evaluative data and analyses can have a great effect on the agency's well-being if they are disseminated to potential supporters and funding sources as well as to agency staff.

Again, in the words of Schorr (1997):

> the moral underpinnings for social action, especially by government, are
> not powerful enough in the cynical closing years of the twentieth century
> to sustain what needs to be done on the scale that it needs to be done.
> In this era of pervasive doubt, public investment of the needed magnitude
> will be forthcoming only on evidence of achieving its purpose and
> contributing to long-term goals that are widely shared. (p. 136)

Acquiring Knowledge Regarding Service Methods

Much of what is termed "program evaluation" historically consisted of routine
monitoring of agency activities. This approach is still common, but fortunately increasing attention is being paid to the assessment of program outcomes. Additionally, program evaluation methods can be used to develop knowledge about the
relationships between interventions and desired outcomes. This has been referred
to, adapting a term from industry, as *social research and development* (Rothman, 1980).
More recently, social work researcher and intellectual pioneer Jack Rothman
(1995), the early leader in social R&D, has used the term *intervention research* to
describe this process of empirically assessing human service interventions.

According to Thomas and Rothman (1994), this method entails three aspects. *Knowledge development* focuses on acquiring practical knowledge regarding
the effects of selected interventions. *Knowledge utilization* is concerned with transforming the results of research into usable practice principles. *Design and development* involve identifying a problem, assessing possible interventions, designing and
testing an intervention, and disseminating results (see also Rothman, 1995).

Controlled experiments help determine whether clearly defined program
technologies can lead to measurable client changes. Although such research-
oriented studies cannot normally be expected to take place with great frequency
in small agencies with limited resources, they do play a major part in establishing
the effectiveness of innovative approaches. Program planners need to be able to
make judgments concerning the effects of specific services. Information concerning such cause-and-effect relationships can be gained through a combination of
activities, including reviewing research completed in other settings, carrying out
ongoing internal evaluations, and utilizing the services of researchers to implement special studies of program innovations.

Producers and Consumers of Evaluations

The purpose of evaluation is to help improve the ways agencies serve individuals and communities. Using methods that are as rigorous as possible is important,
but it is also imperative to understand that evaluation is a means to an end rather
than an end in itself. An elegantly designed evaluative research study is of little

use if it is not recognized as important by the people who have a stake in an agency's efforts. Evaluation efforts involve a number of groups, including not only professional evaluators but also funding sources, administrators and policymakers, service deliverers, and community members. These varying role groups serve as both producers and consumers of evaluations, and they can have tremendous influence on the process if they see themselves as owning it. Patton's (1997) *utilization-focused evaluation* principles and methods have been shown to be very useful in designing and implementing evaluations so that the findings are actually used.

Historically, the various actors in the evaluation process—professional evaluators, funding sources, policymakers, administrators, and services providers—had separate roles and did not often collaborate, or even communicate, with each other. These role distinctions are blurring, however, as practitioners realize they need knowledge about their programs to make improvements and as policymakers and others realize that the complexity of the evaluation process requires multiple methods to be successful (Meier & Usher, 1998). Seidl (1995) describes this trend "toward a more participatory practice model in which evaluators are less often outside authorities and more often colleagues and coworkers" (p. 1932). However, because the traditional roles are still being fulfilled and all involved will have to address current and preferred role expectations, we will review these.

Professional Evaluators

A sizable proportion of the evaluation that takes place in human service organizations is performed by professional evaluators, researchers who use their skills either within the evaluation and research departments of large agencies or as external consultants offering specialized assistance. Whether evaluators are employed by the organization or contracted as consultants, they are expected to bring objectivity to the evaluation process. Their presence brings to the evaluation task a degree of rigor and technical excellence that could not be attempted by less research-oriented human service providers.

The technical virtuosity that professional evaluators offer has both negative and positive implications. At its worst, the evaluation researchers' contribution can sometimes be irrelevant to the ongoing agency work. Evaluators may produce reports that, although accurate, are too esoteric to be readily understood or used by the people who decide among programs or allocate resources. Evaluators who are overly detached from agency decision making often fail to affect services.

Another negative aspect of the use of external consultants as evaluators is agency workers' tendency to place evaluative responsibility totally in the consultants' hands. Evaluation can work effectively only if attention is paid to goal attainment and data collection on an ongoing basis. If no one but the expert evaluator takes responsibility for assessment of progress toward goals, workers see evaluation as unfamiliar, threatening, and potentially unpleasant.

Effective evaluators use their technical expertise not to impose evaluation on unwilling audiences but to work closely with others in developing feasible designs. If consultants work with internal evaluation committees, they can help administrators, service providers, and consumers clarify their goals, expectations, and questions. Then the studies that are designed can meet recognized needs. The external evaluator's objectivity and internal agency workers' active involvement bring the best of both worlds to the evaluation process.

Funding Sources

Funding sources, particularly organizations providing grants to human service projects, have had a positive effect on evaluation in recent years. Human service agencies are often required to evaluate projects as part of their accountability to funding sources. Grant applications are expected to include discussions of evaluation designs, and these sections are carefully scrutinized before funding decisions are made.

Funding sources could have even more positive effects if attention were focused more on evaluation content rather than simply on form. Funders should not expect that the dollar amount spent on evaluation consultants necessarily coincides with the quality of the research, nor should they accept simple process monitoring as sufficient. Rather, funding sources should press for more effective evaluation of program effectiveness, for both direct consumers and communities. The response to this emphasis on results might well be the design of more creative outcome evaluations than are presently in use.

Policymakers and Administrators

Policymakers and administrators are among the primary users of evaluation because they make decisions concerning the lives and deaths of human service programs. Decision makers need evaluation data to inform them concerning alternatives, just as evaluators need decision makers to make their work meaningful. Yet the linkages between administrators and evaluators are often tenuous.

Agency managers, as well as board members, can make evaluation work more effectively for them if they try to identify the real information needs of their agencies. Evaluations do not have to be fishing expeditions. They can be clear-cut attempts to answer the real questions decision makers pose. If administrators and objective evaluators work together to formulate research questions, the resulting answers can prove both readable and helpful.

Human Service Providers

The providers of services have often tended to be left out of the evaluation process, and in some settings they actually feel victimized by it. They are asked to keep accurate records and fill out numerous forms, but they are not involved in deciding what kinds of data are really needed. They are asked to cooperate with consultants making one-time visits to their agencies, but they are not told exactly what these consultants are evaluating. They are asked to make sudden, special efforts to pull together information for use by evaluators, but they are not encouraged to assess their progress toward goal attainment on a regular basis. Many human service workers feel that evaluation is a negative aspect of agency operations, serving only to point out shortcomings in their work, and they tend to provide information in such a way that their own programs are protected.

Human service providers could play a much more active and useful role in evaluation if they were encouraged to design and utilize evaluation processes, using consultants simply as technical assistants. Service providers are familiar with changing consumer needs, the relative effectiveness of varying approaches, and the agency itself. If they form the heart of the evaluation committee, they can ensure that the real goals of their programs, the objectives being evaluated, and the work actually being done form part of the same whole. In fact, agencies are becoming increasingly involved with "agency-based research" (Rathbone-McCuan, 1995) that is valuable not only for conducting evaluation but also for writing grant proposals and issue papers to shape social policy.

Consumers and Community Members

Consumers and other community members need to be involved in planning and evaluating, from initial goal setting through developing evaluation designs and assessments of agency effectiveness. Consumers are in a good position to be aware of the strengths and weaknesses of service delivery systems and the degree to which observed community needs are being met. Just as important is the fact that the power of service providers and consumers should be more equitably balanced in human service systems. Participatory action research, mentioned earlier, is an example of a method that directly involves clients or community members, who have clear and legitimate interests in the performance of human service programs. Citizens might mount their own evaluation efforts or participate along with human service workers on internal evaluation committees.

Regardless of the form their participation takes, citizens have a major role to play in deciding how, why, and for whom human services should be provided. Human service agencies are accountable to the communities they serve. Their purpose is to work toward goals that both helpers and consumers understand and cherish. The function of administration is to make this ideal a reality.

The Scope of Human Service Evaluation _____

Human service evaluation can take many forms. The approach used in any one setting is likely to be a function of several variables, including (1) the resources and expertise available for use in evaluations, (2) the purposes for which evaluation results will be used, and (3) the orientations and philosophies guiding agency decision makers. The two major types of program evaluations are *process evaluations* and *outcome evaluations.*

Human service programs vary tremendously in their orientations to evaluation, running the gamut from simple program monitoring to controlled experiments studying client outcomes. Regardless of their use of resources, depth, or concern for objectivity, however, evaluation efforts need to be reasonably comprehensive if they are to serve any of their stated purposes. Evaluation should provide, at a minimum, basic information concerning program *processes and outcomes.* Sometimes, however, programs as designed and implemented are very difficult to evaluate. Therefore, before discussing process and outcome evaluations in detail, we will briefly review an important preliminary consideration: evaluability assessment.

Evaluability Assessment

The "accountability movement" in the human services gained momentum in the 1970s, and soon policymakers and analysts discovered that social program designs and information systems were often difficult to evaluate. Poorly defined or improperly implemented programs and vague, unrealistic, or conflicting goals were identified as common problems (Rutman, 1980, p. 37). Out of this concern, *evaluability assessment* emerged in the late 1970s and the 1980s as a process to assess a program's "readiness" for evaluation and to enhance evaluability (Rutman, 1980, 1984; Wholey, 1979).

According to Chambers, Wedel, and Rodwell (1992), an evaluability assessment should begin by assessing the purpose and rationale of the evaluation. All key stakeholders (for example, agency staff, funders, representatives of policymakers, community representatives) need to agree regarding expectations, questions, and goals for the evaluation. These elements can be assessed by reviewing documents such as relevant proposals or contracts and by meeting with stakeholders. If misunderstandings, disagreements, or even merely a lack of clarity arises, these need to be addressed before the evaluation proceeds. At this stage, Rutman (1980) suggests focusing on the feasibility of actually achieving the purposes of the evaluation by asking these questions:

1. Who are the potential users of the evaluation findings? . . .

2. What are the various purposes for conducting evaluations of program effectiveness? . . .

3. What are the information needs of the primary user and other potential users? (pp. 124–127)

Next, program documents are reviewed to develop a program documents "flow model" of the program to determine the intended processes and effects.

Program components (service activities) and intended effects (outcomes) are arranged in a flowchart that describes what is intended to happen to clients going through the program. Program staff (direct service and management) are then interviewed to see whether the program is being implemented as designed. Rutman (1980) suggests the following questions to guide interviews with staff:

1. Are any program components missing from the program documents model?

2. How do each of the program components operate?

3. Are any goals and effects missing in the program document model?

4. What is the meaning of each goal and effect?

5. Are there competing or conflicting goals?

6. Are the causal linkages plausible? (pp. 100–104)

The interviewer then prepares and confirms with the manager a "program manager's model" that reflects the manager's view of program operations. The reality of operations is then assessed by observation of the service delivery process. These questions may be asked to staff to clarify the model in operation (Rothman, 1980):

1. How is the program implemented? . . .

2. Who is served by the program? . . .

3. What appear to be the goals and effects of the program? (pp. 110–113)

Results from this data collection phase are collated and analyzed to develop an "evaluable program model" (p. 116) that includes well-defined program components, clearly specified goals and effects, and plausible links of causality between program activities and expected outcomes. The model may be amended to ensure that it reflects the reality of program operations. It is also possible that, if discrepancies in program implementation are discovered, staff may change actual program behavior to better reflect the model as designed. Ultimately, evaluators need to be confident that the program can be implemented as planned, the evaluation will be able to "attribute the findings to particular program components" (p. 128), and research requirements such as access to clients and records can be met.

If a program has been well designed using a valid theoretical model, is appropriately staffed, and has a complete information system, it is likely to be evaluable without further modification. If not, appropriate program and information systems modifications can be made. In addition to identifying aspects of a program that make evaluation difficult, an evaluability assessment may also indicate ways in which service delivery is compromised (Gabor & Grinnell, 1994, p. 22).

Before leaving this topic, we should note some important concerns regarding an overemphasis on evaluability in traditional terms. According to Schorr (1997), some funders may consider programs as evaluable only if they are

> standardized and uniform, . . . sufficiently circumscribed that their activities can be studied and their effects discerned in isolation from other attempts to intervene and from changes in community circumstances, . . . [and] sufficiently susceptible to outside direction so that a central authority is able to design and prescribe how participants are recruited and selected. . . . [But] these are precisely the conditions that are least likely to characterize effective programs. (pp. 142–143)

These concerns can be mitigated by augmenting traditional evaluation methods with qualitative models such as case studies and action research (McRoy, 1995; Patton, 1990) that are more attentive to program complexities and uniquenesses. Ultimately, the best evaluation is likely to address processes and outcomes, quantitative and qualitative aspects, and dynamics of program uniqueness and generalizability.

In any case, at the conclusion of a thoughtful evaluability assessment, there should be a well-conceptualized and -operationalized program that will be relatively easy to evaluate, in terms of both its processes and its outcomes.

Process Evaluation

Essentially, program evaluation has four basic objectives:

1. To provide information that will be useful in improving a program while it is in operation (often called a *formative* or *process evaluation*)

2. To provide information about the achievement of the program goals and objectives (outcomes or effectiveness)

3. To provide information about program outcomes relative to program costs (efficiency)

4. To provide descriptive information about the type and quantity of program activities or inputs (effort)

We will begin a review of these types of evaluation with the process evaluation.

Process evaluation involves assessing agency activities to determine whether programs are operating in accordance with plans and expectations. As Rossi, Freeman, and Wright (1979) point out, "there is no point being concerned about the impact or outcome of a particular project unless it did indeed take place, and . . . was received by the appropriate participants" (p. 38). Perhaps surprisingly,

a large proportion of programs that fail to show impacts are really failures
to deliver the interventions in ways specified. Actually, there are three
potential failures: first, no treatment is delivered at all (or not enough);
second, the wrong treatment is delivered; and third, the treatment is
unstandardized, uncontrolled, or varies across target populations. In each
instance, the need to monitor the actual delivery of services and identify
faults and deficiencies is essential. (p. 132)

Although few administrators would accuse themselves of delivering "non-
programs," anyone with responsibility for human service delivery should recognize that even subtle differences between planned and implemented services can
have major effects on program results. Process evaluation provides a means for determining whether members of target populations were reached in the numbers
projected and whether specified services were provided in the degree and with
the quality expected.

FORMATIVE EVALUATION   Process evaluation also leads the way toward
efficiency assessment by helping specify exactly how agency resources, especially
human resources, have been used. This approach is sometimes referred to as a
formative evaluation, a type of process evaluation intended to "adjust and enhance
interventions . . . to provide feedback and influence a program's ongoing development" (Royse & Thyer, 1996, pp. 51, 52).
    A formative evaluation normally involves a comparison with identified
standards for program implementation. This process depends on the existence of
clearly defined, measurable program objectives. It also depends on the presence of
an information system that can provide answers to the basic process evaluation
questions: exactly what services were provided, by whom, for whom, to how
many, in what time period, at what cost? When this information is used to compare accomplishments with objectives, guidelines for needed program improvements become clear, comparison of alternate methodologies becomes feasible,
and accountability becomes a reality.

MONITORING   Process evaluations are usually ongoing; that is, they require
the continual retrieval of program data. Program goals and objectives are used as
the standards against which the evaluation is conducted. If, for example, Meals on
Wheels states in its annual plan of operations that it will deliver one meal daily to
each of one hundred clients per program year, or an annual total of 36,500 meals,
then it would be expected that approximately 3,042 meals will be provided per
month. A process evaluation would entail the assessment of monthly efforts to
provide the prorated number of meals, including whether they were provided
to eligible clients (for example, the target population). This type of evaluation
would also examine how the agency's human resources were used to provide the
services.

This type of process evaluation is commonly referred to as *monitoring,* which both provides funders, the agency board, and any other stakeholders with information on how the program is doing with reference to previously identified objectives and standards and also helps agency administrators make adjustments in either the means or the targets of service delivery. Feedback mechanisms must be built into the service delivery system to keep managers informed of whether the program is on course, both fiscally and quantitatively.

ACTION RESEARCH   *Action research* is another type of process evaluation that is less formal than a formative evaluation and is focused on quickly learning about what effects actions are having on the identified problem. As its name implies, action research involves, first, gathering data on a problem (a research phase—for example, a needs assessment) and then action—the implementation of a program (French & Bell, 1990). The next cycle of research involves gathering data on effects, analyzing the data, and making program adjustments or planning new activities. Continuing with the modified program and/or new activities constitutes another cycle of action, followed by another research phase of data collection. This process may continue throughout the program, with the intervals between research phases based on the nature of the program activities. Action research often involves community members and other stakeholders. In fact, *participatory action research* has emerged as a refinement of the original action research methodology (Nelson, Ochocka, Griffin, & Lord, 1998; Sarri & Sarri, 1992).

Another advance beyond traditional action research is *appreciative inquiry:* "an innovative theory [of action research] capable of inspiring the imagination, commitment, and passionate dialogue required for the consensual re-ordering of social conduct" (Cooperrider & Srivastva, 1987, p. 131). This innovative approach emphasizes asking positive questions about a situation and visions for the future. In so doing, "serious consideration and reflection on the ultimate mystery of being engenders a reverence for life that draws the researcher to inquire beyond superficial appearances to deeper levels of the life-generating essentials and potentials of social existence" (Cooperrider & Srivastva, 1987, p. 131).

Outcome Evaluation

Outcome evaluations are of two general types (Hatry, 1997, pp. 3–4). *In-depth, ad hoc evaluation,* favored by researchers, may provide relatively strong evidence on outcomes and effects but is very time-consuming and focused intensively on one program at a time. *Regular outcomes measurement* can cover a broader array of programs on a regular basis but is less likely to provide definitive information on causality. The former is possible usually through well-funded research projects, while the latter will be most common for most human service organizations. *Experimental evaluations* in the typology of Meier and Usher (1997) would include in-depth, ad hoc evaluations.

Both process and outcome evaluations depend on clearly specified objectives. In outcome evaluation, however, the objectives are stated in terms of expected results rather than projected activities. Whereas process evaluation typically uses *activity objectives,* outcome evaluation uses *impact objectives* that describe ultimate end results. The basic question underlying outcome evaluation must be "To what degree have clients or the community changed as a result of the program's interventions?"

Community effect might be measured in terms of changes in the incidence of an identified problem. Client change would probably be evaluated in terms of level of functioning before and after receipt of services. Whether services are designed to affect clients' adjustment, skills, knowledge, or behaviors, some type of assessment tool must be used to determine whether change in the desired direction has taken place. Outcome evaluation depends on the routine use of such measures as ratings by service providers, surveys of client satisfaction, gauges of behavior change, and standardized or specially designed instruments.

If program administrators wish to make confident statements about the effects of services, they must also use studies that distinguish between treatment results and chance occurrences. Positive changes in clients can take place as a result of maturation, experiences that are unrelated to the agency's services, or just change. Sometimes what appear to be changes are actually results of the measurement tool's unreliability or even the effects of measurement itself. Accurate outcome evaluation should ideally use statistical or experimental designs that can control for these contaminating influences. Definitive statements concerning program outcomes depend on the evaluator's ability to make a reasonable estimate of the degree to which measured outcomes can be attributed to the service being evaluated. Most human service agencies use routine monitoring devices to assess all clients' development and add controlled outcome studies with smaller samples of clients, especially when special interventions are being tested.

An example of an outcome evaluation (also known as an *impact* or *effectiveness evaluation*) is the following:

> The Children's Haven, a residential treatment center for abused children ages six through seventeen, decided to introduce a new treatment modality (Modality X) that had proved useful in other, similar settings in enhancing the self-esteem of twelve- to fourteen-year-old children. Children's Haven hypothesized that the introduction of Modality X would significantly enhance self-esteem in at least 80 percent of the children exposed to this intervention. From the total residential population of twelve- to fourteen-year-old children, half were randomly selected to be in the experimental group, and half were randomly assigned to a control group. Each group was administered the Index of Self-Esteem (ISE). Modality X was then applied to the experimental group, but not to the control group, for a period of six months. At the end of this period, each group was again administered

the ISE. The results of the first and second administrations of the ISE to each group were then compared and analyzed for statistical significance in variance of outcomes.

In this example, if the program's objective (significant enhancement of self-esteem in 80 percent of the members of the experimental group) were met, and if it varied in a positive and statistically significant manner from the mean score of the children in the control group, confident statements could be made about the effects of this new program intervention.

Efficiency Evaluation

The data gathered through process and outcome evaluations are sometimes adapted to the needs of an efficiency evaluation. *Efficiency evaluations* are meant to connect costs and outcomes. The term has historically had negative connotations in the human services. In the words of Pruger and Miller (1991), writing in a special issue of *Administration in Social Work* devoted to efficiency, "efficiency is both a conceptual tool and a vision of perfection. In the social welfare enterprise; however, the tool is not used and the vision is neither understood nor valued" (p. 5).

The core question involved in an efficiency evaluation is "Can the same program results be achieved *either* by reducing the amount of program effort *or* by choosing other, less costly alternatives (different kinds of efforts)?" (Tripodi, Fellin, & Epstein, 1978, p. 46). The concept of "program effort" involves the amount and kind of activity carried out by service providers as well as the total costs of resource utilization. Level of effort is thus measured as part of the process evaluation. Program effectiveness is determined most accurately through the outcome evaluation.

With these data in hand, the next step is to decide whether the level of effort, or cost, of a program was appropriate given the results that were attained. Administrators or policymakers might compare two programs by examining the results of process and outcome evaluations. Then, if effectiveness seemed to be equal, they might decide to select the less costly of the two efforts for continuation. Efficiency does not involve simple cost cutting; it involves recognizing that alternate methods might differ in the amount of resources used to arrive at the same end. Because of the misunderstandings about efficiency, Pruger and Miller (1991) underline this point:

> The important thing to understand is that a statement about efficiency is a statement about input AND outcome, means AND ends, costs AND benefits, even if as a conversational convenience only one is mentioned. Output maximization bespeaks greater efficiency *only if costs have not risen proportionately.* Exactly analogously, lower costs do not indicate greater efficiency *unless output has not correspondingly declined.* (pp. 10–11, italics in original)

Making these kinds of determinations requires the use of the most accurate possible information and analysis, and careful implementation of evaluative procedures.

Implementing the Process Evaluation _____

Successful implementation of a process evaluation requires careful collection and analysis of information to verify the program's success in meeting operating objectives. As may be clear from previous chapters, well-designed programs, clearly stated goals and objectives (for both outcomes and activities), and a comprehensive management information system that documents and measures outcomes, processes, and other relevant information such as client demographics must precede the implementation of evaluation procedures. To the extent that these systems are well developed, evaluation becomes much easier.

The objectives leading to goal attainment can be considered measurable only if they contain clear criteria and standards that let the evaluator know whether objectives have been met. The *criterion* is what is to be measured; the *standard* involves the desirable quantity or quality of the criterion. One objective might include several criteria for accomplishment; each criterion must have a standard that the evaluator can use as a measurement. In the case of the Support Club, whose information system was described in the last chapter, managers had this key activity objective: to serve one hundred girls (13.2 percent of the target population) between September 1 and June 30. They expected that individual clients would participate in different combinations of program activities, including academic assistance and tutoring, career counseling, female health education, discussion groups regarding female empowerment, recreational activities, and guest speakers. Because they could not predict how many clients would use each service, it was not realistic to specify expected units of service to be delivered, but they wanted to keep such data to be used for program monitoring and possible modifications. For example, one of the objectives listed is "identification of all appropriate services in the community within three months." One of the criteria, services, includes several standards: "all," "appropriate," and "in the community." The other criterion, time, involves the standard "three months." The evaluator can determine whether the objective has been met by examining each criterion in terms of previously established standards for accomplishment. It will be readily apparent whether the services have been identified within the three-month time limit set as a standard.

The data required for evaluation can be identified through examination of the criteria listed as part of the planning process. Each criterion points the way toward information that will be needed to assess agency progress in meeting desired standards. For example, one of the criteria of our hypothetical agency involved client income, with the standard that clients be at or below the federally stated poverty level. Information concerning income must thus be obtained from each client; otherwise, service providers and evaluators have no way of knowing whether the specified target population is being reached. If the correct number of clients is being served but these clients have high incomes, the agency's goal is not being met. Client information is needed to determine whether the targeted consumer group is being served, just as service delivery information is needed to determine whether the correct treatments are being offered.

Process Evaluation Strategies

Process evaluation depends on the active involvement of all human service workers in an agency because they are all required to set objectives, meet those objectives, and continually gather data. The effective agency must be able to retrieve evaluative information as part of its normal procedures so that progress toward meeting objectives becomes clear far in advance of the times when summary reports are required.

Staff should not think of evaluation as a separate function, performed by experts and unrelated to the work of the agency's programs. Evaluation needs to be considered during program planning and implementation. There is also a need, however, to step back from service delivery on occasion and examine progress objectively. Although evaluative information should inform managerial decisions at all times, sometimes more objective and stringent approaches should be used. Process and outcomes evaluations meet this need.

According to Royse and Thyer (1996, pp. 54–57), there are three approaches to conducting a formative evaluation. The first approach is to locate model standards. This is sometimes done automatically by the funders of a program: they may be outlined in the original request for proposals and are likely to be listed in any rules or regulations that the agency must follow upon receipt of a grant or contract. Licensing or other regulatory requirements may also need to be met, such as fire codes and standards for hospitals or residential programs. In some fields, model standards have been developed by professional associations, and these may be reviewed for use in a particular program. For example, the Child Welfare League of America has issued *Standards for Residential Care Centers for Children* (Royse & Thyer, 1996, pp. 54–55). Managers should become aware of any relevant standards in their program areas, to help ensure that they are using the most current best practices in their field.

Another approach is to use expert consultants to review the program using model standards, generic standards such as those for fiscal and management audits (discussed later). Deficiencies can be highlighted and addressed by program staff.

The third approach is to form an evaluation committee of agency staff, board, and community members or clients to design and conduct the evaluation. Such a group can conduct or oversee the data collection and analysis tasks discussed next. Whether evaluations are performed by internal evaluation teams or by outside consultants, specialized information may need to be gathered, and all data should be analyzed with a view to making concrete recommendations for change.

Information Gathering

The evaluation team can use a variety of methods to gather new data or to place existing information in revised contexts. Rossi et al. (1999) suggest that the data sources most helpful for monitoring agency activities include direct observation by the evaluator, use of service records, data from the agency information system, and information gathered from program participants.

Data gathered through direct observation are useful in terms of objectivity because evaluators are freed from the concern that information might be colored by the subjectivity of service providers or consumers. There is the danger also, however, that observation might in itself bring about changes in the activities being carried out. Direct observation can prove useful if systematic methods are used, but it is more helpful in some situations than in others. For instance, unobtrusive observation can be more appropriate in the context of a public educational program than in the case of a private counseling session. Use of audiotapes or videotapes of selected service delivery episodes can prove to be a more effective adaptation of observational data gathering than in vivo observations would be.

Use of service records can be helpful for analyzing the nature of the consumer population as well as for examining the number and nature of service delivery units. Such records as daily, weekly, or monthly activity reports can provide the basis for the development of program statistics concerning number of individuals served, types of services provided, or other aspects of program processes. Client data forms can also be used to determine the degree to which service consumers are members of the population originally targeted for services.

Although the service records that form the bulk of the agency's stored information also provide most of the information needed for evaluation, they are not always adequate for intensive assessments. The evaluation team often finds it useful to gather data directly from service providers, through either questionnaires or interviews. Such procedures can provide deeper or subtler information than that provided through routine forms, especially because differences in service providers' perceptions of program goals can be recognized. Intensive interviews can also point the way toward instances in which services are not delivered in standard ways by different individuals within programs.

Accurate information concerning service delivery can also be obtained through contacts with service consumers. Sometimes samples of entire communities can be surveyed to determine whether information concerning the program is being disseminated adequately and to the targeted consumer group. Interviews with or questionnaires distributed to clients can help determine consumers' perceptions of services, especially if they differ from providers' notions of the same activities. Information about consumer satisfaction with services is normally collected on a routine basis, and these data, too, can prove important for the purposes of comprehensive evaluation.

The varying types of information available to the evaluation team should be compared to verify their accuracy. The accuracy of stored information can be ensured if staff members receive training in record-keeping skills and if samples of forms are routinely checked. Existing and specially gathered information can then form the basis for evaluative analysis.

Analysis

Analysis of the program for a process evaluation most commonly uses some form of monitoring. *Program monitoring,* according to Rossi et al. (1999) is

> the systematic documentation of key aspects of program performance that are indicative of whether the program is functioning as intended or according to some appropriate standard. It generally involves program performance in the domain of service utilization, program organization, and/or outcomes. (p. 192)

Regarding service utilization, data from the information system are used to answer questions such as these:

- How many persons are receiving services?
- Are those receiving services the intended targets?
- Are they receiving the proper amount, type, and quality of services? (Rossi et al., 1999, p. 192)

The result of this analysis should be a descriptive report that allows the reader to form an accurate picture of the agency and its activities as well as of community members and their use of services.

Program processes and structures can be assessed using a *management audit,* sometimes known as an *administrative audit* (Packard, 2000; Sugarman, 1988; also see Chapter 12). Such an audit may be conducted by designated staff or an outside consultant through analysis of agency documents such as program plans and designs, organizational structures, personnel configurations, and budgets. Staff are typically interviewed to assess their understanding of the program's intended goals, objectives, and methods and their own roles and job functions. They are often asked to share their observations regarding how things are working and to suggest possible program or administrative improvements. Through analysis of information concerning program structures and services, evaluators can determine the degree to which the program is operating as intended. The audit also helps point out strengths and weaknesses of program structures because estimates can be made of the degree to which functions and responsibilities of staff members accomplish goals and adhere to plans. *Cultural competency assessments* (Child Welfare League of America, 1993) are in essence management audits focused specifically on an organization's policies and practices regarding diversity and cultural competence.

Another way of assessing the extent to which a program meets identified standards is *quality assurance* (Royse & Thyer, 1996, pp. 73–76). This technique is most commonly associated with the assessment of medical or clinical records and other aspects of the operation of a medical program or facility. Standards are issued by governmental organizations such as Medicare and by accrediting organizations such as the Joint Commission on Accreditation of Healthcare Organizations (Eustis, Kane, & Fischer, 1993, in Royse & Thyer, 1996, p. 73).

Quality assurance assesses organizational processes and systems, which can be a useful component of a more comprehensive evaluation. It is important to note that this method typically looks at process, not outcomes. The value of this approach should not be underestimated, however, particularly if it is used as an action research effort in which problems identified are addressed and reassessed later to ensure that necessary improvements have occurred. Additionally, a proactive administrator will not only do the "bare minimum" to meet outside accreditation standards but will engage in other evaluation activities, particularly regarding program outcomes, as well.

A process analysis using a flowchart is another useful technique to assess how the program is operating (Gabor & Grinnell, 1994, pp. 24–26). A flowchart, such as the one suggested in the previous chapter, where it was used to design the information system, is constructed to outline all the steps of the service delivery process. Staff and the evaluator then assess the extent to which the intended process is being followed, also noting unnecessary steps which are discovered and other possible improvements.

Other analytical techniques such as time and motion studies of staff also provide detailed examinations of the activities performed by human service deliverers, support staff, and administrators, with emphasis placed on analyzing the time allotted and used for various types of services. Analysis of time use, especially in service delivery units, can help point toward more effective use of resources in the interest of meeting agency goals. Often, failures to meet objectives can be diagnosed through such analyses.

Many staff, particularly those with long experience in large bureaucracies, may have had negative experiences with these techniques, which have on occasion been used by consultants to recommend efficiency improvements resulting in staff layoffs. This procedure is in the "mechanistic" tradition of Frederick Taylor, and, if it is used, its purpose should be made very clear to staff, and they should be involved with its design and implementation. Used well, it can highlight wasted staff time that had previously been spent on unnecessary paperwork and can free up staff for more productive, client-oriented tasks.

The process evaluation can use a variety of data sources and analytical strategies. Its basic purpose is to determine what services were delivered, to whom, and whether they were performed in accordance with the schedule set as part of the planning process. It is just as important to determine whether the services that were planned and delivered had the desired effect on the community. For this purpose, an outcome evaluation should be used.

Implementing the Outcome Evaluation ⎯⎯⎯⎯⎯⎯⎯⎯

A comprehensive evaluation must include attention both to activities performed and to the results of those activities. Measurement of both means and ends can lead to appropriate use of the agency's resources because the effectiveness of varying methods can be estimated, if not established. The purpose of the outcome evaluation—also known as *impact assessment*—is to measure, to the degree possible, the results of program interventions.

Routine Outcome Measurements

Outcome objectives, like process objectives, should be specific and measurable. The existence of concrete objectives allows for ongoing evaluation as client outcomes are routinely monitored. If measurements are inexpensive and convenient to use, they can be used even by small agencies with limited resources. The results of services for all consumers can be measured as part of normal program operations.

As was noted earlier, the two major types of measurement of outcomes are effectiveness and efficiency. *Effectiveness* is a measure of the extent of the accomplishment of objectives that attempt to resolve a social problem or condition. For example, effectiveness measures would be used to assess the extent to which clients on welfare have acquired self-sustaining employment, chronically mentally ill clients are able to live independently, or delinquent youth do not become reinvolved with the justice system. *Efficiency* is typically measured in terms of cost-effectiveness or cost-benefit, and it answers questions regarding the amount of resources that are used to accomplish a particular objective. We will first review the common ways in which effectiveness is measured and will then discuss efficiency evaluations.

ACCOMPLISHMENT OF PROGRAM OBJECTIVES   If objectives are clearly written, criteria and standards for success can be developed to relate to them. A training program can measure trainees' skills, with a specific level selected as an appropriate standard. A treatment program for alcoholics can measure its success in terms of long-term client sobriety; a corrections program can measure recidivism rates; a mental health program can assess rehospitalization rates. It is not always simple to determine methods for quantifying outcome objectives and selecting appropriate criteria and standards. Desired client changes often seem impossible to measure, especially when community-wide, indirect services are offered, when it may be necessary to measure outcomes indirectly through assessment of variables assumed to be closely related to desired outcomes. Regardless of the difficulty, it is worth the effort to search for creative ways of measuring the real goals of services rather than to revise objectives so that they describe easily quantifiable but less valued ends.

According to Gabor and Grinnell (1994, pp. 57–62), there are two broad types of objectives: program objectives and practice objectives. *Program objectives,* part of the planning process discussed in Chapter 3, are measurable outcomes that derive from broader program goals. Program outcome objectives can be of three types:

- *knowledge objectives,* such as increasing a teen mother's knowledge of infant nutritional needs;

- *affective objectives,* such as raising client self-esteem; and

- *behavioral objectives,* such as reducing or eliminating incidents of child abuse.

Programs will also probably have *maintenance objectives* that measure factors important to the agency's survival: "these objectives are formulated to keep the program viable and involve such objectives as 'to increase private donations by 25%'" (Gabor & Grinnell, 1994, p. 59).

At another level, *practice objectives* refer to

the personal objectives of an individual client, whether that client is a community, couple, group, individual, or institution. Practice objectives are also known in the professional literature as treatment objectives, individual objectives, therapeutic objectives, client objectives, client goals, and client target problems. (Gabor & Grinnell, 1994, p. 59)

There should be alignment and compatibility among program goals, program objectives, practice objectives, and practice activities. Work with an individual client (an activity, based on the program design or treatment model) should be directly related to accomplishing a client objective, and the aggregate accomplishment of all client objectives should result in the accomplishment of program objectives, leading to the accomplishment of program goals and at least partial remediation of the identified social problem.

Outcome objectives in the human services have been and in many cases still are difficult to develop. As human service technologies are refined and validated by research results, and to the extent that necessary resources are allocated to programs, outcomes will become easier to identify, achieve, and document. Examples of outcome measures are becoming more frequent in the literature in areas including mental health (Corcoran, 1997; Smith, Rost, Fischer, Burnam, & Burns, 1997), child and family services (McCroskey, 1997), and health care (Beckman, 1997). We will now review some other methods of measuring outcomes in terms of client functioning, behavior change, and perceptions.

ASSESSMENTS OF CLIENT FUNCTIONING   A number of standardized instruments are available to serve diagnostic or specialized purposes (see Gabor & Grinnell, 1994, pp. 113–115; Martin & Kettner, 1996, pp. 71–100; and Royse &

Thyer, 1996, pp. 190–193, for examples). Agencies serving clients with varying problems find it helpful to use measurements that are easily interpreted and that can assess clients' general levels of functioning. Such instruments are readily adaptable to varying purposes because they can be used both to assist in working with individual clients and to evaluate the effectiveness of program thrusts with entire groups or categories of consumers. Flexible instruments can be used with each client before and after intervention. Standards can vary in terms of consumers' pretreatment functioning; so the objectives for one client group might differ, in terms of realistically expected outcome, from the objectives for another.

Many such assessments of client functioning are available and in widespread use. Their effectiveness in human service agencies depends on the care with which they are selected and the regularity and assiduousness with which they are used.

SINGLE-SYSTEM DESIGNS   An evaluation method that has become increasingly common in the human services in recent years is the *single-system research design*. While they can be used for needs assessments, formative evaluations, and quality assurance studies (Royse & Thyer, 1996), they are probably most commonly used in clinical practice. The key requirements of a single-system research design are reliable and valid measures of the identified problem or outcome and the repeated use of this measure over time.

Initially, practitioners raised legitimate concerns about research priorities overriding practice concerns, but the method can be designed so that it can be a useful component of the treatment process (Blythe, 1995). One obvious value of the method is that it requires that the human service worker and client develop specific goals for the intervention and that progress toward the desired outcomes be monitored regularly. This method is likely to become even more common, at least as part of service delivery, to guide work with a client, if not for larger-scale program evaluation.

GOAL ATTAINMENT SCALING   *Goal attainment scaling* (GAS) involves the development of specific evaluation criteria for each client based on his or her treatment goals. Evaluation is based not on a dichotomy between success or failure in reaching goals but on a five-point scale, with the target goal at the center of the range, the most favorable expected outcome at one end, and the least favorable outcome at the other end. The client's progress toward attaining each goal is measured, resulting in a score related to each goal as well as a summary goal attainment score that weighs the average of scores on each individual scale.

One benefit of this approach is that widely varying outcomes can be compared. Systematic evaluation does not require that all clients' goals have commonalities. The same is true when GAS is used for evaluating an agency as a whole. Although each program or service might be oriented toward a different goal, the success of goal attainment across programs can be measured, and the scores of a number of individuals can be combined to estimate a program score.

Royse and Thyer (1996, pp. 92–94) note that GAS has therapeutic utility regarding client goal orientation and has been shown to correlate with other outcome measures. However, it also has some notable limitations, particularly the fact that it provides little useful information at the program level.

MEASURES OF CLIENT PERCEPTIONS   Most agencies also use measures of client satisfaction, asking consumers to evaluate the services they have received. Such techniques can be useful only if they are obtained on a regular basis from both people who have dropped out of treatment programs and people who have completed them. Consumers may be asked to rate their overall satisfaction with services or to respond separately to individual aspects of program delivery. Normally, such measures are based on questionnaires using four- or five-point rating scales.

Royse and Thyer (1996) offer the following suggestions regarding the use of client satisfaction surveys:

1. Use a scale that has good reliability and that has been used successfully in other studies. . . .

2. Use the same instrument on repeated occasions, and develop a local baseline of data so that departures from the norm can be observed. . . .

3. Employ at least one and possibly two open-ended questions so that the consumers of your services can alert you to any problems that you didn't suspect and couldn't anticipate. . . .

4. Use a "ballot box" approach in which one week is set aside when every client (old and new) entering the agency is given a brief questionnaire and asked to complete it while waiting for the scheduled appointment. (pp. 97–98)

Clients may also be asked to evaluate their own well-being before and after receiving services. Such evaluations provide an additional way of examining treatment outcomes. Each client's perceptions of his or her own functioning can be combined with standardized measures and service providers' perceptions, resulting in a more accurate picture of the individual's progress.

Implementing the Efficiency Evaluation _____

While the methods described earlier measure effectiveness by addressing program outcomes—the accomplishment of objectives or changes in client conditions or perceptions—outcomes may further assessed by measuring efficiency. Efficiency is typically measured in terms of *cost-effectiveness analysis* or *cost-benefit analysis*. The former assesses costs with reference to program outcomes, while the latter typically represents both costs and benefits in monetary terms.

The simplest efficiency evaluation involves the determination of unit cost. This figure is accomplished by dividing the number of service outputs or, ideally, outcomes into the amount of dollars allocated (input) for that service. For example, an agency receiving $150,000 per project period to provide counseling services to 150 delinquent children per year could project a unit cost of $1,000 if the unit of service were defined as each unduplicated client (child) served. Of itself, the cost per unit of $1,000 is meaningless without accompanying process and outcome evaluations and without a comparison to at least one other, similar program whose services have also undergone process, outcome, and efficiency program evaluations. In this example, if the outcome is preventing recidivism for at least one year after the completion of the program, the cost of the program can be divided by the number of successful outcomes to determine cost effectiveness on that measure.

Royse and Thyer (1996, pp. 165–167) describe a cost-effectiveness study. The first three steps should already have been done as part of good program design and implementation. *Defining the program model and program objectives* is the first step. The second step, *computing costs,* is mostly accomplished through the development of the program budget. This step can be complicated if one program has multiple groups of clients and service packages, but eventually it should be possible to allocate all program costs (staff salaries and benefits, facilities, other nonpersonnel costs) so that they may be related to program outcomes. The third step, *collecting outcome data,* should already be occurring through the program's information system. Step 4 involves *computing program outcomes,* which would generally be the number of clients for whom there were successful outcomes (for example, no recidivism or rehospitalization, acquisition of self-sustaining employment or independent living status). Next, *computing the cost-effectiveness ratio* is done by dividing program cost by the number of successful outcomes. The final step, *conducting a sensitivity analysis,* involves looking at the assumptions about the relationships among program interventions, costs, and effects.

As one axiom puts it, "Some people use statistics like a drunk uses a lamppost—for support rather than illumination," and cost-benefit analysis may be misused by those wanting to either continue or end a program. The real and legitimate limitations of the use of this method need to be noted by all involved, and every effort should be made to do the best job possible of accurately relating costs to results.

Other types of cost analysis, including cost-benefit analyses, cost-utility analyses, and cost-feasibility analyses (Royse & Thyer, 1996, pp. 167–168) are beyond our scope here.

Experimental Design Options

All of the methods just reviewed help measure changes in human service clients. They do not provide information concerning the degree to which these changes can be attributed to service interventions. Actual estimates of program effectiveness (outcomes), especially when one type of intervention is being compared with another, may use more rigorous evaluation methods. These include preexperimental designs, quasi-experimental designs, and true experimental designs (MacEachron, 1995). Preexperimental designs are becoming more frequently used by agency staff, while experimental designs are typically used to test new service delivery methods. These designs will not be discussed in detail here because they are not routinely performed on human service programs. An interested reader can consult the sources listed here or other social science research texts for further information on these models.

Preexperimental designs "are not very rigorous and are best suited for those occasions where an evaluation is needed but those who are requiring it are not expected to be terribly fussy" (Royse & Thyer, 1996, p. 137). They include the One-Group Posttest Only Design, the Posttest-Only Design with Nonequivalent Groups, and the One-Group Pretest-Posttest Design. Although outcome measures alone allow evaluators to recognize whether change has taken place, such methods do not demonstrate that the human service intervention caused the effect.

Experimental designs help do this by comparing groups of people who have received the service in question with control groups who have not received the same intervention. True experimental designs require random selection of experimental and control groups, carefully controlled interventions, and scrupulously examined outcome measures.

Studies that attempt to control as carefully as possible for a number of variables but that do not meet the stringent definition of experimental design are termed *quasi-experimental*. They include the use of nonequivalent control groups, time-series designs, and multiple time-series designs.

Issues in Human Service Evaluation

In response to the clarion call for accountability, managers of human services have grown increasingly sensitive to the need for sophisticated strategies and designs for program evaluation. As human service organizations have increased their involvement in program assessment, they have had to confront a number of issues surrounding the evaluation process. These issues have been alluded to in the preceding sections of this chapter but are more directly dealt with here to emphasize their present and future importance for human service managers. As competition for scarce resources increases, so will the challenge to managers to confront the issues.

Primary among these issues is the meaning and interpretation of *program effectiveness*. Whereas there is general agreement that service effectiveness can be measured by the extent to which program goals are achieved, dissension is growing regarding total reliance on the "one best way" to measure goal attainment— that one best way being outcome evaluations based on controlled experimentation. While experimental evaluative research designs may represent the "ideal type" of program assessment, they may, at the same time, not be reflective of what is practical, affordable, or desirable as a means of demonstrating service effectiveness. Because of logistic, financial, and ethical considerations, some agencies may find themselves having to resort to quasi-experimental or nonexperimental methods of evaluating program effectiveness. How, then, are claims to effectiveness by these services to be treated? What level of credibility of service effectiveness is to be accorded those programs whose measurement criteria fall short of strict scientific research applications? Should these programs be discontinued?

Exclusive reliance, then, on experimental measures of program effectiveness should be seen as a desired goal toward which research and practice can aspire. In the meantime, however—before that time when all things human can be quantified—the answers to what is a reasonable and acceptable measure of service effectiveness may have to remain in the eye of the beholder. Subjective (value-based) perceptions of program effectiveness must therefore be acknowledged and examined as a relevant element of the evaluation process. One way of doing this is to combine both process and outcome evaluation strategies in the evaluation design—that is, to include both subjective and objective measures of service effectiveness.

A second issue has to do with *evaluation inclusiveness,* or the incorporation of divergent perspectives and variables in the evaluation of service effectiveness. In other words, how inclusive can or should a program evaluation be to reflect all significant and relevant aspects of service effectiveness? Evaluations inherently have a political dimension (Royse & Thyer, 1996, p. 232), and including all relevant stakeholders throughout the process can mitigate such dynamics as well as improve the quality of the product. Most writers, including Briar and Blythe (1985) and Meier and Usher (1998), stress the need to involve service providers in all stages of study design and implementation. In fact, a new field, *participatory evaluation* (Whitmore, 1998), offers specific principles and methods for involving staff, clients, and other stakeholders in the evaluation process.

This point was made earlier in this chapter and is being repeated here because of its importance to the entire evaluation process. A point not previously considered is that made by Moller and Graycar (1983) in their discussion of the need to include in effectiveness evaluations the roles of administrators and policymakers in service delivery. Their point is that service effectiveness is not solely a function of the interaction between worker and client. Rather, it is a function of the interactions of all of the elements of the service delivery system, including its organizational and environmental dimensions.

What is needed, according to these authors, is

> a system of direct accountability between all actors in the network as well
> as the external and indirect accountability produced by the democratic
> system. Evaluation of a service delivery agency therefore must include
> all elements of the network if it is to produce a completed path of
> accountability. Failure to do this truncates the path of accountability, a

process which may well lead to the disruption of the evaluation or the rejection of its findings. (p. 76)

This should, consistent with principles of action research, not only result in a better product but also increase the likelihood of the results actually being used (Moller & Graycar, 1983; Reid, 1987).

While historically there has been an absence of a relationship between funding and program effectiveness (McNeece, DiNitto, & Johnson, 1983), human service managers must realize that

as public and private sources diminish and as requests for funding grow, competition for scarce resources becomes more intense. The agency that demonstrates the achievement of intended outcomes is more likely to be funded than the agency that only reports client demographics and service cost. (Briar and Blythe, 1985, p. 27)

In summary, Schorr (1997) asserts that

the new approaches to the evaluation of complex interventions share at least four attributes: They are built on a strong theoretical and conceptual base, emphasize shared interests rather than adversarial relationships between evaluators and program people, employ multiple methods and perspectives, and offer both rigor and relevance. (p. 147)

Summary

Evaluations may have several purposes, from aiding in decision making and improving programs to building support and demonstrating accountability. Evaluations may look at processes, outcomes, or efficiency, with increasing interest in outcomes evaluation. The utilization of evaluation findings for program enhancement, the involvement of all significant actors in the evaluation process, and the use of multiple approaches in determining service effectiveness are key considerations that today's human service manager must address in the quest for organizational achievement.

Our discussion of evaluation takes us full circle—back to the social problems in our environment that human services are intended to address through a responsive strategic plan, well-designed programs that are part of well-designed organizations using effective human resources and supervision practices and financial and information systems to monitor progress and accomplishments, which are assessed by evaluation. In the next chapter, we will look at leadership: the "glue" that holds everything together and facilitates organizational change to adapt to changing conditions.

Discussion Questions

1. What are some of the reasons that may make staff resistant to or fearful of evaluation? How could evaluation be made nonthreatening or even valued for workers in human service agencies?

2. If you were an agency manager, what steps would you take to build evaluation into ongoing processes?

Group Exercise

Working in small groups of no more than six people, imagine that you are staff members of a human service agency serving alcoholics. The group has decided to use a new methodology for working with clients. Previously, each alcoholic client was seen on an individual basis. Now the group is considering a change to a family-oriented service. Services would be offered both to the client and to his or her family. Design a methodology you would use to evaluate the new program and to compare it with the old approach.

CASE 10

Evaluating the Consultation and Education Department

At the Greenby Community Mental Health Center, the Consultation and Education Department was about to go under. Although consultation and education are required for all community mental health centers, not all centers have fully staffed and active departments. Instead, they implement consultation and education as a percentage of each professional's work. That was what Henry McDonald, the executive director, was suggesting for Greenby.

"You have to understand my position," he exclaimed to a distraught consultation and education director. "Our funding has been cut back. We're more dependent than ever on fees for service and third-party payments. Consultation and education are luxuries we really can't afford. They don't bring in the funds we need, and we've got to put our resources into programs that carry their weight."

"But you know that C and E programs are a high priority. Every center has to have one to keep up its funding," Andy Cutler replied.

"Andy, let's not play games here. You know we don't have to have a C and E department with a full-time director. We only have to provide the service. The real issue is whether your program stays in operation the way it is now, and I'm saying it can't. Now, stop worrying. Your job isn't in jeopardy. You'll be able to move over to the clinical program."

"Henry, believe it or not, it's not my own job that I'm concerned about. No matter what kind of measurement you use, you have to see that the C and E department does pull its weight. We've developed liaisons with every major employer in the area, we've got preventive programs going in the schools, and our divorce and family workshops are attracting more people every time we put them on. Word is getting around in the community."

"Sure, the workshops attract people. At five dollars a head, why shouldn't they? The program is self-supporting, I'll grant you that, but it's not pulling in enough capital to pull its weight with the center as a whole. There's no way it can."

"But what you're not recognizing, Henry, is that this program is supporting the other programs. You've had an increase in the number of people referring themselves for alcohol and drug abuse programs. I'm telling you that this is because of the preventive programs we've been doing at the factory. You've had an increase in self-referrals for family therapy. I think they're coming from our workshops. The programs we offer help people recognize their problems, and when they recognize them, they start to come in for more help."

"That's very possible, Andy. But I've got a board of directors to deal with, and I don't know whether they're going to buy that line of reasoning. They're not professionals, you know, and they don't necessarily see those relationships that way. What they can see is the difference between what a person pays to participate in a workshop and what the same person would pay for one of the other programs. Its a good thought to say that you're feeding into the other services, but we don't really know that. We don't really know anything about the impact you're having. Give me something I can tell the board. Give me something I can tell the state. Just give me something."

1. What steps might you take if you were Andy Cutler, the consultation and education director?

2. How might a more effective evaluation program have helped the consultation and education program?

3. What methods might prove helpful in demonstrating the effectiveness of Cutler's preventive programs?

References

Beckman, B. (1997). Outcomes measurement for social work research and practice in health care. In E. Mullen & J. Magnabosco (Eds.), *Outcomes measurement in the human services* (pp. 218–223). Washington, DC: NASW Press.

Blythe, B. (1995). Single system designs. In R. Edwards (Ed.), *Encyclopedia of social work* (19th ed., pp. 2164–2168). Washington, DC: NASW Press.

Briar, S., & Blythe, B. (1985). Agency support for evaluating the outcomes of social work services. *Administration in Social Work, 9*(2), 25–36.

Burck, H. D. (1978). Evaluating programs: Models and strategies. In L. Goldman (Ed.), *Research methods for counselors: Practical approaches in field settings.* New York: Wiley.

Chambers, D., Wedel, K., & Rodwell, M. (1992). *Evaluating social programs.* Boston: Allyn & Bacon.

Child Welfare League of America. (1993). *Cultural Competence Self-Assessment Instrument.* Washington, DC: Author.

Cooperrider, D., & Srivastva, S. (1987). Appreciative inquiry in organizational life. *Research in Organizational Change and Development, 1,* 129–169.

Corcoran, K. (1997). Use of rapid assessment instruments as outcomes. In E. Mullen & J. Magnabosco (Eds.), *Outcomes measurement in the human services* (pp. 137–143). Washington, DC: NASW Press.

Eustis, N., Kane, R., & Fischer, L. (1993). Home care quality and the home care worker: Beyond quality assurance as usual. *Gerontologist, 33*(1), 64–73.

French, W., & Bell, C. (1990). *Organization development* (4th ed.). Upper Saddle River, NJ: Prentice Hall.

Gabor, P., & Grinnell, R. (1994). *Evaluation and quality improvement in the human services.* Boston: Allyn & Bacon.

Hatry, H. (1997). Outcomes measurement and social services: Public and private sector perspectives. In E. Mullen & J. Magnabosco (Eds.), *Outcomes measurement in the human services* (pp. 3–19). Washington, DC: NASW Press.

MacEachron, A. (1995). Experimental and quasi-experimental design. In R. Edwards (Ed.), *Encyclopedia of social work* (19th ed., pp. 909–916). Washington, DC: NASW Press.

Martin, L., & Kettner, P. (1996). *Measuring the performance of human service programs.* Thousand Oaks, CA: Sage.

McCroskey, J. (1997). Outcomes measurement for family and children's services: Incremental steps on multiple levels. In E. Mullen & J. Magnabosco (Eds.), *Outcomes measurement in the human services* (pp. 189–197). Washington, DC: NASW Press.

McNeece, C. A., DiNitto, D. M., & Johnson, P. J. (1983). The utility of evaluation research for administrative decision-making. *Administration in Social Work, 7*(3/4), 77–87.

McRoy, R. (1995). Qualitative research. In R. Edwards (Ed.), *Encyclopedia of social work* (19th ed., pp. 2009–2016). Washington, DC: NASW Press.

Meier, A., & Usher, C. (1998). New approaches to evaluation. In R. Edwards, J. Yankey, & M. Altpeter (Eds.), *Skills for effective management of nonprofit organizations* (pp. 371–405). Washington, DC: NASW Press.

Moller, J., & Graycar, A. (1983). An eye for evaluation. *Administration in Social Work, 7*(2), 69–77.

Nelson, G., Ochocka, J., Griffin, K., & Lord, J. (1998). "Nothing about me, without me": Participatory action research with self-help/mutual aid organizations for psychiatric consumers/survivors. *American Journal of Community Psychology, 26*(6), 881–912.

Packard, T. (2000). The management audit as a teaching tool in social work administration. *Journal of Social Work Education, 36*(1), 39–52.

Patton, M. (1990). *Qualitative evaluation and research methods* (2nd ed.). Newbury Park, CA: Sage.

Patton, M. (1997). *Utilization-focused evaluation: The new century text* (3rd ed.). Thousand Oaks, CA: Sage.

Pruger, R., & Miller, L. (1991). Efficiency and the social services: Part A. *Administration in Social Work, 15*(1/2), 5–23.

Rathbone-McCuan, E. (1995). Agency-based research. In R. Edwards (Ed.), *Encyclopedia of social work* (19th ed., pp. 136–142). Washington, DC: NASW Press.

Rossi, P., Freeman, H., & Lipsey, M. (1999). *Evaluation: A systematic approach* (6th ed.). Thousand Oaks, CA: Sage.

Rossi, P. H., Freeman, H. E., & Wright, S. R. (1979). *Evaluation: A systematic approach.* Beverly Hills: Sage.

Rothman, J. (1980). *Social R&D: Research and development in the human services.* Upper Saddle River, NJ: Prentice Hall.

Rothman, J. (1995). Intervention research. In R. Edwards (Ed.), *Encyclopedia of social work* (19th ed., pp. 1521–1527). Washington, DC: NASW Press.

Royse, D., & Thyer, B. (1996). *Program evaluation: An introduction* (2nd ed.). Chicago: Nelson-Hall.

Rutman, L. (1980). *Planning useful evaluations: Evaluability assessment.* Newbury Park, CA: Sage.

Rutman, L. (1984). *Evaluation research methods: A basic guide* (2nd ed.). Beverly Hills: Sage.

Sarri, R., & Sarri, C. (1992). Participative action research. *Administration in Social Work, 16*(3/4), 99–122.

Schorr, L. (1997). *Common purpose.* New York: Anchor Books Doubleday.

Seidl, F. (1995). Program evaluation. In R. Edwards (Ed.), *Encyclopedia of social work* (19th ed., pp. 1927–1932). Washington, DC: NASW Press.

Smith, G., Rost, K., Fischer, E., Burnam, A., & Burns, B. (1997). Assessing effectiveness of mental health care in routine clinical practice. In E. Mullen & J. Magnabosco (Eds.), *Outcomes measurement in the human services* (pp. 124–136). Washington, DC: NASW Press.

Sugarman, B. (1988). The well-managed human service organization: Criteria for a management audit. *Administration in Social Work, 12*(4), 17–27.

Thomas, E., & Rothman, J. (1994). An integrative perspective on intervention research. In J. Rothman & E. Thomas (Eds.), *Intervention research: design and development for human services* (pp. 3–20). Binghamton, NY: Haworth.

Tripodi, T., Fellin, P., & Epstein, I. (1978). *Differential social program evaluation.* Itasca, IL: Peacock.

Whitmore, E. (Ed.). (1998). *Understanding and practicing participatory evaluation.* San Francisco: Jossey-Bass.

Wholey, J. (1979). *Evaluations: Promise and performance.* Washington, DC: Urban Institute.

Windle, C., & Neigher, W. (1978). Ethical problems in program evaluation: Advice for trapped evaluators. *Evaluation and Program Planning, 1,* 97–108.

CHAPTER 11

Leading and Changing Human Service Organizations

Summary

Discussion Questions

CASE 11: Budget Cut

References

We have now reviewed all of the core managerial functions, from planning and program and organization design, to human resources management and supervision, to financial management and monitoring and evaluation. Leadership will be presented in this chapter as the force holding these elements together, *aligning* them, and enabling the organization to function as an integrated system. Because human services must be constantly adapting, we will also look at common methods of organizational change that a manager or other staff member may use to improve organizational operations or responsiveness.

As the human service manager ascends the ladder of power and authority in the human service organization, the technical knowledge and skills of management require expansion and honing, and the expectations for leadership increase. Hierarchical ascent is usually accompanied by increased responsibility and decision-making authority. In-depth mastery of all of the elements of the managerial process, not necessarily required at the lower management levels, may become essential. Increased positional power and visibility attract greater attention to and reliance on the manager's leadership style. In fact, from an organizational perspective, leadership is the key element that integrates management functions from planning to evaluation.

The relative importance of the technical elements (planning, organizing, and so on) vis-à-vis the leadership function will, of course, vary with the particular position occupied by the leader in the organizational hierarchy. Some leadership positions require considerable involvement and proficiency in all areas, while more specialized jobs may call for expertise in only one area. For example, the executive director of a small nonprofit agency may need to possess technical knowledge and exercise leadership skills in program planning; organizational design and development; recruiting, hiring, and training staff; fund-raising and financial management; clinical supervision; and program evaluation. On the other hand, a human service manager in a large public agency assigned to the directorship of the program planning department will certainly need to possess in-depth knowledge and skills in the planning process. At the same time, however, that manager may also be responsible for organizing, staffing, supervising, and evaluating his or her department and for complying with some sort of budgetary constraints. Specialization, therefore, does not necessarily relieve the human service manager from involvement in the other managerial functions or from leadership responsibilities.

Leadership is a complex phenomenon that can be examined and explained from a variety of perspectives. The perspective presented here addresses responsiveness to the organization's environment and both the efficiency and the effectiveness issues confronting today's human service administrators. We will now review some of the current perspectives on organizational leadership and then look specifically at change management, a key aspect of leadership in the current dynamic human service environment.

Transactional and Transformational Leadership

In a classic work, Burns (1978) distinguishes between two basic forms of leadership. *Transforming leadership* is based on the ideal of unified effort, with leader and follower both working on behalf of goals to which each subscribes. In the words of Burns, transforming leadership (now more commonly referred to as *transformational leadership*) "occurs when one or more persons *engage* with others in such a way that leaders and followers raise one another to higher levels of motivation and morality" (p. 20). *Transactional leadership,* in contrast, does not require a common goal for leader and follower; instead, divergent interests are recognized, and the leadership process becomes a kind of quid pro quo bargain in pursuit of separate but complementary aims. This is essentially an exchange relationship between leader and followers, with each agreeing to do things to accommodate and to some extent meet the needs of the other.

Transactional leadership is easier and more common, whereas transformational leadership is more challenging and time-consuming but is likely to be more effective in bringing out higher potentials in all involved. Transformational leadership is often seen as more desirable, because it emphasizes important principles such as shared values, motivations, and higher purposes.

Leadership principles such as those articulated by Burns can be complemented by behaviors based on some of the theories of management discussed in Chapter 4, such as human resources approaches of McGregor and Likert, and participative supervisory styles presented in Chapter 7 regarding supervision. We will now look at additional ways in which managers as leaders can work with staff to help them do their best work and make their organizations more responsive and effective.

In a summary of leadership theory as it is relevant to the human services, Bargal and Schmid (1989) outline leadership roles that managers can fill, and we will adapt this framework here. Because of the importance of values in the human services, we will first look at managers as articulators of values. Next, we will examine managers as creators and shapers of organizational culture. We will then see how managers can fulfill their leadership roles as visionaries, teachers, designers, and consultants. We must also consider the manager as a political actor, a role that many regard as unsavory and distasteful but is a fact of organizational life.

Running an efficient unit, program, or agency is a necessary but insufficient requirement for today's human service manager. It has been said that efficiency is doing things right and effectiveness is doing the right thing. In other words, in addition to doing things right—that is, mastering the managerial knowledge and skill of planning, organizing, and so on—human service managers must also be able to "do the right thing." They need to be not only proficient managers but also astute leaders.

The Manager as an Articulator of Values

If doing the right thing is indeed the distinguishing characteristic between a good manager and a good manager/leader, then one must examine what doing the right thing means. Doing the right thing connotes action taken within the context of what is "right" and what is "wrong." Seen in this light, doing the right thing transcends the technical imperative of doing things right, which most leadership paradigms address. Doing the right thing becomes a matter of judgment exercised within some framework of personal and/or professional values.

The importance of values as guides for leadership and organizational effectiveness has been receiving increasing attention in the business literature in recent years. In a book published by the Peter F. Drucker Foundation for Nonprofit Management (Hesselbein, Goldsmith, & Beckhard, 1996), many cutting-edge thinkers discuss values in ways that are very compatible with human service management. Kouzes and Posner (1996) emphasize the importance of "character" in organizational leadership, asserting that "the first milestone on the journey to leadership credibility is *clarity of personal values*" (p. 103, italics in original). They add that "leaders must be able to gain consensus on a common cause and a common set of principles. They must be able to build a community of shared values" (p. 105). Heskett and Schlesinger (1996) put this in terms of leaders "defining, shaping, and using core values" (p. 116): leaders must help the organization explicitly define its core values and talk about these on a regular basis so that they can guide behavior and decision making. From a human service perspective, Frances Hesselbein (1996), a former chief executive of the Girl Scouts of America, asserts that "the leader for today and the future will be focused on *how to be*—how to develop quality, character, mind-set, values, principles, and courage" (p. 122).

Another leading thinker in the business sector, Noel Tichy (1997), studied successful leaders and found that they had in common clear ideas for how their organizations should operate strategically, high levels of personal positive energy, the willingness to make difficult decisions, and "strong values that everyone understands and lives up to" (p. 20). Popular writer Steven Covey (1990) has agreed with the importance of values but suggests this does not go far enough (even Hitler, according to Covey, had values, one of which was a unified Germany; p. 95). He believes we must go further to the notion of *principles,* which he describes as "proven, enduring guidelines for human conduct" (p. 94).

Whereas personal values can and often do play a part in managerial decision making, managers who are members of the helping professions are guided in their work primarily—and, in the ideal, exclusively—by values emanating from a professional philosophy. Whereas managers in the human services can turn to the "science" of management in "doing things right"—that is, in the appropriate application of managerial technology to enhance organizational *efficiency*—they must rely on their profession's values and ethics for guidance in "doing the right thing"—that is, in the *effective* delivery of service, as measured by the extent to which clients' needs are met, their rights respected, and their dignity and integrity honored. Patti (1985) considers service effectiveness as the "primary object of social welfare administration." He argues that service effectiveness "should be the principal criterion of a model of social welfare management practice." Service effectiveness, he continues, "is most fully congruent with the values and purposes of the human service professions" (p. 3).

The centrality of client needs as a reflection of professional values and purpose, and therefore as an essential ingredient of service effectiveness, can be inferred from Gummer's (1987) observation that a "major legitimating criterion for a profession is a primary orientation to the needs of clients as opposed to the self-interests of its members or the concerns of society-at-large" (p. 22).

Ethics: The Implementation of Values

Professional values provide the human service manager with the navigational bearings necessary to maintain a steady course in the pursuit of organizational effectiveness. Professional values help managers focus their technical, efficiency-oriented decisions and actions on clients' needs rather than on production quotas or political exigencies. It is not that productivity and politics are without import. However, they count among the various *means* of achieving the *goal* of quality service delivery. The values of a profession in turn serve to define the profession's code of ethics, which are essentially behavioral guidelines for practice. In addition to ethical guidelines in a profession's code of ethics, several writers have offered specific guidance for human service managers.

Perhaps reflecting the difficulties in prescribing in advance what a manager should *do*, Lewis (1988) outlines some "thou shalt not" principles:

1. Managers should not advocate against the interests of the organization that employs them. . . .

2. Managers should not assume or accept responsibilities which they are not competent to fulfill. . . .

3. Managers should not allocate resources in a manner that promotes distrust of their motives among the various clientele they must serve. (p. 282)

The first principle can allow for a manager who strongly disagrees with an organization's actions and attempts to change this through acceptable methods such as
those discussed later in this chapter. In extreme cases, a manager may become
aware of illegal or unethical behavior of the agency that cannot be corrected, and
the choices narrow to leaving, with or without *whistleblowing* (publicly accusing
one's organization of illegal conduct). Whistleblowing is an extreme step that
should be taken only after careful consideration.

Lewis's second guideline highlights the notion that managerial competence
can be a ethical issue. Expecting to be absolved of financial irregularities because
of not knowing proper procedures is a poor defense and bad management. His
third principle is perhaps the most fundamental: "of all the personal attributes one
can look for in a manager, the one most relevant for judging ethical behavior is
trustworthiness" (p. 276).

Specific questions that may help identify ethical issues in the area of philanthropy are provided in a framework developed by Rudolph (1995): "used as an
ethical instrument, it is a conceptual mirror to reflect upon standard operating
procedures in an ethical context" (p. 365). Specific areas addressed include the relationships between ends and means, raising funds, distribution of funds, community involvement in fund distribution, and program design.

Lowenberg and Dolgoff (1995) suggest considerations that should *not* be
used in ethical decision making: personal preferences, feelings, and statistics (for
example, "If most social workers in your agency use sick leave for vacation purposes, does that make it ethical behavior?"; p. 371). They then list the following
questions to ask at each step of dealing with an ethics issue:

A. What are the ethical issues involved? What are the principles, rights,
   and obligations that have an impact on the ethical question?

B. What additional information is needed to properly identify the ethical
   implications?

C. What are the relevant ethical rules that can be applied? Which ethical
   criteria are relevant in this situation?

D. If there is a conflict of interest, who should be the principal
   beneficiary?

E. How would you rank-order the ethical issues and ethical rules you
   have identified?

F. What are the possible consequences that result from utilizing different
   ethical rules?

G. When is it justified to shift the ethical decision obligations to another
   person (not the social worker)? To whom should it be shifted in this
   case? (p. 372)

These questions will be easier to answer if the manager has clarified in advance her or his key values and those of the organization. Two procedures suggested by Lowenberg and Dolgoff for this are the "least harm" principle ("choose the option that will result in the least harm, the least permanent harm, or the most easily reversible harm" [p. 377]) and the rank-ordering of ethical principles (for example, life protection, autonomy, quality of life, confidentiality, truthfulness).

Ultimately, according to Rapp and Poertner (1992), "ethical analysis involves identifying competing values, specifying accompanying obligations, recognizing the consequences of the obligations, weighing the relative effects of the consequences, and making a considered judgement" (p. 106). Ethical issues tend to arise when they are least expected, and thinking through in advance key guiding principles may expedite the process of resolving an ethical issue when it emerges.

That the profession of social work has been cited to illustrate and develop the argument for values-driven leadership is not to slight the other professions in the human services or to imply that they are not client centered or effectiveness oriented. The professions that claim membership in the field of human services, by definition of such membership, commit themselves to the goal of service effectiveness. Moreover, they also have, as members of professions, codes of ethics that govern professional conduct.

Ethical dilemmas can sometimes be avoided or made easier to deal with if an organization has clearly articulated values that are used regularly to guide decision making, as discussed earlier. Another way in which values and ethical guidelines may be communicated, demonstrated, and put into effect is through the management of an organization's culture. In recent years, the articulation of values and organizational culture are increasingly seen as important functions of organizational leadership.

The Manager as an Architect of Culture

Since the term *organizational culture* is now part of common discourse in human service organizations, with all the attendant risks for misunderstanding and misapplication, a definition will be helpful here. Organizational culture can be seen as

> the *shared pattern* of beliefs, assumptions, and expectations held by
> organizational members, and their characteristic way of perceiving the
> organization's artifacts and environment, and its norms, roles, and values
> as they exist outside the individual. (Bowditch & Buono, 1997, p. 286,
> italics in original)

These are reflected in several "dimensions" described by Bowditch and Buono (1997, pp. 292–293). First, *organizational values* provide guidelines for how people should behave in the organization. Next, *managerial culture* is reflected in dominant leadership styles and management philosophies, such as authoritarian or participative approaches. *Organizational heroes* "represent what the company stands for and reinforce the values of the culture by underscoring that success is attainable, acting as a role model for others." *Organizational myths and stories* and *organizational taboos, rites, and rituals* such as awards ceremonies are very useful for passing on belief systems and for shaping beliefs and values. Finally, *cultural symbols* reflected in the organization's physical layout, furniture, logos, and elsewhere provide clues as to what is rewarded and who has the most power.

Observing these dimensions can provide rich information regarding expectations about how people should behave in an organization. Several caveats are in order, however. First, according to Schein (1992), there are three levels of culture: the level of *artifacts* reflects visible structures and processes; *espoused values* include the stated strategies, goals, and philosophies of the organization; and *basic underlying assumptions* include "unconscious, taken-for-granted beliefs, perceptions, thoughts, and feelings" that are the "ultimate source of values and action" (p. 17). Artifacts are the easiest to observe and change, while the basic underlying assumptions are often difficult to discern and more difficult to change if a culture is seen as dysfunctional.

To complicate matters further, organizations may have unique *subcultures* in different programs, divisions, or offices of a large organization. These may be assessed and targeted for change just as a larger organizational culture can be. A subset of organizational culture, climate, is easier both to describe and change. *Climate* has been described as "psychological environments in which the behavior of individuals occurred" (Trice & Beyer, cited in Ott, 1998, p. 118) and is generally seen as a general representation of the perceptions and feelings of members of an organization. Climate can thus be described as tense, hostile, fun-loving, formal, rigid, or stimulating. It is most easily measured through employee attitude surveys, which are discussed later in the section on organization development consultation and in Chapter 12. As is the case with culture, climate may vary in different parts of the organization. Also, unlike culture, it can change more easily and rapidly, based on factors such as budget cuts and newly appointed managers.

There is, of course, no "ideal" culture, but managers can and should identify those that are dysfunctional (such as process cultures in an era of increased accountability and tight resources) and try to change them. A human service manager would be wise to engage staff in thoughtfully examining the organization's culture and determining which aspects of it are holding back the agency and need to be changed, as well as identifying positive aspects of the culture which should be celebrated and nurtured.

In their study of organizations with strong cultures, Kotter and Heskett (1992) found that some made successful adaptations to new environments and others did not. In successful organizations, they found top management that clearly articulated core values and desired behaviors, personally made effective adaptations in their practices and behaviors, did not tolerate arrogance in others, and kept their own egos under control. In the corporate cultures of those organizations, managers valued leadership at multiple levels, valued all key constituencies/stakeholders including employees, changed strategies and practices as needed to fit the changing environment, and engaged in many specific practices that fit the needs of the environment.

Schein (1996) and others have noted that changing culture is very difficult; this task nevertheless represents a real opportunity for a human service manager to impact the way an organization operates. Schein (1996) suggests that different approaches are needed at different life cycle stages of an organization. In a new organization, the manager (often a founder) can create culture through hiring choices, enacting indoctrination and socialization procedures, and serving as a role model. Later, the strengths of a founder (for example, energy and vision) can become a liability if the manager resists letting go of leadership and holds back from necessary change. According to Schein (1996), "the successful leaders at this stage are the ones who either have enough personal insight to grow with the organization and change their own outlook or recognize their own limitations and permit other forms of leadership to emerge" (p. 63). Eventually, the manager needs to become a change agent, helping "*evolve* culture by building on its strengths while letting its weaknesses atrophy over time" (p. 64, italics in original).

Strategies for a manager to use as a change agent will be outlined later. The study of organizations from the standpoint of culture and climate represents a powerful "school of thought" of organizational theory. Because of its potential for the development of valuable insights into the behavior of organizations, especially as that behavior relates to organizational effectiveness, this approach deserves serious study by the student of the human service organization and by the manager of the human service organization.

The Manager as Developer of Vision ⎯⎯⎯⎯⎯⎯⎯⎯⎯⎯⎯

According to Eadie (1997), "widely shared organizational values, a vision, and a mission are critical to, if not the preeminent producer of, a nonprofit organization's unity" (p. 47). We previously discussed mission, which answers the question "Why does the organization exist?" and values, which respond to "How should the organization and its members behave?" We will now examine *vision,* which answers the question "What future does the organization desire to create?" Strategic and operational plans will answer questions regarding what the organization intends to accomplish, but an organizational vision goes beyond the details of strategies and objectives to describe an inspiring and desirable future toward which staff are motivated to pursue with commitment.

In their influential book on leadership, Bennis and Nanus (1985) assert:

> To choose a direction, a leader must first have developed a mental image
> of a possible and desirable future state of the organization. This image,
> which we call a *vision,* may be as vague as a dream or as precise as a goal
> or mission statement. The critical point is that a vision articulates a view
> of a realistic, credible, attractive future for the organization, a condition
> that is better in some important ways than what now exists. (p. 89)

Visionary leadership has become enormously popular in the management
literature, with growing evidence (much of it in the form of case studies, however) of its value (Hesselbein et al., 1996). To add to the expanding literature on
the importance of vision in the business sector, one study of nonprofit executives
(Shin & McClomb, 1998) found that managers using a visionary leadership style
reported higher levels of innovation in their organizations. Bargal and Schmid
(1989) also highlight visionary leadership as a key perspective in leadership theory.
It will therefore behoove the human service manager to understand this perspective and use it to develop a personal vision and work with staff to develop a com-
pelling vision for the organization.

According to Bryson (1995), a vision

- Focuses on a better future

- Encourages hopes, dreams, and noble ambitions

- Builds on (or reinterprets) the organization's history and culture to
  appeal to high ideals and common values

- Clarifies purpose and direction

- States positive outcomes

- Emphasizes the organization's uniqueness and distinctive competence

- Emphasizes the strength of a unified group

- Uses word pictures, images and metaphors

- Communicates enthusiasm, kindles excitement, and fosters
  commitment and dedication (p. 163)

The vision for an organization often originates with or is first conceptualized by the founder or, later in its life cycle, the chief executive. However, staff in
most organizations will not uncritically "get behind" a vision given to them from
on high. Staff need to be able to articulate their own visions, and mechanisms

need to be in place for dialogue about everyone's visions leading to a unified vision for the organization. This may begin with discussions among the agency's executive team and/or board of directors, but after a preliminary draft is developed, it should be circulated widely for discussion and amendments. In fact, "shared vision" is one of Senge's (1990) five "disciplines" of a learning organization. According to Senge, shared visions start with individuals sharing their visions and listening to each other. The process of building true commitment to a vision is time-consuming and lacking in glamour but should pay off through staff's common understanding of where the organization is headed and their determination to work toward it. And, of course, a vision is unlikely to be implemented unless effective management systems and well-defined strategies to move the organization forward are in place (Blanchard, 1996).

The Manager as a Teacher

The retired CEO of the Herman Miller furniture company, Max DePree (1989), said, "The first job of a leader is to define reality. The last is to say thank you" (p. 9). Defining reality is done through teaching: helping staff develop a view of the world and their organization in which things make sense and in which people confidently work toward achieving the goals of the organization. According to Senge (1990), "leaders are responsible for building organizations where people continually expand their capabilities to understand complexity, clarify vision, and improve mental models—that is, they are responsible for learning" (p. 340). In fact, fostering learning on the part of everyone is the real point of teaching.

From a slightly different perspective, Tichy (1997) found in his research that the ability to teach was a key characteristic of the successful leaders he studied. He suggests that each leader needs to have and articulate a "teachable point of view": a combination of clear ideas about where the organization needs to go and how it should operate, strong values, high levels of energy, and the ability to make tough decisions. According to Tichy, leaders teach primarily by telling stories about their own experiences and things they have learned, by speaking at workshops and training classes about how people should think and behave to be successful in the organization, and by finding teaching opportunities in the daily operation of the organization.

Human service managers can facilitate organizational learning by reflecting on their own values and ideas and how they have shaped who they are as managers and leaders, and by sharing these with staff in ways that help clarify organizational purpose and reinforce the desired culture of the organization. In the next chapter, we will talk a bit more about developing and maintaining the abilities of employees to continually learn and thereby keep the organization dynamic and adaptive to new conditions.

The Manager as a Designer

Senge (1990, pp. 341–342) uses the metaphor of a ship to illustrate the importance of another function of a leader: as a designer of the organization's systems, strategies, and policies. He found that when he asked managers what role on a ship was "the leader," the common answer was "the captain" or, more rarely, another role such as navigator or engineer. The neglected role, according to Senge, is the designer: the person who determines what the ship will look like and be able to do. In this sense, the design of an organization would include not only structures and processes as outlined in Chapter 5 but also integrating everything so that the whole system works. In this sense, the "crucial design work for leaders . . . concerns integrating vision, values, purpose, systems thinking, and mental models" about how the organization works (p. 343).

This function of leadership is essential in ensuring integration of and alignment among all aspects of the organization. Things will not function well if staff are rewarded based on their performance but goals and objectives are unclear or if managers are held accountable for the results of their programs but not given control over their own budgets. We will look in more detail at the integrating function of leadership in the last chapter.

The Manager as a Political Actor

As was discussed in earlier chapters on strategic planning and the environment, an effective human service manager must at times consider the political aspects of a situation, whether it be the demands of conflicting stakeholders or power struggles within the agency. Other leadership perspectives such as those just reviewed may in some ways be effective in mitigating dysfunctional political dynamics, but a manager must nevertheless be able to identify and deal with issues of organizational power and politics (Gummer, 1990). In the words of Perlmutter (1985–1986), "as the external environment is becoming simultaneously more complex, dense, and unpredictable, special attention must be paid to new skills and strategies appropriate for a new political reality" (p. 3).

In responding to environmental influences on organizational goals and services, Perlmutter (1985–1986) proposes four "approaches for proactive leadership," each of which requires political sophistication. These approaches include working with the appropriate political subdivisions, utilizing the voluntary sector, mobilizing external constituencies, and pursuing legal options. Patti (1987) suggests three strategies to "mobilize the support of external resource providers around the criterion of service effectiveness" (p. 380). The first is to demonstrate that the agency "can be effective on its own terms. A second strategy to increase the autonomy of an agency is to reduce its dependency by diversifying its sources of support." The third strategy involves the assumption by social administrators of active roles in the political and legislative processes that influence the formulation of social policies.

Internally, a human service manager can appropriately use power tactics in several ways. First, the manager can be alert to political dynamics in any context. This is usually most obvious in budgeting, where fighting among program managers for scarce resources can become not only blatant but dysfunctional. Political aspects appear in other organizational processes as well: who gets what functions in a restructuring, what the hiring criteria for staff are and who makes the decisions, and what data are collected for program evaluation are important decisions in which many have a stake. A manager who can become aware of possible power and politics dimensions in any issue or process can then act on at least two levels: by thinking and behaving politically and by empowering others. While these actions may be seen as contradictory, an effective manager can and probably should do both.

According to Gummer (1990) and Gummer and Edwards (1995), "thinking politically" involves diagnosing the interests and power bases of various actors on a particular issue and then attempting to control the agenda (for example, who can attend a meeting, what questions are open for discussion) and the decision making process (options, constraints, decision criteria, and staff involvement). "Behaving politically" includes assessing and effectively using the psychological and motivational profiles of oneself and others, building good working relationships with others, communicating effectively and sharing information strategically, and creating influence networks throughout the organization. This can involve framing requests or proposals in terms of how they will benefit the target of influence and building up "chits" by doing favors for others. If such behaviors seem distasteful to human service professionals socialized with values of support, openness, and cooperation, remember that the use of power can be, as described by McClelland in Chapter 7, personalized or socialized, with the former seen as inappropriate and the latter as a legitimate way to accomplish shared organizational goals.

Also, Gummer and Edwards (1995) suggest that effective and appropriate political behavior involves playing by the rules, performing useful functions for the organization, and managing impressions:

> Managers can increase the positive political consequences of their work by carefully adhering to organizational norms, particularly those concerning the proper exercise of power and authority; identifying tasks that their units can do which are considered important to the overall organizational mission; and seeing that their accomplishments and those of their units are accurately and fully conveyed to others within and outside the organization. (p. 145)

It is also legitimate to develop one's own personal sources of power, such as one's reputation, technical abilities, clear personal objectives, positive relationships with others, communication effectiveness, and self-confidence and optimism (Lynch, 1993, pp. 39–44). This process can include developing the power bases discussed in the context of motivation in Chapter 7, particularly referent power (having qualities that others admire) and expert power (having valued knowledge and skills).

Perhaps even more important for managers is their ability and willingness to develop the power in others, commonly known as *empowerment*. Of course, client empowerment is a commonly discussed principle in the human services (Guterman & Bargal, 1996), but our interest here is in the empowerment of workers in the conduct of their jobs. Cohen and Austin (1997) assert that empowerment of staff should be formally sanctioned by the organization and built into organizational processes and the worker's job role. Staff empowerment as a way of life can enhance the possibilities of organizational effectiveness and change by more fully using the creativity and resources of all staff.

Terms such as *participative decision making* (PDM) (Packard, 1989) or *participative management* (Weinbach, 1998, pp. 66–72) are often used to describe techniques of empowerment. PDM is often based on human resources theories such as those of Likert and McGregor discussed in earlier chapters. There is growing evidence of the value of PDM or participative management (Pine, Warsh, & Maluccio, 1998; Ramsdell, 1994), including its perceived effects on organizational performance (Packard, 1989) and service outcomes (Guterman & Bargal, 1996). Managerial strategies for increasing PDM are available at the microlevel through supervision methods that use participative leadership styles (see Chapter 7) and at the macrolevel through employee involvement in organizational change, as discussed later.

Organizational Change in Human Service Organizations

Needs and demands for organizational change, coming from the agency's environment, staff, clients, and often from its own leaders, are so widespread as to be considered a constant of human service administration. Welfare reform, managed care, results-based accountability, reinventing government, and change efforts such as reengineering are realities affecting managers in a wide range of agency settings. Factors within the organization such as low morale, burnout, inadequate management skills, and high turnover can also present change opportunities. Program redesign, agency restructuring, developing program evaluation systems, enhancing diversity, and changing an obsolete or dysfunctional organizational culture can all be done more effectively using planned change processes.

In recent years, organizational change has received increasing attention in the human service literature. For example, Galaskiewicz and Bielefeld (1998) studied change in charities in Minneapolis–St. Paul, and Hagedorn (1995) profiled change activities in public social services in Milwaukee. Eadie (1997, 1998) has outlined a model for change and innovation in not-for-profit organizations. Bargal and Schmid (1992) summarize other work in this area, and a few applications of change attempted by lower-level staff (Brager & Holloway, 1978; Moren, 1994; Resnick, 1978) and administrators (Shera & Page, 1995) have been published. Organization development has been increasingly used in human service organizations (see, for example, Colon, 1995; Latting & Blanchard 1997; Norman & Keys, 1992; Packard, 1992; Resnick & Menefee, 1993), and several cases of generic organizational change efforts in public child welfare have been reported (Cohen & Austin, 1994, 1997; Gowdy & Freeman, 1993; Hugman & Hadley, 1993; Pine et al., 1998). Perlmutter (2000) has summarized several change approaches, notably those of Patti and Resnick (1985) and Kotter (1996), including a review of political and professional change strategies. These examples notwithstanding, most agency administrators have received little or no training in organizational change processes and models.

Three overall methods of organizational change will be presented here: *leaders as change agents* who both lead and empower staff, staff-initiated *organizational change* used by lower-level employees, and various *consultation* models. These are based on a comprehensive framework for describing types of organizational change in human service organizations developed by Resnick and Patti (1980), who grouped change approaches into change from below (also known as *staff-initiated organizational change*), administrative change, and organization development. Organization development has been expanded here to incorporate other forms of consultation.

Resnick and Patti note that each approach has unique uses, strengths, and weaknesses. Over the years the distinctions among these are becoming less prominent. For example, lower-level employees are often empowered as change agents through initiatives such as TQM or group problem solving in organization development. Furthermore, a middle manager in a large agency may end up using staff-initiated organizational change tactics with superiors in executive management if she or he is not sanctioned to initiate change as part of the managerial role.

A first step in planning organizational change is to decide which approach to use. More than one may be used, simultaneously or sequentially. It is not uncommon for a leader to be acting as a change agent while also using consultation such as organization development or reengineering. Table 11-1 outlines the approaches and critical factors to consider when choosing an approach.

TABLE 11-1
Approaches to Organizational Change

Critical Intervention Variables	Administrative Change	Consultation	Staff-Initiated Organizational Change
Change agent/action system	Administrators with officially prescribed authority to initiate change	Outside consultant retained by agency administration to facilitate change	Employees with no prescribed authority or responsibility to initiate change
Primary sources of legitimacy	Legislative order, formal roles and authority, agency policies	Contract with agency administration	Professional ethics and values, employee or professional associations
Primary sources of power	Formal authority, control over resources & information	Expertise (knowledge and skill regarding change processes)	Other workers, knowledge of the problem, professional expertise
Common tactics	Directives, budgetary control, personnel changes, visionary leadership, restructuring, consensus building through staff participation	Data feedback and problem solving, team building, strategic planning, employee empowerment, TQM, reengineering, analysis of processes	Participation on agency committees, fact finding, building internal support through education and persuasion
Major constraints and sources of resistance	Subordinate inertia stemming from fear or skepticism, entrenched interests, scarce resources, lack of external support, limited control of implementation	Limited time involvement, lack of administrative support, employee distrust of outsider, employees' prior negative experiences with consultants	Superiors' disagreement, insufficient time or energy, uncertain legitimacy, fear of reprisal and disapproval, job insecurity

Adapted from Resnick and Patti (1980, pp. 18–19).

Administrative Change through Leadership _____

In the turbulent environment of the human services, good leadership and employee empowerment or participative management are inherently change tools, but a general discussion of them here is beyond the scope of this chapter. The focus here will be on current research regarding leaders specifically as change agents.

Many current models of leadership are explicitly focused on creating change. Prominent examples include visionary leadership, transformational leadership, and participative management. Bargal and Schmid (1989) summarize current leadership research as it could be applied to human services, highlighting the leader as a creator of vision and strategic architect and as a creator and changer of organizational culture. Pearlmutter (1998) emphasizes the importance of self-efficacy (believing in one's ability to complete a task) in a leader acting as a change agent and suggests ways of developing it. In a study of nonprofit human service organizations, Shin and McClomb (1998) found that visionary leadership correlated highly with organizational innovation. Other examples of leaders as change agents are found in Hesselbein et al. (1996), Katzenbach et al. (1995), Kotter (1996), Nadler (1998), Nanus and Dobbs (1999), and Rapp and Poertner (1992, Chapter 6).

Use of Consultants

In situations in which an administrator or the agency does not have the knowledge or skills to respond to a particular need for change, consultants can be an appropriate, effective, and efficient alternative. Just as experts in management information systems are used to aid in automation or fund-raising specialists assist with development of a fund-raising strategy, organizational change consultants provide expertise in specific organizational change methods.

According to Rieman (1992), consultation in the human service arena is a method and a process to

1. enhance knowledge,

2. improve skills,

3. modify attitudes, and

4. change behaviors for providing better services to clients.

"A *consultant* is a change agent who brings special content or knowledge to change the consultee. The *consultee* may be an individual, group, organization, or community" (p. 9, italics in original).

Patti and Resnick's third change approach, organization development, will be broadened here to include other forms of consultation or organization-wide change such as business process reengineering, reinventing government initiatives (Osborne & Plastrik, 1997), and total quality management (Gummer & McCallion, 1995). Organization development is typically more client driven, whereas the other forms just mentioned use more specialized change technologies in which consultants play a more active role. However, this distinction is becoming increasingly blurred, with the agency as the client taking the dominant role in deciding what to do and consultants providing methods to accomplish jointly determined goals. After a review of generic consultation approaches, some of the most common of these methods will be reviewed. Those presented here are the ones most likely to be applied in human service organizations and are included so that an administrator in an agency who has brought in such consultants will know something of what to expect and how to deal with the particular process being used, and so that an administrator wanting to initiate change requiring outside expertise will have some ideas on where to begin.

Types of Consultation

Schein (1988) has made a distinction between the consultant's role as a content expert who can solve immediate problems and his or her role as a process facilitator who attempts to enhance others' abilities to solve their own problems independently. He describes three consultation models, each with its own underlying assumptions.

1. Purchase of expertise model—In this situation, the consultee has little involvement in the process. The consultant is hired to perform a specific task or solve an identified problem. This approach is workable only if the client, or consultee, has clearly and correctly diagnosed the problem and if the consultant can arrive at an acceptable solution. Installing new bookkeeping software would be an example of this model.

2. Doctor/patient model—In this model, the consultee (termed the *client*) asks the consultant both to diagnose and to solve an organizational problem. The approach assumes that the client has provided all necessary diagnostic information and that the organization is willing to accept the "prescription." This situation leaves the consultee somewhat dependent on the consultant and often stops short of planning for the maintenance of organizational "health" after the consultant leaves. Industrial engineering is an example of this model, sometimes known as the "expert" approach.

3. Process consultation—This approach, which Schein tends to recommend for most situations, involves the consultee in all stages of problem solving, with the consultant acting as a facilitator who can help in the development of effective problem-solving processes. The assumptions here are that active involvement will increase the consultee's problem-solving skills, thus providing more long-term benefit, and that the consultee will benefit from being involved in diagnosing the situation. Organization development best exemplifies this model.

Consultants and clients should thoughtfully consider the needs of the situation and arrange for the best approach. The purchase of expertise model can be used, for example, if a program has identified a specialized need such as training on working with incest victims. The agency can then solicit consultants with this expertise. For complicated situations ranging from poor morale to funding crises, process skills will likely be needed, because there will be no easy "right" answer. Ideally, a consultant would have both process skills and expertise in selected areas. For example, in a funding crisis, process skills would be needed to help the client organization sort things out, identify issues, and consider actions; expertise skills in areas such as strategic planning, budgeting, and fund development would be valuable as well. In any case, a consultant should keep the client's needs paramount and, if she or he lacks needed expertise, suggest the use of other consultants.

We will now look at some of the consultation approaches currently being used in organizations. These are all probably more frequently used in for-profit businesses, which usually have greater resources to be used for consultation. However, as we will see, they are becoming more common in human service organizations.

ORGANIZATION DEVELOPMENT   Organization development (OD) has historically been one of the most common consultation methods in business and industry and is being increasingly used in human service organizations. In OD, the consultant and the client organization jointly assess an organization's change needs and develop an action plan for addressing them. Organization development represents Schein's "process" model, although OD consultants often provide technical expertise in areas such as strategic planning, reengineering, and total quality management (TQM, covered in a later section), which vary on the "process" to "expert" continuum.

To change the way an organization solves its problems, the OD consultant may use any one of a vast number of interventions, including these common ones:

1. **group process interventions** such as team building;

2. **intergroup process interventions,** including conflict resolution strategies, intergroup confrontation meetings, and joint problem-solving sessions;

3. **training programs,** designed to enhance organizational skills and using innovative educational strategies such as simulation and gaming;

4. **survey feedback,** or the gathering and sharing of diagnostic data about the organization and its current norms and processes;

5. **action research,** which involves broad participation in the development of change strategies based on structured research and behavioral science technologies; and

6. **changes in the organizational structure** based on group agreement about suggested alterations.

The key to defining an intervention as OD is not the specific strategy used but the democratic involvement of the organization members who might be affected by a change. All strategic planning is done under the assumption that the organization must be enabled to deal effectively with future needs. This assumes that the organization and its members must gain purposeful control over the change process. Also, regardless of specific consultation activities, an effective OD consultant will follow clearly laid-out procedures that include problem identification, contracting, assessment, planning, intervention, and evaluation.

In many situations, the diagnostic process leads not to training or group process interventions but to changes in organizational structure. Although structural changes may, in many instances, have broader influence than process interventions, the ideal situation is typically one in which technostructural adjustments are part of a broader OD process. If the members of an organization are actively involved in problem diagnosis, they are likely to be as actively involved in supporting the implementation of structural solutions.

In addition to organization development, consultants are used for business process reengineering and total quality management (TQM) implementation. These approaches may use either expert or process models, while other forms of consultation, including management analysis, typically use the expert approach. These are briefly defined later.

Some Common Consultation Technologies

REENGINEERING   Reengineering, or *business process reengineering,* has reached fad status in the business and government sectors in the United States, in spite of evidence that many such efforts fail (Hammer & Champy, 1993). It has been defined as "a fundamental rethinking and radical redesign of business processes to achieve dramatic improvements in critical contemporary measures of performance such as cost, quality service, and speed" (Hammer & Champy, 1993, p. 32).

Reengineering typically involves a thorough examination of the whole organization, focusing on structures and processes. The current organization is assessed, and a new, ideal organization is proposed that eliminates all processes that do not add value for customers. Through the 1990s it came to be seen as a euphemism for downsizing, but reengineering experts asserted that they are not equivalent processes, although a common result of reengineering is the elimination of management layers and positions. Some of the concerns related to reengineering were discussed in Chapter 4. Since it typically requires the use of an outside consultant who can suggest a complete process, we will provide only a brief outline here.

The reengineering process typically begins with the organization developing a vision of a preferred future, identifying change opportunities, forming reengineering teams, and focusing resources. At the next stage, the current processes are assessed, often known as defining the *current business model:* the way the process identified for reengineering is done at present. After choosing processes that seem to be good opportunities for reengineering, *benchmarking* and *identifying best practices* can locate organizations whose practices can be used as standards and goals. Sometimes the organization conducts a *gap analysis* to show the differences between the current state and the ideal state (sometimes known as the *future business model*), which is based on benchmarks and the organization's vision. Next, reengineering teams solicit input from customers and employees and redesign existing processes, by eliminating steps that do not add value to the product or service. This stage usually includes getting rid of the "silo mentality" of many organizations in which staff from different functions or units do not communicate or work well together. Often management positions are seen as not adding value but rather slowing things down, and positions can be eliminated. Here is where reengineering got its reputation as a euphemism for downsizing. When positions are eliminated, an organization should do everything possible to retain employees in still-needed positions. After viable proposals for change are approved, the organization needs to transition to the new designs and systems. Monitoring continues to see whether changes are having the intended effects and to identify other change opportunities.

TOTAL QUALITY MANAGEMENT   TQM is an organization-wide philosophy and process of continuous improvements in quality by focusing on the control of variation to satisfy customer requirements, including top management support and employee participation and teamwork (Gummer & McCallion, 1995). As contrasted with reengineering, TQM focuses on the line worker level rather than the larger administrative systems and structures. This approach, too, was discussed in more detail in Chapter 4.

MANAGEMENT ANALYSIS   *Management analysis* is a generic term involving expert analysis and audits of management structures, goals and objectives, and processes including organization charts, staff utilization, coordination mechanisms, roles and responsibilities, and work methods to improve efficiency and reduce costs. Recommendations often include reorganization, consolidation, downsizing/rightsizing, and, in government settings, sometimes privatization.

Industrial engineering is the profession most associated with this type of analysis: experts observe and analyze work processes using techniques such as work measurement studies, work standard setting, work simplification, and work unit and job-task analysis to recommend the most efficient methods of accomplishing tasks. This is a clear example of Schein's "expert" model, although some management analysts attempt to include employees in analysis of findings and preparation of recommendations to have "buy-in." Regardless of these efforts, such analysis is usually seen as primarily focused on cutting costs and positions with less emphasis on client service and meeting community needs.

Selecting and Using Consultants

Now that we have reviewed the types of things consultants can do and the ways in which they can operate, we will offer some guidelines that can be used when engaging a consultant. Rieman (1992) provides a useful set of criteria for a consultant that a manager or staff may use in assessing possible consultants:

1. Professional competency and experience in a human service field

2. Psychological and emotional security. Personal and professional maturity are more important than chronological age. Some are mature at 20; some are immature at 75!

3. Nonauthoritarian, flexible, open attitude

4. Humility in large measure—the strength, courage, and honesty to say "I don't know"

5. Lots of intestinal fortitude

6. Informal, relaxed comfortable behavior with individuals and groups

7. Understanding and acceptance of the consultee and ability to convey this feeling

8. Willingness to make personal/professional interests subordinate to consultee's interests and needs

9. Skill in interviewing, both individual and group

10. Willingness to show appropriate emotion

11. Nonjudgemental, tolerant attitude

12. Moderate (healthy) amount of aggressiveness so as to intervene, for example, when a group is in trouble during the consultation process

13. Conciseness of thinking and expression—thinking well on one's feet

14. Articulateness

15. Ability to consolidate information quickly—learn, feel, observe, give

16. Good judgement and intuition (p. 25)

Yankey (1998) provides useful guidelines for selecting and using consultants, noting that consultants are normally identified through personal relationships or the issuance of a request for proposals. Regardless of the method used, clear criteria for the qualities of a consultant, such as those outlined here, should be in hand. There should also be clarity regarding the consultation itself, reflected both in the RFP, if one is used, and in the contract with the consultant chosen. A contract should outline responsible parties and their roles, the problem and goal, individuals and/or units or programs to be involved, consultant "deliverables" (for example, a report, recommendations, services provided) ground rules, fees, and a schedule.

Frequently a change opportunity is identified by someone in the organization, and a consultant is not available. Many organizational concerns can be addressed by staff without outside expert help. When such change activity is conducted by staff at or near the line level, it is referred to as *staff-initiated organizational change.*

Staff-Initiated Organizational Change

Change strategies initiated by lower-level employees, typically referred to as "change from below" or "change from within," are summarized by Holloway (1987) as *staff-initiated organizational change* (SIOC). This process was originally defined by Resnick (1978) as

> a series of activities carried out by lower or middle-echelon staff in human service organizations to modify or alter organizational conditions, policy, program, or procedures for the ultimate improvement of service to clients. The activities engaged in are legitimized by professional purposes as well as by organizational norms. (p. 30)

The process is typically initiated by line workers and involves five steps.

First, for the *initial assessment,* a problem is identified, an action system consisting of individuals who have a commonality of interests and concerns is formed, data are gathered, a change objective is set, and possible solutions are considered. The potential influence of change agents is assessed, as are the organizational context, risks and benefits to change agents, and driving and restraining forces, with particular attention to the interests and concerns of the organizational decision makers involved.

The next stage, *preinitiation,* involves workers assessing and developing their influence and credibility ("social capital") and inducing or augmenting stress so that the problem will be addressed.

At the *initiation* stage, the change goal is introduced, with consideration of how it will be seen as conforming to the interests of key decision makers. Change agents develop alliances with and support from other key individuals and groups and prepare specific proposals that conform to interests and values of key actors. They select representatives to meet with decision makers and introduce the change goal and proposal.

Assuming that the change goal is approved, the *implementation* stage includes gaining support and commitment of staff involved and managing resistance, ensuring that implementation expectations are understood.

Finally, *institutionalization* involves making any necessary adjustments to the plan and then developing standardized procedures for the proposal and linking it with other organizational elements (for example, human resource systems, information systems).

This summary may make the process seem too easy, and, in fact, Holloway also acknowledges the risks faced by lower-level employees proposing potentially controversial ideas. An additional critique of the assumptions on which this model is based is presented by Cohen and Austin (1997), who suggest a new model in which worker participation in decision making should be formally sanctioned, with participation in organizational improvement built into social workers' jobs and with a commitment to individual and organizational learning throughout the change process. Their proposed strategies, encouraging dialogue, opportunities for "taking stock" and off-site retreats, line workers "looking at the data," and action research, are, in fact, elements of the administrative change model outlined earlier.

Now that we have reviewed the way organizational change can be accomplished by leaders, consultants, and lower-level staff, we will look briefly at why so many planned change efforts fail. We will then review a model of organizational change that addresses these possible pitfalls and can be used by anyone in the hierarchy, from executive to line worker, with or without consultants.

Why Organizational Change Efforts Often Fail _____

Because substantive organizational change often confronts indifference or resistance and leads to discomfort or stress on the part of employees or larger units in the organization, it is not surprising that many change efforts fail. Change from below often cannot sufficiently move the existing power structure, and many top-down initiatives fail because they are introduced in an authoritarian way. Kotter has (1996) found several commonalities in failed change efforts:

1. **Allowing too much complacency**—Change agents need to establish a high level of urgency in others, to motivate them to want change.

2. **Failing to create a sufficiently powerful guiding coalition**—Key leaders need to support the change effort publicly.

3. **Underestimating the power of vision**—As in the case of visionary leadership, "vision plays a key role in producing useful change by

helping to direct, align, and inspire actions on the part of large numbers of people" (p. 7).

4. **Undercommunicating the vision by a factor of ten (or one hundred or even one thousand)**—People need to clearly see that the benefits to them will outweigh the costs, and they need to see their leaders behaving consistent with their stated intentions and values.

5. **Permitting obstacles to block the new vision**—A change vision can be stalled by existing systems such as organizational structure and rewards systems that are not in alignment with the change.

6. **Failing to create short-term wins**—Staff need to see some quick successes to combat complacency or discouragement.

7. **Declaring victory too soon**—Large-scale change, usually involving culture change, takes years to accomplish fully.

8. **Neglecting to anchor changes firmly in the corporate culture**— The results of change need to be visibly connected to improved organizational performance, and new behaviors and systems need to be based on the new norms and values.

The change model described in the next section is intended to address factors that may lead to failed efforts, and it is based on the key elements of successful change models: leadership, staff-initiated change, and consultation (particularly organization development and other participative approaches).

A Comprehensive Change Model

Regardless of the location and role of the change agent, core principles of assessment, strategy development, implementation, and institutionalization apply. Consultants may also be brought into any change process as appropriate to augment agency expertise.

This process begins with a preliminary action system (perhaps only one person at first) determining the existence of important preconditions, assessing the current state, and defining an ideal future state. This may be limited or broad, based on the change agents' perception of the change goal. Examples include changing a procedure, training staff, developing an evaluation system, enhancing diversity, doing a strategic plan, or changing the agency's culture. The gap between the present and the future is analyzed to identify what needs to be changed. Next, an analysis of driving and restraining forces and of the perspectives of key stakeholders and decision makers provides guidance regarding selection of strategies and tactics. At the initiation stage, the desired future state is presented for a decision on implementation. If the proposal is approved, implementation begins, followed by activities to ensure institutionalization of the change.

Preconditions

Before embarking on a planned change initiative, the prospective change agent should determine the extent to which important preconditions for change are present. In a human service organization, a core level of management competence, clearly articulated humanistic values, and a participative management philosophy would usually be necessary preconditions. The organizational culture and the state of labor relations should also be considered. Substantive change will be less likely with ineffective or authoritarian management, an excessively bureaucratic or political culture, or heavily conflictual management-staff relations. If these conditions exist, they should be the first targets for change and will require outside help. Those who think there is no need for change in one's organization are advised to consider the axiom of Tom Peters (1988): "If it ain't broke, you just haven't looked hard enough" (p. 3).

Action System Development and Maintenance

A change idea often begins with one person: the agency's executive, some other manager, or a line staff member. This person should immediately involve others in the discussion of the current situation and the need for change. This group will provide the initial energy for the change initiative and may be involved throughout the process. Eventually there should be a "guiding coalition" (Kotter, 1996) whose members have the power, expertise, credibility, and leadership to make change happen. Key stakeholders, decision makers, and others with knowledge of the situation may be added over time. In large-scale administrative change, this may involve formation of a steering committee, labor-management committee, and/or design team. There is typically a "sponsor," ideally the chief executive, who makes it clear that the change initiative is a priority, and a "champion" who keeps the process moving on a daily basis. In staff-initiated organizational change, there would not usually be a sponsor, but there would be at least an informal process champion. Line workers from other units or programs and eventually managers and support staff would be invited to participate, typically forming an informal action team. As Resnick and Patti (1980) note, attention will need to be paid to both analytical tasks such as data collection and interactional tasks such as team building and clarification of decision-making processes.

Current State

An assessment of the current state often starts by looking at trends or pressures—from the environment (funding cutbacks, expectations for more and/or better services) or from within (staff morale or burnout, inadequate management systems, lack of strategic direction). Regardless of the scope of the perceived problem or change goal, the organization's purpose (mission and core values) should be reviewed, with particular attention to performance expectations from funders, clients, and other stakeholders and to quality of working life priorities from the point of view of managers and line workers. Any change goal will be easier to sell and implement if it is seen as contributing to enhanced client service, program effectiveness, or other priorities of the organization.

Future State

While the traditional approach to change begins with a problem, current thinking suggests that a better place to begin is the development of a vision of a desired state, in this case a change goal. At the organizational level, Nanus (1992) defines *vision* as a mental model of a desirable, realistic, credible, and attractive future for the organization. Such visions typically focus on the entire organization, a program or division, a work unit, or an organizational process or system, but staff-initiated change may begin with a vision of a new procedure or policy that enhances organization effectiveness. Ultimate performance expectations, such as a new level of quality or effectiveness to be reached or the existence of a new system, need to be clearly defined.

Gap Analysis

Data need to be gathered to identify specifically where things stand at the present and what changes will be needed to reach the future state. Nadler (1998) describes this stage as "recognizing the change imperative" (p. 109). Program performance data may be reviewed, and a cost-benefit analysis may be done to show the value of a proposed change. Data can also be used to demonstrate a sense of crisis or urgency. A budget deficit, high staff turnover, the impending end of a major grant, or documentation of wasted energy on nonproductive processes can all provide evidence that a change is needed.

Analysis of Driving and Restraining Forces and Stakeholders

After a change goal has been identified, the action system can use a *force field analysis* (Brager & Holloway, 1992) to identify *driving forces,* which aid the change or make it more likely to occur, and *restraining forces,* which are points of resistance or things getting in the way of change. The change goal, or desired future state, is represented by a line down the middle of a piece of paper. To its left, a parallel line represents the current state of the organization. The change process involves moving from the current state to the ideal future state. To the left of the second line (the current state) are listed all driving forces (individuals, key groups, or conditions) which may assist in the implementation of the change. On the other side, restraining forces which will make the change implementation more difficult are

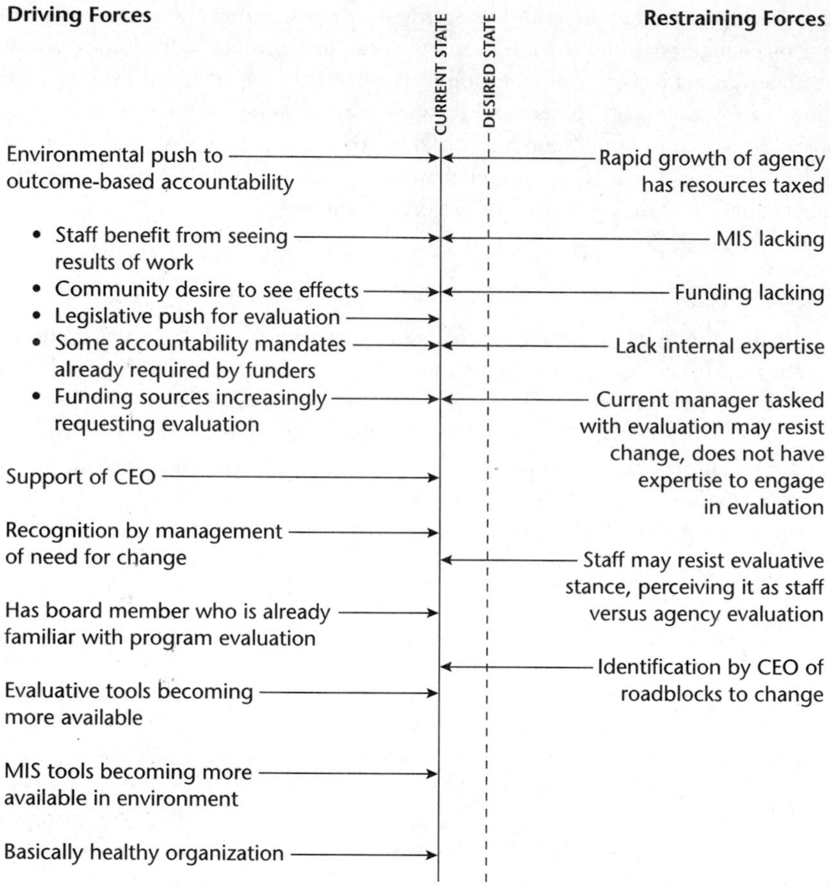

Driving Forces   **Restraining Forces**

CURRENT STATE | DESIRED STATE

Environmental push to ———————→|←——|————— Rapid growth of agency
outcome-based accountability   has resources taxed

- Staff benefit from seeing ————→|←——|————————— MIS lacking
  results of work
- Community desire to see effects ——→|←——|———————— Funding lacking
- Legislative push for evaluation ———→|
- Some accountability mandates ——→|←——|———— Lack internal expertise
  already required by funders
- Funding sources increasingly ————→|←——|——— Current manager tasked
  requesting evaluation   with evaluation may resist
                                                     change, does not have
Support of CEO ————————————→| expertise to engage
                                                            in evaluation
Recognition by management ——————→|
of need for change   ←——|———— Staff may resist evaluative
                                             stance, perceiving it as staff
Has board member who is already ————→| versus agency evaluation

                                             ←——|——— Identification by CEO of
Evaluative tools becoming ————————→| roadblocks to change
more available

MIS tools becoming more ——————————→|
available in environment

Basically healthy organization ————→|

FIGURE 11-1
Force Field Analysis: Implementing a Program Evaluation System

listed. An example is presented in Figure 11-1: a force field analysis of a change goal to implement a program evaluation system (Linn, 2000). Stakeholders may be listed here as well: managers, bureaucratically oriented staff, or others likely to prefer the status quo. Arrows from both sides touching the "current state" line represent the constellation of forces.

Each force is then assessed in two ways: its potency or strength and its amenability to change. More potent forces, especially restraining ones, will need greater attention. Those not amenable to change will have to be counteracted by driving forces. The analysis of the force field involves looking at which driving forces may be strengthened and which restraining forces may be eliminated, mitigated, or counteracted. The change plan would include tactics designed to move the relevant forces.

Initiation

This stage builds on the development and maintenance of the action system by engaging all relevant stakeholders in dialogue about the desired future state. Change goals are refined to reflect their interests and build consensus and alignment while remaining true to the original visions. This step often involves analysis and problem solving regarding what will be necessary to take the situation from the current state to the desired future state.

Problem solving may seem to be a simple process, but in organizations things are usually more complicated than initial observations may suggest. Although the existence of a problem is noted, the definition of the problem is less clear. There is a tendency to identify potential solutions prematurely or even to state solutions as problems. For instance, an agency administrator might state a problem as "The counselors need training in group work" rather than "There is a long waiting list of clients who desire counseling. Could working with clients in groups, rather than individually, provide a partial solution? Do counselors need more training to implement this potential solution?"

In fact, the definition of the core problem is not always easily found. Greater attention to determining the real nature of the problem can make a great deal of difference in the generation of alternative solutions. When focus is placed initially on a discrepancy rather than on a potential solution (the current state versus the future state), more creative decision making can result. Analyzing potential causes can help ensure that the most important underlying factors are identified. Brainstorming can then be used to develop possible solutions. The purpose of brainstorming is to identify many ideas, so the following rules should be followed:

1. No evaluation is permitted.

2. Wild ideas are encouraged.

3. Quantity, not quality, of ideas is encouraged.

4. Piggyback on (modify or adapt) others' ideas.

5. Only clarification questions may be asked.

After many ideas are brainstormed, they may be assessed, adapted, modified, combined, or rearranged. The most viable ideas are chosen, based on assessing the extent to which they will facilitate reaching the stated goal.

For example, suppose a career counseling program for youth had failed to attract the number of young people expected. Without further analysis, the problem might be stated incorrectly as "There is a need for career counseling services for young people in this area," "The quality of the counseling and placement services has not lived up to expectations," or "We need to improve our mechanisms for getting information about the program out to young people." If, however, the problem were stated in terms of the discrepancy between the desired and existing states ("There are 500 unemployed youth in our geographic area, and we are serving only 125 clients"), planners would be free to explore a number of possible explanations and solutions. If one likely solution were to be tried, planners would be able to evaluate it by measuring its effect on the specific problem. The agency might still "improve mechanisms for getting information about the program out to young people," but the alternatives would have been carefully considered and the likelihood for a successful solution would be increased.

Solutions or change proposals may range from recommending solutions to specific problems to changing procedures or program methods, computerizing, providing new training programs, implementing a quality program, or changing the agency's culture. Any proposal should include relevant background material and descriptive data as well as details on how it would be implemented, who would be involved, and what resources will be needed.

The proposal should then be presented to relevant decision makers for approval. In the case of staff-initiated change, these would be a management team or executive group; for administrative change, organization-wide meetings may be used to announce the proposal after consultation with stakeholder groups such as labor organizations. Dialogue and consensus strategies are preferred, but the use of inducements or power tactics may need to be considered under certain conditions.

Implementation

After approval of the plan, possibly as modified based on concerns raised by decision makers or other stakeholders, implementation can begin. In large-scale change this often involves the formation of teams to implement approved changes in programs, systems, or policies. Similar processes are part of staff-initiated change, although usually on a smaller scale. Getting some short-term wins, in which all employees can see results of the effort, is necessary to build momentum and broaden support for the new vision. More staff should become involved and developed to raise commitment to change. Gains are consolidated as more difficult aspects of the plan are addressed, producing further change.

Institutionalization

Ultimately, changes need to be locked in by becoming part of existing strategic plans, standard operating procedures, and the organization's culture. They need to be linked with other systems: resource needs should be addressed through the agency budgeting process, and new positions, roles, or reward systems need to be formalized in the human resources system. All changes should be fully and regularly communicated to all staff through bulletins, newsletters, or meetings, to ensure that all are aware of the change and are able to answer all questions about it. A client- or customer-oriented perspective and a focus on the impacts on key organizational outcomes should be maintained at all times. Because agencies operate in turbulent environments, change management becomes ongoing and a way of life for the organization.

Summary

We began this chapter by examining the role of leadership in tying together all organizational processes into a coordinated whole. The various roles of leaders, as articulators of culture, creators of vision, and so forth, were noted as important variables in organizational effectiveness. In the dynamic human service environment of today, change is a constant, and leaders play key roles as change agents in their organizations. In addition to leaders, other staff, even at the line level, can and should function as change agents. Occasionally consultants can provide valuable outside expertise to aid change processes engaged in by staff. Finally, a change process that may be used by change agents at any level, with or without consultants, was presented.

In the final chapter, we will review where we have been, with particular attention to the effectiveness of key organizational processes. Assuming that change will be constant, we will look at how a human service manager may remain competent through continuing development into the future.

Discussion Questions

1. Think of a leader of a human service organization whom you have seen in action. What did that leader do that was effective and ineffective? What would have made that leader more effective? What examples of leadership theories or models did you see?

2. Think of an opportunity for organizational change in an organization with which you are familiar. Define a change goal and outline a strategy and process for accomplishing it. What role would you play?

write notes to answer Q's

CASE 11

Budget Cut

The Women's Agency of Schaefer City offered a full range of services to women, including counseling, educational interventions, and career development programs. Services were offered by a combination of professionals, paraprofessionals, and volunteers, with self-help and peer counseling important components of most programs.

The one agency program that depended solely on professional service deliverers was the health center, located in a separate building but overseen by the same board of directors and administration. The health center dealt with a variety of women's health needs and offered family planning and first-trimester abortions. Although medical service was provided by physicians and nurse practitioners, all counseling was provided by women with degrees in psychology, counseling, or social work.

For the abortion clinic, this approach worked very well. Each woman who came in for the abortion procedure talked first with a counselor, who took a medical history, answered any questions about the procedure, and explored the woman's readiness for taking this step. The process of exploration often led women to reconsider their options; certainly the decision-making process was enhanced.

This program was placed in jeopardy when severe cutbacks in funding for the total agency took place. There was no consideration of eliminating the abortion clinic itself; the cutbacks, however, were to affect the counseling aspect of the program. By cutting the number of professional counselors from nine to three, enough money could be saved that the number of women served could remain constant. The agency's administrator chose to limit the intake counseling interviews to twenty minutes each. In that time, medical information could be obtained and information about the procedure given.

The reaction to this cutback was immediate and strong. All of the professionals associated with the abortion clinic recognized that the suggested change in staffing patterns would be devastating, not just for the women losing their jobs but for the program itself.

From the patients' viewpoint, the problem involved the fact that they would be deprived of the opportunity to consider their decisions with assistance from skilled helpers. Although they would have factual information, many of them would regret their decisions, which could have lasting effects.

The change also seemed serious in terms of the well-being of the professionals still offering services. No longer would they have the opportunity to provide empathy and help to people in crisis. Instead, they would be spending their time with person after person, giving and getting information in an assembly-line approach. They would not be able to stay with patients through the medical procedure or provide emotional support later. Instead, they would stay in their offices, maintain business as usual, and quickly burn out.

1. Given the fact that the agency had to survive with fewer resources, how could financial cutbacks have been implemented more effectively?

2. What possibilities might there be for maintaining the quality of services while cutting back on expenditures?

3. What effect might this situation have on the long-term health of the agency?

References

Bargal, D., & Schmid, H. (1989). Recent themes in theory and research on leadership and their implications for management of the human services. *Administration in Social Work, 13*(3/4), 37–54.

Bargal D., & Schmid, H. (Eds.). (1992). Special issue: Organizational change and development in human service organizations. *Administration in Social Work, 16*(3/4).

Bennis, W., & Nanus, B. (1985). *Leaders*. New York: HarperCollins.

Blanchard, K. (1996). Turning the organizational pyramid upside down. In F. Hesselbein, M. Goldsmith, & R. Beckhard (Eds.), *The leader of the future* (pp. 81–88). San Francisco: Jossey-Bass.

Bowditch, J., & Buono, A. (1997). *A primer on organizational behavior*. New York: Wiley.

Brager, G., & Holloway, S. (1978). *Changing human service organizations: Politics and practice*. New York: Free Press.

Brager, G., & Holloway, S. (1992). Assessing the prospects for organizational change: The uses of force field analysis. *Administration in Social Work, 16*(3/4), 15–28.

Bryson, J. (1995). *Strategic planning for public and nonprofit organizations* (rev. ed.). San Francisco: Jossey-Bass.

Burns, J. (1978). *Leadership*. New York: Harper & Row.

Cohen, B. & Austin, M. (1994). Organizational learning and change in a public child welfare agency. *Administration in Social Work, 18*(1), 1–19.

Cohen, B., & Austin, M. (1997). Transforming human services organizations through empowerment of staff. *Journal of Community Practice, 4*(2), 35–50.

Colon, E. (1995). Creating an "intelligent organization" in the human services. In L. Ginsberg & P. Keys (Eds.), *New management in human services* (2nd ed., pp. 98–114). Washington, DC: NASW Press.

Covey, S. (1990). *Principle-centered leadership*. New York: Simon & Schuster.

DePree, M. (1989). *Leadership is an art*. New York: Doubleday.

Eadie, D. (1997). *Changing by design*. San Francisco: Jossey-Bass.

Eadie, D. (1998). Building the capacity to lead innovation. In R. Edwards, J. Yankey, & M. Altpeter (Eds.), *Skills for effective management of nonprofit organizations* (pp. 27–44). Washington, DC: NASW Press.

Galaskiewicz, J., & Bielefeld, W. (1999). *Nonprofit organizations in an age of uncertainty: A study of organizational change*. New York: Aldine de Gruyter.

Gowdy, E., & Freeman, E. (1993). Program supervision: Facilitating staff participation in program analysis, planning, and change. *Administration in Social Work, 17*(3), 59–79.

Gummer, B. (1987). Are administrators social workers? The politics of intraprofessional rivalry. *Administration in Social Work, 11*(2), 19–31.

Gummer, B. (1990). *The politics of social administration*. Upper Saddle River, NJ: Prentice Hall.

Gummer, B., & Edwards, R. (1995). The politics of human services administration. In L. Ginsberg & P. Keys (Eds.), *New management in human services* (2nd ed., pp. 57–71). Washington, DC: NASW Press.

Gummer, B., & McCallion, P. (Eds.). (1995). *Total quality management in the social services: Theory and practice*. Albany, NY: Rockefeller College Press.

Guterman, N., & Bargal, D. (1996). Social workers' perceptions of their power and service outcomes. *Administration in Social Work, 20*(3), 1–20.

Hagedorn, J. (1995). *Forsaking our children: Bureaucracy and reform in the child welfare system.* Chicago: Lake View Press.

Hammer, M., & Champy, J. (1993). *Reengineering the corporation.* New York: HarperBusiness.

Heskett, J., & Schlesinger, L. (1996). Leaders who shape and keep performance-oriented culture. In F. Hesselbein, M. Goldsmith, & R. Beckhard (Eds.), *The leader of the future* (pp. 111–120). San Francisco: Jossey-Bass.

Hesselbein, F. (1996). The "how to be" leader. In F. Hesselbein, M. Goldsmith, & R. Beckhard (Eds.), *The leader of the future* (pp. 121–124). San Francisco: Jossey-Bass.

Hesselbein, F., Goldsmith, M., & Beckhard, R. (Eds.). (1996). *The leader of the future.* San Francisco: Jossey-Bass.

Holloway, S. (1987). Staff-initiated organizational change. In A. Minahan (Ed.), *Encyclopedia of social work* (18th ed., pp. 729–736). Washington, DC: NASW Press.

Hugman, R., & Hadley, R. (1993). Involvement, motivation, and reorganization in a social services department. *Human Relations, 46*(11), 1319–1348.

Katzenbach, J., Beckett, F., Dichter, S., Feigen, M., Gagnon, C., Hope, Q., & Ling, T. (1995). *Real change leaders.* New York: Random House.

Kotter, J. (1996). *Leading change.* Boston: Harvard Business School Press.

Kotter, J., & Heskett, J. (1992). *Corporate culture and performance.* Boston: Harvard Business School Press.

Kouzes, J. & Posner, B. (1996). Seven lessons for leading the voyage to the future. In F. Hesselbein, M. Goldsmith, & R. Beckhard (Eds.), *The leader of the future* (pp. 99–110). San Francisco: Jossey-Bass.

Latting, J., & Blanchard, A. (1997). Empowering staff in a "poverty agency": An organization development intervention. *Journal of Community Practice, 4*(3), 59–75.

Lewis, H. (1988). Ethics and the managing of service effectiveness in social welfare. *Administration in Social Work, 11*(3/4), 271–284.

Linn, S. (2000). *Agency change plan.* Unpublished manuscript, San Diego State University.

Lowenberg, F., & Dolgoff, R. (1995). Guides to making ethical decisions. In J. Tropman, J. Erlich, & J. Rothman (Eds.), *Tactics and techniques of community intervention* (3rd ed., pp. 370–386). Itasca, IL: Peacock.

Lynch, R. (1993). *LEAD! How public and nonprofit managers can bring out the best in themselves and their organizations.* San Francisco: Jossey-Bass.

Moren, S. (1993). Social work organizations from within. *International Social Work, 37*(3), 277–293.

Nadler, D. (1998). *Champions of change.* San Francisco: Jossey-Bass.

Nanus, B. (1992). *Visionary leadership.* San Francisco: Jossey-Bass.

Nanus, B., & Dobbs, S. (1999). *Leaders who make a difference.* San Francisco: Jossey-Bass.

Norman, A. & Keys, P. (1992). Organization development in public social services— The irresistible force meets the immovable object. *Administration in Social Work,* *16,* 147–165.

Osborne, D., & Plastrik, P. (1997). *Banishing bureaucracy: The five strategies for reinventing government.* Reading, MA: Addison-Wesley.

Ott, J. S. (1998). Understanding organizational climate and culture. In S. Condrey (Ed.), *Handbook of human resource management in government* (pp. 116–140). San Francisco: Jossey-Bass.

Packard, T. (1989). Participation in decision making, performance, and job satisfaction in a social work bureaucracy. *Administration in Social Work, 13*(1), 59–73.

Packard, T. (1992). Organization development technologies in community development: A case study. *Journal of Sociology and Social Welfare, 19*(2), 3–15.

Patti, R. (1985). In search of purpose for social welfare administration. *Administration in Social Work, 9*(3), 1–14.

Patti, R. J. (1987). Managing for service effectiveness in social welfare organizations. *Social Work, 32*(5), 377–381.

Patti, R. & Resnick, H. (1985). Leadership and change in child welfare organizations. In Laird, H. & Hartman, C. (Eds.), *Handbook of child welfare.* Glencoe, IL: Free Press, 269–288.

Pearlmutter, S. (1998). Self-efficacy and organizational change leadership. *Administration in Social Work, 22*(3), 23–38.

Perlmutter, F. D. (1985–1986). The politics of social administration. *Administration in Social Work, 9*(4), 1–11.

Perlmutter, F. (2000). Initiating and implementing change. In Patti, R. (Ed.), *The handbook of social welfare management.* Thousand Oaks, CA: Sage Publications, 445–457.

Peters, T. (1998). *Thriving on chaos.* New York: Knopf.

Pine, B., Warsh, R., & Maluccio, A. (1998). Participatory management in a public child welfare agency: A key to effective change. *Administration in Social Work, 22*(1), 19–32.

Ramsdell, P. (1994). Staff participation in organizational decision making: An empirical study. *Administration in Social Work, 18*(4), 51–71.

Rapp, C., & Poertner, J. (1992). *Social administration: A client-centered approach.* New York: Longman.

Resnick, H. (1978). Tasks in changing the organization from within. *Administration in Social Work, 2*(1), 29–44.

Resnick, H., & Menefee, D. (1993). A comparative analysis of organization development and social work, with suggestions for what organization development can do for social work. *Journal of Applied Behavioral Sciences, 29,* 432–445.

Resnick, H., & Patti, R. (1980). *Change from within.* Philadelphia: Temple University Press.

Rieman, D. (1992). *Strategies in social work consultation: From theory to practice in the mental health field*. New York: Longman.

Rudolph, L. (1995). Framework for ethical decision making in philanthropy: A matrix of relationships. In J. Tropman, J. Erlich, & J. Rothman (Eds.), *Tactics and techniques of community intervention* (3rd ed., pp. 365–370). Itasca, IL: Peacock.

Schein, E. (1988). *Process consultation: Vols. I and II*. Reading, MA: Addison-Wesley.

Schein, E. (1992). *Organizational culture and leadership* (2nd ed.). San Francisco: Jossey-Bass.

Schein, E. (1996). Leadership and organizational culture. In F. Hesselbein, M. Goldsmith, & R. Beckhard (Eds.), *The leader of the future* (pp. 59–70). San Francisco: Jossey-Bass.

Senge, P. (1990) *The fifth discipline: The art and practice of the learning organization*. New York: Doubleday Currency.

Shera, W., & Page, J. (1995). Creating more effective human service organizations through strategies of empowerment. *Administration in Social Work, 19*(4), 1–15.

Shin, J., & McClomb, G. (1998). Top executive leadership and organizational innovation: An empirical investigation of nonprofit human service organizations (HSOs). *Administration in Social Work, 22*(3), 1–21.

Tichy, N. (1997). *The leadership engine*. New York: HarperCollins.

Weinbach, R. (1998). *The social worker as manager* (3rd ed.). Boston: Allyn & Bacon.

Yankey, J. (1998). Selecting and using consultants. In R. Edwards, J. Yankey, & M. Altpeter (Eds.), *Skills for effective management of nonprofit organizations* (pp. 504–520). Washington, DC: NASW Press.

12

Meeting the Challenge of Organizational Achievement

CHAPTER OUTLINE _____

The purpose of this book has been to provide professionals in human service programs with an introduction to the field of management. Several assumptions underlie this purpose. One is that professionals in service delivery, although for the most part trained as direct practitioners, stand a good chance of moving into managerial positions relatively early in their careers and therefore should have at least a rudimentary exposure to the theory and practice of administration. Part of this assumption—that many direct practitioners will join the managerial ranks—finds empirical support in at least one of the helping professions, social work. One study (Chess, Norlin, & Jayaratne, 1987) revealed that "full-time social workers . . . are more likely to be engaged in the practice of social work administration than in any other single form of practice" (p. 70), including casework, group work, and case management—all direct practice technologies.

The second assumption is that the helping professions, as a result of the first assumption, are responding to the challenge of management facing their members by providing formal training in this method of practice. Over half of all schools of social work offer management specializations (Brilliant & Holloway, 1995). This book is intended to contribute to the managerial content of the educational programs not only of social work but of the other helping professions as well.

A third assumption is that, given that almost all human service workers operate in agencies, direct service staff with some management training and knowledge will be more aware of the context, system dynamics, and views of managers and other stakeholders of the organization. Such direct service workers, to the extent that they understand a managerial perspective and can incorporate this into their own worldview, will be more effective in influencing managers to make better decisions or to create or allow change to benefit clients and the community. These workers will also have deeper insight into the heretofore mysterious or inexplicable behavior of the managers in their organizations, which should help them both influence these managers and accept some organizational realities that cannot be changed, such as responding to accountability requirements of funding organizations.

In this chapter, we will review where we have been, starting with planning as a response to the complex human service environments and needs for service. We will look at how organizations and programs should be designed based on chosen strategies and at the importance of other subsystems (human resources, information and evaluation, and financial systems). Finally, the need for constant organizational change and the essential role of leadership in pulling things together will be emphasized. Continuing in this vein, we will examine ways in which continuing growth and renewal can occur at the individual, group, and organizational levels. After discussing the skills and education that human service managers will need in the twenty-first century and how they can effectively make the transition to management, we will close with some observations on prospects in the future for human service administration.

Human Service Management Functions:
A Systems Perspective _____

The most salient elements of the human service managerial process have now been covered in some detail. Together, these elements, or functions, constitute a *managerial system*. As part of a system, the managerial elements, or *subsystems*, comprise a set of interrelated and interdependent parts operating synergistically to produce efficient and effective organizational outputs and outcomes. All subsystems of the managerial process—planning, budgeting, designing, staffing, supervising, evaluating—are critical to the viability of the overall system. *Synergy* means that the effect of all the parts working together is greater than the sum of the effects of the subsystems taken independently: the whole is greater than the sum of its parts. At the same time, however, synergy implies that a system's strength is diminished by the weaknesses of its parts. Additionally, all the subsystems must be aligned with one another: they must be based on similar design principles and values and must be oriented toward the same goals.

The important implication of the systems approach for human service managers is that proficiency in all of the functions of the managerial process is essential for successful managerial performance. We will now take a final look at the human service management model presented in Chapter 1 (see Figure 12-1).

Managing the Environment

A human service manager will need to monitor trends in the environment constantly, from the local and state levels to the federal and, sometimes, the global level. Political trends including devolution of formerly federal responsibilities, privatization of services, and increased accountability demands are likely to continue. Macroeconomic trends will always be relevant: in good times there may be increased funds for prevention, and in bad times less funding will be available when it is needed most. The "marketization" of human services and the increasing globalization of the economy will continue to impact human service agencies and clients. Social and organizational complexity will, if anything, increase, requiring managers to look clearly at wider aspects of society and anticipate further into the future. Needs assessments, asset mapping, community collaboration, and marketing and public relations strategies will all help the manager and the agency deal with the environment.

Planning and Program Design

For the human service manager to survive and achieve in today's human service organizations, he or she must have knowledge and skills in the planning process, including assessment of the environment; the determination of strategy and goals, and their alignment with organizational mission and purpose; the specification of

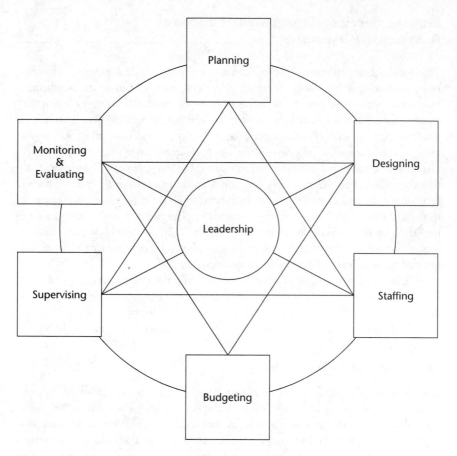

FIGURE 12-1
A Conceptual Framework for Human Service Management

program objectives, based on program goals, and their formulation in measurable terms. Strategic planning has emerged as an effective method for integrating the organization's mission and internal strengths and weaknesses with opportunities and threats in the environment. Thoughtful attention must be paid to the consideration and selection of program models and activities (including their possible social, economic, political, and legal consequences) designed to meet program objectives and goals and to satisfy the organization's mission.

Organizational Theory

Organizational theories—from the traditional bureaucracy and scientific management approaches, through the human relations insights from the Hawthorne studies, to contemporary human resources approaches that maximize employee involvement—are all in evidence today. Systems theory and emerging developments such as the excellence movement, business process reengineering, and learning organizations also offer useful perspectives for human service organizations. Contingency theory enables organization designers to select the most appropriate theories and models for a particular situation.

Organization Design

Organization design, as we pointed out earlier, is both a noun and a verb. As a noun, it describes the two components of an organization's design: structures, represented by organizational charts, and processes such as decision making and communication that cannot be seen on a chart. As a verb, *organization design* is the process for determining how the different parts will be organized and work together. Staff task forces can be formed to develop a design that proposes the best structures and processes for an organization at a given time.

Human Resource Development

After the overall organization is designed to fit agency strategies and programs, individual jobs must be designed to fit the model chosen for a particular program. Jobs should be designed to accomplish program purposes and be fulfilling for staff. Then, criteria for jobs must be developed and staff must be hired. New staff need to be oriented, and an ongoing program of staff training and development should be available, based on a needs assessment. Staff should be evaluated annually, using techniques such as behaviorally anchored rating scales, management by objectives, or critical incidents. Striving for a diverse agency workforce is important. This will ensure compliance with relevant laws and executive orders and also increase the likelihood that the workforce will be able to respond to clients in culturally appropriate ways. The use of volunteers, prevention of burnout, and employee assistance programs are other important aspects of human resource management.

Supervision

Human resources are nurtured through the supervision process. An effective supervision relationship begins with the use of appropriate models of motivation and leadership. Contingency theory operates here: no two workers are motivated in the same way, and various styles of leadership may be appropriate depending on the situation. Staff also need to be rewarded fairly and appropriately. Attention to all of these factors will contribute greatly to the effectiveness of a program's services by valuing and fully using staff—the agency's most important resource.

Financial Management

After determining the program model to be used and selecting necessary staff, budgeting can begin, usually by estimating expenditures. An annual budget is created and may be updated during the year. Specialized techniques such as cutback management, zero-based budgeting, and cost-effectiveness analysis can at times be useful as aids to decision making. Fund-raising and writing proposals for grants or contracts are key management activities. Part of the accountability process is the preparation of periodic financial reports and the completion of an annual fiscal audit.

Information Systems

A well-designed information system can enhance an organization's effectiveness and responsiveness and raise an employee's sense of satisfaction and purpose. Managers should bear these points in mind to avoid having an information system designed only to meet external accountability and evaluation needs and not fully valued or supported by staff. An IS should be designed with careful attention to information needs (related to program outcomes, for example) and should include significant participation by staff who will be using the system. Such a system will probably involve computers, the potentials of which are increasing daily. An IS should meet both internal needs (for feedback, program modification, and employee satisfaction) and external needs related to accountability and program evaluation.

Program Evaluation

Evaluations may have several purposes, from aiding in decision making and improving programs to building support and demonstrating accountability. Evaluations may look at processes, outcomes, or efficiency. There is increasing interest in outcomes evaluation. Using evaluation findings for program enhancement, involving all significant actors in the evaluation process, and taking multiple approaches in the determination of service effectiveness are key considerations that today's human service manager must address in the quest for organizational achievement. Evaluation takes us full circle—back to the social problems in our environment that human services are intended to address through a responsive strategic plan, well-designed programs that are part of well-designed organizations using effective human resources and supervision practices and financial and information systems to monitor progress and accomplishments, which are assessed by evaluation.

Leadership and Organizational Change

Leaders who effectively fill various roles, such as articulators of culture and creators of vision, can make essential contributions to organizational effectiveness. In the dynamic human service environment of today, change is a constant, and leaders play key roles as change agents in their organizations. In addition to leaders, other staff, even at the line level, can and should function as change agents. Occasionally consultants can provide valuable outside expertise to aid change processes. Planned change, conducted by a leader, lower-level staff, or consultants, can help keep the organization maximally effective and responsive to its environment.

We will now take a final look at the importance of leadership in human service management and then review some specific ways in which individuals, groups, and the organization as a whole can engage in ongoing change and development.

Putting It All Together through Leadership _____

The human service managerial system of interdependent and interacting elements is depicted in model form in Figure 12-1. It should be clear that leadership, at the center, is the unifying force among all the organizational subsystems. A key challenge for the organization, and particularly for managers/leaders, is to achieve and maintain *alignment* among the functions. According to Labovitz and Rosansky (1997, pp. 170–175) leadership is the "glue" of alignment. As we suggested in the previous chapter, top-level leadership is essential, but leadership *throughout* the organization, by many individuals, is equally essential. Leaders need to make sure that each subsystem is functioning well and that the subsystems are aligned, or functioning in harmony.

For example, a well-conceived strategic plan will go nowhere if there are not well-designed programs to implement strategies. Well-designed programs cannot be monitored unless an outcome-based information system is in place to allow tracking of activities and results. If staff are not trained to implement the service delivery models in use, good results are not likely. If funds are not allocated to high-priority activities, failure and cynicism may result. If teamwork is preached but staff are rewarded only based on individual performance, teamwork will not occur. If effective evaluation systems are not in use, managers and other staff will not be able to answer questions regarding what has been accomplished: whether client and community problems have been solved and strategies have been successful. If there is a culture of attention to process rather than to results, or if going through the motions rather than innovating seems to be the norm, the organization will stagnate.

Leaders need to pay constant attention to all the subsystems and to organizational climate and the quality of working life to ensure that success will occur. This includes, first, good management and good management systems. Leadership to articulate organizational purpose, visions, and values and to manage constant change will be needed as well. We will now look at some of the ways that organizational excellence can be achieved and maintained at the individual, group, and organizational levels.

Growth and Renewal for the Manager _____

A human service worker intending to enter management should expect to develop skills in the areas outlined in this book. Additionally, some studies have been conducted about the particular skills needed on the part of human service managers. For example, Menefee and Thompson (1994) found that the social work manager's role is varied, requiring a multitude of technical and interpersonal skills. Some of the skills found to be both important and frequently used were communicating, supervising staff, boundary spanning, strategic planning, empowering and developing staff, building teams, and managing meetings.

A similar study of Chicago area social work administrators revealed the importance of thirty-seven management skills (Hoefer, 1993). Nine management skills were common to each of the entry-, middle- and top-level administrators who were surveyed. Deemed to be "important" were group dynamics, leadership, conflict resolution, identifying with the agency, oral and written communication, professionalism, commitment to clients, and decision making (Hoefer, 1993).

In one study to identify factors that mental health teams wanted in their leaders (Corrigan, Garman, Lam, & Leary, 1998), important skills noted were the ability to define clear team goals and the individual roles necessary for their accomplishment, the ability to "assume responsibility and make appropriate decisions" (p. 120), transformational leadership skills (see Chapter 11), effective management of diversity issues, and attention to staff development.

In reviewing the management knowledge and skills outlined in this book and some of the literature, human service managers clearly will need a good deal of education, development, and training. One debate in this field—and, in fact, any field in which professionals work in organizations—is the relative importance of technical knowledge of a field or profession and generic management knowledge. In social work, there is consideration of the best degree for social work managers: the MSW, MBA, or MPA. Cupaiuolo, Loavenbruck, and Kiely (1995) found, consistent with Hoefer (1993), that at lower management levels the MSW may be preferable, with the MPA or MBA more desirable for upper management. Related to this point, Brilliant and Holloway (1995) conclude that "management training generally has had a marginal place in social work education" (p. 242), finding in their study that 59 percent of the MSW programs they studied had concentrations in administration or macro practice with an administration component.

This discussion suggests that MSW education can be a viable way to develop human service managers, depending on the specifics of a particular master's program, but that other development opportunities will need to be available. A human service manager can take advantage of workshops, continuing education, or certificate programs locally or nationally. A large city may have a resource such as the Support Center offering workshops on not-for-profit management subjects ranging from leadership and strategic planning to financial management and writing grant proposals. Nationally, professional organizations such as the Child Welfare League of America in Washington, DC, and the National Network for Social Work Managers in Columbia, SC, are valuable resources. The latter has established the Academy of Certified Social Work Managers to help ensure the competence of social work managers.

Training and development opportunities in the business sector are too numerous to mention, but one prominent example will illustrate some common management development techniques that should be useful to the human service manager. The Center for Creative Leadership, with offices in Greensboro, North Carolina, and other cities, is a national model for comprehensive management development (McCauley, Moxley, & Van Velsor, 1998).

Training offered by the Center for Creative Leadership and similar programs often includes assessment activities for individual managers. One technique that is growing in popularity is *360-degree feedback,* which involves using standardized management style or behavior instruments that are filled out by the manager and his or her supervisor, subordinates, and peers (Lepsinger & Lucia, 1997; Tornow, London, & CCL Associates, 1998). Instruments used typically let raters describe managerial behaviors observed and an assessment of their perceived effectiveness. Results are collated by a consultant or training organization and fed back to the manager anonymously. The consultant providing the feedback then helps the manager process the results and decide on action steps to improve skills or adjust styles.

Instruments used in 360-degree feedback may describe a manager's behaviors (for example, their perceived effectiveness in delegating, assigning work, supervising, working with others) or their personal styles of interacting with others. Two common instruments for the latter are the *Myers-Briggs Type Indicator* (MBTI) (Hirsh & Kummerow, 1987), and the *Strength Deployment Inventory* (SDI) (Porter & Maloney, 1981). The MBTI, based on the work of C. G. Jung, measures eight personality preferences on four bipolar scales. *Extraversion-Introversion* addresses preferences for drawing energy from the outside world or one's internal world. *Sensing-Intuition* looks at preferences for gathering information through the five senses or through the "sixth sense" of intuition. *Thinking-Feeling* contrasts organizing information logically or personally. *Judgment-Perception* indicates one's preferences for being more planned and organized or spontaneous and flexible. The SDI looks at different behavioral traits: the *altruistic-nurturing* person is trusting, idealistic, and helpful; the *assertive-directing* person is self-confident, ambitious, and persuasive; and the *analytic autonomizing* person is practical, methodical, and analytical.

Each of these profiles, in the MBTI and the SDI, has unique sets of strengths and weaknesses and tends to work best under particular circumstances. The challenge is not to change to a "better" style but rather to become aware of strengths and cautions in one's preferred style and perhaps develop other styles, and then to use styles consciously, deliberately trying to fit the needs of a situation.

Another common management development technique is familiar to human service workers: the *experiential leaderless group.* When used for management development, such groups are given a problem-solving task and observed by the trainers as they complete their work. Each participant receives feedback from group members and the trainers, with the hope of improving his or her group process skills. These behaviors are particularly valuable for a manager participating in an organizational team, which is receiving increasing attention as a relevant arena for organizational effectiveness.

Team Development

The importance of group dynamics has been acknowledged in organizations since at least the Hawthorne studies of the 1920s. More recently, it has become clear that in today's complex and dynamic organizations, teams are becoming an essential element of ensuring that the work of the organization is getting done. In organizations, many *work groups* hold meetings and perform activities involving communication and discussion. However, as any member of an organization can attest, not all work groups are teams. According to Johnson and Johnson (1997), in a work group

> interdependence is low and accountability focuses on individual members, not the group as a whole. The product of a working group is the sum of all the work produced by its members. Members do not take responsibility for results other than their own. Members do not engage in tasks that require the combined work of two or more members. In meetings, members share information and make decisions that help each person do his or her job better, but the focus is always on individual performance. (pp. 507–508)

In contrast, Johnson and Johnson suggest that a *team* "is more than the sum of its parts" (p. 508) and that a team's performance

> includes team work products that require the joint efforts of two or more members as well as individual work products. Teams not only meet to share information and perspectives and make decisions, they produce discrete work products through members' joint efforts and contributions. The focus is primarily on team accountability. (p. 508)

Of course, not every work group needs to be a team in this sense: many work units meet to exchange information, solve problems, and make decisions without needing to become a team in the pure sense. However, as organizational environments become more complex and staff become more interdependent, the extra effort it takes to truly become and operate as a team may pay off in greater organizational effectiveness and efficiency, and perhaps an improved quality of working life for staff. Researchers have noted the value of teams in settings in which work is nonroutine (see Chapter 4 regarding theories of organization) and particularly where "knowledge work" predominates: characteristics of most human service settings.

Teams can be intact work groups that do some amount of shared work (for example, staff in a residential program), interdisciplinary teams in which people from different professions work with common clients (such as in a mental health program), cross-functional teams that meet to coordinate across organizational boundaries (management teams consisting of different program managers in an agency, for example), problem-solving groups (ad hoc groups to solve particular problems), or permanent teams (for instance, quality improvement groups).

Johnson and Johnson offer several suggestions for forming teams:

1. Keep the size of teams small. . . .

2. Select team members on the basis of their (a) expertise and skills and (b) potential for developing new expertise and skills, not on the basis of their position or personality. . . .

3. Bring together the resources the team will need to function, such as space, materials, information, time-lines, support personnel, and so forth. (pp. 520–521)

For structuring and nurturing the teams, they suggest the following:

1. Present the team with its mission, structure. . . .

2. Have frequent and regular meetings that provide opportunities for team members to interact face-to-face and promote each other's success. . . .

3. Pay particular attention to first meetings. . . .

4. Establish clear rules of conduct. . . .

5. Ensure accountability by directly measuring the progress of the team in achieving its goals and plot it on a quality chart. . . .

6. Show progress. . . .

7. Expose the team to new facts and information that helps them redefine and enrich its understanding of its mission, purpose, and goals. . . .

8. Provide training to enhance both taskwork and teamwork skills. . . .

9. Have frequent team celebrations and seek opportunities to recognize members' contributions to team success. . . .

10. Ensure frequent team-processing sessions. (pp. 521–523)

Other useful guidelines for building and managing for teams have been offered by Siegel (1995), who emphasizes the team's organizational context and group process skills, and Tropman (1998), who focuses on decision making and meetings management.

Work groups wanting to move toward becoming teams may benefit from an organization development intervention known as *team building* (Dyer, 1995). In this context, team building consists of including identifying team members, making a commitment to the process, gathering data from team members, feeding data back to the team, joint problem solving or visioning, and action planning. This is best accomplished in a workshop setting, away from the work site, for a one- to three-day block of time, and usually involves an organization development consultant (see Chapter 11). Such a workshop, if successful, can provide the foundation for teamwork on an ongoing basis in the work setting. Team-building sessions can be used for existing work groups wanting to improve their functioning or a newly formed team.

A variation of team building, *new manager orientation* (Huse, 1980) or *supervisory transition* (Zugel, 1983) sessions, can be held with a team that has a new leader. Such a workshop usually involves preliminary data collection regarding the work style preferences, issues, concerns, and visions of the new leader and the team; data feedback and discussion in a workshop setting; and joint action as in a regular team-building session.

Any work group or team operates within the context of the larger organization, which, depending on organizational culture and leadership, can enhance or stifle team behavior. A manger leading a team also functions as a boundary manager with other parts of the organization, which may at times involve negotiating on behalf of the team in furtherance of team goals. In an organization that is not supportive of team functioning, this role will, of course, be difficult and may need to be addressed through one of the organizational change activities discussed in the previous chapter. Fortunately, organizational cultures supportive of team behavior are increasingly seen as not only desirable but essential to the accomplishment of the work of today's complex organizations.

In fact, the use of teams is in some cases being taken to the level of the entire organization. Such *team-based organizations* (Mohrman, Cohen, & Mohrman, 1995) are particularly appropriate to organizations doing nonroutine, knowledge-based work. Becoming such an organization will usually require a major redesign of the organization and change of its culture. In spite of the challenges in becoming a team-based organization, this approach will probably become more commonly used as a way of more fully tapping the abundant resources of all employees and of eliminating non-value-added activities such as traditional management control activities.

Ensuring the Ongoing Growth of the Organization ———

Organizational Life Cycles

Theories of organizational life cycles suggest that organizations must be constantly alert to changes in their environments and internal conditions and must adapt effectively to survive and grow. Hasenfeld and Schmid (1989) provide a useful model for describing the life cycle stages of a human service organization. At the *formation/entrepreneurial stage,* the organization has little structure and uses informal managerial processes. In another model (Bailey & Grochau, 1993), this is described as the *entrepreneurial stage,* characterized by innovation, the design of programs, and the acquisition of resources.

In Bargal and Schmid's *development/collectivity stage,* resources and services have been identified and an organic structure evolves. This is Bailey and Grochau's *team-building stage,* at which more participative leadership becomes appropriate. Organizational systems (planning, budgeting, personnel, and so forth) then need to be developed. This occurs at Bargal and Schmid's *maturation/formalization stage,* in which a transactional leadership style is common. Next comes *elaboration of structure,* in which the search for new opportunities can be enhanced by strategic planning, decentralized organizational designs, and transformational leadership.

As the growing organization moves toward this stage, it may risk taking a turn toward a *bureaucratic stage,* in which standardized procedures may stifle initiative and creativity. If this happens, the organization enters a stage of *decline* (Bargal and Schmid) or *stagnation* (Bailey and Grochau) in which the status quo is protected. If this situation is not corrected, both models predict *death* as the final stage. The important point is that decline and stagnation can be prevented by *renewal* (Bailey and Grochau), which can occur in Bargal and Schmid's model through successful management of the elaboration stage. Renewal involves quick and appropriate responses to environmental changes and a reexamination of the organization's mission, programs, and operations so that appropriate organizational changes may be made.

The mature organization needs to develop renewal capabilities including proactive management of the environment such as strategic management and client responsiveness, visionary leadership, and attention to managerial succession (developing lower-level staff as leaders of the future). This strategy will lead to new strategies and programs, with mergers or collaborations with other agencies becoming increasingly common. Employee empowerment and increased involvement with the community are additional activities that can contribute to renewal. In addition to performing environmental intelligence-gathering activities such as strategic planning, the manager also needs to monitor internal organizational conditions to be able to adapt effectively.

Employee Attitude Surveys

A popular method for assessing the internal climate of an organization is the *employee survey,* sometimes known as an *attitude* or *organizational survey* (Kraut, 1996). This is an organization development intervention with a rich history of usefulness. As is the case with other organization development activities such as team building, such a survey is best conducted with an experienced consultant's assistance. It should begin with a serious discussion within the organization, ideally at all levels, about the organization's need to learn about its functioning and level of commitment to making change. Top management support will be required (the "sponsors" of the process discussed in the previous chapter), and there will need to be "champions" in the form of staff assigned to fill leadership roles in the design and implementation of the survey. An organization-wide steering committee may be formed to provide overall policy and direction and guidance, and a survey team is often responsible for the design of the survey and its implementation.

A number of standard surveys may be used, or an organization may design a survey specifically for its unique uses. The advantages of a standardized survey are known validity and reliability of the instrument and perhaps industry-wide norms that may be available for comparison. For example, the state of Texas has extensively used a Survey of Organizational Excellence in state agencies and private organizations (Lauderdale, 1999), and Cohen and Austin (1994) have used the Human Resource Audit in a child welfare agency. Validity and reliability may be disadvantages of a "home-grown" survey, which has the advantages of being uniquely tailored to the needs of the organization and a greater sense of staff ownership over the process (Packard, in press).

An employee survey may have questions that solicit employees' opinions on any aspect of an organization's functioning, including views on the mission, leadership behavior, processes such as hiring and promotions, facilities and equipment, supervisory styles, work group climate, and quality of working life factors ranging from pay to the job itself. Surveys are completed anonymously and returned to the consultant for data collation and analysis. Consistent with the action research process reviewed in the previous chapter, data are fed back to the organization for discussion and action planning. Data feedback begins with the executive management team, the steering committee, and the survey team. Data are then fed back to all work groups in the organization. Members of a work group normally receive data for the organization as a whole and for their own work group. The use of the survey in identifying opportunities for change is crucial: if no actions follow the survey, employees are likely to become disillusioned. Problem solving in the context of a change process as discussed in the previous chapter should occur, and the survey should ideally be repeated after an appropriate interval—usually, twelve to eighteen months—to assess changes. Some organizations do surveys on a regular basis to monitor organizational conditions.

The Management Audit

Another way to assess how an organization is functioning is the *management audit* (Allison & Kaye, 1997; Packard, 2000; Sugarman, 1988). Traditionally, management audits are conducted by consultants who examine agency documents, observe agency processes, and interview staff. They then prepare a report for management outlining findings and recommendations. This is the "expert" consultation mode described by Schein in the previous chapter. An alternative is to have a management audit done participatively, with staff involved with its design and implementation, much as an employee survey is conducted. The key factors are that the method used and the criteria being assessed need to be seen as valid and appropriate by members of the organization, so that the findings will be seen as relevant and legitimate.

A management audit format that has been used in human service organizations (Packard, 2000) appears in the appendix. Such a form may be filled out by any members of the organization who have knowledge of the factors under consideration. As in the case of a survey, results can be collated by a consultant for feedback to staff. Of course, any staff who have provided data for a management audit will expect to see the findings and will expect to see action taken. Problem-solving groups or task forces can be formed to address weak areas in the agency's management systems. For example, in one agency, a management audit revealed deficiencies in the agency's evaluation system, which gathered data only on client demographics and units of services. The executive director formed a task force to improve the evaluation system, and recommendations from the task force were implemented by the agency.

Cultural Competence Assessment

Another way in which the organization may evaluate its internal operations is a *cultural competence assessment* (Child Welfare League of America, 1993). This tool may be implemented using the same procedures as those used in a management audit. Usually such an assessment looks at all aspects of cultural competence, from governance and policy to management and service delivery concerns. In one agency, an assessment of cultural competence made explicit what had been obvious but unacknowledged: the agency's staff were almost all white women, and the agency's client population had become increasingly diverse. Highly committed to being responsive to the community, the agency formed a diversity committee, chaired by the agency executive, to develop strategies for making the agency more diverse and culturally competent.

The Learning Organization

One final strategy for helping an agency remain adaptive and vital is the *learning organization,* mentioned in Chapter 4 as a growing phenomenon in organizations since the publication of Senge's (1990) *The Fifth Discipline.* A similar term, *organizational learning,* has also become popular (Easterby-Smith, 1997). Definitions of these terms and the distinctions between them are still evolving (Tsang, 1997). In the simplest terms, "organizational learning is a concept used to describe certain types of activity that take place in an organization while the learning organization refers to a particular type of organization in and of itself" (Tsang, 1997, pp. 74–75). More specifically, organizational learning, according the Argyris and Schon (1996), "refers broadly to an organization's acquisition of understandings, know-how, techniques, and practices of any kind and by whatever means" (p. xxi). They also make a distinction between *single-loop* and *double-loop* learning, with the former involving relatively simple adaptations and changes and the latter requiring an examination of the underlying theory in use that determines why the organization acts as it does. For example, discovering that 275 sign-offs are necessary to approve an innovation and changing this procedure would involve single-loop learning, while examining how people in the organization allowed this situation to begin with would involve double-loop learning (p. 21).

According to DiBella and Nevis (1998):

> there are three essential criteria of organizational learning: First, new skills, attitudes, values, and behaviors are created or acquired over time. . . . Second, what is learned becomes the property of some collective unit. . . . Third, what is learned remains within the organization or group even if individuals leave. (pp. 25–26)

They suggest that organizational learning involves ten factors or steps. First, information is gathered about conditions outside the work unit, followed by an assessment of the identified gap between current and desired performance. Discussion about how key factors are defined and measured ensues, followed by discussion of creative new ides. The organization must foster a climate of open communication and provide resources necessary for continuous education. Members must be open to the consideration of new and different ideas and methods, and leaders need to be personally and actively involved in maintaining the learning environment. Finally, a systems perspective is necessary to recognize interdependence among units.

The systems perspective is Senge's "fifth discipline": the essential element in integrating the other four disciplines. The first discipline, *personal mastery,* involves "continually clarifying what is important to us" and "continually learning how to see current reality more clearly" (Senge, 1990, p. 151). The gap between the current reality and one's vision is creative tension, which provides energy for change. *Assessing mental models,* the second discipline, involves looking at our underlying assumptions about a situation and discussing these with others so that we can clarify and adjust them as needed. The third discipline is *shared vision,* in which team members discuss their personal visions and reach alignment on a shared vision to which all are truly committed. *Team learning,* the fourth discipline, requires "the need to think insightfully about complex issues . . . , the need for innovative, coordinated action . . . [and a learning team that] continually fosters other learning teams through inculcating the practices and skills of team learning more broadly" (pp. 236–237). *Dialogue,* as distinct from discussion, is required here: suspending assumptions and working to truly understand each other as colleagues. The fifth discipline, *systems thinking,* involves seeing interrelationships, going beyond blame for current conditions, and looking for fundamental rather than symptomatic solutions.

This material is obviously very complicated stuff, and Senge and his colleagues have published two guidebooks (Senge, Kleiner, Roberts, Roth, & Ross, 1999; Senge, Roberts, Ross, Smith, & Kleiner, 1994) and provide training through the Society for Organizational Learning in Cambridge, Massachusetts. There have been some applications of organizational learning principles in the human services. Cohen and Austin (1994) report the formation of "learning laboratories" in a change initiative in a public child welfare organization. Kurtz (1998) applies Senge's disciplines to the study of an interorganizational human service network, and Cherin and Meezan (1998) suggest how evaluation can be used as a form of organizational learning.

Learning organization applications are likely to become more common in human service organizations, and managers should become aware of these ideas so that they can make thoughtful choices about attempting to use them and avoid incomplete or inadequate applications of a complex process. Finally, Rapp and Poertner (1992, p. 93) offer these requirements for a learning organization: a culture supportive of organizational learning, managers with learning organization knowledge and skills, and an information system to collect relevant information on organizational performance.

We have now reviewed growth and development concerns and strategies at the individual, group, and organizational levels. One final developmental process remains for our consideration: the transition that a human service worker makes from direct service to management.

Transitioning to Management

As direct service workers face the challenge of management and the need to broaden their managerial knowledge and skills, they concomitantly become increasingly aware of the complexity of their organization and its environment. Ascending the agency hierarchy often reveals issues and dimensions of organizational life previously obscured at the worker level. The move from service provider to manager affords the nascent incumbent a wider panorama of the constraints and contingencies facing the organization. The higher the ascent, the broader the view; the broader the view, the greater the responsibility for dealing with the issues relevant to that level of the organization's hierarchy.

If the profession of social work is at all representative of the helping professions, almost half of all graduate-level human service providers will find themselves in managerial positions four to five years after obtaining their professional degrees (Chess et al., 1987). Therefore, it is incumbent on students of the human services to study management theory and practice in preparation for the probable transition from clinician to manager early in their careers.

Moving from human service direct practitioner to manager entails a number of challenges. Not only must the neophyte manager learn to master a new technology—the technology of managing human service programs—the manager-cum-clinician must also direct his or her attention to a new client system—an organizational unit or program. Promotion also means, in most cases, the acquisition of positional authority and responsibilities much greater than those that devolve to the direct practitioner. If the manager is to be effective, he or she must develop skill in the use of newly acquired authority and power. Moreover, the manager must be able to exert expert power; that is, he or she must demonstrate to subordinates mastery of the technology they employ. In addition, the manager is expected to embrace the agency's mission and goals and to represent administration in the implementation of policy formulated at the top.

Perlmutter (1990) notes the importance of role changes that are experienced by a worker promoted to management: the direct service worker focuses on individual clients or client groups, whereas the perspective of the administrator gets broader at each level up the hierarchy. An important implication here is that a manager may have a more difficult time setting priorities, but also he or she has staff to whom tasks may be delegated.

Another factor that changes with a rise in the hierarchy is the orientation toward time. Whereas a line worker is more concerned with the present, a manager must look further into the future, anticipating strategy implementation and budget expenditures. Many clinicians are trained as facilitators or enablers, while administrators are expected to be more decisive in providing leadership and vision.

In a related vein, line workers may be less comfortable with or accustomed to using power to accomplish tasks. As we noted in Chapter 7, there are different types of power, and a wise administrator will become comfortable with and skilled in the use of power to advance the organization's mission.

A new supervisor will be able to move more easily into a managerial role by being aware of these changes in role expectations and perspectives. As was pointed out in the first chapter, managers moving up in the hierarchy need a broader array of conceptual skills (for analyzing the environment, assessing connections among systems, and so forth) and less knowledge in technical areas such as service delivery methods. People skills, of course, remain essential at all levels.

Perlmutter (1990) offers additional guidelines for those moving up beyond supervision into middle management. Upper management can augment the effectiveness of middle managers with an agency-wide management philosophy of empowerment (Cohen & Austin, 1997; see also the discussion of empowerment in Chapter 11). In an article regarding mental health professionals becoming managers that was originally published in 1980 and republished in 1999 because of its continuing relevance, Feldman (1999) discusses the conflicted feelings that human service managers often have about the use of power and related issues of clinician autonomy versus allegiance to the organization. He suggests that managers strive for the optimum amount of employee participation in decision making, being sensitive to both employee and organizational concerns.

A more recent source of conflict for mental health managers has been created by pressures for cost containment and subsequent increases in managed care. Gabel (1996) has suggested that the manager experiencing these conflicts needs first to confront them personally and reach a satisfactory level of resolution (for some, this may mean leaving the organization). Then, increased attention to the clarification of new roles and expectations may help staff deal with difficult situations.

Middle managers can also be helped through ongoing formal and informal organizational communication. Perlmutter suggests that monthly meetings with executive management, a suggestion box system to keep upper management informed of staff concerns, and management development seminars can all make managers more effective. At the personal level, a new middle manager should take advantage of management development opportunities such as external workshops and training. Formation of a network of peers to allow discussion of problems and offer support can help enhance skills and prevent burnout.

Networking and mentoring (Kelly & Post, 1995) can be immensely helpful for both new and experienced managers, with mentoring (Bell, 1998) being particularly valuable for new managers. *Mentoring*—"a relationship of growth, development, and sharing between two individuals" (Kelly & Post, p. 152)—can be either informal or formal. A formal mentoring program must include matching mentors and protégés, creating time for mentoring, evaluating the process, and, most important, sanction by the organization (Kelly & Post, 1995). *Networking* in an organizational setting, according to Kelly and Post (1995), is "a relationship between one individual and another individual, group, or organization that provides a reciprocal benefit in terms of information, advice, knowledge, or collaboration" (p. 156).

Key elements of either a mentoring or networking program are clarity of goals (such as reducing turnover, improving communications); clear roles for mentors, protégés, and supervisors; and an evaluation design. In the case of a mentor program, mentors need to be carefully selected, ensuring that they are not in the chain of command of their protégé. Mentoring and networking are particularly valuable for managers who are women or people of color—traditionally underrepresented in the management ranks and often lacking for role models they can easily relate to (Morrison, 1992). These two strategies can be of great value to individual managers and to the organization as a whole, as those managers are able to add more value to the organization through their increasing abilities.

Professional advancement in organizations provides not only challenges but anxieties as well. The better prepared the clinician is to accept these challenges, the more manageable the anxieties. Direct services workers who enter the ranks of management bring with them essential professional values and ethics and important knowledge of the realities of human service work, from which the organization can benefit as these new managers develop managerial skills.

The Need for Managerial Excellence

Given the turbulent environments in which most of today's human service organizations find themselves—environments characterized by competition, ambiguity, and uncertainty—one of the issues revealed to the manager in the move up the managerial tiers is that of organizational survival. Mandates for accountability, demands to do more with less, and shifting political and economic priorities all constitute additional challenges to managers of contemporary human service organizations.

Managerial excellence requires not only technical mastery of the functions of planning, designing, developing human resources, budgeting, supervising, and evaluating but also the ability to address the social, cultural, and political dimensions of management. This includes knowledge of and attention to the values, beliefs, customs, and traditions of the organization and its environment, including the organization's client system. Managerial excellence, therefore, requires both technical and sociopolitical acumen.

Managerial excellence involves an expanded conceptualization of the human service enterprise. It involves being able to conceive of the organization—the agency and its various levels and programs—not only as a rational, technical instrument designed to carry out certain functions. Involved as well is the ability to see the human service organization as an evolving, adapting response to social needs, as an institution "infused with values" symbolic of societal aspirations. Managerial excellence thus includes both technical competence and leadership competence.

Bennis (1989, p. 45) has made the following distinctions between managers and leaders:

Manager	Leader
Administers	Innovates
A copy	An original
Maintains	Develops
Focuses on systems and structure	Focuses on people
Relies on control	Inspires trust
Short range	Long range
Asks how and when	Asks what and why
Bottom line	The horizon
Imitates	Originates
Accepts status quo	Challenges status quo
Good soldier	Own person
Does things right	Does the right things

Bennis tends to disparage managers and management training, suggesting that only leadership is important. We assert that both sets of skills are essential. Clearly, education of administrators, including those in the human services, has traditionally focused more on management than on leadership. For that reason alone, leadership warrants increased emphasis today. Furthermore, the challenges facing organizations in the twenty-first century are more complex than those of the past, when management skills were adequate. It is now even more important than ever that traditional management thinking should not override the need for leadership.

Leadership complements technical knowledge of management with skills that at this stage of organizational knowledge have more characteristics of "art" than "science" (DePree, 1989). According to DePree:

> The measure of leadership is not the quality of the head, but the tone of the body. The signs of outstanding leadership appear primarily among the followers. Are the followers reaching their potential? Are they learning? Serving? Do they achieve the required results? Do they change with grace? Manage conflict? (p. 10)

Whether defined as an art relying on intuitive skills and professional judgment or as a science operating from empirically verified knowledge, management is central to organizational viability. Whereas organizational *efficiency* is more a function of technical competence, organizational *effectiveness* is more a function of leadership competence. The combination of both usually translates into managerial excellence. Leadership competence, a more elusive goal, is built on technological expertise but usually depends, in addition, on a variety of other attributes, including personal style, acquired knowledge, and on-the-job experience.

Another challenge facing the human service manager is that posed by the philosophy, values, and ethics of that person's profession. For human service managers—most of whom share a humanistic, client-oriented philosophy based on such concepts as social justice, self-determination, the right to privacy, and the dignity and worth of all individuals—the challenge is to align organizational values and behavior with professional values and ethical dictates. Fortunately, most human service organizations are founded on the same service philosophies and values shared by human service providers. Unfortunately, not all organizations that espouse humanistic, client-centered philosophies and values always translate them into action, in terms of the treatment of either their staff or their clients. It is the obligation of the professional manager to steer organizational behavior in the direction of humanistic values, standards, and goals at all levels of the organization, but most certainly at the line operations level, where the functions of the organization and the needs of its clients converge.

Conclusion

Organizational achievement in the human services is more than a function of an efficient managerial technology; it is a function of several variables in synergistic interaction. One of those variables is the quality of the managerial leadership of the organization. Another is the nature of the organization itself—not just its structure and the sophistication of its direct service technology but also its culture and commitment to service effectiveness. A third variable is the organization's environment and its legitimation and support of agency values and goals, as well as its provision of material resources that enable the organization to achieve service effectiveness. Although other variables influence organizational achievement, these are three of the most critical ones.

The administrator, the agency, and the environment constitute an interactive and interdependent triad. When they share the same values and aspire to the same goals, and when these values and goals center on the true needs of clients, the job of the managerial leader is facilitated and the results are gratifying. Disagreement and conflict over values and goals will create challenges that the administrator will need to address.

Whereas managerial competence and excellence are necessary criteria for organizational survival and achievement, they are in and of themselves insufficient conditions. Without economic, social, and political support from the environment, the manager of human service programs, no matter how knowledgeable or skilled, will find it difficult to achieve organizational effectiveness. The human service manager's job must therefore include attention to these larger issues. Managed care, as one example, may remain a reality, but professional administrators should continually advocate for changes in social policy to ensure high-quality services for all in need, particularly those disadvantaged by poverty, racism, or other forms of oppression.

The shift from direct practice to administration by professionals in the human services should be made in full awareness of the challenges and demands associated with the new role. Today's managerial leaders in the human services need not only the technical knowledge and skills related to managerial efficiency but also the sociopolitical talents associated with effective leadership. While the responsibilities are great, so are the rewards.

Pioneer social work administrator Mary Parker Follett stated the challenge of integrating professional values, ethics, and standards with the expectations of the organization in these words, written in 1925:

> What I am emphasizing here is that in the profession it is recognized that one's professional honour demands that one shall make this integration. . . . When, therefore, I say that members of a profession feel a greater loyalty to their profession than to the company, I do not mean that their loyalty is to one group of persons rather than to another; but that their loyalty is to a body of principles, of ideals; that is, to a special body of knowledge of proved facts and the standards arising therefrom. What, then, are we loyal to? To the soul of our work. To that which is both in our work and which transcends our work. (cited in Graham, 1995, pp. 272–273)

Human service managers face profound challenges. First, we must do all we can to identify service delivery technologies with proven effectiveness and learn as much as we can about the organizational conditions under which staff can be effective in addressing the social problems and needs that shape our agencies' purposes. We must advocate for social policies that enable these methods to be effectively deployed, and we must effectively and efficiently operate our programs with managerial skill and leadership elan. We must remain true to our professional values and be responsible stewards of the resources entrusted to our agencies. We must make difficult decisions and always treat our staffs with respect.

We fervently hope that some of today's students and line workers as well as newly promoted managers will be the human service organization managers and leaders of the future. We hope that current managers will continue to enhance their skills and retain the professional commitments and passions that brought them into the human services. We hope that human service management educators will recognize the current and evolving realities of organizational life and continue to provide students with the cutting-edge knowledge and skills they will need to become managers and remain lifelong learners.

The challenges and opportunities ahead will be massive and unprecedented, and it will take great talent, skill, and commitment to respond effectively. Managers will need simultaneously to enhance their own skills and quality of working life as well as those of their staffs and to both maintain and increase the effectiveness and responsiveness of their agencies. We hope that these skilled managers and leaders can maintain their visions, optimism, and energy under challenging circumstances, to lead fulfilling lives and to help their staffs, clients, and communities do so as well.

Discussion Questions

1. What do you think are the key challenges facing human service organizations today? How well are our organizations and professions adapting to a dynamic environment?

2. What are your current career goals and visions? What additional skills and knowledge do you think you will need to continue to grow and develop professionally?

CASE 12

Deinstitutionalization

For several decades, an important force in mental health programs has been "deinstitutionalization." Many people who were formerly patients in large state hospitals have been leaving them to be placed in smaller, community-based facilities.

Window on the World (WOW) is one of the new agencies that arose in response to deinstitutionalization efforts. It was designed to act as a halfway house for people recently released from the nearby state hospital. Although the funding for WOW comes from a number of sources, the primary source involves third-party payments from the state vocational rehabilitation agency and the state and local departments of social service. Essentially, these agencies pay room, board, and fees on behalf of the clients they place in the halfway house.

The WOW facility is clean and well kept. Staff members have real concern for the clients, and efforts are made to keep the surroundings comfortable. Yet some of the staff members have begun to question the treatment plans for individual patients.

In one such recent situation, John Billings, a staff member, asked to see Harmon Fisk, the executive director, about one of the patients.

"I'd like to talk to you about Gail Drew," he began. "I'm positive she's ready to get on her feet and start moving. If we could just cut back on her medication, I think we might really see an improvement in this case. She might even be ready to be placed in a part-time training program and come back here in the evenings.

Maybe nothing really major at first, but if we could just give her a chance, just give it a try."

"Just what do you want me to do, John?"

"Well, I thought you might be able to check with Dr. Freund about whether he could change her medication. You know, the stuff she's taking now is keeping her kind of knocked out, and . . ."

"Look, John. Carl Freund has been the consulting psychiatrist here since the word go. You come in here with a fresh master's degree and want to tell him his business. Don't you think he knows what he's doing?"

"It's not that, Mr. Fisk. Of course I think he knows what he's doing. I'm just saying that I'm seeing a subtle change in this one patient, and I think she's ready to move toward a less sheltered existence. We won't know that unless we cut down on her medication. We can always change it back again if it doesn't work out. What have we got to lose?"

"I'll tell you what we've got to lose. We've got Gail Drew's fees to lose. She's a Social Service patient. They pay her way. But they pay her way only when she's incapacitated. If she's on her feet and out there being trained, the fees are cut to a quarter of what they are now, and we can't support her on that. And if she's out there working, her fees are cut to nothing. She can't support herself on that. Now, what do you want me to do? Put this woman out there on her own in the cold? On your say-so?"

"Wait . . . wait a minute, Mr. Fisk. We can't just keep someone doped up because that's the only way we can make money off her."

"No, now just *you* wait a minute. For one thing, you sound plenty noble, but I don't see you turning down your paycheck on Fridays. Where do you think that money comes from?"

"I know, but . . ."

"I didn't make this system. If you don't like the way it works, talk to the government. The thing is, I don't like seeing a patient like that lying around all day any more than you do. But believe me, we wouldn't be doing her any favor cutting off her medication, getting her out there on the streets with her hopes up, and then having her lose the support that she's got. Face it. These people are chronic. They're not going anyplace. But at least here it's clean, it's comfortable. They've got a roof over their heads, and they're not piled one on top of another in an institution like they were monkeys in a cage."

"But Mr. Fisk, Gail Drew should have a chance. . . ."

"Have a chance for what? To starve out there on her own? Look, we need fees to run this agency. If we don't get the fees, we don't get to exist. Then what happens to Gail Drew and to the rest of the patients we've got in those beds upstairs? You think our going under is going to do them any good? Where do you think they'll go except back to State, where they came from?"

1. What ethical considerations exist in this case? How would you address them?

2. What does this case illustrate concerning the connections between funding sources and services?

3. Are there ways that differing funding patterns might be developed to make deinstitutionalization work more effectively?

4. If you were John Billings, what would you do now?

5. If you were Harmon Fisk, the director, would you be able to come up with any better answers?

6. Are there insurmountable differences between human service professionals and managers?

References

Allison, M., & Kaye, J. (1997). *Strategic planning for nonprofit organizations.* New York: Wiley.

Argyris, C., & Schon, D. (1996). *Organizational learning II: Theory, method, and practice.* Reading, MA: Addison-Wesley.

Bailey, D., & Grochau, K. (1993). Aligning leadership needs to the organizational stage of development: Applying management theory to nonprofit organizations. *Administration in Social Work, 17*(1), 23–45.

Bell, C. (1998). *Managers as mentors.* San Francisco: Jossey-Bass.

Bennis, W. (1989). *On becoming a leader.* Reading, MA: Addison-Wesley.

Brilliant, E., & Holloway, L. (1995). Social work education for nonprofit management: Do we want it? In L. Ginsberg & P. Keys (Eds.), *New management in human services* (2nd ed., pp. 233–245). Washington, DC: NASW Press.

Cherin, D., & Meezan, W. (1998). Evaluation as a means of organizational learning. *Administration in Social Work, 22*(2), 1–21.

Chess, W. A., Norlin, J. M., & Jayaratne, S. D. (1987). Social work administration 1981–1985: Alive, happy, and prospering. *Administration in Social Work, 11*(2), 67–77.

Child Welfare League of America. (1993). *Cultural Competence Self-Assessment Instrument.* Washington, DC: Author.

Cohen, B., & Austin, M. (1994). Organizational learning and change in a public child welfare agency. *Administration in Social Work, 18*(1), 1–19.

Cohen, B., & Austin, M. (1997). Transforming human services organizations through empowerment of staff. *Journal of Community Practice, 4*(2), 35–50.

Corrigan, P., Garman, A., Lam, C., & Leary, M. (1998). What mental health teams want in their leaders. *Administration and Policy in Mental Health, 26*(2), 111–123.

Cupaiuolo, A. A., Loavenbruck, G., & Kiely, K. (1995). MBA, MPA, MSW: Is there a degree of choice for human services management? In L. Ginsberg & P. Keys (Eds.), *New management in human services* (2nd ed., pp. 45–56). Washington, DC: NASW Press.

DePree, M. (1989). *Leadership is an art.* New York: Doubleday.

DiBella, A., & Nevis, E. (1998). *How organizations learn.* San Francisco: Jossey-Bass.

Dyer, W. (1995). *Team building.* Reading, MA: Addison-Wesley.

Easterby-Smith, M. (1997). Disciplines of organizational learning: Contributions and critiques. *Human Relations, 50*(9), 1085–1113.

Feldman, S. (1999). The middle management muddle. *Administration and Policy in Mental Health, 26*(4), 281–290.

Gabel, S. (1998). Leadership in the managed care era: Challenges, conflict, ambivalence. *Administration and Policy in Mental Health, 26*(1), 3–19.

Graham, P. (Ed.). (1995). *Mary Parker Follett: Prophet of management.* Boston: Harvard Business School Press.

Hasenfeld, Y., & Schmid, H. (1989). The life cycle of human service organizations: An administrative perspective. *Administration in Social Work, 13*(3/4), 243–269.

Hirsh, S., & Kummerow, J. (1987). *Introduction to type in organizations* (2nd ed.). Palo Alto, CA: Consulting Psychologists Press.

Hoefer, R. (1993). A matter of degree: Job skills for human service administrators. *Administration in Social Work, 17*(3), 1–20.

Huse, E. (1980). *Organization development and change.* St. Paul: West.

Johnson, D., & Johnson, F. (1994). *Joining together: Group theory and group skills* (5th ed.). Upper Saddle River, NJ: Prentice Hall.

Kelly, M., & Post, K. (1995). Mentoring and networking in human services. In L. Ginsberg & P. Keys (Eds.), *New management in human services* (2nd ed., pp. 151–161). Washington, DC: NASW Press.

Kraut, A. (1996). *Organizational surveys.* San Francisco: Jossey-Bass.

Kurtz, P. (1998). A case study of a network as a learning organization. *Administration in Social Work, 22*(2), 57–73.

Labovitz, G., & Rosansky, V. (1997). *The power of alignment.* New York: Wiley.

Lauderdale, M. (1999). *Reinventing Texas government.* Austin: University of Texas Press.

Lepsinger, R., & Lucia, A. (1997). *The art and science of 360° feedback.* San Francisco: Jossey-Bass.

McCauley, C., Moxley, R., & Van Velsor, E. (Eds.). (1998). *The center for creative leadership handbook of leadership development.* San Francisco: Jossey-Bass.

Menefee, D. T., & Thompson, J. J. (1994). Identifying and comparing competencies for social work management: A practice driven approach. *Administration in Social Work, 18*(3), 1–25.

Mohrman, S., Cohen, S., & Mohrman, A. (1995). *Designing team-based organizations: New forms for knowledge work.* San Francisco: Jossey-Bass.

Morrison, A. (1992). *The new leaders: Guidelines on leadership diversity in America.* San Francisco: Jossey-Bass.

Packard, T. (in press). Enhancing site-based governance through organization development: A new role for school social workers. *Journal of Social Work in Education.*

Packard, T. (2000). The management audit as a teaching tool in social work administration. *Journal of Social Work Education, 36*(1), 39–52.

Perlmutter, F. (1990). *Changing hats.* Washington, DC: NASW Press.

Rapp, C., & Poertner, J. (1992). *Social administration: A client-centered approach*. New York: Longman.

Senge, P. (1990). *The fifth discipline: The art and practice of the learning organization*. New York: Doubleday Currency.

Senge, P., Kleiner, A., Roberts, C., Roth, G., & Ross, R. (1999). *The dance of change*. New York: Doubleday.

Senge, P., Roberts, C., Ross, R., Smith, B., & Kleiner, A. (1994). *The fifth discipline fieldbook*. New York: Currency Doubleday.

Siegel, D. (1995). The dynamics of team management. In L. Ginsberg & P. Keys (Eds.), *New management in human services* (2nd ed., pp. 72–97). Washington, DC: NASW Press.

Sugarman, B. (1988). The well-managed human service organization: Criteria for a management audit. *Administration in Social Work, 12*(4), 17–27.

Tornow, W., London, M., & CCL Associates. (1998). *Maximizing the value of 360° feedback*. San Francisco: Jossey-Bass.

Tropman, J. (1998). Effective group decision making skills. In R. Edwards, J. Yankey, & M. Altpeter (Eds.), *Skills for effective management of nonprofit organizations* (pp. 244–261). Washington, DC: NASW Press.

Tsang, E. (1997). Organizational learning and the learning organization: A dichotomy between descriptive and prescriptive research. *Human Relations, 50*(1), 73–89.

Zugel, R. (1983). Managing supervisory transitions. In L. Goodstein & W. Pfeiffer (Eds.), *The 1983 annual for facilitators, trainers, and consultants* (pp. 231–240). San Diego, CA: University Associates.

Management Audit

Indicate the degree to which each factor is present in your organization. Use a rating of "4" if all aspects are fully present with positive effect; use a "1" when the factor is absent or not at all effective; use a "2" or "3" to reflect relative amounts of the factor being present/effective or problematic.

Scale
1 = To a little or no degree
2 = To some degree
3 = To a great degree
4 = To a very great degree

Planning

To what degree:

1. _____ does your organization have and use a strategic plan?

2. _____ does your organization have a clearly defined mission that is well known, well understood, and well accepted by staff?

3. _____ are the strategies, goals, and objectives of your organization based on the mission?

4. _____ are the goals and objectives complete and clear?

5. _____ do the objectives reflect measurable client benefits and other outcomes?

6. _____ are the plans of your organization used on a regular basis?

Management of the Environment

To what degree:

7. _____ can you identify the problems or needs your organization is intended to address?

8. _____ can you define the target population (for example, demographics, geographic boundaries) your organization is intended to serve?

9. _____ are key stakeholders (funders, other agencies, regulators) satisfied with agency programs and services?

Client Relations _____

To what degree:

10. _____ can you define what consumers of your services perceive their needs to be?

11. _____ is the relationship between your organization and its clients clearly defined and communicated to both?

12. _____ are clients satisfied with the services as delivered by your organization?

Program Design/Technology _____

To what degree:

13. _____ is each service appropriate to meet identified client or community needs?

14. _____ are service delivery technologies appropriate to achievement of the mission, strategies, and objectives?

15. _____ does the agency base its service delivery methods on the most powerful proven models and theories?

16. _____ is each service effective in accomplishing its stated goals and objectives?

17. _____ are there clear program standards that describe the quality and efficiency of services expected for clients?

18. _____ does your organization specify objectives and outcomes for each client?

Structure and Design _____

To what degree:

19. _____ are all staff's role and performance expectations clear and agreed to?

20. _____ are the organization structure and reporting relationships clear to all?

21. _____ does your organization have clear, written policies and procedures that are consistent with the mission and goals and that drive expected behavior?

22. _____ is your agency's structure clearly aligned with strategy?

23. _____ is your agency's structure flexible and minimally bureaucratic?

24. _____ does your organization's structure facilitate cross-function collaboration, teamwork, and support?

25. _____ does your organization have communication mechanisms or processes to keep all staff informed about current and anticipated activities or developments?

Management Information Systems

To what degree:

26. _____ does the agency have a computerized client data collection and processing system for demographic, services, and outcome data?

27. _____ does your organization have a way of identifying and aggregating client outcome data (effectiveness)?

28. _____ does your organization have clearly defined units of service that can be used to measure the types and amounts of services provided (efficiency)?

29. _____ are there clear performance standards for which aggregated client data are used in ongoing service monitoring and feedback?

30. _____ are data produced by your organization's management information system considered in rewarding staff and in making program changes?

31. _____ can your MIS measure productivity, cost-benefit, and cost-effectiveness?

Budget and Financial Management

To what degree:

32. _____ can you calculate program costs from budget data?

33. _____ can you calculate the cost per successful client outcome from budget data?

34. _____ do financial reports provide managers with effective, accurate and timely information?

35. _____ do expenditures consistently match program budgets and actual income?

36. _____ has an external audit been conducted within the last year, have results been shared, and have problems been corrected?

37. _____ are administration and program budgets clearly aligned with strategies and objectives?

Staffing and Human Resources Management _____

To what degree:

38. _____ is your organization staffed with persons fully qualified to perform their duties?

39. _____ is your organization staffed with persons carefully oriented and supervised?

40. _____ are there appropriate and adequate staff development opportunities for staff?

41. _____ does your organization recruit and select staff whose professional ideology and training are compatible with the mission and style of the agency?

42. _____ does your organization respect the professionalism of the staff?

43. _____ does the agency have a formal performance appraisal system which is appropriate and regularly used?

Leadership _____

To what degree:

44. _____ do leaders in your organization regularly interact with staff ("manage by walking around," attend meetings)?

45. _____ do leaders project a positive attitude (via trust and respect, for example) toward staff?

46. _____ does your organization have clearly defined values that are well known, well understood, and well accepted by members?

47. _____ do leaders help develop and articulate an inspiring and shared vision, purpose, and mission for the agency that drives strategy and programs?

48. _____ do leaders in your organization use appropriate management styles that motivate you to achieve high performance?

49. _____ do leaders articulate high ethical standards and ensure that they are maintained?

Organizational Culture and Change

To what degree:

50. _____ do managers work to create an organizational culture conducive to organizational effectiveness?

51. _____ do managers pay attention to informal group and organizational processes that affect the agency's operations?

52. _____ are you satisfied with the conflict management approach used by your organization?

53. _____ does your organization regularly discuss what changes should be made to improve the system and then make appropriate changes?

54. _____ do staff feel empowered to take initiative and be creative?

55. _____ does your organization monitor costs and ways to reduce them without adversely affecting the quality of service?

Program Evaluation

To what degree:

56. _____ are the outcomes of specific program activities evaluated?

57. _____ is program efficiency evaluated?

58. _____ are less formal methods of evaluation used (for example, collection and review of staff impressions, client complaints and suggestions)?

59. _____ is the impact of the program compared to the need for the program (program adequacy)?

60. _____ does your organization follow up with consumers to collect data that indicate long-term effects of your services?

61. _____ are the results of program evaluations used to make changes?

62. _____ are all relevant accreditation, licensing, or regulatory standards currently met?

Quality of Working Life _____

To what degree:

63. _____ do salaries provide an adequate income?

64. _____ do salaries provide fair compensation?

65. _____ does your organization provide safe and healthy working conditions?

66. _____ does your organization allow for individual worker autonomy?

67. _____ do jobs permit the learning and exercise of a wide range of skills and abilities?

68. _____ do job assignments contribute to employees expanding their capabilities?

69. _____ does your working environment provide freedom from prejudice?

70. _____ does your organization provide egalitarianism?

71. _____ does your organization provide upward mobility?

72. _____ does your work environment provide supportive groups?

73. _____ does your organization possess a sense of community that extends beyond face-to-face work groups?

74. _____ does your organization provide the right to personal privacy?

75. _____ does your organization allow for free speech?

76. _____ does your organization provide procedures for due process and access to appeals?

77. _____ does your organization provide equitable treatment in all matters?

78.   do the demands made by your organization allow for a balanced role of work that allows the worker to have leisure and family time on a regular basis?

79. _____ do you perceive your organization to be socially responsible?

Author Index

Subject Index